Di**M**ent

Join**nking for frag**ted times

Tony Morden

M^CNIDDER | & GRACE

Published by McNidder & Grace
21 Bridge Street
Carmarthen
SA31 3JS
UK
www.mcnidderandgrace.com

Original paperback first published 2020

A catalogue record for this work is available from the British Library.

ISBN: 9780857162014
Ebook: 9780857162021

Designed by JS Typesetting Ltd, Wales
Printed and bound in the United Kingdom by Short Run Press Ltd, Exeter

Some Quotations

'It is difficult to get a man to understand something when his salary depends upon his not understanding it'.
Upton Sinclair (US Author)

Do you understand what the Peter Principle is? If <u>Yes</u>, apply it to yourself and to your colleagues. If <u>No</u>, why do you not understand it?

There is no such thing as a "Systemic Failure" – only a failure of responsibility, a failure of process, or a failure of Dilemma Management (or all three).

Who is responsible for protecting the vast majority of UK working people, NHS employees, hard-working farmers (etc) against (i) the bad science and (ii) the risky consequences of any acceptance of the extreme demands of aggressive single-interest groups or self-publicists who have developed the ability to employ influential Voices in the media in order to promote their propaganda? Not for them the Bigger Picture described in this Book, nor any of its "joined-up thinking"?

Q. Or, where is all of the electricity going to come from?
A. ???

Coronavirus

The publication of this Book was finalised during the global Coronavirus Pandemic of 2020. Although the Book was unavailable during the early stages of that Pandemic, it is very clear that its contents (i) would then have been, and (ii) currently remain of direct relevance to the subsequent management of that critical event, and to the very serious Dilemmas to which it has given rise.

The Book describes Event Characteristics, and alludes to the dynamic of change (sometimes called a "Kondriatev Wave") undoubtedly caused by the Pandemic.

It also deals with the consequences of extreme individualism in the UK, with the widespread lack of personal or social responsibility, and with the influence of both the media and so-called "social media". These were amongst the causes of the refusal of some members of the public to accept and to act upon reasonable warnings based on the science-based government risk assessments issued at the time.

DILEMMA MANAGEMENT
TABLE OF CONTENTS

Preface

"We are continually faced with great opportunities brilliantly disguised as unsolvable problems" – *Margaret Mead*

WHAT THIS BOOK IS ABOUT

The subject of this **Book** is *the management of dilemmas*. Hence its **Title**. The Book defines and describes the process of **Dilemma Management**. And it illustrates this **process** with a variety of **Case Examples** for instance from business, politics, healthcare, security, sport, and more generally from the taxpayer-funded public sector.

Management Dilemmas may be categorised as a real-world decision type that:

❑ are non-routine, non-programmable, strategic, political or policy-orientated. In this they are likely to be characterised by the issues of Time Span Discretion (level of responsibility or orientation) described in Chapter 21;

❑ derive from the flow and reality of events as they unfold, or as they may be predicted (forecast) to occur;

❑ will in some way or other have to be dealt with, however that may be; *and also*

❑ may incur cost or a need to allocate scarce resources;

❑ will require focus on processes of implementation and action as a priority over mere talk, analysis or the exhortation of others to take responsibility;

❑ may or may not have a convenient or mutually acceptable resolution, if any at all; *and*

❑ may prove uncomfortable, challenging or difficult to deal with.

Dealing with Management Dilemmas is likely to require the exercise of:

❑ appropriate personal and professional capability (defined in this Book as capacity plus willpower); *to include*

- ❑ leadership (however this is defined);
- ❑ management competence;
- ❑ risk management;
- ❑ performance evaluation and management.

Dealing with Management Dilemmas will also require the exercise of personal, group or corporate authority allied to the acceptance of proper accountability and responsibility.

Management Dilemmas are at the very least likely to be significant in the scheme of things. Or indeed they may be **the norm** where for instance financial management, resource allocation, political decision making or processes of performance management are concerned.

Management Dilemmas are defined, and the reasons for managing them are described in detail in Part One of this Book.

THE BOOK'S PRACTICAL PURPOSE
This Book has been written in order to meet (fulfil) the following criteria:

Practicality and Professionality – the Book is practically and professionally relevant to its real-world context and conditions. These conditions are now characterised by the existence of a variety and diversity of major dilemmas (some highly risky or dangerous) which cannot be ignored and which have in some way to be dealt with, however that may be.

Relevance and Usefulness – the Book will be relevant and useful to people, whoever they are, wherever they may be, and at whatever stage in their careers who have (or will in the future have) a professional or role-defined responsibility (i) to identify and to understand dilemmas, (ii) to manage such dilemmas (or their consequences) or (iii) to attempt their resolution. Such people will include those in political, elected, leadership, governance, managerial, specialist, advisory or administrative roles. It will also include those responsible for resource allocation, financial management, the taxation of electorates, and so on.

Implementation Orientation – the Book is written to meet practical and professional needs for the *implementation* of management process and the achievement of whatever results may be obtained from Dilemma Management. Thus, the Book poses such standard questions of the "who", "what", "where", "when" and "how" of the matter. At the same time it deals with such issues as "what is it going to cost", "who is going to pay" (or "who is going to subsidise"), "what is the performance management criteria?" or "will it make any money?"

The Book also places a very strong emphasis on *capability issues* (where capability is defined to equal capacity plus willpower), decision making and leadership. This emphasis will in turn require a focus on issues of responsibility, whether individual or corporate. Thus, there may have to be (i) a rejection of naïve appeals (exhortation) "for someone else (but not me)" to do something, or calls for "the government to act". It will (ii) also imply a refusal to accept any "passing the buck".

The Book accepts the critical fact that whilst some dilemmas may be resolved, there will be occasions where such a resolution cannot (for whatever reason) be achieved.

Usability – the ISO defines *usability* as 'the extent to which a product can be used to achieve specified goals with effectiveness, efficiency, and satisfaction in its specified context of use'. Effectiveness may in turn be seen as a function of the appropriateness and cost of the item relative to its purpose and to the time constraints under which the user must operate. Usability may also be defined more specifically in terms of the accessibility, fitness for purpose, ease of use, and learnability of any human- made object.

In the case of this Book, such ease of use and learnability is relevant to its role in *the process of facilitating knowledge development and transfer* in applied and practical conditions, at the same time as creating a degree of utility or satisfaction on the part of the Reader. In this sense, a parallel objective for the Book is to create *added-value in professional terms*.

SOME KEY WORDS

Here is an A to Z of *key words* that the Reader will find throughout this Book. They are **dilemma:-**

- ❑ **attitudes**
- ❑ **behaviours**
- ❑ **capability**
- ❑ **causes**
- ❑ **concepts**
- ❑ **cultures**
- ❑ **debate and dialectics (talk for talk's sake; windbaggery)**
- ❑ **decision**
- ❑ **diagnosis**
- ❑ **identification**
- ❑ **illustration (Case Examples)**
- ❑ **implementation**
- ❑ **leadership**
- ❑ **management**
- ❑ **mapping**
- ❑ **opinions**
- ❑ **perceptions**
- ❑ **process**
- ❑ **professional competence**
- ❑ **reality**
- ❑ **resolution, non- resolution, or delay**
- ❑ **responsibility**
- ❑ **risk**
- ❑ **urgency or necessity**

SOME BASICS OF THIS BOOK

This Book draws on, and is to some degree underpinned by *all four of the Author's existing published works*, as listed below. These books are available from Bookpoint, from Routledge, and from Amazon. Amazon also sells Kindle versions of some of these books, whilst some are also available in e-format.

Principles of Management and **Principles of Strategic Management** are well-established works which describe, analyse and explain the various concepts, principles and practices of the management process.

Equality, Diversity and Opportunity Management and **A Short Guide to Equality Risk** deal with issues of equality, diversity, opportunity and discrimination that are classic sources of dilemmas. The process of Dilemma Management described in this Book is frequently required to seek resolutions to these issues, and thereby to assure the maintenance of people's Human Rights.

Principles of Management is published by Ashgate, an imprint of Routledge;

Principles of Strategic Management is published by Ashgate, an imprint of Routledge;

Equality, Diversity and Opportunity Management is published by Gower, an imprint of Routledge;

A Short Guide to Equality Risk is published by Gower, an imprint of Routledge.

BOOK PLAN

This Book comprises five main parts. These are:

- ❖ **Part One – What are Dilemmas, and why Manage them?**
- ❖ **Part Two – Some Dilemma Sources (I): Big Pictures, People and Culture**
- ❖ **Part Three – Some Dilemma Sources (II): Time, Finance, Security, and Risk**
- ❖ **Part Four – A Dilemma Management Process**
- ❖ **Part Five – Endgame: Some Final Dilemma Management Issues**

Figure 1 refers.

BOOK FORMAT

The format of this Book is based on *clear and sharply focussed chapters*. Each chapter has its subject matter and *Case Examples* by way of illustration. The Author has at the same time made every effort to ensure the internal consistency of the entirety of the Book's contents.

One of the aims of this format is to make it *commutable* – some chapters may be read in a single or return journey to and from work.

The Author states unequivocally that the construction of this Book is based (i) on the reality of the relevant facts as they are interpreted by him to be, and (ii) irrespective of whether or not this interpretation is likely in any way to be consistent with the Reader's own views.

Next, the Author states unequivocally that the construction of this Book is not based on:

❖ **any use of the process of "dumbing down", trendiness or over-simplification;**

❖ **any intention to avoid the use of long words and complex syntax where required;**

❖ **any avoidance of the use and application of necessary or appropriate technical or managerial terms. Thus, for instance, the leadership and functioning of one very large UK Public Service Organisation is clearly characterised by serious failures of operational co-ordination and integration. This organisation can be categorised as *segmented, fragmented and dissociated*. See the Author's *Principles of Management* for an explanation;**

❖ **any reluctance to employ bullet points or checklists where this will facilitate usability, focus, or reader-friendliness.**

SOME ILLUSTRATIVE DILEMMA EXAMPLES

Here are four illustrative dilemma examples:

Example One: **applying for a promotion** – Bill (or whatever name or gender you prefer) learns of a promotional opportunity for which he thinks he is qualified. He is tempted, but should he actually apply for the job? Here are some of the components of the dilemma he may now have to deal with:

❑ is he an effective performer in a selection or an interview situation? What evidence of his suitability for the post could he demonstrate?

❑ would he boost his pension if he got the job (and is this his <u>sole</u> motivation)?

❑ how clear is the job description? What would be the volume, variety, responsibility and accountability of the work?

❑ equally importantly, is the job a management or a leadership role? Would the job require him to take on staff supervisory responsibilities, and how well could he demonstrate his ability to handle them? Is he good at treading on eggshells, dealing with the self-opinionated or the inevitable awkward squads, or soothing those who have been passed over for the promotion that he has obtained?

❑ could he cope with criticism, staff appraisal, performance evaluation (etc)?

❑ could he actually <u>do </u>the new job (because, in the end, there is only one way of finding out)? Is he a *chancer*? Would he be found out and got rid of?

❑ how much additional pressure would be involved in doing the job compared with what he does now?

❑ could he handle this pressure, and how can he be sure of that now, before even applying? Could he always keep his cool, especially if being deliberately tested by his superiors to see what he is made of?

❑ what would happen to him (and to his career and to his family) if he couldn't handle the pressure (ie risk of dismissal, illness, nervous breakdown, family break-up, etc)?

❑ does he discuss the application with his family beforehand; does he listen to their concerns; or does he go ahead anyway (even if being appointed will mean moving jobs, house, schools, etc)?

Or do the proverbs encouraging Bill *(i) not to jump out of the frying pan into the fire,* or *(ii) to keep out of the kitchen if he cannot stand the heat* come to apply, if he can't know beforehand?

Bill's dilemma (as well as that of those people who might recruit him) may in part be described by the "Peter Principle", to which reference is made in Chapters 2 and 21.

Example Two: **culling cats** – controversy continues to engulf the domestic cat. Accused of wiping out large number of wild birds (which are of critical importance to the environment and climate change issues) arguments have been put forward for a cull at least of stray and feral domestic cats in order to safeguard essential wildlife. Others demand that pet cats be kept indoors at all times. These proposals have not gone down well with cat lovers, nor with people who hold strong opinions about what they think are more important environmental or climate change issues, and to which they tell us that we ought to be paying more attention.

Example Three: **Citizens Advice (or "dicing with debt")** – the work of the UK's excellent Citizens Advice Bureaux (sometimes called "Citizens Advice") is now dominated by the two issues of *personal debt* and *benefits*. Each is of course related to the other. Figures published in 2017 by the Bank of England and the Financial Conduct Authority (FCA) record a dilemma-laden (and frightening) national situation, as follows:

❏ £203 billion – is the amount of unsecured debt owed by Britons on credit cards, car finance and other loans. This compares with the £208 billion peak before the 2008 financial crisis. The issue is also dealt with in later chapters;

❏ 14 million – is the number of people "just surviving" financially. By the FCA's definition "they would struggle to get by" if they lost their job or received a large unexpected bill. Crucially, some of these people are now likely to be officially categorised by lenders as "persistent debtors";

❏ 1.2 million – the number of homeowners likely to be unable to continue paying their mortgage if payments rose by less than £100 per month;

❏ 6.5 million (one in eight) – the number of UK adults with no cash savings at all;

❏ 31% – the proportion of Britons facing a potentially "bleak retirement" because they are not paying into a pension fund, or not paying enough. This issue is also dealt with in later chapters;

❏ 3.1 million – the number of people who had taken out one or more (exorbitantly priced) "payday" or "doorstep" loans in the year.

Example Four: **Social Welfare and some Emergency Services?** – there is growing evidence that the UK's Police Service, NHS and School System have become the *Emergency Providers of Last Resort* in matters of social welfare, nutrition, safeguarding, and care in the community. This may for instance apply to any or all of:

❏ children who as Minors are legally the responsibility of parents;
❏ people who are suffering from mental health issues in the community;
❏ the elderly, who may end up in a hospital bed because they have no one to look after them, no resources, and nowhere else to go;
❏ people suffering from the consequences of substance abuse and drug addiction;
❏ others who for whatever reason are on the margins of society.

That is, these services appear to be becoming society's "dumping grounds" for those who are seen as unwanted, "weak", marginalised or even "redundant"?

Introduction

A LOGIC FOR THIS BOOK

One of the Author's objectives in writing this Book is to explain and assert the logic for the implementation and use of a Dilemma Management capability in the critical context of an urgent UK requirement for a <u>significant upward step-change in the professionalisation</u> of leadership, entrepreneurial, managerial, political, public, healthcare, charitable, Third Sector and administrative process.

The Author argues, reasonably and obviously enough, that the UK is now a post-Imperial / post-colonial nation that has (whether it likes it or not) no choice but to rely on itself to earn its own keep. It can (i) no longer take for granted, nor (ii) rely on others (such as the various international sources of borrowed funds; wealthy UK taxpayers who can easily enough transfer their money to offshore or to British-controlled tax havens; the European Union; the traditional sources of oil-based wealth; the so-called "special relationship" with the USA (?); or a rapidly globalising China) to assist it or to bail it out from the historical consequences (iii) of unsustainable policies, expenditures or commitments; and (iv) the complicating fact of having lived for so long beyond its means in the pursuit of what are now routinely described as individualistic, consumerist, materialistic, and (v) ultimately non-communitarian, non-neighbourhood, and environmentally unfriendly ends.

The need for this step change is likely to be made all the more critical in any post-Brexit UK scenario characterised (i) by the developing consequences of an obsolescent, and outdated "installed base" of (so-called "elite"?) social class and academic conditioning; (ii) by the inevitable reduction of material, social, cultural, and media expectations or complacency; (iii) by the future need for the making of harsh political, commercial and economic choices in an increasingly resource-constrained and internationally competitive environment; and in which (iv) there are guaranteed to be (politically significant) losers as well as winners within communities and neighbourhoods; all of this exacerbated (v) by a growing North – South and London-centric divide in the UK.

WHY DILEMMA MANAGEMENT

This Book can justify the current and critical **need** for Dilemma Management in such prevailing circumstances as:

❏ a history of significant (and costly) *failures of leadership, responsibility and accountability* in the UK, whether in the management of the affairs of business, finance, politics, healthcare, or the civil, public, charitable and Third Sector service (etc); *associated with*

❏ a widespread, entrenched, out-dated, and continuing arrogance, complacency and *amateurism* in matters of the responsibility for leadership and management process ("it's all really a game or a joke");

❏ entrenched, out-dated and continuing arrogance, complacency and amateurism in matters of financial management, taxation and taxation policy, exacerbated by an ongoing failure to assure an efficient provision of *taxpayer value*; *associated with*

❏ the potentially unsustainable expenditure of enormous sums of public (taxpayer plus borrowed) money by governments; by institutions such as the UK National Health Service (NHS), the military and security services, by benefit, charitable and social care agencies; also by sub-contracted companies (for instance GEC or Carillion); etc;

❏ a politically, ethically and socially unsustainable level of personal greed at the level of corporate CEOs in respect of bonus payments received;

❏ an unsustainable development of individualism and consumerism; *and*

❏ rapid and potentially highly damaging developments associated with Big Data, the Attention Economy, and social media; *and in particular*

❏ the catastrophic impact of such developments on Minors subject to parental authority;

❏ rapidly increasing needs to manage all manner of diversity and complexity;

❏ intense domestic and international competition, whether in business, politics, the provision of international charitable aid, or defence (etc);

❏ major issues that need resolution and decision, such (i) as the UK's Brexit programme and the *future nature* of its international political and trade relations, or (ii) the nature of healthcare, pension and social welfare provision during the years to (say) 2060, or (iii) of housing provision, or (iv) of the sources of electricity supply, food and the stewardship of the UK countryside in the context of environmental and climate- change concerns;

❏ continuing national and global pressure on people's Human Rights;

❏ terrorism, hostility, cronyism, corruption, crime, and a continuing risk-laden lack of accountability;

❏ divided opinion and fragmented sentiment, leading to a state of almost permanent controversy and disagreement (and so- called "rage"), for instance as represented in (or encouraged by) the behaviour of what has become in some instances an opinionated, hostile, non-responsible and self-serving media or social media; *and associated with*

❏ an apparently increasing (and naïve) cultural UK penchant for, or actual **distraction / displacement activity** in finding refuge in talk and exhortation (*windbaggery* and *gobbery*) rather than action; in argument, looking backwards rather than forwards, in entrenched opinionation and complacency; in febrile dialectics, so-called "conversations" and "debate"; in futile and meaningless analysis-paralysis; and in prevarication, obfuscation and "passing the buck"; *as compared with*

❏ again, the urgent need to accept personal, collective and corporate accountability and responsibility for proper process, behaviour, leadership, decision, enterprise, safeguarding, implementation, cost-management, taxpayer value, and action (etc).

SOME ARTIFICIAL AND UNNECESSARY DILEMMAS

The Author makes no apology for categorising the following as *artificial, created and unnecessary dilemmas*. These dilemmas have to be dealt with, wasting precious time, energy, goodwill and resources. They may also be risk-laden. The management of such dilemmas also constitutes an significant example of the value loss described in a later chapter. These artificial and unnecessary dilemmas include:

- ❏ personal and professional complacency, amateurism, obsolescence, or laziness;
- ❏ bad science, in any form;
- ❏ binary thinking;
- ❏ denial of reality, whether for instance by the media, politicians, organisations or pressure groups;
- ❏ so-called "Political Correctness" – which is really a destructive form of opinionation;
- ❏ excessive individualism, narcissicism, self-indulgence and cynicism;
- ❏ the creation or promulgation of artificial and unnecessary emotion, division and / or anxiety;
- ❏ concepts of so-called "celebrity";
- ❏ any failure to identify and to accept the personal, collective or corporate accountability already described above. This constitutes irresponsibility; *and may be associated with*
- ❏ **blame / "pass the buck" cultures in which it is always somebody else's fault;** *and / or*
- ❏ **so-called "systemic failures" in which no-one is prepared to accept responsibility.** *In reality there is no such thing as a "systemic failure"*;
- ❏ journalistic or social media opinionation, "spin" and so-called "fake news";
- ❏ trendiness for its own sake unrelated to facts and circumstances as they stand, but used to enrich someone at the expense of others.

AND FINALLY

The Author has written the Book in as a fair and an objective manner as the subject will allow. The Book has most certainly not been written to be "nice". The Author has tried to avoid making over-much reference to his own personal prejudices (eg as a voter, taxpayer or customer, etc) where this has been possible. The Book also tries to avoid making use of hype, exaggeration and sensationalism in dealing with its subject.

The Author has drawn upon his experience as (a responsible) Trustee and Trustee Board Member of a major UK Charity, and subject to the requirements of the **Nolan Principles** described in Chapter 24.

AUTHOR'S NOTE

The Author is categorised as disabled within the meaning of the UK Equality Acts. He has in writing this Book used (i) relevant medico-legal understanding, (ii) an understanding of certain NHS protocols and procedures, and (iii) a knowledge of high level medical consulting practice.

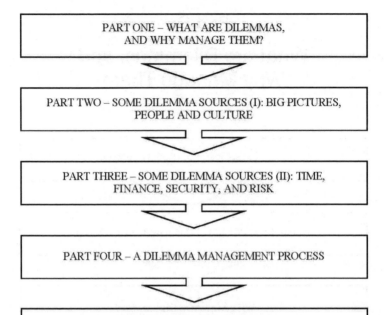

Figure 1
Book Plan

Part One

What are Dilemmas, and Why Manage Them

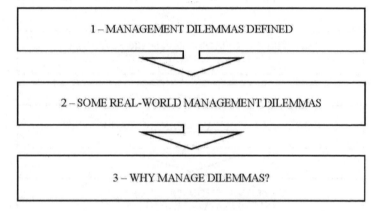

Figure 2

Chapter One
Management Dilemmas Defined

The Oxford English Dictionary (OED) defines a Dilemma as 'a form of argument involving an adversary in a choice between two (or … more) alternatives, both equally unfavourable to him; … a choice between two (or … several) alternatives which are equally unfavourable; *also a position of doubt or perplexity'*.

A MANAGEMENT DILEMMA DEFINED

A Management Dilemma is defined here as a set of circumstances in which a choice *may* have to be made, or instead *must* be made by a responsible person or persons between decision alternatives that are at the same time any or all of:

❑ favourable or unfavourable to the decision-maker; *and / or*
❑ likely to put the decision-maker into a position of doubt or uncertainty as to the resolution or resolutions that might be possible; *and / or*
❑ which may or may not be resolvable to the complete satisfaction of all parties affected by the dilemma; *and / or*
❑ were created by others whose motives may or may not coincide with those of the decision-maker, or indeed may be actively competitive or hostile to them

and in which:

❑ the identification or fixing of the occasion for decision (or its timing) may be unclear or not agreed; *and / or*
❑ the choice between making the decision, delaying it, or not making it may be unclear or not agreed by the parties to the dilemma

DILEMMA CAUSES

There are likely to be two or more variables which must be taken as determinants of diagnosis, policy choice, decision or action; but at the same time:

❏ which may, or may not be congruent, coterminous or conflicting; *and also*

❏ whose interaction may, or may not be congruent or conflicting; *or*

❏ whose interaction may preclude certain other actions, or increase the level of risk associated with such other actions;

❏ *but* **whose inter-disciplinarity or requirement for co- ordination are essential features in policy-making, decision-making, assurance or practice (for instance as in the case of child or mental health care in the community, or of housing or educational policy)**

and which will (i) act as drivers of the choice of options or objectives from which diagnoses, decision choices or modes of implementation may have to be made; but (ii) to which the relevant stakeholders may be more or less attached in their scale of priorities; and (iii) whose necessary identification or solution may be associated with varying perceptions of:

❏ what "should (or should not) be done" as compared with "what could be done"; *or*

❏ what is politically possible; *or*

❏ what is consistent with available finance, resources, capability and willpower; *or*

❏ prevailing and alternative views based on the concept of opportunity cost (such as that of the Best Value approach to public expenditure); *and*

❏ which render subject specialist, single interest, high power distance, self-publicist, emotional, or so-called "politically correct" approaches to finding, implementing or assuring solutions as undesirable, invalid, ineffective, or unsustainable.

The causes of Management Dilemmas are analysed in more detail in Parts Two and Three of this Book.

THE SIGNIFICANCE OF MANAGEMENT DILEMMAS

Management Dilemmas will be significant where:

❑ they force the parties to the dilemma into a position of doubt about the degree to which that dilemma may be resolved to the satisfaction of all; *and / or*

❑ they are likely to impose a degree of Risk and Uncertainty on the decision-maker and the parties involved; *and / or*

❑ the apparent resolutions may be shown to have the characteristic of mutual exclusivity or non-resolvability; *and / or*

❑ they ultimately prove to be mutually exclusive or unresolvable.

The significance of Management Dilemmas is analysed in more detail in Chapter 3 of this Book.

MAPPING A DILEMMA

A dilemma may be conceptualised and shown as a continuum between two polar extremes. The decision options that comprise the dilemma may then be mapped at various points between these extremes. *For the **specific purposes of this chapter** the extent of the dilemma **might be shown** as more negative on the left and more positive on the right*, as shown in Figure 3.

The more that the contents of the dilemma continuum can be described and the more that in this case:

❑ there are relevant variables to the centre or right of the continuum; *and*

❑ the more congruent (internally consistent) are the descriptors to the centre or right of the continuum

the more likely it may be that effective decisions may be made and the dilemma resolved. This process is described in Part Four of this Book.

CASE EXAMPLE

Motorists take photos and videos at the wheel – an RAC survey showed an alarming increase in the number of UK motorists illegally using mobile phones whilst driving. One third of all drivers admitted to one form or other of this potentially lethal practice, which is now described by the RAC as the biggest safety concern amongst other road users. The causes of this increase included:

❑ a belief amongst respondents that it was increasingly unlikely that offenders would be caught (which offenders therefore thought that they would get away with it unchallenged); *partly because*

❑ there were not now enough road policing officers to enforce the law, and roadside cameras would most likely not to be functioning; *and in any case*

❑ offenders considered that their use of mobile phones was more important (or more necessary) to them personally than obeying the law of the land.

The immoral and anti-social practice of using a mobile phone whilst driving was described by the UK's Department for Transport as a contributory factor in 492 accidents during 2014. Of these, 21 were fatal and 84 were classed as serious. One senior police officer commented of the dilemma revealed by the survey that people needed to start taking proper personal responsibility for their behaviour behind the wheel, and to exert strong social pressure on family, friends and colleagues who childishly and complacently put others at serious risk by persisting in the use of their mobile phones whilst driving.

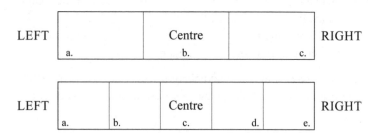

Figure 3
Mapping a Dilemma

Chapter Two
Some Real-World Management Dilemmas

This chapter contains an illustrative selection of real-world Management Dilemmas, for instance as evident at the time of writing this Book.

THE PETER PRINCIPLE (I)

The Peter Principle, described by Laurence Peter, relies on a perception that any process that seems to work effectively *now* may be used in progressively more challenging applications *until (eventually) it fails*. People may use what has always worked for them before, until they discover (for instance as a result of professional complacency, inertia, laziness, an outdated knowledge/ competency base, or even bad luck / serendipity) that the approach is no longer appropriate or viable in the present circumstances. That is, the application of past paradigms or methodologies now gives rise to a serious current dilemma. *How next to proceed? Or how to encompass and manage inevitable change?*

The application of the Peter Principle is for example well known for the recruitment and selection dilemma to which it gives rise. The case of **Bill** was described in the Introduction to this Book. The assessment of someone's potential for promotion may have to be based on some kind of evidential assessment of performance in their current job (particularly if they come from outside; are not well known to the recruiting organisation; and justified scepticism about the value of employer references, or worse testimonials received exists amongst the recruiters).

Eventually, all things being equal, applicants might over time be promoted to their highest level of competence. After that, they *could* be promoted to a role in which they are not competent, because (i) there are no prior precedents upon to which judge their activities;

(ii) remedial training and development may not work; or (iii) they are shown to lack the necessary competence, or physical and mental stamina for the task. After this point, promotions might only result in an enhanced incompetence. Or instead the person may at best have reached a *career ceiling or plateau*.

Peter then suggests an organisational scenario in which many (or even all) roles become occupied by employees who are incompetent to carry out their required duties. In consequence the work has actually to be accomplished by those employees below them who have not yet reached their level of incompetence.

Peter noted that the newly revealed incompetence of promotees might result from the work being more difficult than they had expected (that is beyond their capacity).

Or the incompetence might instead be explained by the fact that the Knowledge and Skills required in the role are different from what sustained them in the past, for instance for the reason that:

❏ an excellent engineer, doctor or accountant may prove to be a poor line or executive manager because (i) they possess a damaging tendency to develop professional jealousy or a contempt for subordinates; (ii) they do not have the necessary communication or interpersonal capabilities, or (iii) lack the emotional intelligence, willpower and positive motivation effectively to lead a department, or a team, or hospital staff (etc); *and*

❏ their *installed base of thinking* does not encompass the necessary knowledge or experience of critical managerial and leadership processes needed to fulfil their new role, as for example described in the Author's texts *Principles of Management* and *Principles of Strategic Management* to which reference is made in the Introduction to this Book; *and*

❏ they are also unfamiliar with the process of Dilemma Management being described in this Book.

The Peter Principle as a cause may also be relevant in the case of potentially very serious dilemmas to which major organisational investments or *commitments to decisions* may give rise. Such commitments are analysed in Chapters 15 and 26. Issues of leadership are dealt with in Chapter 21.

THE PETER PRINCIPLE (II), BULLYING, AND TYPE "A" BEHAVIOUR

Peter also comments that incompetent managers as bosses may be unwilling to promote evidently effective and competent subordinates into positions of responsibility in order to assist in running the department, hospital or institution (etc). Such an appointment could reveal their own weaknesses to all, potentially threatening the tenure they hold.

Worse, the boss may deliberately place the subordinate in a situation where for whatever reason they are sometimes bound to fail. Or they may adopt practices of bullying and harassment in which a promising subordinate is treated so aggressively that they leave. This is a feature of "Type A" behaviour, to which reference is made in later chapters of this Book; and also in the Author's texts *A Short Guide to Equality Risk* and *Equality, Diversity and Opportunity Management* recorded in the Introduction.

FOOTBALL STARS OR ACADEMIES?

Professional football clubs in the UK are under immense short- term pressure from their owners to show quick results, to win trophies, and above all to qualify for the European Champions League. As a result, a Premier League manager is in particular almost certain to face the risk of being sacked if his team has a poor run of form. Top clubs and their managements are in consequence likely to be tempted to buy-in the best players that they think that they (and their money) can get their hands on, irrespective of where these players come from (and irrespective of the future prospects of UK national teams). This strategy has been encouraged by the huge increases in annual income received by Premier League clubs from TV rights and sponsorship deals. It may as a result be tempting for club managements to downgrade the importance of developing young British players in academies because the reward (the pay-off) is long-term and uncertain. This may in turn lead to a lethal downward spiral in which:

❏ clubs do not have young players coming through their academies who have any chance of making the grade at the top level (or who could instead be sold on at a profit); *at the same time as*

❏ expensive bought-in (or "mercenary") players conspicuously fail to live up to expectation; *with the result that*

❏ clubs face the "double whammy" feared by chairpersons and CEOs at the end of the season in which they are left empty-handed, with no trophies, committed to expensive player contracts or transfer losses, massively overspent; and perhaps worst of all relegated to the Championship.

NEW PRODUCT, SERVICE, OR BRAND DEVELOPMENT

Company managements may be under pressure to introduce new products, new services, or new brands. This pressure might be market driven. Or equally, it might come from company staff who wish to make their own mark or make a name for themselves (for instance to improve their chances of promotion within the company, or to move on to one of the competitors).

A dilemma may emerge where the new development is likely to take place at the expense of, or indeed result in the withdrawal of popular existing lines. The elimination of such lines, services or brands may be met with market scepticism or customer hostility, particularly if the new lines are not perceived as being conspicuously better in terms of usage context or application, or the quality of the recipe appears to have been reduced in order to save money (as in the case of the UK vegelate substitute for proper chocolate), or the change is seen as purely cosmetic. The trade may instead dismiss the new offer as change for change's sake. Worse, the whole process may result in reputational losses, create a vacuum, and allow competitors to displace the company's offer with their own well-established lines.

Certainly, controversy surrounded Unilever's decision to re-brand one of its "Vim" multibrand family cleaning products. The well-known British brand "Jif" became "Cif" in an attempt to create a European brand. The globalisation of brands was fashionable at the time, but the scatological nature of the new brand name seemed to have escaped Unilever's marketing department!

Concerns about the potential impact of new product development or rebranding also seem to explain Procter & Gamble's wariness about the process. Any development proposal is subjected to a rigorous process of questioning in order to identify any potential knock-on effects on existing lines, whilst brand names and formulations such as "Arial" are treated as sacrosanct by the company.

Recent controversy has also surrounded the Government enforced reduction of the sugar content of soft drinks in the UK, leading in one instance to an occurrence of panic buying and hoarding by traditionalists of supplies of the iconic Scots drink "Irn Bru"!

EUTHANASIA (A "QUIET AND EASY DEATH" – OED)

Creates a dilemma which contains either a legal or an illegal choice for an individual:

❑ who is of fully sound mind (which can be certified); *and*
❑ who is suffering pain and distress from an incurable and terminal illness (which illness can be certified); *and*
❑ for which illness there is no known cure, and no probability of any cure being developed within the remaining life span of the individual (which can also be certified); *and*
❑ whose key relatives, representatives or executors are in agreement with, and supportive of that person's desire for euthanasia; *in order to*
❑ relieve their personal suffering; *and*
❑ to remove what they now perceive to be an unwanted and unnecessary burden on themselves, on family and on the healthcare system.

Ethical and legal restrictions may prevent members of the medical profession from assisting the sufferer in taking their own life. This might mean that such members of the medical profession are placed in an impossible position, because (i) they will not be able to relieve suffering, and may even (ii) be obliged to prolong it against the will of the individual concerned and the wishes of their relatives.

At the same time, the sufferer is uncontrollably exposed to the application of the ethical priorities of other people to their own personal case, when they simply wish to die in order to end their pain and misery.

HOLDING A REFERENDUM

In a parliamentary democracy, political parties may be perceived by the electorate as having to accept the responsibility of governing a country once they have been elected to power. For the government of the day then to announce that it wishes to hold a referendum about some particular issue (such as the UK's membership of the European Union) may raise a number of unforeseen dilemmas. Is the government of the day likely to be seen as trying to duck an issue or to evade the responsibilities for which it was elected, and for which it might instead be punished at the next General Election? Is it instead admitting to the electorate that it is unable or unwilling to make the decision that underlies the question posed by the referendum? Will voters accept what they might then perceive as "passing the buck" when they might not otherwise expect to have any direct or immediate ability to influence the outcome? Reference is also made in Chapter 30 to the issue of passing the buck.

Does the electorate fully understand all of the issues at stake, and does it wish to consider the complexities or implications of the question? Or will at least some voters reduce the matter to its simplest, most convenient and (to them) most understandable common denominator, such as jobs or immigration in the case of the 2016 UK's EU Referendum; or hostility to the "Westminster" (UK) Government in the case of the 2014 Scottish Independence Referendum?

In any case, how might the electorate respond to the referendum itself? Will it accept it on the stated terms? Or might the response develop into a broad protest movement against either or both the issue concerned and the political party who called for the referendum?

Ultimately, the referendum may prove to be like Pandora's Box, letting out who knows what when forced open in the process of asking the electorate what it really thinks. Such unpredictability may backfire. It may solve nothing, create new dilemmas, and leave the aftermath of the referendum in an even more unsettled condition than before the question was asked.

HEALTHCARE

The concept and process of healthcare may mean different things to different people. And at the same time the providers of the necessary funding may face dilemmas about what they think they should want for their money, and how healthcare performance may be monitored and measured. Healthcare dilemmas might include:

❑ deciding whether **prevention** or **cure** takes precedence;
❑ deciding whether acute physical care is seen as more important than mental health care. Sufferers of mental health issues tend to have a weak *Voice of the Victim* (as described in later chapters), may be regarded as an unwanted burden, or perceived only to be found at the margins of society;
❑ identifying the attitudes of consultants towards the relative prestige of their practice. The palliative care of the elderly (sometimes called "bed-blockers", "crumble" or "crumblies" in the UK National Health Service) might be seen as unattractive and boring when compared with the development of cutting-edge medical processes, drugs and technologies;
❑ deciding what performance measurement criteria should be used, for instance in comparing the relative merits of prevention or cure as priorities. Anti-smoking or anti-alcohol campaigns may be vital but expensive, unpopular, and carry no guarantee of success;
❑ deciding what level of financial and resource provision is needed, compared with what the society or insurance holders can afford; *and*
❑ deciding what counts as "efficient" or "cost-efficient" practice, for instance in terms of public access to services; Accident & Emergency capability; the regional grouping of specialities; or the achievement of Excellence and World Class practice, or Six Sigma (the latter for instance as a critical component of the priority healthcare discipline of *infection control*).

PRIVATE AND FAMILY COMPANIES (I)

Such companies may be highly successful. They may be able to harness entrepreneurial and other capabilities without having to operate within public shareholder constraints, and may be free to pursue ventures which shareholder corporations could (or would) not. They do not necessarily have to make money at any particular time. But such organisations do face a number of key dilemmas which they may have to try to resolve. These include:

❑ ensuring management succession, particularly when reliant on family members. The phrase "shirtsleeves to shirtsleeves in three generations" describes the syndrome in which increasingly wealthy offspring lose interest in running the family business, do not need the money, or lack the founder's drive to make matters succeed;

❑ coping with the consequences of having children or private company partners who are simply not up to the job. Does this mean bringing in outsiders, and are there any suitable sons or daughters to marry them off to? Or can the proprietors of a highly successful business afford to buy out ineffective family members, partners or private shareholders in order to reassert control?

❑ managing the threat of powerful internal family members, partners or private company shareholders (such as the representatives of private equity companies or investment trusts) realising the value of their interest by selling out to another party;

❑ dealing with the distraction (or threat) of family feuds, personality clashes, excessive high power distance (see Chapter 6) or leadership paranoia, resistance to change, perceptions of superstar status, or a developing unwillingness to innovate leading to threats to future business viability. Such threats might be easier to deal with in a public shareholder corporation where disruptive or ineffective elements might more easily be removed.

Such dilemmas may be resolvable, or they may not. If not resolved, they are likely to threaten the continued existence of the organisation.

PRIVATE AND FAMILY COMPANIES (II)

Where private or family companies are well run and resourced, they may (i) use cost advantages and (ii) the fact that they do not have to pay dividends as competitive weapons against their shareholder-based rivals. Cost may be managed on a strategic basis, with low to zero profitability or even loss leading being used to build market share.

Profitability may be a concept that is only monitored over a period of time, taking one year with the next. That is, such companies may be able to take a *long-term* view of events, free from the short-term annual obligation to reward shareholders (and in particular, large institutional shareholders).

A spectacular UK example lies in the behaviour of grocery retailers such as Aldi and Lidl (the "discounters") who have used their private status to achieve large increases in market share and put enormous pressure on their shareholder corporation rivals, such as Tesco, Sainsbury and Asda.

HIGH STREET WOES?

The concept of an retail-oriented *High Street* has for many decades been at the heart of UK urban development policy. This concept is based on a model in which people travel to the location (for instance by bus or tram) to do much of their shopping, to seek services, or to access entertainment (etc). This model was subsequently developed to include large scale retail centres with good road access and copious parking. The model was designed:

❑   to meet shoppers' needs as knowledge of the consumer behaviour of the time seemed to require; *and*
❑   to provide local employment; *and*
❑   to assist the localised development of the skills of retail management; *and*
❑   to provide a key local source of property taxes as income for for local government.

This traditional UK model is now under very serious threat, with all of the dilemmas that this implies. *Threats* have appeared variously:

❑   from the rapid growth of online marketing / sales competition and its effect on the competition strategy described in Chapter 23;
❑   from the rapid recent closures of High Street Bank branches. This reduces the level of service available to shoppers, for instance disadvantaging (i) those who do not (or cannot) for

whatever reason access the internet to manage their financial affairs; or (ii) those local retailers who have to manage cash transactions that result from their trading activities; *and*

❏ from the high and rising level of retail property rents and taxes, increasingly affordable only by large and powerful national retailers. This may have the effect of reducing consumer choice (and reducing the level of price competition).

LOCALISED RETAIL OR SERVICE ENTREPRENEURSHIP

The high and rising level of retail property rents and taxes described immediately above may become affordable only to large and powerful national retailers. This may have the effect of hampering or discouraging the development of *localised retail or service entrepreneurship*, except (i) where rental subsidies are available or (ii) local authorities choose as a matter of policy to secure premises specifically for the development of such localised entrepreneurship. This is a Human Capital issue which may lead to, or secure new employment, training and development in the face of decline elsewhere in the region.

SURVEILLANCE AND POLICING (I)

The prime objective of which is to keep people safe from harm caused by terrorists, criminals, knife-carriers, or other wrong- doers. As such, surveillance and policing must represent some kind of intrusion (such as "stop and search") into people's lives as the system monitors what they do and where they go. If there is no intrusion then there is no effect. This is the first dilemma. Then, a decision must be made as to whether the process (i) is to be discreet, so that people do not necessarily know that it is happening; or instead (ii) is to be invasive and intensive, so sending a clear message that wrong-doing will be identified and thereby discouraged. Decisions must therefore be made as to how far the process of surveillance and policing is carried out, and to what degree. Should the process monitor people's private lives, their electronic and computer communications, their consumption habits, who they are friendly with and what their social life is like? And what will be done with such information? Who will have access to it? Also see Chapter 5.

SURVEILLANCE AND POLICING (II)

In many Third World and totalitarian countries surveillance and policing is seen as essential to identifying and controlling dissent, or punishing what is seen to be deviant behaviour, for instance within people's own homes, their relationships, religious practice (or lack of), and circles of friends. Indeed, will these circles of friends be likely to contain informants, and what will happen to them if they are discovered? This may be related to:-

CORRUPTION AND CRONYISM

Which occurs in most places and at many levels, from deciding who gets what contracts right up to the wholesale theft of a country's budget (which is sometimes termed "kleptocracy"). Corruption could be defined as an immoral and illegal practice from which one person (or set of persons) can profit at the expense of others. One candidate may be favoured over another so that he or she gets a job. An examiner may be bribed to ensure that a particular student gets a high mark or receives a scholarship.

Corruption gives rise to the dilemma in which there is a need to have someone or some entity (such as a member of the judiciary or police, an auditor, or an external moderator) who or which (i) is honest but also in a sufficiently powerful or influential position to be able to identify and to "blow the whistle" on corruption such that those responsible are openly forced to do something about it, without (ii) subsequent attempts being made to corrupt such whistle-blowers or ultimately to silence them by such means as imprisonment or homicide.

The dilemma may then become circular or self-reinforcing. Corruption may breed more corruption until it becomes an endemic feature of organised society, requiring ever more powerful people or institutions to try to resist the wrong-doing and break the cycle. But at each turn, these people may too be pressured into succumbing to what by then might have become an enormous financial or political temptation, or instead an uncontrollable threat to their personal safety. Corruption may be associated with the *cronyism* to which reference is made in later chapters of this book.

LOCAL GOVERNMENT

The establishment and running of any system of local government may give rise to a host of dilemmas and decision alternatives. Some of these **will have to be resolved** as best may be the case.

A decision has to be made as to how "local" local government is to be. Should it attempt to encompass all of neighbourhood / ward / parish delineations, districts and counties; or only a selection of each (as is increasingly happening in the UK). And what does local democracy actually mean? How far and by what means can communities / neighbourhoods reasonably be involved in decision-making that affects them? What about housing, redevelopment and industrial plans deemed to be essential to the area; or the housing of immigrants; or potentially controversial major or strategic infrastructure developments involving the construction of roads, rail, airports, waste disposal, or electric power generation facilities? Should a mine or fracking facility that will create many new jobs be located in a National (Country) Park close to an area that has suffered major industrial decline?

Should local government provide services directly, or should it act to commission them and act as quality controller for external or sub-contract suppliers? Or, instead, should standardised operational, welfare or social type services be provided by national agencies, perhaps at a lower cost based on mandated economies of scale and experience effect benefits (described in Chapter 23) accessed from large but very tightly controlled sub-contractors? Should one size fit all when it comes to choice of practice and performance assessment, or should local government be free to choose from the various available practices those which they feel suit them best? What structures of organisation and processes of management should be applied – from the traditional mechanistic bureaucracy to the de-integrated or virtual company based on core and sub-contracted components?

This brings us to the matter of *relationship architecture*. What, firstly, is to be the nature of the relationship with central government, whether in setting priorities or in establishing funding arrangements? Is there to be a degree of equality between local and central government, or is local government simply seen as a tool (whether willing or not) of central government implementation with only a pre-defined level of acceptable performance variation. Indeed, should there be national statements of permitted (and non- permitted) variation in local government provision, cost and performance, monitored centrally or assessed by some kind of external agency or auditor? And who decides what quality standards should apply to the process of quality assurance?

How important is to be the relative cost of provision of local and central government service providers (because in the end, all government services have to be funded by the taxpayer)? And who sets performance standards? Does central government have the right to interfere (for instance by appointing commissioners) if performance falls below standards set nationally by (or for) central government? Indeed, who sets these national standards and to what extent are local government representatives to be consulted or involved in the process? This has become particularly critical in recent years in the UK when aggressive central government policies of stretch and leverage have been imposed in order to achieve greater economy, efficiency and effectiveness. Local governments, like some in Australia, have been forced to do much more with much less.

A decision may have to be made as to whether local government should have a powerful national voice (such as the UK's Local Government Association). What should its influence be relative to central government, for instance in establishing strategy and policy, or deciding performance standards? How influential should be the role of independent or neutral agencies (such as the Institute of Fiscal Studies) in setting standards or monitoring local government performance?

And finally, how are disagreements within the local government system (for instance between neighbouring local authorities), or between local and central government to be resolved? Who has the last word and who has the right to make the final decision?

MEDIA MANAGEMENT

Individuals, politicians, enterprises and institutions may have to deal with the Media (whether broadcast, newspapers or internet- based, etc). Such a requirement to deal with the Media may (for whatever reason) have become a part of the relationship architecture considered necessary (or instead self-imposed) in order to function.

Dilemmas may then characterise the decisions deemed to be required as a part of the management of this relationship architecture. Such dilemmas might include any or all of the following:

❏ what is the need for, and the purpose of any such requirement for interaction with the Media? That is, why are the Media to be involved, or why should they be involved?

❏ can the Media be trusted (or does the story come first)?

❏ to what degree can the interaction be managed on a proactive basis? To what extent can the Media be controlled (if at all) in order to achieve a required outcome?

❏ what, in outcome or Performance Management terms (Chapter 24) are the expectations from any decision to interact with the Media; *or*

❏ what are the estimates of the costs or risks versus the likely benefits of the interaction?

❏ to what extent is the relevant Media considered to be excessively London-centric, and what is the estimate of the likely consequences of this bias?

Ultimately, an interaction with any Media raises a basic question for the decision maker. Is the Media there to meet your requirements (and what might this cost?). Or is your role instead to feed the Media with information and stories to suit its own purpose? How will that Media react to attempts to implement proactive control and management on your part. This issue became a fundamental (and almost certainly a destructive) feature of discussions about Brexit.

A dilemma continuum – a judgement may therefore have to be made as to (i) where on any dilemma continuum (illustrated in Figure 3) the relevant Media is perceived to be located; and (ii) what this Media's role is seen to be by those people charged with the responsibility for interpreting the matter. Issues of Perception are dealt with in Chapter 9.

Thus, for example in a dilemma continuum of three compartments as identified in Figure 3, and using the **Left – Centre – Right** version shown there, decision maker perceptions might be mapped as follows:

❖ **Left** – a particular Media may be categorised as inappropriate, febrile or hostile. Worse, that Media may be characterised by a syndrome in which all news or stories are deliberately talked up (exaggerated) to crisis proportions. Control / crisis management protocols may therefore have permanently to be kept in place in order to manage any "fake news" or unavoidable interaction with this Media. Crisis Management is described in Chapter 18 of this Book.

❖ **Centre** – use the Media pragmatically on a case by case basis. A view might be taken that some degree of proactive control might be negotiable.

❖ **Right** – the Media may be judged to be any or all of useful, trustworthy or compliant. Some degree of control is likely to be available.

The Reader may choose to identify examples from his or her own experience. Reference to Media management is also made in Chapters 8 and 18.

Chapter Three
Why Manage Dilemmas?

Michael Wolff asserts in his book Fire and Fury *(pps263-264) that President Trump 'was impetuous and yet did not like to make decisions ... and no decision hounded him so much as what to do about Afghanistan. It was a conundrum that became a battle ... [there] was an approaching need to make a decision on Afghanistan – a military quagmire he knew little about ... [and] having inherited it did not make his feelings warmer or make him to want to dwell on it further. He knew the war was cursed [and] put the responsibility for it on two of his favourite people to blame: Bush and Obama. [As] for Xxxx, Afghanistan represented [yet] one more failure of establishment thinking. More precisely, it represented the establishment's inability to confront failure.'*

This chapter describes key reasons for the proactive management of dilemmas; and introduces the concept of the Management Dilemma as driver of events, action, or reaction. The significance of Management Dilemmas was identified in Chapter One.

DILEMMAS REQUIRING DECISION

A judgement may have been made that a particular dilemma needs to be resolved. That is, a decision will have to be made by those people responsible for dealing with, or sorting out the matter, however difficult it may be. For instance, a country with active environmental policies will have to bite the bullet about future electricity generation. Once a decision to phase out power generation by burning hydrocarbon fuels has been made, replacements will have to be put in place. Their construction will take many years, and part of the decision will involve accepting or rejecting the use of nuclear power generation as a part of the package. In the end, whatever the alternatives, and however unpopular those alternatives might be, a country's government dare not let the lights go out.

DILEMMAS PUT ON HOLD

Alternatively, a decision may be made that a particular dilemma does not at this point of time need to be resolved. The UK Government, for instance, prevaricated for years over the expansion of London's airport capacity. Whichever decision it made (such as expanding Heathrow or Gatwick) would have been unpopular. At the same time the various airports carry on their work and ship passengers in and out. Canvassing or lobbying for one option or another does not necessarily persuade decision- makers who may yet to be convinced of the need to do anything, or to spend huge sums of money.

To put the resolution of a dilemma "on hold" implies a knowing, deliberate or strategic side-stepping or avoidance of decision or action by those responsible. In the UK, such a strategy has been used for instance in the case of proposed investments in potentially disruptive and expensive infrastructure projects, regional super-hospitals, or expenditure on high cost or controversial weapons systems.

Just because a decision *could* be made does not necessarily mean that it *should* be made, or *will* be made.

DILEMMAS RESULTING FROM PAST COMMITMENTS

A specific dilemma decision requirement may result from the making of *past commitments* to courses of action which it has since proven difficult (or impossible) to abandon, but whose current viability or justification is now being questioned. This for example is an issue for the military, for whom new weapons systems may take years to develop or build, but which may be obsolete (or excessively expensive) before they can be deployed.

Reference is made in Chapter 26 to the work of Staw & Ross in analysing the effects of *commitments to decisions* on the Dilemma Management process.

DILEMMAS AS CONTINGENCIES

Once defined, a dilemma may come to be seen by decision-makers as a key *contingency* which is likely to shape the outcome of the decision choice process. The nature of the dilemma, and the way in which it might be resolved may come (i) to *constrain* what alternatives might be identified as possible, or (ii) to act as a *limiting factor*. **The need to take contingencies, constraints and limiting factors into account is a standard part of any resource allocation, financial management, or decision- making process.** That is, the nature of the dilemma may place restraints on what type of decision could be made, or what might be financed or resourced.

As an example, post Brexit decisions on UK trading relationships will fall into this category. The decision to leave the European Union must by definition provide dilemmas about the country's future international trading relationships, as well as about the nature of the long-term relationship between Northern Ireland and its Irish neighbour; and with Scotland.

DILEMMAS AS ENTITIES INCONSISTENT WITH RECEIVED WISDOMS

These received wisdoms might include:

❏ the assumption that progress follows an inevitable straight line towards future improvement (that is, that progress must always be linear rather than demonstrating what may equally be the reality of a cyclical, regressive, repetitive, or circular dynamic);
❏ the probability that all problems contain their own solution ("there is nothing that we can't solve for you");
❏ the probability that "win-win" will always be possible;
❏ the probability that all exigencies can be forecast, avoided, dealt with, or their potential effect mitigated. This syndrome is for instance at the heart of the UK Webbist, Fabian and 1930's (or President Allende's subsequent Chilean) corporatist concept of the "public administration" of central and local government matters, healthcare, etc. Everything can be predicted or pre-planned. The civil servants or experts who run the show will reign supreme in managing the affairs of the "ordinary people" who should in return happily believe what they are told, pay their taxes, and trust those in charge! Management Dilemmas will never happen. Or if they do they will be resolved. The concept of management process is redundant – an American import

merely suitable for people "in trade", retailers and the like (!). This issue is dealt with in later chapters;

❏ the probability that compromise will be available. It will always be all right on the night;

❏ the probability that administrators and managers are always right, in particular the higher up they are in the organisation hierarchy!

DILEMMAS AS SOURCE OF RISK, THREAT OR CRISIS

The need to manage dilemmas is reinforced where their diagnosis shows them to be a likely source of risk, uncertainty, threat or crisis. Decision-making processes need in this case to be fully cognisant with the disciplines of risk and crisis management, and with the ability to recognise and to deal with threats. Past UK, US and European military involvement in the Middle East and Afghanistan, however well-meant and politically justified, has thrown up a variety of dilemmas associated with religious-based terrorism which pose a major threat to people's welfare. Does a country become involved in international military ventures, or should it pursue a policy of strict non-intervention and hope to keep out of trouble? Is such a choice even possible?

The issue of dilemmas as a source of risk, uncertainty, threat or crisis are dealt with in more detail in Chapters 17 and 18.

DILEMMAS AS SOURCE OF OPPORTUNITY

By the same token, dilemmas may serve to act as sources of opportunity, if recognised as such. For instance, lateral thinking about the issue of housing shortages in the UK might reveal the possibilities of making more use of prefabricated or off the peg construction (for instance using structural steelwork, wood or composites), or the hire of redundant passenger or cruise ships as speedy solutions to what is becoming an urgent and divisive problem affecting young people in urban areas.

Certainly, where one institution fails to recognise or do something about an extant dilemma, there is no guarantee that somebody else will make the same mistake. They may fill the vacuum for instance by:

❏ establishing market entry by the introduction of new knowledge, new paradigms, new processes or new products that respond to the circumstances of the dilemma; *or*
❏ forming a new political party, such as UKIP, (etc);
❏ etc.

The issue of the exploitation and management of opportunities is given detailed treatment in other books written by this Author, as listed in the Introduction.

DILEMMAS AS A SOURCE OF COMPLEXITY
The existence of one or more dilemmas may introduce complexity into a situation where a decision on resolution may, or instead may not be required, as described above. For instance, the NATO membership of East European and Baltic countries formally under the sway of the USSR, and the stationing of multinational armed forces in those countries is bound to complicate the management of the already difficult political relationship with the neighbouring Russian Federation.

The impact of the addition of such complexity will be relevant to the effectiveness of the processes of diagnosis, decision-making and resolution described in later chapters of this book. Complexity as a source of dilemmas is identified in Chapter 4.

DILEMMAS AS BANANA SKINS
Dilemmas may turn out to be unseen banana skins under the feet of unwary or unprepared decision-makers (or simply people who have not read this Book!). Such banana skins may for instance trip up stakeholders, politicians, managers, administrators, individual members of staff, or those responsible for brand or corporate reputation, (etc). They may expose shortcomings in performance management, leadership, or quality assurance. Such banana skins might be based on any of the following:

❏ a failure to take a full range of variables into account in situation analysis or decision-making. This was clearly the case in the 2016 UK Brexit Referendum dilemma when London-centricity, and both of the prevalent media and political opinionation blinded government thinking to popular sentiment about globalisation, immigration and the European Union in (what in some cases had been the) industrial heartlands of England and Wales. This is in turn related to:-

❑ being taken by surprise by the turn of events, again indicating a failure to anticipate the potential damage that may be caused by ineffective dilemma decision analysis and process. This issue is dealt with in later chapters;

❑ 20-20 vision in hindsight (or the "Chilcot Effect") in which a failure to properly recognise and explore the nature of current dilemmas will result in decision-making whose consequences *now* will come back in *future hindsight* to haunt those responsible. This was the case of UK military involvement in Iraq and the subsequent criticisms of the Chilcot Report. Criticism based on hindsight is easy but its effect may still be devastating for the people, politicians or institutions involved, such as the British Army which faced severe criticisms for sending troops to fight without proper and effective equipment. Creating a defensible position now, however difficult, may be the only security against being badly "bitten on the bum" in the future;

❑ rigid opinionation, complacency, failure to think laterally and to "think out of the box", or to accept ideas "not invented here" which may be relevant to managing the dilemma. These are classic decision-making problems dealt with in later chapters of this book and given extensive treatment in other books written by this Author and listed in the Introduction. The identification of dilemmas, however difficult or intransigent they are, may force people to have to think the unthinkable or to get ahead of the game, whatever that game may be. *That is:-*

❑ dilemmas may provide *reality checks*, however much people dislike them or fear their consequences. The UK Brexit vote provided just such a reality check. Certain decisions might have to be made and unpopular choices considered, because the real world will force them on the country irrespective of the sentiment towards them.

DILEMMA MANAGEMENT AS INDICATOR OF COMPETENCE

This chapter has described a number of reasons why the proper identification and management of dilemmas may be necessary. Some dilemmas may need resolution; others will act as constraints on what is possible or desirable; and so on. Where, however, those responsible either fail or refuse to recognise or acknowledge the existence of Management Dilemmas that will inevitably affect or constrain what is possible, then quite reasonably, personal or organisational competence may come to be questioned. It may become clear to the outside world, to voters, to the media, or to political opponents (etc) that inaction is variously due to personal or committee dithering, incompetence, lack of effective leadership, hand-wringing, infighting, analysis-paralysis, or pure indecision. Such indecision may manifest itself in courses of action (or rather, simple lack of progress) that can be characterised at best as *muddling through*, or at worst the burying of corporate or decision-maker heads "in the sand" in the hope that the problem will just go away. This issue is dealt with in more detail in Parts Four and Five.

Case example: the UK NHS – sadly, it can be argued that this competency syndrome has been, and is still characteristic of the management ("administration") of the UK's state healthcare system (the NHS), for instance in coping with pressures for improved performance and financial management, or in the likely rationalisation of hospital capability into fewer more expert locations universally characterised (i) by excellent status in their allocated specialism and research, and (ii) by world class standards of infection control as described in an earlier chapter.

DILEMMAS AS DRIVERS OF EVENTS

Ultimately, and whether decision-makers or administrators like it or not, some dilemmas will act as the *drivers* or determinants of events. This is true of resource allocation at a time of politically limited funding and performance management pressures based in part on imposed strategies of stretch and leverage ("doing more with the same, or with less"). It is true for police force numbers and knife crime. And it is true for international relationships with friend or foe. It is true of the need for national defence, security, terrorism management, or international peacekeeping.

CASE EXAMPLE

Gun control – countries such as the USA have laws that establish and protect the rights of citizens to purchase and carry firearms. In the case of the USA, these laws were laid down in post- Revolutionary times when the new and independent American Government feared re-invasion by the British for instance from the remaining Royalist territory that is now called Canada, and decided to maintain fully armed militias as a key line of defence against such threat. Having subsequently established effective formal military forces (for in- stance during the American Civil War) successive US Presidents have since tried to restrict what is now widely perceived to be un- necessary and highly dangerous individual gun ownership, only to fail under circumstances where lobbying by the American National Rifle Association (NRA) and US gun manufacturers (with some sup- port from the Republican Party) has defeated all political attempts at gun control. What is left is a spiralling carnage resulting from the individual freedom to purchase and use even the most high powered rifles and semi- automatic weapons, such as those legitimately used by the military. Certified mental instability may be no bar to gun ownership. An individual might simply buy a gun and ammunition by post from a newspaper. Deaths and injuries from weapons acci- dentally discharged by young children also abound.

Gun ownership in the USA has created what appear to be highly dangerous and insolvable dilemmas given (i) intransigent popular attitudes for and against gun ownership and (ii) the dysfunctional nature of the US Government system, which was created at a time when fear of the British and their allies was uppermost in the minds of American legislators, but which now no longer appears to be fit for purpose. But a civilised society cannot function properly without the most strict gun control (there can for instance be no justification for the individual ownership of handguns, high powered rifles, or military assault weapons capable of rapid fire). There can be no place and no justification for any dilemmas affecting the degree to which that society protects its members from entirely avoidable harm caused by unnecessary gun ownership.

Part Two

Some Dilemma Sources (I): Big Pictures, People and Culture

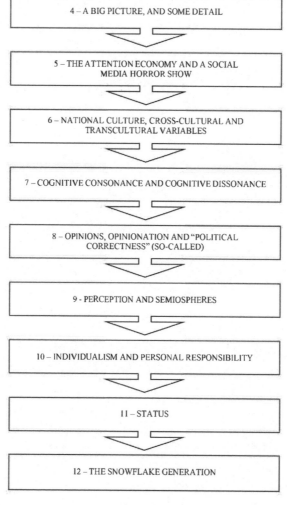

4 – A BIG PICTURE, AND SOME DETAIL

5 – THE ATTENTION ECONOMY AND A SOCIAL MEDIA HORROR SHOW

6 – NATIONAL CULTURE, CROSS-CULTURAL AND TRANSCULTURAL VARIABLES

7 – COGNITIVE CONSONANCE AND COGNITIVE DISSONANCE

8 – OPINIONS, OPINIONATION AND "POLITICAL CORRECTNESS" (SO-CALLED)

9 - PERCEPTION AND SEMIOSPHERES

10 – INDIVIDUALISM AND PERSONAL RESPONSIBILITY

11 – STATUS

12 – THE SNOWFLAKE GENERATION

Figure 4

Chapter Four
A Big Picture, and Some Detail

This is the first of the chapters of this Book that identify, categorise, and illustrate *different sources of dilemmas*. Chapter 4 commences this analysis on a basis from the *general or generic* (macro) and "Big Picture" to the *specific* (micro), the *detailed and the directly useable*.

The necessity for such an analysis is quite simple. If decision-makers and the people responsible for the process of Dilemma Management cannot identify and properly diagnose the causes and character of the dilemmas they face, and with which they will have to contend, then they will not be able to resolve them.

A BIG PICTURE (THE MACRO)

GENERAL OR GENERIC <u>EXTERNAL</u> DILEMMA SOURCES

General or generic dilemma sources may be identified at a **Big Picture or macro** level scale by such *boundary management* processes as *external* scanning or event monitoring. Such processes may identify broad contingent factors, determinants or drivers such as:

❑ **PREMSTLE**, a standard acronym that stands for **P**olitics and political drivers; **R**esource or financial conditions; **E**conomy; **M**arket; **S**ociety, language and culture; **T**echnology, **L**aw and legal regulation; **E**nvironment.
❑ Specific issues associated with the Defence of the Realm, Policing and Security, Counter-Terrorism, Crime and Corruption.
❑ The impact of the Media.
❑ The impact of the Attention Economy (Chapter 5).
❑ The impact of Social Media (Chapter 5).

These external sources may create dilemmas in such practical contexts as:

❏ Knowledge Management;
❏ the political and regulatory frameworks to which people and organisations are subject, and the resource allocation implications associated therewith;
❏ the existence of mutually exclusive or incompatible stakeholder expectations;
❏ the degree of risk, uncertainty and complexity as characteristics of the external environment;
❏ the market, trade, and the competition that characterises them;
❏ perceptions of external threat or opportunity;
❏ technology change and requisite innovation, including Kondriatev Waves and S Curves that may or may not require a response (as dealt with in a later Section of this Chapter);
❏ informatics and the applications of information and communication technologies (ICTs), "Big Data", etc;
❏ the ethical, *whether moral, amoral, or immoral*; *and*
❏ the social and the cultural; *and*
❏ the specific and increasingly critical impact of social media on young people in the UK (which is dealt with at various points in this Book);
❏ competitive access to sources of funding eg for Public or Third Sector;
❏ the paradigms upon which work methodologies are based, such as excellence, lean or stretch, economy, efficiency, usability, the search for competitive or comparative advantage, the relative emphasis on customer or client satisfaction, performance management, (etc).

CASE EXAMPLE
UK Higher Education – educational developments occurring at a time of increasing global competition, pressure to demonstrate performance in line with increasingly prescriptive government targets, and tougher financial or performance measurement methodologies may put pressure on the classic British Higher Education Model. Demands for vocationality, usability and work relevance may for example result in the erosion of the traditional non-science and

non-engineering streams in the longer-established universities. Such streams might become marginalised into an expensive niche status available only to wealthy and self-funding middle class and international students in favour of an increased vocational and competency-based emphasis on entrepreneurship, business, finance, technology or Information Technology routes; and to which government funding may or might again become attached.

The precedent was established by Napoleon Bonaparte who set up the (now well-established and prestigious) Grandes Ecoles in France to provide the practical expertise needed to run his empire. The German Fachhochschule follow a similar emphasis on vocationality, adding foreign language teaching as a priority.

GENERAL OR GENERIC <u>INTERNAL</u> DILEMMA SOURCES

General or generic internal dilemma sources may be identified at a Big Picture scale or macro level by such features, processes or variables as:

- ❑ stakeholder variety and complexity;
- ❑ stakeholder ideology;
- ❑ political expectations and behaviour;
- ❑ political or corporate governance;
- ❑ leadership style;
- ❑ processes of policy formulation or strategic management;
- ❑ management process;
- ❑ resource allocation or financial and asset management;
- ❑ the degree of complexity;
- ❑ the prevailing degree of variety and diversity eg in political party memberships, voter electorates, social segmentation, religious practice, immigration and associated transcultural variations present in society, etc;
- ❑ service provision and attitudes towards customer service;
- ❑ quality assurance and management;
- ❑ organisation and structure;
- ❑ workplace, employment and training;

❏ operational and performance management;
❏ requirement for change and improvement;
❏ language and perceptions;
❏ equality, diversity and opportunity management, such as impacts on recruitment and promotion criteria;
❏ etc.

THE CREATION OF DILEMMAS BY OTHERS

An organisation and its management may face, and have to deal with dilemmas *deliberately created by others*. Typically, such dilemmas are put in place to embarrass, to discomfort, or to disrupt those against whom the dilemma is targeted, or instead to create an unwanted crisis to which a response will have to be made. This Section lists seven illustrative examples, as follow.

Market competition – as in the case (i) of UK grocery discounters (Aldi and Lidl to whom reference has been made in an earlier chapter) using the advantage of cost, price, and a limited product line against those shareholder-based competitors such as Tesco or Sainsbury who choose to stock a wider range of lines and whose cost / price strategies must generate profits to pay dividends and maintain share values on the Stock Market. At the same time, (ii) retailers such as Tesco and Asda have, by selling clothing lines at low prices in their supermarkets created a dilemma for clothes retailers who choose to retain High Street or shopping centre locations. Such retailers must finance overheads such as rents and local taxes out of their revenues in a consumer behaviour situation where they hope that many customers will continue to distrust (or can be persuaded to continue to distrust) the process of shopping for clothes by mail order or on-line, and retain a preference to go shopping for clothes. The case of "High Street Woes" was described in Chapter 2.

Technology obsolescence – in which newcomers who are not committed to an existing technology that is fast becoming obsolete may place original suppliers (who have not yet developed new capabilities associated with the replacement technology, and about the existence of which they may remain in denial) in a terminal dilemma. Such was the case of locomotive manufacturing when traditional manufacturers of steam locomotives such as Baldwin and North British disappeared under the onslaught of the introduction of more efficient diesel-electric and electric locomotives manufactured by English Electric, GEC, General Motors, GE Corp, Siemens and Alsthom, etc. Similarly, the market for expensive electro-mechanical cash registers, dominated by NCR, disappeared in a few years as superior electronic versions were introduced to retailers by manufacturers such as Burroughs. The issue of technology dynamics and technology obsolescence as dilemma sources needing management is also dealt with at various other points of this Book.

Dialectics and debate – a reasoned or reasonable debate may be necessary in order to define the parameters of an issue or a dilemma and to identify decision choices associated with it. A dialectical process may carry this debate forward, for instance within a parliamentary or an institutional context, into an exercise of disputation and criticism based upon logical or rational principles and dogmas. Such a process of scrutiny, aimed at yielding the "truth" about a subject may also clarify matters and permit a thorough identification of relevant or appropriate courses of action. **However, what the Oxford English Dictionary calls "logical disputation"** *may become an end in itself.* **This may have a number of unforeseen, non-useful, non-usable, or unwanted** consequences. These might include:

❏ delay by "analysis-paralysis" in which nothing ever gets done. The debate is what matters. It becomes an end in itself; the decision can be put off in favour of more debate. This *stalemate syndrome* is also described in other chapters of this Book; *or*
❏ more and more dilemmas are identified, increasing complexity (perhaps unnecessarily) making resolution even more difficult;
❏ the loss of sight of "Occam's Razor", which states that entities should not without good reason be complicated. Occam's Razor as a decision rule prescribes simplicity. Keep it simple!
❏ necessary compromises, such as those associated with resource allocation and financial stewardship (particularly of taxpayer or shareholder monies) become more difficult to fashion;

❏ those involved losing sight of the over-riding priority for policy and decision-makers of responsibility, application, usefulness, implementation and action in respect of issues; or the defence and security of the realm; or other Big Picture type dilemmas which must be dealt with.

Matters may be made worse in the context of media interactions (e.g. as described in Chapter 2) in which an aggressive media, with journalists under intense pressure to file ever more eye-catching stories, stokes up discussion and debate as a way of meeting their own targets for impact. Ultimately, a febrile atmosphere may be created in which the priorities of policy and decision-makers are shaped by media pressures which, for instance, politicians find impossible to resist, and which creates further (but unnecessary) dilemmas for them to resolve. This syndrome itself creates an anti- democratic dilemma.

Yet Voters don't vote for journalists, but for parliamentary candidates of their choice!

Political dilemmas – in which ongoing shifts in ideology or party position may put MP's who were elected at the immediately previous election into a personal dilemma. Do they conform to any new ideology or policy now being touted (and which did not necessarily prevail at the last election) if they, their constituency representatives, or their trade union do not approve of it? Do they publicly use their Parliamentary position to resist the changes? And if so, do they run the risk of deselection before the next election in favour of more acquiescent constituency candidates? Or do they split away from the party and form a rump, or even a new party? Only at the next election will they reap the rewards of their decisions, whether for good or ill.

Media or Single-Interest / Pressure Groups – who may create dilemmas to which other parties perceive that they are forced to respond. For instance, media or passenger representatives may create financial or resource allocation dilemmas associated with the sentiments and opinions of rail commuters who have to use a franchised rail service deemed (i) by operator and franchisor to be cost-effective but (ii) seen for whatever reason by customers to be unsatisfactory and expensive. Such dilemmas may be created in order deliberately to force the franchisor to change the franchise, or to increase the level of public subsidy in order to provide what media or pressure groups consider to be a better, and preferably a cheaper subsidised service.

Another example is illustrated by the actions of media, single-interest or pressure groups that campaign on behalf of certain types of groups identified by Equality Legislation. Those classified under the headings of race, gender or sexual orientation may find that their **Voices** are well represented and heavily publicised. Other categories may find themselves with a much lower level (or no) championing. The Voices of the elderly and the disabled (in particular the mentally ill) as **Victims** may be heard with difficulty, if at all. For instance, as a result, the elderly are called "crumble" or "bed-blockers"; whilst the mentally ill may be at the bottom of everyone's pile. The issue of **Hearing Voices** is dealt with in a later Section below.

Terrorism and security – in which the strategy and actions of terrorists and terrorist organisations may have the effect of creating security dilemmas associated with resource allocation. Should security agencies concentrate their efforts on intelligence seeking as preventative strategy; or on providing a very high level of visible and armed presence as a means of avoiding major incidents such as those that have affected France, the USA, and Spain during recent years. Similarly, what are the legalities of permitting members of the armed forces (as opposed to police officers) to fire plastic / rubber bullets, or instead to shoot to kill in circumstances in which they and civilians are under threat? These issues are dealt with in Chapters 16 and 25.

Military strategy – in which dilemmas derive from decisions as to how governments might choose to structure, to resource, and to deploy their armed forces in conditions where external aggression takes the form of cyberwarfare (such as attacks on weapon system weaknesses that result from an self-imposed or manufacturer-led reliance on over-complicated computerised technologies); psychological and media threat; undeclared warfare; or territorial creep (as for example practiced at this time of writing by Russia and China). Conventional military thinking and process may be of limited use, needing augmentation or replacement (i) by advances in intelligence seeking, or (ii) by aggressive diplomacy, increasingly likely to be backed up by very tough economic sanctions as responses.

HEARING VOICES

The *Voice of the Victim* was described in a previous Section above. It may be the case that such Voices are simply hard to hear given the welter of competing communications calling for attention or support. Even if the Voices can be heard, their effectiveness as communications creating attention and action (the marketer's AIDA) may be a function of the degree to which their source can effectively *be identified and interpreted*. Who are the people involved and what do they want? Recognition and interpretation may be a source of dilemmas. One example lies in the consequences of *the raising of the retirement age*. Where state pensions are payable, this may save the Government money. But raising the retirement age assumes that people are still physically and mentally capable of doing their jobs. It also overrules people's plans for their retirement, a subject which may be very dear to their hearts and have significant political consequences at future elections. Such overt favouring of *fiscal benefit* as against *individual benefit* may give rise to the dilemma as to what is the *public benefit* of Pension policy (and who should define it?). Later retirement keeps experience in the system but delays progress for the younger workers behind. And which age group of workers are likely to be more motivated?

Other Voices whose identification and interpretation may be likely to give rise to dilemmas might include any of the following:

❏ the Voice of the Voter;
❏ the Voices of Stakeholders;
❏ the Voice of Families and Households;
❏ the Voice of the Taxpayer;
❏ the Voices of the Rich, the Powerful, and the Influential (and their Networks);

- ❏   the Voices of the Customer, Client, or Patient (etc);
- ❏   the Voice of "Youth", however this is defined;
- ❏   the Voices of those who are in Debt, or in receipt of state Benefit Payments; or those who for whatever reason consider themselves to be Marginalised, Disenfranchised, Dispossessed, or on the edge of Society.

The *Voice of Opinion* is described in Chapter 8. The *Voice of Threat* is dealt with in Chapter 18.

SOME DETAIL (THE MICRO)

EVENT AND CONCEPT CHARACTERISTICS

The identification and resolution of dilemmas being described in this Book will next depend on *specific* (**micro**) *cognitive and collective processes of perception, definition, value assessment and assurance*, for instance as described in Chapter 9. **Is everybody agreed about what the dilemma is and what its implications are?** This detailed process of identification, validation and assurance may depend on the nature of the characteristics of the *events* or the *concepts* which best represent the dilemma upon which focus is being brought to bear. These events or concepts may contain a variety or diversity of possible interpretations, about which agreement must be reached and disagreements overcome. The Author lists some of these event and concept characteristics in his Book "Equality, Diversity and Opportunity Management" and illustrates some of them here with specific examples from a national Equality Agenda, thus:

Absence or presence – by which a decision (for whatever reason) may not, will not, or cannot be made as to the actual existence or otherwise of the event or concept. Dilemmas resulting from the event or concept are unlikely to be dealt with if their existence (i) is unknown or uncertain, or are (ii) unacknowledged, or (iii) are denied. *Example:* strong management resistance has frequently characterised UK workplace attitudes (i) towards the existence of mental health issues; or instead (ii) to the widespread incidence of crippling employee back pain (for instance in the nursing profession) or poor back health caused by certain types of work practice, poor posture, damaging seating, or ineffective ergonomics.

Ambiguity – by which the event or concept is characterised by a variety of potentially conflicting definitions or interpretations, and presents alternative meanings from which the decision-maker may have to choose. *Example*: the understanding of work-related stress and mental health disability issues in the workplace, which can typically suffer from multiple conceptualisations (or misconceptions) and viewpoints.

Change – by which the concept or event, and the variables that define it, are subject to a dynamic or pattern that is characterised by any or all of on-going variation, originality, novelty, inconsistency, instability, and uncertainty. There may be *no precedent* or relevant past experience by which to make decisions based on the concept or event, whose interpretation could in any case be ambiguous. *Example*: the appointment of women and gay people as bishops or imams in Christian or Muslim religious organisations.

Complexity – by which the components of the event or concept are characterised by a wide variety of inter-related variables, each of which (as well as the inter-relationship between them) must be considered in any decision-making process. *Example*: the specification and high cost of "disability friendly" public buildings or transport infrastructures where the likely pattern of usage of disabled facilities cannot be predicted in advance.

Entropy – by which the nature and outcomes of the concept or event are likely to be characterised by such negative features as stagnation, decline, or deterioration. Open Systems Theory states for instance that systems which do not receive, internalise and apply an adequate quantity or variety of relevant or novel information and stimulus from the external environment may be subject to entropy. *Example*: the negative humanitarian, social or political impacts of out-dated or inappropriate cultural traditions or religious orthodoxies, for instance as described in more detail in Chapter 6.

Equifinality – by which it may be proposed on a contingency basis that there is **no** "one", "only", or "best" way of doing something. *A task may be carried out, or an objective achieved in a variety of different ways.* What matters is the end result. The detail of the process involved might vary according to circumstances, experience, capability or choice. *Example:* the achievement of compliance with UK Equality Law (eg in respect of the treatment of daughters, wives, widows, and women in general) may have to be assured in different types of communities by means that are deemed *to be most appropriate* to their specific cultural or religious circumstances. This issue is dealt with at various points in this Book.

Inconsistency – by which the event or concept possesses varying and unpredictable features over time. The concept or event is likely to be characterised by change or a lack of clear precedent, so decision-making about it may not always be able to be the same. *Example*: the unpredictable legal outcomes of actions at UK Employment Tribunals or courts in respect of protected Equality categories, such as women or members of ethnic groups, and the resulting potential for inconsistencies between judgements upon which Case Law is then accumulated. Such inconsistency may provide law-makers with dilemmas as to decisions on the framing of new laws that follow developments in Case Law.

Negotiability – which is defined by the OED as an event or a concept possessing the property of being subject to *negotiation* and a subsequent agreement (or disagreement) between two or more parties. It is also defined as a process (i) of one party conferring with another for the purpose of arranging some matter by mutual agreement; (ii) of discussing a matter with a view to achieving a settlement or compromise as outcome; (iii) of dealing with, managing or conducting a matter requiring capability and consideration; and (iv) of overcoming obstacles by means of skilful interaction or manoeuvre.

Originality, novelty or innovation – by which the concept or event presents new features for which there is again no decision-making precedent; or which require the development of new thinking, new experience, or new capability before any agreement on effective decisions can be made about them. *Example*: the potential impact of genetic testing. Genetic testing can be used to identify the medical history of an individual or their family. Such tests may be used to predict the likelihood of future health problems, life expectancy, and to quantify the risks to a supplier of health or life insurance. This may be seen by the financial services industry to be reasonable because it is efficient. Should law-makers therefore permit genetic information to be used in making decisions about the sale (or refusal to sell) health or life insurance, or to prohibit its use?

Priority (or urgency) – by which the definition of the concept or event may be perceived to have characteristics of *relative urgency* when placed in comparison with other events or concepts to which some kind of response may also be needed. The concept of priority may present the decision-maker with perceptions of an apparently unavoidable choice between taking action sooner rather than later. At the same time, therefore, perceptions of urgency may force the decision-maker to reduce the priority with which other events are being treated. This is a classic operations management dilemma faced by healthcare agencies dealing with acute or mental illness, sickness or disability (etc), who must juggle the use of available treatment capacity in accordance with an unpredictable and changing demand pattern (for instance associated with a major accident, an act of terrorism, or a flu epidemic). There is always going to have to be someone at the head of the queue, and someone near to the end of it. Dilemmas may thus be associated with (i) variations in attitudes or (ii) the consistent choice of decision options towards what, in the overall scheme of things, constitutes *an order or degree of relative priority* in the case of allocation (or reallocating) staff and resources, the analysis of performance compared to standards or expectations, or strategies for engaging with the media (etc).

Priority is likely to present dilemmas associated with the issues of Safeguarding, as described in Chapter 16.

Concepts or events characterised by priority or urgency may also be likely to be associated with Risk, as described in Chapter 17. They may instead contain a potential for Threat or Crisis, as described in Chapter 18.

Stability, instability, or the pattern of relative stability – by which the characteristics of the concept or event do not only display inconsistency over time, but are to some degree variable and unstable. Unstable concepts will show a degree of change and uncertainty, and that change or uncertainty may be more or less predictable. *Example*: the nature of UK attitudes to immigration issues, and to the kinds of political decisions made about them in the face of unstable public attitudes.

Value implications – the concept or event may possess characteristics of value (or *values*) whose potential outcome may shape the choice of decision or resolution. *Example*: the issue of what can be defined as "reasonable" or "proportionate" in legal, resource or behavioural terms may provide key dilemmas for policy or decision-makers. For example, what is a reasonable sum of money to spend on a national health service; should that money be spent on prevention or cure (as described in a previous chapter); and how much of the cost should be contributed by voters, taxpayers and households? Also see Chapter 25.

Variety or Diversity – by which the decision-making process based on the event or concept is likely to be characterised by a degree of variation of circumstance or experience, thereby giving rise to potential dilemmas. The greater the degree of variety or diversity, (i) the more important it will be to be able to identify and differentiate the various features of the decision requirement; (ii) the greater may be the decision-making load; (iii) the more critical will be the capability to deal with, or possess experience of these conditions of variety and diversity; and (iv) the more important it will be to seek agreement about them. *Example*: complexities associated the management, care, and funding of an ageing community; and of age as a protected category, giving rise to policy and resource allocation dilemmas. This dilemma may be exacerbated where it can be shown that the elderly have been very long-term taxpayers, and that they constitute a large voting block.

Volume – the nature, timing, and pressure of the dilemma resolution or decision-making process may depend on the volume or scale implied in the concept or event. The greater the volume or scale of the concept, (i) the greater the decision-making load; (ii) the greater the risk of managerial overload, process confusion, or time delay; and (iii) the more likely will be the risk of the occurrence of filtering and over-simplification as pressure for action mounts on individuals or departments. *Example*: national healthcare arrangements, whether preventative, restorative, or palliative are likely to be characterised by multiple issues, multiple debates, and multiple dilemmas. Some of these are dealt with at various points in this Book.

Issues of *Risk and Uncertainty* as event or concept characteristics are dealt with specifically and in more detail in Chapters 15, 16, 17 and 18; also in Parts Four and Five of this Book.

Chapter Five

The Attention Economy and a Social Media Horror Show

A prior knowledge of such dystopian works as "Brave New World", "1984", "Lord of the Flies" and "Fahrenheit 451"; or the films "A Clockwork Orange", "Blade Runner", "Soylent Green" and "The Matrix" might be useful for this chapter?

A TRULY HORRIFIC SOCIAL MEDIA SHOW (I)

A 14-year-old <u>Minor</u> committed suicide after she had viewed images of self-harm and suicide on the internet sites of Instagram and Pinterest. The girl, Molly Russell, had seemed to her parents to be well and happy. But she <u>believed</u> that she was depressed – a <u>perception</u> she had hidden from her parents because she felt that she did not want to burden them with her anxieties. Instead, she had gone online to explore her feelings. There, her father believes, she was bombarded by graphic images of self-harm and references to suicide that led her to kill herself. Indeed, a month after she died Pinterest sent her an e-mail containing a photo of a slashed thigh and a caption stating that 'I can't tell you how many times I wish I was dead' [Source: *The Week*].

Author's note – this is the most shocking example in this Book of a failure of corporate Dilemma Management. Given his own personal and professional experience of anxiety and mental health issues the Author insists that all UK parents reading this Book must in future exert a totally robust, strongly proactive, and undisputed control over the access of Minors such as Molly to any form of internet or social media interaction. He reminds parents that if the Safeguarding (Chapter 16) of their children requires urgent expenditure on the services of child psychiatrists, then such expenditure must of necessity displace the non-essential luxuries of (unnecessary) holidays, new kitchens or new cars (etc).

ANOTHER HORROR SHOW (II)

The progress of an appalling attack on a mosque in New Zealand in which about fifty worshippers were murdered *was recorded as it took place*. It was uploaded on to the Internet for all to witness as it happened. There was a delay before the recording was deleted by so-called "Moderators", but it is likely still to be lurking somewhere or other in the ether as a testimony to the degree to which the nature of social media has become non-controllable, sinister, corrupted and brutalised. This is "Fahrenheit 451" territory.

THE ATTENTION ECONOMY

The *Attention Economy* treats **people's attention** as a scarce resource, to be competed for at a time of man-made information overload. Enormous investments in this so-called economy are now acting as a serious dilemma source.

The Attention Economy was described by the *Guardian Newspaper* as the "largest, most standardised and potentially the most centralised form of personal attention (mind) control ever invented".

The Attention Economy is described as a globalised internet. It is shaped in part by the demands of the advertising industry and by advertising-led consumer marketers acting on behalf of their clients. It has also been exploited by politicians such as Donald Trump. Its roots lie in ongoing developments in US behavioural and information psychology which identifies ways in which technological design may be used (i) to persuade people, (ii) to retain their attention, and (iii) to re-orient their thought processes.

Internet technology companies such as Apple, Facebook, Google, Twitter, Instagram and Snapchat have in consequence responded to the values, incentives and paradigms of advertising companies. In particular they have developed techniques *that are designed to capture, and to hold a proportion of people's attention*. This may graphically be illustrated by the disastrous (addictive and corrupting) practice of selling *on-line gambling*, for instance with fixed-price odds and the potential for rapid iteration. It explains why the *Guardian's* correspondent noted that "there's a reason why many of us can't put our phones down: the technology is designed to be addictive". He notes that US research shows that some people touch, swipe or tap their phones *over two thousand times per day.* Quite apart from taking them to bed with them at night.

The technology developed for the Attention Economy has also come to encourage frequent communication (*whether good, bullying or bad*) between *teenagers as key Attention Economy customers and consumers of the future.* Its specifications allow a degree of personalisation. Companies can identify when they think that a teenager feels "insecure", "worthless", or in need of a "confidence boost". They can then manipulate when people receive "likes" for their posts, ensuring that they arrive when cues are indicating when or whether an individual feels vulnerable, fearful, in need for approval, or just bored.

The Guardian suggests that the same forces that have led tech firms to be able to "hook" users with design tricks are now used to depict the world in a way that may make for compulsive viewing. This means favouring *the instantaneous, the sensational, the emotional, the dialectical, the disputational* (as described in a previous chapter), *the apparently crisis-laden, and the outraged.* "Boring but necessary" is not news anymore, even if it deals with vital issues such personal debt (for instance caused by on-line gambling), benefits, trends in employment statistics, pensions, and the progress and success of the agricultural or fishing year upon which we all depend, etc.

The newspaper suggests that media companies are now being forced to follow the imperatives of the Attention Economy – they need to sensationalise, bait, entertain, and create apparent crises in order to survive. And they and their journalists must do it *now.* The Attention Economy is thus ideally set up to promote a political phenomenon like President Trump, whose teams are skilled at getting the attention of supporters and critics alike, quickly promoting strong feelings of *daily* involvement, commitment, outrage or hostility

This "distracting technology" may then be contributing towards the social and psychological development of a *continuous partial attention,* limiting people's willingness and ability to communicate, to focus and to concentrate. Chapter One of this Book describes the risks of distracted driving in the UK.

Thus, the forces of the Attention Economy may be in the process of eroding our ability and willingness to remember or to reason. It may discourage thinking for oneself and taking personal initiative. It may potentially lower personal IQ. It may unreasonably (i) raise expectations and (ii) lower boredom thresholds. Or it might stop us talking to our partner over a nice meal together in a favourite restaurant (look at diner behaviour the next time you are there). And you don't need to be able to read maps if you have what you are told is a completely accurate (!??) Sat Nav?

The Guardian suggests that some people are becoming programmed, and unable (or worse unwilling) to control their own minds. They are being manipulated (for good or ill) (i) by their peers, (ii) by advertising agents and their clients, (iii) by so-called "influencers", and (iv) by their politicians.

Like "Brave New World", "1984", "Lord of the Flies" and "Fahrenheit 451", or the films "A Clockwork Orange", "Blade Runner", "Soylent Green" and "The Matrix" to which reference is made above, the Attention Economy may have come to portend a terrifying and dilemma- laden future of anomie, social control and dystopia?

SOCIAL MEDIA DILEMMAS AND MINORS (I) – DAMAGED SCHOOLCHILDREN?

Whilst UK schools can and do prohibit the use of mobile phones, tablets (etc) when their pupils are on school premises, they cannot mitigate the effects of the Attention Economy described immediately above when children are not there. If the parents of these children **(as Minors for whose welfare these parents are legally responsible)** (i) are unable, (ii) unwilling, or (iii) cannot even be bothered to control the domestic use of electronic devices to access the internet (irrespective of what form this interaction might take) then there is for instance no guarantee that any home-based learning as is required will occur. Equally, there may be no guarantee that children will get a *proper night's sleep*, making them (cumulatively?) drowsy and inattentive at school. In the worst case, children may have become so distracted by their use of the internet that they are unable to focus on the necessary realities of the educational process going on around them. They may have by then (and again for good or ill) passed into the realms and control of an artificial *semiosphere* as described in Chapter 9 of this Book.

SOCIAL MEDIA DILEMMAS AND MINORS (II) – EMOTIONAL PRESSURE, BULLYING AND CORRUPTION

Social media type dilemmas under this heading for instance include or derive from any or all of:

❑ **the ongoing and open bullying and corruption of under- age children (again, being legally protected Minors);**

❑ **an artificially imposed, entirely unnecessary and dangerous mental health risk (for instance as described at the beginning of this chapter);**

❑ **a gratuitous image distortion, personal devaluation, and character assassination;**

❑ **the casualisation, trivialisation, de-humanisation and even glorification of violent or degrading behaviour (for instance as portrayed in computer games);**

❑ **gross, illegal (and immoral / evil) child exploitation and pornographication;**

❑ **failures of operator moderation;** *and*

❑ **issues of the personal / parental / educational / and state safeguarding responsibilities for young children as Minors;**

❑ **etc.**

A recent report suggested that schools in the UK should play an enhanced (and belated?) *safeguarding role* in rectifying parental failures to prepare children *aged eight to eleven* (again as Minors legally subject to parental control) who are moving from primary to secondary school. This safeguarding role would deal with the (totally artificial) **"emotional demands"** of social media that such pupils may face when they change schools. Apparently, some UK pupils are finding it hard to manage the transition, in their words facing (an unnecessary and unwanted) "cliff edge" as they transfer to secondary school where the report opines that "social media becomes more important in their lives".

The Children's Commissioner for England has at this time of writing also expressed her concern that some primary school pupils have already, and critically become over-dependent on social media approbation. Such children are becoming anxious about their identity, as well as their appearance online and offline. These children perceive themselves to be obliged to chase "likes" and to seek the online validation of themselves by peers (*or much more dangerously by others unknown to them*). They may also feel that they cannot disconnect from this so-called media because it will be perceived by their peers as socially unacceptable, or (more damagingly) an act of personal weakness on their part.

Suggestions (whether or not remedial) to such social media dilemmas facing Minors and those who are responsible for them include:

❑ firstly that the apparently well-meaning but ineffective and "nice" behaviour of some parents, schools, and educational authorities in the UK may be leading in the near future to individualistic, anti-social, and potentially catastrophic consequences. These may be associated with dilemma conditions associated with (i) a limited politico-social focus; (ii) the well-intentioned middle-class "conversations", distracting and fruitless "debates", endless talk and a fearful "politically correct" inaction to which reference is made in Chapters 4 and 8 of this Book; (iii) an entrenched middle class fear of personal, social and political conflict, and leadership responsibility; and (iv) an apparent and dilemma-laden public finance naivety to which reference is made in Part Four. **Indeed, the dilemmas associated with social media and under-age children may now be posing a direct threat to the future of UK Democracy itself?**

❑ the *critical and urgent need specifically* for parental and school reinforcement of the message that a person's real value *is not in any way whatsoever defined* by "likes" or how they appear to others in the limited, opinionated, artificial, consumerist (and now corrupted) "bubble" of the social media world; *and*

❏ that schools and parents should be required on a safeguarding basis to prepare children (again as Minors) *proactively, cognitively and critically / sceptically* as well as *emotionally* for the evident, "significant", distorting, corrupting and dangerous risks of social media that may affect them as they move schools, meet new classmates and grow up; *to include*

❏ the universal introduction by primary schools of compulsory lessons for year six and seven pupils in digital literacy and online resilience, so that these pupils can be prepared (and a strong degree of personal scepticism instilled) for this artificial emotional and distorting side of social media; *assisted by*

❏ the safeguarding requirement for strongly proactive parental, school and governmental instruction to ensure that children as Minors identify and to navigate "rollercoaster" attacks by the variously narcissistic, individualistic, consumerist, negative, bullying, violent, pornographic, destructive and also criminalised aspects of social media; *and as necessary to include:*

❏ the necessity for the absolute (or instead statutory reinforcement of?) acceptance by parents of their personal safeguarding responsibility for the *proactive monitoring and management* variously of the sites and apps used by their children, their children's lists of so-called "friends", the privacy settings used, and the personal images or family images to which other users have / might be able to gain access (etc).

CASE EXAMPLE

But do we enjoy our online obsession (I)? – *The Week* noted that apparently not all of us do. It commented that '63% of [UK] secondary school pupils say that they wouldn't mind if social media didn't exist; 56% describe themselves as being on the edge of addiction to it; [and] 71% say they've been on temporary "digital detoxes" to try to get over it … it doesn't stand you in good stead with your boss either: 19% of employers say they've rejected a candidate for a job on account of their online activity. Almost 48% of girls between 11 and

18 say that they've been bullied or abused on social media. [And] 21% of women in the UK aged 18 to 55 say they've experienced abuse or harassment online'.

CASE EXAMPLE
But do we enjoy our online obsession (II)? – *The Week* also reports that 45% of Britons aged 18 to 24 would feel "weird" without their smartphones for a day – because they "would not know what to do".

BIG DATA MEETS BIG BROTHER?
The Chinese Government has established a **Social Credit System**.

This uses "Big Data" to reward "good citizens" who follow the Country's "socialist core values" and "behave decently". It can of course instead be used as a threat to disadvantage those deemed by the State to be lazy, unpatriotic or politically unsound. The system is based on a partnership between (i) the Chinese Government's oversight and (ii) the entrepreneurial capabilities of Western and Chinese informatics capitalism.

The Week comments of this Social Credit System that Western societies could easily enough travel in the same direction if they chose so to do, given the plethora of personal credit and Attention Economy type information already available to governments about their own people.

The Chinese system uses a *National Trust Score* that *from the viewpoint of the State* rates (i) what kind of citizen a person is, and (ii) how trustworthy that person is. *The Week* writes that its readers might 'imagine a world where many of your daily activities were constantly monitored and evaluated: what you buy online; where you are at any given time; who your friends are and how you interact with them; how many hours you spend playing video games; and what bills and taxes you pay (or not). It's not hard to picture in the West, because most of that [already] happens, thanks to data-collecting behemoths like Google, Facebook and Instagram, or health-tracking apps such as Fitbit. But now imagine a system where all of these behaviours are rated as either positive or negative and distilled into a single number, according to rules set by the government. That would create your *Citizen Score*, and it would tell everyone whether or not you were trustworthy. Plus, your rating would be publicly ranked against those of the entire population and used to determine your eligibility for a mortgage or a job, where your children can go to school – or your chances of getting a date' (in a country with a statistically large male to female imbalance) … 'Beijing is pitching the system as a desirable way to measure and to enhance "trust" nationwide and to build a culture of "sincerity". The policy states that "it will forge a public opinion environment where keeping trust is glorious. It will strengthen sincerity in public affairs, commercial sincerity, social sincerity, and the construction of judicial credibility". By 2020 [it is proposed that] the behaviour of every citizen in China will be ranked [in this way], whether they like it or not'.

Ultimately, Chinese State policy towards political or social trust is evolving in a particular way. *This is that if a trust is broken in one place, restrictions could then be imposed elsewhere.* People with low ratings may have to accept slower internet speeds; restricted access to restaurants, nightclubs or golf courses; or have the right to travel by rail or air removed. Scores could be used in determining rental applications, the ability to get insurance or a loan or even social security benefits. Citizens with low scores might not be hired by certain types of employers, or be stopped from obtaining certain types of work; or they might be unable to enrol their children in certain types of schools. The Social Credit system will "allow the trustworthy to roam everywhere under heaven whilst making it hard for the discredited to take a single step".

Fukuyama's concept of *Low Trust* is described in Chapter 6 of this Book. The Chinese Government and its various informatics partners may in justification of its Scheme point to the country's lack of past experience (compared with Western Governments) with issues of what may to them:

❑   be the relative novelty and risk of personalised credit ratings and the management of credit card usage. Credit card accounts were not used in China in the past. Indebtedness resulting from uncontrolled credit card usage has now become a major dilemma source in the UK; *and*

❏ be State concerns expressed about the relative quality and risk
of past contractual compliance and fulfilment amongst Chinese
businesses and their customers.

The role of the *Chinese Family Business (CFB)* is described in
the Author's text *Principles of Management*, to which reference is
made in the Introduction to this Book. Such businesses have traditionally managed risk-related matters of customer creditworthiness
and contractual supplier compliance by means of the honour-based
concept of *xinyong* between family-owned suppliers and buyers. The
significant limitations of this familistic or clan-orientated "available
credit" and trustworthiness profile are however clear in a country
now operating as a critical player in a globalised economy.

Fukuyama's description of a "saddle-shaped" business structure
as described in the Author's *Principles of Management* includes (i)
numerous small or familistic businesses at one end, and (ii) large
state-owned organisations at the other. The Chinese have made
enormous strides during recent decades in bridging this gap by the
entrepreneurial encouragement of the establishment of both large-
scale capitalist (however owned), international, state, and semi-state
manufacturing and service enterprises. Issues of the effectiveness of
the management of debt, payments, and national and international
contractual compliance are critical to this development.

One yearly report, published at this time of writing, shows that 17.5
million "discredited" Chinese citizens were banned from purchasing
airline tickets, whilst 5.5 million were banned from travelling by
train. The report justifies these figures as a means of "encouraging
proper and lawful behaviour".

Chapter Six
National Culture, Cross-Cultural, and Transcultural Variables

This chapter identifies, categorises, and illustrates different sources of dilemmas that derive from the existence of *national culture, cross-cultural, and transcultural variables*.

Any analysis of Dilemma Management that is carried out in a country such as the UK, Australia, Canada, the USA (etc) which (i) must, of trading necessity be internationalised in its outlook; and (ii) whose population is to some degree polyglot (made up of all sorts of different races and backgrounds) will have to be subject to interpretations that are cross-cultural. To ignore national, cross-cultural and transcultural variables is simply naïve and unrealistic.

Dilemmas may arise because of the existence of these national, cross-cultural, and transcultural differences in a society. These differences are also described in other books written by this Author as listed in the Introduction to this Book.

NATIONAL CULTURE DEFINED

Geert Hofstede defines national culture as "collective mental programming". The people of any particular nationality are culturally conditioned by particular patterns of socialisation, education, and life experience. Cultural conditioning is stable and resistant to change. This is because national culture resides (i) collectively in the mental make-up of the people in the society; (ii) in their institutions (family, education, religion, forms of government, institutions and associations, law, work organisations, art, literature, settlement patterns, towns and cities, buildings, etc.); and (iii) in their ideologies, technology, and scientific theories.

Hofstede suggests that although individuals are conditioned by cultural influences at many different levels (family, education, social group, locality, work group, profession, etc.), they share a *collective national character* which represents their cultural mental programming. This *collective mental programming* shapes their values, attitudes, capabilities and competencies, behaviours, and perceptions of what is important.

Hofstede, Hampden-Turner & Trompenaars, Fukuyama, and Lessem & Neubauer propose that national culture and values, as they are likely to be the source of dilemmas, could be categorised on the basis of any or all of the following "cross-cultural" variables, namely:

High and Low Power Distance – the concept of Power Distance describes how a society deals with dilemmas associated with the perception that people are in any way unequal in a social and status sense. Power Distance is used to describe the degree to which a society accepts or rejects an unequal distribution of power, whether in politics and governance, in decisions on resource allocation and the distribution of wealth, or in the management process. Societies with *high power distance* stress inequality, develop structures and systems in which everyone has and knows his place, and reinforce the existing status quo.

Societies or cultures with high power distance will exhibit a large degree of centralisation of political authority and economic power. They may favour autocratic, hierarchical and authoritarian attitudes to leadership and decision-making.

Societies or cultures characterised by *low power distance* on the other hand regard social inequality as undesirable and try to reduce it. The apparently unconstrained exercise of power by one person may be looked at by others with scepticism or suspicion, legal challenge, or open resistance.

Uncertainty Avoidance – the concept of Uncertainty Avoidance describes how a society copes with dilemmas associated with uncertainty about the future, and deals with the reality of risk. Uncertainty Avoidance indicates the extent to which a society feels threatened by uncertain, novel, or ambiguous situations, and tries to "avoid" dilemmas associated with these situations for example by the use of such stabilizing mechanisms as:

❏ placing heavy reliance on professional and technological expertise, "expert" judgement and opinion, systematic processes of forecasting, or technological attainment;

❏ the establishment of formalised and standardised rules and regulations that for example "cover all eventualities", "establish policy and contingent decision", or "eliminate the need to exercise discretion" in conditions of risk and uncertainty;

❏ the provision of long-term career prospects and stability of employment; *or instead:-*

❏ encouraging belief in the existence of "absolute" (and unchangeable) "truth";

❏ refusing to tolerate new or "deviant" ideas or behaviours;

❏ resisting innovation; ignoring concepts "not invented here".

Strong uncertainty avoidance societies teach their people to try to anticipate the future; to create institutions that establish and reinforce security and stability; and to avoid or manage risk. Such security may be established by education (as evidenced by the emphasis on the application of mathematics and statistics in France or the USA, or the analysis of risk in The Netherlands). It may instead be established by laws and statutes; collective international agreements (such as those establishing the European Union, or world free trade); technological expertise; religion; ideology; the pursuit of economic or market power (eg. by dominating it); military power and NATO style treaties; control of resources (eg. gold or diamonds) or access to resources (eg. oil, copper).

More negatively, strong uncertainty avoidance societies may be characterised by religious dogmas or political ideologies that are resistant to change. This resistance is likely to be associated with the high power distance identified in the previous section, above.

Weak uncertainty avoidance societies may instead encourage people to tolerate uncertainty, to accept what the day brings, and maybe to take risks. Such people can tolerate and deal with dilemmas associated with behaviour, values and opinions different to their own. They do not feel threatened by the cultures of others. More negatively, some weak uncertainty avoidance societies are associated with low expectations and a fatalist outlook on life, which may give rise to dilemmas which are very strongly resistant to resolution.

Collectivism and Familism versus Individualism – is a concept which indicates the relative closeness of the relationship between one person and others in a society. It anticipates fundamental dilemmas associated with the nature of the role, place, and motivation of the individual in relation to their membership of families, clans, tribes, teams, groups, the neighbourhood or the community, and the wider collective that is society.

In *collectivist* societies such as those in South East Asia, people are socialised into a collective orientation to life experience. In such a culture the responsibility is placed on the individual to put the collective or corporate interest first, ahead of individualistic priorities. In return, the individual has the right for instance to expect that the community will look after his or her interests when times are difficult. The individual – collective dilemma is also found in strongly *familistic* societies, such as those of Italy, Spain, and the Indian sub-continent. Pressure is placed on each member to ensure that family interests take precedence over individual preferences.

In *individualistic* societies, personal demands and desires take precedence. There may be an expectation that the purpose of political, business and social institutions is to ensure that these demands can be met, for instance by an officially relaxed attitude to the availability of consumer credit, low interest rates, the effective discouragement of personal saving, and disinterest in investments in future pension prospects.

Similarly, in individualistic societies such as the UK and the USA, employers and employees may view their obligations towards each other as instrumental or legalistic, and therefore lacking in commitment. At its most basic, the employment relationship may be perceived in terms of a "spot contract" which is based on standard terms and takes place at market prices. The individual can always go off to seek better things elsewhere if he or she so chooses. This then, however, gives rise to the dilemma in which personal expertise and proprietary knowledge built up over the time of the employment may as much be perceived to belong to the individual as it does to the employer. The individual may regard it as a personal asset to be traded as necessary for the best price in the market. This syndrome is frequently noted in the financial services sector in which highly experienced individuals are effectively free to transfer their skills to the highest bidder on a global scale.

Hofstede suggests that as nations become wealthier their people tend to become more individualistic in character and attitude. This increases the likelihood of the occurrence of dilemmas that are the subject of this Book, and may decrease the likelihood that these dilemmas can be resolved in a government / political context in which the interests of the many must be balanced against those of the individual and the few. How is the contribution of the individual to be seen within the wider context of the community? How (if at all?) does society manage that relationship? Ultimately, whose interests are defined within the prevailing value system to come first?

Why should the individual be permitted to buy high-powered firearms and ammunition when, clearly, it is not in any way desirable from the viewpoint of the society that has to cope with the consequences?

CASE EXAMPLE

Personal pensions – the almost certain likelihood of *shortfalls in personal pension provision* will provide a huge dilemma for the UK Government during the period 2040 onwards, requiring expensive and potentially divisive decisions to be made about the need for enhanced taxpayer support of those (already called "the new poor") who for *the specific reasons here* of their own consumerist short-sightedness will not have accumulated anything like the necessary investments from their own income to secure even a half-decent retirement, some at the very worst having frittered away their life's income on expensive cars, online gambling, computer games, holidays, and TV box sets (etc). *Pensions are not seen by such people as a matter for personal responsibility. It is for the state (and the taxpayers who fund it) to provide for their comfortable old age.*

Masculinity versus Femininity – describes the division of roles between the sexes in society, and the degree to which a society allows overlap between the roles of men and women. It anticipates the dilemma associated with decisions or actions that are to be based on the relative values that society places upon the sexes, and on the roles that they are perceived to carry out.

Hofstede defines masculinity and femininity as two ends of a dilemma continuum. Measurement in terms of this dimension expresses the extent to which the dominant values in society are *masculine* (assertive, acquisitive, or competitive) rather than *feminine* (caring, serving; concerned with people, the quality of life or the environment).

In strongly masculine societies men are dominant, and deal with "things" and money. Men may attempt to, or be expected to portray an authoritarian, patriarchical, competitive, rational, or unemotional character. The woman's feminine role is expected to be caring, serving, emotional, intuitive, and modest. Indeed, "management" *as an entity* (**but not the concept of Management Process upon which this Book is based**) may itself be seen as a traditionally masculine activity.

Hofstede suggested that Japan was the most masculine society. Japanese women, traditionally, were not expected to reach senior management positions in politics or business organisations. Women in Anglo-Saxon countries, on the other hand, may be showing increasing signs of masculinity in their orientation and behaviour. There are rapidly increasing expectations in Anglo- Saxon countries that women will come to reach positions of leadership and management in Government, in public institutions, and in companies.

In feminine societies or institutions, men as well as women may be involved in caring and serving type activities, for instance in aspects of healthcare management, customer service, or hospitality management. They may expect to display feminine, emotional, intuitive, and modest characteristics.

Impose Rules or Allow Exceptions – organisations, institutions and the wider society must to some degree formalise, standardise, or codify their operations. There exists a minimum (or "requisite") level of bureaucracy without which any activity (such as running a regulatory, a licencing, or a healthcare institution) cannot be consistent or systematic. Policies, procedures, rules, and routines provide the basic framework for organised and accountable work. This basic framework is a part of enterprise structure, technology, and relationship architecture.

At the same time, however, there needs to be a necessary recognition of exceptions, changes, and the need for innovation. Relationships, policies, rules, operations, and technologies may need to be capable of:

❏ short-term adjustment (in order to deal with new or exceptional cases, new demands, or political readjustments); *or*
❏ long-term evolution; *or*
❏ rapid and wholesale change (for instance when there is a sudden redefinition or shift in the knowledge, technological, or market base, such as happened with the development of computing, information, and telecommunications technologies; or in response to major shifts such as the UK decision to leave the European Union).

Case Example: does a professional football club maintain a policy of never paying the fees of agents who "represent" the players whom it wishes to buy (instead insisting that the player as client of the agent pays fees out of the transfer fee, which then reduces the sum received by the player)? Or does it makes exceptions to its own rules in the case of some players whose services it is keen (or desperate?) to secure?

Achieved Status versus Ascribed Status – any given society will have to choose how to determine the basis for allocating status and reward. This may place that society or its institutions in a dilemma. For instance, to whom should Knighthoods or CBEs be awarded in the UK, and for what reason? And what criteria should be in place to permit the removal of such rewards in the case of (i) subsequent lawbreaking by recipients, or instead (ii) apparent breaches of the spirit of the law and culturally expected behaviour by them?

The allocation of status and reward may (firstly) depend upon the *achievement* of certain types of criteria directly associated with governmental or institutional performance in its operating context (such as the number of patients successfully treated), or in its marketplace (such as sales volume or profitability).

Or instead, the *allocation* of status and reward may depend upon some other characteristic that is seen to be culturally important, and whose demonstrated achievement those who make the decisions on behalf of society wish to be seen to reward. Such criteria might include age, seniority, caste or tribal membership, wealth, gender, membership of a particular family, length of service, education, or past service to the party or commitment to the state.

The choice between these two bases for allocating prestige and reward depends upon what society, or those who control that society define to be important, and on what example it wishes to set to aspirants for such status. Such examples are criteria of fundamental importance, and may vary widely across any international perspective. They are likely to be a key source of cultural dilemmas, for instance at times of rapid social change.

Analysis versus Integration – any cognitive or intellectual process may require *either or both* of (i) the analysis of concepts or phenomena into constituent parts; and (ii) the integration of such concepts or phenomena into whole patterns, relationships, processes and wider contexts. Analysis and integration are the opposite ends of an intellectual process. Anglo-Saxon societies tend to analyse (or to "deconstruct"); Eastern and some European societies (such as the Germans) tend to seek cohesive patterns (to integrate or to "construct").

This dichotomy may give rise to an intellectual or cognitive dilemma. Societies, cultures and education systems that are orientated to analysis or deconstruction may demonstrate weakness in terms of their ability to co-ordinate or to integrate what they know into a coherent and useful whole. Issues of a failure to "join up" thinking provide clear *wholistic or holistic dilemmas* for instance for the UK's National Health Service (NHS), and for the security services of many countries. At the same time, any culture, society or institution must be capable of deconstructing and reconstructing its base of Knowledge, its concepts, its technology, its products and services, its policies, and its processes in order to redefine, re-imagine, re-engineer, adapt, update and improve them. Deconstruction, reconstruction and integration are essential to the processes of refinement and continuous improvement (*kaizen*), and recycling (*sairiyo*) described elsewhere by this Author. Thus, for instance, concepts based upon life cycles (such as the marketer's Product Life Cycle) are "tidy" and "logical" in the terms of Western analysis. Such concepts may however be counterproductive to the development of the apparently more successful evolutionary, adaptive, and incremental approaches to the development of knowledge, technologies, and processes favoured by the Germans and the Japanese. What we consider "obsolete" may to them simply be a resource to be recycled and adapted within a wider context of prevailing capability, competence, tradition, and market development.

Equality versus Hierarchy – different cultural value sets may give rise to dilemmas concerning whether emphasis should be given to the achievement of *social and personal equality and empowerment*; or instead to the use of the *high power distance and institutionalised inequality* described by Hofstede, above.

For instance, the contribution of the individual may, as a matter of principle, be valued highly. If the individual feels that his or her contribution is valued, he or she may make strenuous personal or entrepreneurial efforts on behalf of society, the body politic, or the institution. This might however:

❏   create a potentially chaotic environment in which skills of diplomacy have to be used in order to fashion compromises among competing individuals, and to smooth individual "ruffled feathers", for instance in a political, a university, or a parliamentary context;

❏   slow down decision-making, because of the over-riding need for consultation. Everyone's opinion has to be listened to, and delays to action may have to be tolerated;

❏   the concept of management process may have to be perceived in terms of a complex package comprising leadership, the identification of professional equality and "useful" contribution, and inter-personal or inter-organisational mediation, accommodation and compromise. The concept of "hierarchy" may be seen as unhelpful, whilst urgent decision- making may be seen as unachievable.

Alternate cultures will emphasise the precedence of the authority and judgement of the hierarchy, the state, the CEO, the Leader, the family, or the proprietor (the "owner"). Individuals and subordinates must accept their place in the prevailing "pecking order", and accept the evaluative criteria of those above them who are seen to be entitled to command and to judge what others must do.

This in turn may raise dilemmas about the effectiveness of hierarchical judgement, and about the (well documented) risk that strongly centralised structures may go unchallenged in ignoring potential threats represented by the external influence of political realities, the market, technology, international relationships, corruption, crime, and the wider environment (etc). This issue is also dealt with in later chapters.

Neutrality versus Emotion – Hampden-Turner and Trompenaars note that 'members of cultures which are *neutral* do not telegraph their feelings but keep them carefully controlled and subdued. In contrast *emotional* cultures show feelings plainly by laughing, smiling, scowling and gesturing: they attempt to find immediate outlets for their feelings'. The degree to which behaviour is openly emotional (expressive), or instead unemotional (neutral) is a major difference between national cultures. For instance, there may be a tendency for those with norms of emotional neutrality to dismiss displays of anger, delight or intensity in interactional settings or the workplace as "unprofessional".

Hampden-Turner and Trompenaars suggest that there are two issues involved in the issue of emotional display. These are:

❏ the question of whether emotion should be openly exhibited in political, institutional, business, leadership, military, or managerial relationships; or instead be deliberately suppressed ("stiff upper lip please, old boy"); *and*

❏   the question as to whether emotion should (or can) be deliberately separated from the processes of thought and reasoning
lest it reduce objectivity, increase subjectivity, or even 'corrupt
them'.

The two Authors suggest that 'Americans tend to exhibit emotion,
yet separate it from "objective" and "rational" decisions. Italian and
South European nations in general tend to exhibit emotion and not
separate it from their reasoning. Dutch and Swedes tend not to exhibit and to separate. There is nothing "good" or "bad" about these
differences. You can argue that emotions held in check will twist
your judgements despite all efforts to be "rational". Or you can argue
that pouring forth emotions makes it harder for anyone present to
think straight. Similarly you can scoff at the "walls" separating reason from emotion, or argue that because of the leakage that so often
occurs, these walls should be thicker and stronger'.

They go on to warn that strongly neutral or emotional 'cultures
may have problems in doing business with each other. The neutral
person is easily accused of being ice-cold with no heart; the emotional person is seen as out of control and inconsistent. When such
cultures meet, the first essential is to recognise the differences, and
to refrain from making any judgements based on emotions, or the
lack of them'.

Inner-directness versus Outer-directness – social, cultural and
institutional value sets will determine what their purposes, strategies
and direction should be.

Purpose, strategy and direction may on the one hand come firmly
from *internal* driving or leadership forces (for example ideological
or entrepreneurial) *from within* the body politic and / or the governance of organisation. Relationships with external stakeholders,
the media, and other relevant parties may be perceived as requiring
positive (and maybe aggressive) management. Outside pressures,
such as from international, market or technological environments, or
those from legislative or judicial regulation may be "filtered" to suit
the perceptions and convenience of institutional decision-makers.
"Foreign" ideas, concepts "not invented here", or ideas that are

considered to be ideologically unsound may be rejected. Or at least such ideas or concepts may be regarded with suspicion or complacency, for instance on the (arrogant) grounds that "we have nothing to learn" (or "we do not want to learn" anything) from their originators.

Alternatively, the body politic or institution may operate in a *symbiotic relationship with its environment*, absorbing and adapting from it as it moves through time and process. It may, for example, prefer at any one time to appoint a significant proportion of its staff from outside. This was the case when a highly qualified Canadian financial specialist, Mr Mark Carney, was appointed as Governor of the Bank of England. It can be argued that internal candidates for certain types of government, specialist or managerial posts will have become too "set in their ways". They may be perceived to have become out of touch with the external "reality" of politics, of the marketplace, the knowledge base, or technology as it now exists, and be incapable of generating the new ideas for which they themselves were perhaps recruited in the past. Such internal candidates (such as those in the football industry) should themselves look to leave and "move on" to other institutions or organisations to update their knowledge and competence base, and thereby usefully to further develop their own expertise and careers.

Idealism and Rationalism versus Pragmatism – some societies and cultures are characterised by the belief that policies and actions may directly be determined by *prevailing ideals*. Such ideals include (i) the belief in universal Human Rights, social justice or social care; or (ii) the values that underpinned the formation of NATO or the European Union; or (iii) the belief in equality amongst all, whether in terms of gender, caste or race, (etc); or (iv) the right to bear arms in the USA. Such idealism may then be reinforced by the *rational belief* that idealistic values and policies may be handed down without further ado, for example to administrators or civil servants for their direct implementation. Because the ideals are seen as correct or appropriate to society's scale of priorities, the issue of the realities of this implementation are of no concern to policy-makers. Nor is the management process that may be needed. *The necessary leadership* *and management will be an afterthought.* Matters will follow to plan. Indeed, plans (such as so-called "corporate plans") are simply seen as an expression of the reality that is to follow. The UK's Groundnut Scheme in 1940's East Africa was for instance based on the ideal of turning weapons into ploughshares. Nothing could go wrong. But instead the groundnuts, so vital to the feeding of post-World War Two Britain, never arrived. The crops failed, as did the plan.

Pragmatists will counter that *no plan survives contact with reality*, for example citing the expensive construction and subsequent abandonment of the mighty corporate plans of the 1960s. What matters to pragmatists is the *detail of implementation.* Who is going to do it? How are things to work? How much is it going to cost? Is the venture sustainable; and if not (like the UK's NHS) how can it be made so? Who will lead and who will follow? What form will the management process take? *What are the key performance objectives and who will be held personally responsible for achieving them?* What is the Risk (Chapter 17 of this Book) and what happens when something goes wrong? Who carries the responsibility and who is to clear up the mess afterwards?

Some circumstances call for idealism, for instance in setting standards for national health, equality, security, safeguarding, or social care. *But the realities of their implementation then require an intense degree of realism and pragmatism.* The dilemma comes in deciding on how best to reconcile the two approaches. Does for instance the European Union remain a grand (and rationalistic) scheme for the political reconciliation and federalisation of European countries in what has been a war-torn continent? And is it still a pragmatic response to the need for free trade in which at least some of the competitive playing field should be level for all of the players?

Case Example: should a government, as well as any particular individual, live within the financial means available to it? Or should for whatever reason that government or individual borrow as much money as they can in order to spend, putting off thought about the need for repayment to another day, another time, another person, or another government?

Low Trust versus High Trust – Fukuyama differentiates between *low trust* and *high trust* cultures.

Fukuyama notes that the leaders and decision-makers of societies, governments and institutions characterised by a *low degree of trust of others* may hold an attitude to uncertainty, unpredictability or equality that takes the form of fencing their people in, and controlling them with a series of hierarchical, behavioural, legalistic or bureaucratic rules. He suggests that, as a result, advanced industrial societies have created comprehensive legal and contractual frameworks for economic transaction, resource allocation, business organisation, financial and risk management. Legal systems are in place *to guarantee the compliance* of those with whom governments and organisations have to interact or to transact affairs. Transactional and behavioural requirements are pre-specified in codes, and backed up by law. Fukuyama suggests that 'people who do not trust one another will end up co-operating only under a system of formal rules and regulations, which have to be negotiated, agreed to, litigated, and enforced (if necessary by coercive means)'.

Fukuyama notes that such rules and laws impose their own dilemmas. They cost money. But they create little if any, positive benefit or added value. Fukuyama comments that 'legal apparatus, serving as a substitute for trust, entails "transaction costs". Widespread distrust in a society imposes a tax on all forms of economic activity' and behaviour. Such transaction costs include any or all of:

❑ the costs of holding together entities, communities, organisations, agencies, architectures and value chains that are neither characterised by mutually agreed values, nor trust, nor compliance. Such costs include mechanisms of governance, regulation and control within the management process, and the legalistic specification of contractual agreements within and outwith the organisation;

❑ the costs of finding trustworthy employees, agents, or suppliers;

❑ an increased burden of monitoring and decision-making;

❑ the costs of enforcing compliance; *and*

❑ the costs of non-compliance, disputes, litigation, compensation and payoffs;

❑ societal and institutional mechanisms of supervision, policing and control, for instance as described in terms of McGregor's "Theory X" style of management.

Case Example: Fukuyama suggests that liberal Anglo-Saxon societies like the UK and the USA now exhibit a serious dilemma caused by the growing tendency (described elsewhere in this Chapter) 'towards individualism and a potentially debilitating social atomisation'. He cites the rising (and expensive) use of litigation (such as in the case of the so-called "compensation culture") within the business, medico-legal, and social environments in these countries as an indicator of the declining level of trust that is associated with increasing individualism and personal self-absorption, and as evidence of the erosion of the communal values and the social capital that are dependent on trust amongst colleagues, partners, customers, parents, patients, and the wider community.

Other reasons for this low trust view towards society, its institutions and its people might include any or all of:

❑ cumulative experience and evidence of low trust attitudes and behaviour (for instance as shown by the development of the criminal justice system, or accumulated in case law);

❑ the continuing reluctance or outright failure of governance bodies, corporations, and executives to comply with entirely reasonable and necessary requirements for example associated with the Capitalist, Human Rights, or Equality Agendas;

❑ the ineffectiveness of strategies of voluntary self-regulation or restraint in the arenas of employment and service provision, or of policies of so-called "social responsibility";

❑ pressures from influential opinion formers and opinion leaders who have become adept at using and manipulating the media (for instance using the "Black Arts" of journalism as described in Chapter 8) in order to make their case for change in attitudes towards the Individualism versus Collectivism agenda described elsewhere in this Chapter;

❑ the widespread emergence in organisations of the processes of Risk Management described in Chapter 17 of this Book,

associated with an increasing awareness of the potential consequences and costs of *crises* deriving from failures of compliance
(described in detail in Chapter 18).

Case Example: the growing and lethal use by road users in the UK
of mobile phones whilst driving cars, or worse driving HGVs, was
described in Chapter 1.

Case Example: healthcare adherents to a belief in the low trust
nature of society may insist on a very strongly prescriptive and
interventionist attitude to the generic health of the populace. The
precedent for this approach was established in the UK during World
War Two. But since many people in the UK now appear to believe
that their personal health and welfare is the responsibility of their
doctor and the National Health Service (*and not their own*), then it is
entirely reasonable to assume that such people *will not take personal
responsibility* for their own behaviour, smoking, fitness, weight
management (etc). Healthcare agencies might therefore insist that
there should be aggressive government regulation of such matters as:

❑ the access to, and pricing of undesirable products such as to-
  bacco and alcohol;
❑ the sugar, fat, and vitamin content of foodstuffs;
❑ the formal certification of, and direct monitoring by GPs
  (personal doctors) of personal diets, and particularly those of
  children;
❑ the imposition of direct additional healthcare charges for treatment of smokers, the clinically obese, drunks (for instance in the
  establishment and client funding of official "drunk tanks"), etc;
❑ the annual publication of accurate costs to the taxpayer of collective non-conformance.

Fukuyama notes that the leaders and decision-makers of societies,
governments and institutions that are instead characterised by a *high
degree of trust of others* may not require extensive contractual or
legal regulation of their relationships and architectures because an
established and working consensus gives members of the group a
basis for *mutual trust*. Fukuyama for instance states that 'if people

who have to work together trust each other because they are all operating according to a common set of ethical norms, doing business costs less. Such a society will be better able to innovate organisationally, since the high degree of trust will permit a wide variety of social relationships to emerge'. At the same time, there may be:

❏ fewer incidences of litigation and a reduced likelihood of disputes, compensation and payoffs;
❏ a decreased burden of monitoring and decision-making; *and*
❏ trust-based societal and institutional mechanisms of supervision and control;
❏ leadership and management styles based on participative and personal responsibility-orientated approaches for instance characterised by Theory Y or Theory Z; *and hence*
❏ reduced transaction costs.

Case Example: Premier League Football Clubs in the UK employ some players whose annual incomes can only be described as "eye-watering" (if not obscene?). It might therefore be reasonable for such Clubs to expect such players to internalise their terms and conditions of employment to the absolute letter, and to *require total personal responsibility* in living up to them. They might be expected to refrain from gambling on football games; from tweeting their opinions as if these were the views of their employer; from making illegal, negative, drunken, racist, or sexist public exhibitions of themselves calculated to inflict reputational damage on their employer; not to become embroiled in UK tax avoidance schemes; and most certainly from eating the wrong sort of food. Yet, year after year, some players return to pre-season training overweight and have then to be sent away to lose the excess kilos (pounds in old money). Does this mean that the Club (i) applies one set of (high trust) expectations to the majority of its (lower paid) staff, but (ii) is forced to treat its (much more highly paid) players as *naughty children* who are to be deemed to be incapable of taking responsibility for themselves, and *must aggressively be minded on a Theory X basis?* Reference is also made in Chapter 8 to dilemmas caused by the behaviour of professional footballers; and in Chapter 11 to issues of celebrity status.

Transcultural Variables – which for the purposes of this Book may be regarded as a subset of the National and Cross-Cultural Dilemma Sources being described in this Chapter.

Transcultural variables may be defined to include influential traditions, orthodoxies, dogmas or socially imposed stigmas (such as those affecting women as mothers, widows or divorcees; female genital mutilation (FGM); young girls forced into household slavery or marriage against their will; familistic-based "honour violence", or familistic "blood money" payments, etc). Such behaviours may derive from what to us are cultural influences based on foreign religious tenets (such as the highly aggressive, gender-intolerant and conservative Saudi Arabian Wahhabis' sponsorship of the international proselytism of Islam), or established fatalism, or animist beliefs.

Such transcultural differences provide serious dilemmas in dealing with, or confronting what to us may be unacceptable or illegal patterns of behaviour. Forced marriage, familistic inter- breeding, honour–based violence, female genital mutilation, female feticide, the allocation of reduced status to widows and divorcees, and the patriarchical sponsorship of the male-only prioritisation of educational opportunities require proactive legislative action to be taken against the male dominated values of immigrant groups and ethnic minorities. This action will be based for example on well-established Western Human Rights values of equality and tolerance, and the absolute belief in the need for *genetic diversity and requisite variety* in society.

CASE EXAMPLE

Transcultural psychiatry – the Oxford Handbook of Psychiatry (Edition Three, 2013) notes the professional need to take a conventional, Western and *evidence-based* medical approach towards the treatment of psychiatric ailments whose source must be defined in transcultural terms. Genuine mental health problems may be diagnosed (and *properly re-categorised*) as for example having been caused (i) by a history of familistic inbreeding; (ii) by patient perceptions of the influence of "the evil eye"; or (iii) of mischief by witch doctors paid to place curses (for whatever reason) as a means of taking revenge on the victim; or (iv) of a criminal failure to uphold proper family values and commitments (for instance by sacrificing [murdering] children, or by committing violence against someone who is deemed to have damaged family honour).

Chapter Seven
Cognitive Consonance and Cognitive Dissonance

In his theory of "Cognitive Dissonance" (1957), Leon Festinger proposed that human beings strive for, or are instead driven towards the establishment of some degree of internal psychological consistency between (i) *their personal cognitions* (defined below) and (ii) *the actual reality and demands of the world* with which they are faced at the time.

This is because a person who is experiencing an internal psychological inconsistency with that reality is described by Festinger as suffering *Cognitive Dissonance (CD)*. In order to function in a manner which is perceived to most effectively cope with external reality *(however in their minds this might be)*, that person will have to seek some kind of balance or congruence between (i) their mental set as cognitions and (ii) their perceptions of the reality confronting them.

CASE EXAMPLE
"No platforming" – reacting to an official invitation to the French politician Marine Le Pen to speak at Cambridge University, some students there called for the "no-platforming" of the speaker. This action corresponds with the "Snowflake Behaviour" described in Chapter 12. In spite of the negative implications for the concept of free academic and political speech that lie at the heart of democracy as well as the university concept, this "no-platforming" behaviour seems to have been rooted in a severe (and self-imposed) Cognitive Dissonance between (i) the proper and reasonable demands of democracy and (ii) the gross intolerance of deliberately limited (or fascistic) student mindsets unable and unwilling to accommodate to, and to respect views that for whatever reason differ from their own?

THE CONCEPTS OF COGNITIVE CONSONANCE AND COGNITIVE DISSONANCE

The concepts of Cognitive Consonance and Cognitive Dissonance (the latter sometimes here abbreviated by the acronym "CD") describe *the relationship between two broad groups of variables, as listed below.*

[1] Cognitions: *to include any or all of:-*

- ❏ the nature of the mental / psychological / psychiatric functioning of the person or group;
- ❏ awareness, ideas, knowledge and understanding;
- ❏ perceptions (Chapter 9);
- ❏ value and value set;
- ❏ beliefs;
- ❏ attitudes;
- ❏ philosophy;
- ❏ ideology;
- ❏ opinions and opinionations (Chapter 8);
- ❏ self-perception; *also to include:-*
- ❏ any sense of entitlement; *and / or*
- ❏ level of boredom threshold; *and / or*
- ❏ level of expectations;
- ❏ semiospheric make-up (Chapter 9); *to include:-*
- ❏ social class, reference group; *and*
- ❏ groupthink; *and*
- ❏ adherence to family, clan or tribe values;
- ❏ etc.

[2] Behaviours: *to include any or all of:-*

- ❏ the effect of mental / psychological / psychiatric functioning;
- ❏ decisions on how to define and to deal with reality;
- ❏ acceptance or rejection;
- ❏ adjustment or adaptation;
- ❏ the choice of specific actions;
- ❏ the application of established or necessary paradigms, protocols or policies;

❏ the adherence to regulations or laws;
❏ strategies;
❏ etc.

RELATIVE CONSONANCE

The relative degree of congruence (*consonance*) between the two groups of variables may then be described in such terms as:

❏ consonant (ie congruent or harmonious);
❏ neutral;
❏ contradictory; *and / or*
❏ dissonant (ie not congruent or harmonious); *and / or*
❏ constituting a source of mental stress as driver of behaviour or action; *and / or*
❏ perceived to require some degree of adjustment, adaptation or decision on one or other side (or both) of the two groups of variables. This level of adjustment may depend on whether the perceived level of CD is (i) increasing or (ii) reducing in strength.

MANAGING COGNITIVE DISSONANCE

The relative degree of CD may (or might) be managed, or instead an attempt made to restore a perception of desired balance (consonance, congruence or harmony) by either or both of:-

❖ the reinforcement of cognitions or behaviours; *or*
❖ the changing of cognitions or behaviours.

Reinforcing cognitions or behaviours – might include:

❏ justifying the cognition and / or the behaviour. *Example:* "I have always smoked cigarettes. I cannot stop smoking now. I see no point in even trying to do so. I must be able to smoke whenever I need to";
❏ justifying the cognition and / or behaviour by adding new cognitions. *Example*: "I get seriously stressed when I can't smoke whenever I need to – I can't do without it";

❑ ignoring, denying or defying information that conflicts with cognitions. *Example*: "I do not believe all the negative propaganda about smoking cigarettes. It is all about creating scare stories to try to stop people like me smoking. It is my right to choose to smoke if I choose, and it is nobody else's damned business if I do. And the local hospital should put up proper heated smoking zones on their premises if they don't want people to smoke on the wards";

❑ belief disconfirmation or contradiction, thereby reducing CD. *Example*: "I don't need to undertake Continuing Professional Development (CPD). I know what I am doing and I have plenty of experience. These training/HR people can't teach me anything";

❑ demonstrating the relative benefits of adhering to the cognitions causing the Cognitive Dissonance. *Example*: "undertaking CPD is not worth it for me. I am not going to get a promotion or a salary increase out of it".

Changing cognitions or behaviours – might include:

❑ directly changing the cognition and / or the behaviour (however this is achieved). *Example*: "I now absolutely refuse to continue smoking. I don't want to die young – which I will around here if I do not stop";

❑ demonstrating the relative benefits of changing the cognitions causing the Cognitive Dissonance. *Example*: "I have decided that undertaking CPD could be very worthwhile for me. It will enhance my professional standing. I might even get a promotion or a salary increase out of it". *This might also be related to:-*

❑ a strategy of incentivising or inducing compliance. For instance, an exterior stimulus such as a threat or a reward may be perceived to be sufficiently significant / worthwhile that the individual or group actively reduces the influence of the cognitions causing the CD. *Example*: "we have been told by the company's new owners that we must sign up for intense programmes of CPD in order to update our competencies. We have also been told that we are expected to demonstrate a significant and rapid enhancement in our motivation and commitment to the job. Otherwise we might be sacked on capability grounds" **(from an actual case example known to this Author from an American truckmaker upon its acquisition of a high-value UK heavy goods vehicle brand which was at the time (i) a major defence contractor to the British Army, and (ii) which was a preferred supplier of tank transporters).** *This might also be combined with:-*

❏ managing the consequences of the choices or decisions (behaviours) which give rise to the Cognitive Dissonance. This might for instance be achieved by the provision of (cognitive or behavioural) justification for choosing one course of action rather than another. *Example*: "we / you are going to have to get involved in serious CPD. On the job / in house activities may have to be augmented by the completion of Part-Time college or university studies, perhaps to HND, Degree or Masters / Professional Level Four (etc). *This may also be associated with:-*

❏ *effort justification*, by which cognitions and / or behaviours might be adjusted, adapted or changed where the individual or group engage in *effort justification*. Whilst or whereas the particular effort involved might otherwise be a source of Cognitive Dissonance, this effort may be forthcoming because it can (or has to be) justified (ie takes on a character of cognitive consonance) for instance as being (i) worthwhile, necessary, requisite or rewarding; *and / or* (ii) any failure to engage in it may come to be perceived by self or others as a significant likely increased source of CD as compared with the current level; *and / or* (iii) any failure to engage in it may ultimately come to be perceived as representing a potential source of failure or career damage for individual, group or semiosphere.

Case Example: post 18 school examinations such as Advanced ("A") Levels, Higher Examinations (Scotland), university entrance examinations, matriculation, Baccalaureate, tests of English language and / or mathematical competence etc – are widely used as tests of post-school exit performance. They may be used to gain university entrance, employment apprenticeships, funding scholarships, etc. This type of examination or test has taken on a critical national and international role in the direction of Higher Education and professional education and training. Failure at the level of this hurdle may simply be unacceptable, for instance to the British Middle Classes. Or even totally disastrous in the case of pupils from China and South East Asia.

SOME DILEMMAS ASSOCIATED WITH COGNITIVE DISSONANCE

Reference is made in this Book to dilemmas that (at least in part) result from the presence of Cognitive Dissonance (CD) as a contributory or variable factor in the make-up of that dilemma. These could include any of the following illustrations.

Cognitions associated with expectations and boredom levels – attitudes and behaviours associated (i) with the nature of personal expectations and (ii) the level of boredom that can be tolerated by individuals, groups, or semiospheres (Chapter 9) may be significantly dissonant to / with the conditions or circumstances that actually present themselves. This may for an example be an issue for so-called "Snowflakes" (Chapter 12).

Cognitions associated with the Peter Principle – cognitions and behaviours associated with the currency of occupational or professional practice may over time become dissonant to / with the actual requirements of work as they develop. The Peter Principle may come into effect when the *gap* between (i) existing cognitions and (ii) the reality of the behaviours or competencies that are now needed to accomplish key objectives has (iii) developed variously into emergent conditions of outdatedness, obsolescence, the consequences of a failure to pursue CPD (etc); or worse has resulted in the establishment of the technology discontinuities and "S" Curves described elsewhere by this Author.

Bill's promotion – Bill was described in the Introduction as applying for a promotion to a job perhaps (i) with supervisory or leadership responsibilities, and / or (ii) with what would to him be a significantly increased work remit. Quite apart from the question of whether or not his cognitive set encompasses the necessary additional capabilities, competences or motivations, Bill's existing cognitions may urgently have to be adapted by him to potentially new, alien or even unwelcome behaviours associated for instance with:

❏ an enforced and drastic change in work – life balance which will affect all aspects of his personal, family and occupational circumstances;
❏ staff motivation, capability evaluation, discipline or dismissal;
❏ leadership in hostile circumstances where he is certain to come under criticism; *perhaps to include:-*
❏ the making of unpopular or controversial decisions about the allocation of scarce resources between equally justifiable but competing personal or departmental claims on what is available; *or:-*
❏ managing conditions of enforced organisational change, staff redeployment or redundancy, or wholesale technological and business change.

Managing funding decisions – decisions on funding or the allocation of limited resources may require the people who make them to cope with a variety of forms of Cognitive Dissonance. This CD may characterise any or all of the decision-maker(s) involved, the people to be affected by the decision(s), stakeholders, scrutineers and / or commentators, the news media (etc).

What people want, or would like to receive may have to be weighed against alternative cognitions and behaviours for example associated with:

❏ the concepts and management of what are deemed in Chapter 15 to be risks of negative value or failure;
❏ the concepts and management of security issues, risk, uncertainty and crisis described in Chapters 16 to 18;
❏ the formal requirement to use the concepts of "reasonability" and / or "proportionality" described in Chapter 25;

❏   the ability to manage commitments to a successful conclusion in line with objectives and budgets, for instance as described in Chapters 15, 24 and 26;

❏   the ability to engage successfully in "eggshell management" (Chapter 31) under conditions of intense controversy, debate, politicisation or stalemate as described throughout this Book.

A CHAPTER CONCLUSION

The process (i) of recognising or dealing with any of the dilemmas described in this Book, or (ii) of proposing any kind of resolution to them may give rise to some degree of Cognitive Dissonance on the part of individuals, groups, semiospheres or entities. This was very clearly a feature of the Brexit process.

This Cognitive Dissonance may then itself become a variable, an influence or a determinant in any attempt to deal with that dilemma. In other words, the issue of Cognitive Consonance and Cognitive Dissonance will have become factors in the Dilemma Management process.

Chapter Eight
Opinions, Opinionation, and "Political Correctness" (So-Called)

'You know, it's a terrible thing to appear on television, because people think you actually know what you're talking about.'
– Sir David Attenborough

OPINIONS AND OPINIONATION

OPINION DEFINED

The OED defines *opinion* as a judgement, ideology, dogma, or belief about someone or something that is deemed to be likely or to be true in the mind of one person, or of many like-minded persons. This judgement, ideology, dogma or belief is based on theory, thought or supposition; it is reckoned to be the case about something *irrespective of its relationship to the facts as they stand.* That is, opinion may be a form of evaluation, value judgement, speculation or prejudice based on grounds that are insufficient as proof of truth or veracity. Ultimately, an opinion may be a self-conceit, an arrogance, an obduracy, a myth, a fantasy, a chimera, or instead an overconfidence. *There is no guarantee whatsoever that the opinion will bear any relationship to objective Fact.*

CASE EXAMPLE

Cashing in on foreign students?? – writing to **The Times** newspaper, a former Vice-Chancellor of the UK's prestigious Newcastle University expressed the opinion that he strongly disagreed with the continued influx of foreign students into UK universities. Whilst as a result these universities provide very significant export earnings (and contribute massively to employment statistics), this was not seen by the correspondent as 'the purpose of our universities, which is to educate our citizens and to pursue research. An element of cosmopolitanism is, of course, essential, but we are taking it too far, to a point at which it impairs the indigenous character of our universities. A recent walk around the London School of Economics reminded me more of an international airport than a seat of learning. Ironically, we are impairing the character that makes British universities so attractive abroad.'

A very vigorous response to (and rebuttal of) these opinions by the President of Universities UK was subsequently published by **The Times [Source: The Week]**.

THE VOICE OF OPINION

Opinions may be held or communicated on any of (i) an individual basis; (ii) an aggregated or collective basis for instance through social media; (iii) through the process of media journalism, or (iv) collectively on a groupthink basis. This "Voice of Opinion" may derive from any or all of:

❏ personal socialisation, culture, class, status, inclination, and power;

❏ the nature of current trends, and of contemporary "received wisdoms";

❏ the influence of the excessive individualism and groupthink that now characterises some Anglo-Saxon societies, especially when associated with the self-orientated influence of the Attention Economy, journalism, the media, or social media;

❏ the degree of personal arrogance or perceived self-importance, complacency, or self-satisfaction (and possible fear of change to the status quo);

❏ the ideologies or prejudices which people have chosen (or been coerced) to believe;

❏ the religious beliefs or prejudices which people have chosen (or been coerced) to believe;

❏ membership groups;

❏ executive conditioning, often associated with consensual or enforced groupthink amongst senior officers, civil servants, journalists and broadcasters, etc;

❑ so-called "celebrity" status, whether of performing artists, footballers, self-publicists, etc. Also see Chapter 11;
❑ so-called "political correctness", which in reality is now no
   more than one form of personal opinion or collective groupthink, based on a particular ideology, preference, prejudice,
   current social trend, or received wisdom to which reference was
   made above. The concept of "political correctness" is dealt with
   in a later section of this chapter.

**This list must exclude the concept of "professional opinion", as
communicated by consulting engineers, lawyers or healthcare
professionals. Such "opinion" is in fact a statement of perceived
fact, based on the professional's <u>legal right</u> to make judgements
informed and assured by externally validated qualification and
experience.**

The issue of *Hearing Voices* was analysed in Chapter 4.

OPINIONS AS POSITIVE
Opinions are a manifestation of peoples' rights to think and to say
what they like in a free society. This contrasts with non- democratic
societies characterised by oppression and a lack of personal freedom
of expression.

The expression of opinions may act as a safety valve, draining off
socially hostile or negative sentiments. Opinions may instead be useful and constructive, for instance contributing to dilemma diagnosis
and resolution. Opinions may be innovative or progressive, taking
such forms as "thinking outside of the box", for instance in the case
of the UK's Brexit, or the need for social, benefits, or healthcare
reforms.

THE POWER AND APPLICATION OF OPINIONS
The more that the Voice of Opinion is characterised by any or all of
the following, the more it may be categorised as a "hard" opinion,
and the more influential (whether with a positive or a negative effect)
this Voice will be in dilemma diagnosis or resolution:

❑   the more effectively it is formulated and communicated;
❑   the more powerful and influential is the source;
❑   the more its promotion is supported by influential opinion leader or lobbying type behaviour; *or*
❑   the more it commands Attention Economy and media attention, or media adherence, or is backed by such adherence (sometimes described in terms of the "black arts" of journalism); *and*
❑   the more that other people recognise or understand the meaning of the Voice, are affected by it, or wish to be affected by it.

The better-formulated and the harder is the opinion, and the stronger is the resolve of those who adhere to it, the more that this opinion may be put forward as constituting "Fact".

It may also serve (i) as a means of *testing the water* in a decision-making context, or (ii) as a *negotiating ploy* in determining eventual outcomes. This syndrome seems to have come into prominence in the UK's Brexit negotiations to leave the European Union.

CASE EXAMPLE

The curiosity of attributed opinion – the customers of newspapers, the broadcast media, journals, or the social media may have noticed a dilemma associated with the use of *attribution* by correspondents. For instance, in communicating his views to **The Times** newspaper, an (imaginary) academic called Dr Jones has the legal right in the UK to add that he is a Professor of Politics at Loamshire University. On the other hand (but with no such right) Ned Boggles, an (equally imaginary) player with Loamshire All Stars Premier League Football Club is now likely to ensure that as far as the tabloids and social media are concerned, a reference to his employment as a first team player with that club is always made in his media interactions. Whilst in neither case may the employer have been consulted about the communications of Messrs Jones or Boggles, the recipient of the opinion is perfectly within their rights to assume (correctly or otherwise) that the views of Messrs Jones and Boggles do actually reflect those of the people who employ them.

This syndrome of attributed opinion was described in the Case Example given at the beginning of this Chapter. On another occasion it landed a very senior executive of Saatchi & Saatchi (a global advertising agency) in hot water during 2016. That case is described in Chapter 18.

It was also illustrated by the case of a Liverpool FC footballer who openly used social media to accuse his club (ie his employer) of lying about the reasons for its decision not to select him to play in certain matches. This resulted in the Manager, Mr Jurgen Klopp, warning 'the entire Liverpool squad of the standards he expects on social media' following his player's outburst on Snapchat. He decreed that all of the Club's players were required 'to work hard and keep quiet' in order to pursue their careers as employees **[Source: The Guardian]**.

THE DILEMMA OF OPINIONATION

People have their right to opinions. But as in the case of debate and dialectics (Chapter 4), what others may categorise as the promulgation of excessive, negative, obstructive, aggressive or vexatious opinionation (*perhaps as forms of influence without responsibility*) may instead:

❏ distort the clarity of thinking, or act as an unnecessary source of confusion and complexity; *and*

❏ reduce objectivity; *or*

❏ trivialise or "dumb down";

❏ slow down, or stop things getting done that need to be done, for instance as in the case of the proposed UK use of Skype to carry out remote medical consultations in sparsely populated areas;

❏ constitute a source of analysis-paralysis as displacement activity or obstructive strategy; *or*

❏ be pointless, representing wasteful argument or debate *as distraction for its own sake*. This may be described in terms of an "it's all really a joke, or a game" syndrome for instance as still evidenced in parts of UK politics or its public sector, and in the stereotyping of life by the advertising industry. Work may still be seen by some as an extension of middle class university life. *It all has to be fun.* Nothing really matters that much, nothing really needs to get done urgently, and there is no over-riding sense of personal responsibility towards employer, client or taxpayer. You can always "wing it", perhaps in a hurry to get away to the pub; *or*

❏ deliberately to divert or distract attention *away* from things that are seen as more important in the scale of priorities of other people whose ability to bring influence to bear is limited, for instance because they are victims, or the underemployed (etc) with the weak voices described in the next Case Example and also in Chapter 4;

❏ misdirect, mislead or delude others (whether deliberately or not) because the opinion expressed is actually ill-informed or wrong. This may be the case with attitudes to mental health and the equality issues associated therewith; with discussions about immigration; or with opinions about the nutritional or calorific value of foodstuffs, etc. The latter syndrome has had calamitous effects on UK farming and food supply industries, whether in the case of eggs, beef, the use of gluten in foodstuffs, and the proliferation of potentially unnecessary food imports with high environmental costs (etc); *and also*

❏ be a source of, or become an item of so-called "fake news";

❏ be used (i) as defensive bluster in reaction to unpopular new ideas or policies, or (ii) as a tactic of aggression to try to back their proponents into corners from which it may be difficult to escape except by giving up on the proposition that gave rise to the hostility in the first place;

❏ be presented (deliberately or otherwise) as inconsistent or irreconcilable with the "Facts" as others may perceive them. This is a syndrome skilfully used by some UK educationalists, for instance in influencing attitudes to school tests and league tables, competitive team games, the teaching of skills and competencies, higher level vocational education, grammar school proposals, independent secondary academies, etc;

❏ be used deliberately to create complexity, for instance as described in Chapters 4 and 17 (the latter in respect of the concept of "wicked mess" risk);

❑ be used deliberately as a source of dilemma creation (for instance in politics or competition strategy), as described in various chapters of this Book;

❑ be used to talk matters up into apparent crisis proportions (also see Chapter 18);

❑ be used to create unnecessary anxiety, as described at various points in this Book;

❑ be used to downgrade the process of dilemma resolution at best to conditions of "muddling through", or the achievement of the lowest common denominator compromise, as described in various chapters of this Book; *or*

❑ ultimately to create circumstances that are at some stage irreconcilable with necessary decision-making processes, dilemma resolution, and implementation.

CASE EXAMPLE

Opinion, reality and do they actually give a f**k about it?? – the opinionation of a particular or powerful class, group or media may have the effect of diverting or distracting attention away (i) from the issues that really matter to a majority of others (such as jobs, benefits, debt, or housing); or (ii) away from issues that are seen as more important in the scale of priorities of people whose ability or influence is limited, for instance because they are "ordinary working people" or "just about managing"; or have lost their (at least half- decent) jobs or pensions in the process of government cuts, takeovers, or globalisation; be perceived as "poorly educated" or disenfranchised; live in an unfashionable place with apparently limited employment prospects and a perceived lack of entrepreneurial drive; or are in some way marginalised.

So, do politicians or the news media promote stories which deal with the great issues of the day (and which may make good TV), which are of passing interest to journalists, opinion formers, the politically correct, "news junkies", the excitable, and those who are categorised as the "chattering classes"?

Or should the prevailing opinionation at least accept some of the harsh realities of working class life and try to address them? One fan of the 2016 US Presidential Candidate Donald Trump commented that in approving 'of all his ideas – even his threat not to honour America's commitments to NATO – "who cares" she shrugs. "Maybe you guys are losing sleep over what happens to Ukraine, but I promise you that out-of-work steel workers (in the USA) could not give two f**ks'" **[Source: The Week].**

SO-CALLED "POLITICAL CORRECTNESS"

The widespread use of the term "political correctness" has developed into a *significant, human-made, and potentially destructive source of dilemmas*. Many of these dilemmas distract. They may well be totally unnecessary, but will nevertheless require some kind of decision or resolution on the part of other people, irrespective of their relevance or importance to, or urgency in the current circumstances. As such they may for instance be seen as examples of:

❏   the contingencies; sources of risk, threat or crisis; banana skins; or indicators of incompetence (etc) described in Chapter 3;
❏   the dialectics or debate described in Chapter 4; *and / or*
❏   the induced catastrophes described in Chapter 18; *and*
❏   an avoidable drain on available resources which may go unnoticed, unquestioned or unchecked.

"POLITICAL CORRECTNESS" DEFINED
The concept of *political correctness was originally defined* to describe language, policies or measures that were intended to avoid giving offence to, or disadvantage members of certain groups in society. The purpose of the concept was (*and as enshrined in Law remains*) to avoid the use of language or behaviour (etc) that can be can be interpreted to exclude, to marginalise, or to insult certain groups of people who are considered to be disadvantaged, at risk, or discriminated against.

So-called "political correctness" and the Voice of the Victim [I] – however, a subsequent view is that the undoubted ethical pressure to behave in an appropriate manner was then seized upon by groups (for instance at first in the USA) in particular representing the categories by race, gender, or sexual orientation. Such groups have proven themselves capable of demonstrating a powerful and effective "Voice of the Victim" as described in Chapter Four of this Book; and also in the Author's two **Equality Books** to which reference is made in the Introduction. This in comparison, say with the elderly, the sufferers of dementia, or the mentally disabled (etc) whose Voice of the Victim is for whatever reason much weaker (and more dependent on others) in the scheme of things.

UK EQUALITY LEGISLATION

UK Equality Legislation sets out *to assure the implementation (i) of the proper management of diversity and (ii) the proper promotion of equality and opportunity*, thus:

❏ the concept of equality is concerned (i) with ensuring that people are treated equally in the sight of the law, (ii) are not discriminated against unfairly, and (iii) are afforded the same and equal opportunities as others; *and*

❏ there is a respecting and valuing of diversity and difference, whether this difference is visible or not.

In order to achieve this implementation of the management of diversity, and the promotion of equality and opportunity the State *has mandated*:

❏ a *General Duty* to ensure that Equality Legislation is applied in the employment, service provision, educational, and neighbourhood / community management contexts (etc) to which it applies; *and*

❏ a specific *Public Sector Equality Duty* requiring political and public authorities to eliminate discrimination, harassment, victimisation and any other unacceptable conduct that is prohibited in respect of persons having the *protected category status* described immediately below, and (ii) to advance equality of opportunity (etc); *and*

❏ that the statutory *Commission for Equality and Human Rights* (CEHR) monitors progress in Equality matters and reports as a scrutiny body in respect of issues arising, progress made, etc.

The Protected Categories – the UK and the EU have categorised the following as "protected" categories against whom any failure by others to comply with Equality Law is *illegal*:

❏ the elderly (*age*);
❏ the *disabled* (for instance as designated by a consultant medical practitioner under the WHO's ICD, or the US DSM, etc);
❏ the *married* or the *civil partner*;
❏ the *pregnant* and those entitled under the Law to *maternity / paternity leave*;
❏ *racial difference*, whether by colour, ethnic background, or origins. This category may also include caste differences that are the subject of discrimination (as in India);
❏ *religion and belief* (or any lack of, which for example may have significance to members of closed fundamentalist sects who are trying to free themselves from external communal, transcultural or psychological control in order to live an alternative lifestyle);
❏ *gender and sexuality* based on male and female categorisation, but with controversy arising at this time of writing about the potential dilemma concept of so-called "gender neutrality"?
❏ those who have undergone, or are undergoing *gender reassignment*.

Other Protected Categories – which, internationally, could include any of the following:

❏ caste members;
❏ people whose *genetic information* is known;
❏ First Nation peoples;
❏ former prisoners with "spent" criminal convictions;
❏ married women with children, who may culturally be unemployable in some countries.

The Standard Categories of Discrimination – there are four standard categories of discrimination, thus:

❏ *direct* – in which one person is for whatever reason treated less favourably than another in comparable circumstances, eg for reasons of age, disability, race, gender, etc as described above;

❏ *indirect* – which is defined to occur where a "provision, criterion or practice" is applied equally to all but has a differential impact, eg discriminating against women in promotion situations because they have children or plan eventually to become pregnant;

❏ *harassment* – which is defined as unwanted conduct that violates a person's dignity or exposes them to an intimidatory, hostile, bullying, degrading, humiliating or offensive environment on the grounds of a failure to accommodate to any of the relevant categorisations eg "dirty old men" groping pretty girls, the bullying of defenceless residents in care homes, racist attacks, so-called "gay bashing", etc;

❏ *victimisation* (or *retaliation*) – which is defined as treating a person less favourably because they have taken action in respect of some incident of discrimination, for instance by bringing a complaint or activating a proper and formalised institutional grievance procedure.

THE APPLICATION OF UK EQUALITY LEGISLATION

This legislation lays down required behaviours in respect of Equality issues, and specifies what is meant by *compliance*. Case Law has then given flesh to the bones, addressing *in detail* (i) what compliance involves, and (ii) what may be the consequential risks and costs of any failure of that compliance.

UK Equality Law is enforceable across the board in the spheres of politics, employment, service provision, governance and performance measurement, housing, neighbourhood and community management (etc).

It is people's individual, political, organisational and collective responsibility to know what the law requires, and fully to comply with it. This applies, inter alia, to employers and employees, sub-contractors, service providers, political party members and Parliamentarians, members of the media as well as users of social media, membership groups (etc). **Ignorance is no excuse at law.**

WHAT IS REASONABLE AND PROPORTIONATE?

Chapter 25 describes what may be defined as *reasonable and pro-portionate* behaviour, policy choice, resource allocation, or financial management for example in respect of the issues being dealt with in this chapter. This subject is given detailed treatment in the Author's text *Equality, Diversity and Opportunity Management*, published by Routledge, and to which reference is made in the Introduction to this Book.

"POLITICAL CORRECTNESS" AS CHIMERA AND DILEMMA SOURCE

The concept of so-called "political correctness" **as a chimera** in respect of Equality and Opportunity issues has come to constitute (i) a damaging distraction or displacement, and (ii) a highly partial mirror of the real-world legal responsibility of individuals and institutions described above. *As such it now constitutes a critical and human-made Dilemma Source needing proper diagnosis, confronting, management, and resolution.*

So-called "political correctness" cannot replace statutory obligation for Equality compliance, nor can it in any way qualify it.

At worst, the concept as a source of human-made dilemmas has become a distracting, destructive and wasteful use of resources, for instance doing damage to families and relatives of innocent people caught up in its artificial web.

The concept of so-called "political correctness" also appears to have become redundant relative to the original purpose created for it. It is now applied indiscriminately to anything or anyone with whom there is disagreement in what has become an excessively opinionated society, wedded to talk, discourse, argument and debate. It might be based on a collective or semiospheric groupthink (described in Chapter 9). It might instead be based on a particular distraction, ideology, set of values, prejudice, preference, current social media trend, campaign, political weakness, or received wisdom (for instance derived from, or motivated by the use of the *Attention Economy* described in Chapter 5).

**So-called "political correctness" as form of information filter-
ing** – the application of "political correctness" is based on processes
of *information filtering and distortion* (for instance as described
in detail in the Author's *Principles of Management* and *Equality,
Diversity and Opportunity Management* to which reference is made
in the Introduction). Its arbiters:

❑ select what is to them appropriate data by means of filtering
out whatever information is incongruent to, or inconsistent and
incompatible with a selected ideology, prejudice, or "angle";
❑ manipulate or distort the remaining data or information to augment and to enhance its usefulness (eg as "Fact") in meeting a
particular purpose or objective. *This might also mean:*
❑ the deliberate creation of Cognitive Dissonance (Chapter 7) or
CD; *and*
❑ sensationalising, trivialising, grabbing attention, or even "sexing
up" the "Facts" (or *the fake news* as it may have now become),
for instance to meet the requirements of the Attention Economy,
advertisers, the media, or the specific needs of dissemination
by social media. Again, this may involve talking matters up to
perceived crisis proportions, or creating anxiety.

**So-called "political correctness" and the Voice of the Victim
[II]** – the concept of "political correctness" is in part now used as
a dilemma source deliberately to exploit variations in the relative
strength of the Voice of the Victim described in Chapter Four and in
the Author's two *Equality Books*.

The more powerful is the Victim group, and the more "politically
correct" it has by now managed to categorise itself, the harder it may
be for others to comment on matters championed by it. *The Week*
gives the example of discussion about the family and family status as
a policy issue. Some politicians or commentators have become wary
of dealing with such issues because they fear upsetting, or giving
offence to single mothers, lesbians and gay communities. Having or
raising children for these latter groups (who have powerful voices in
the media, in social media, and in politics) may effectively be an artificial, individualistic, non-familistic, and defensive matter involving

issues of assessment, donors, potentially hostile public opinions or bullying, and the reaction of children's school peers (etc).

It was also the Author's contention in his two *Equality Books* that those with a weak Voice of the Victim suffer as a result of what has by this time of writing become entrenched "political correctness" on the part of the influential Voices described above. Campaigning for the elderly (*aka* "crumble", "bed-blockers", or "wrinklies"), people with Alzheimers or dementia, the mentally disabled, people on benefits or homeless, those who have lost their dignity, or the victims of hate crime, (etc) may seem to others to be "boring", "pointless", "un-fashionable", "non-trendy", and unrewarding to the media in the current scheme of things.

An alternative view of so-called "political correctness" – political correctness as a human-made dilemma may now be seen as:

❏ an opinionated, prejudicial, and destructive hammer used to crack the nut of another person's belief. This might be the case (i) of a significant disagreement with that alternative belief, or instead (ii) represent an unwillingness to accept the existence of that belief as being in any way relevant or valid; *or*

❏ a means of attempting to downgrade the perceived importance of some thing or some issue for instance in order to undermine it in the eyes of others; *or*

❏ a deliberate method of creating argument and dispute, ideally to become vexatious, for instance as described as a form of distraction in Chapter 4; *or*

❏ a deliberate means of crisis creation, again as described in Chapter 18; *or*

❏ a form of intellectual fascism or totalitarianism in which "political correctness" is used to attack anything that a group, a political party, a media, or semiosphere does not like, does not approve of, or is prejudiced against.

The concept of the "Snowflake Generation" is analysed in Chapter 12.

Case Example: it has apparently become "politically correct" in some quarters to criticise people who pay their bills in cash.

Paying bills by cash is quite legal in the UK. Some of the "politically correct" however believe that the use of cash in transactions may lead to tax avoidance. This is a gross insult to the small traders and farmers (etc) who for whatever reason use cash. The *real tax avoidance* is carried out by wealthy individuals and multinational companies – usually operating in a strictly legal manner according the laws of some country or other! *How many banks are left on your High Street? Where do you now get your small change and pound coins?*

Case Example: should you use a black emoji?

Case Example: at this time of writing some supporters of Brexit are being criticised for their Referendum choice. Supporting Brexit has, in some quarters, become "politically incorrect"! So much for democracy? Also see Chapter 2.

CASE EXAMPLE
Self-censorship – to what extent should politicians, journalists, or media commentators (or Authors like myself) *self-censor* in such UK cases as the large-scale and carefully planned sexual abuse of vulnerable under-age white girls, as happened in Rotherham or Newcastle-upon-Tyne? These crimes, for which the participants received heavy custodial sentences, were carried out mostly by men from one particular ethnic community. There appears however to have been some subsequent political reluctance to comment on these cases (i) for fear of being accused of "racism" (even though these racist crimes were proven in Court), and (ii) equally for risking the loss of what may traditionally have been a large ethnic block vote favouring one particular political party or other in the location.

Chapter Nine
Perception and Semiospheres

DILEMMA PERCEPTION, DEFINITION, AND ASSURANCE

The nature of the diagnosis, definition, and / or resolution of dilemmas being considered in this Book is likely to be subject to *cognitive processes of perception, definition and assurance*. These cognitive processes may take place at any or all of personal, group, group-think, organisational, communal, cultural or cross-cultural levels to which reference is made both in previous and later chapters.

The application of these cognitive processes may (i) result in clear agreement, or instead (ii) in an acknowledged uncertainty about the meaning or consequence of any particular dilemma issue, such as those associated with fully implementing the Human Rights of women or dealing with roboticisation.

Alternatively, the application of these cognitive processes may (iii) result in a variety or diversity of interpretation, or (iv) in a significant disagreement about the nature of the issue at hand. Hence the discussion in Chapter 8 about what constitutes *fact* (as ***Knowledge***) as might be agreed by parties to the perceptual process; or fact as some people would instead like it or prefer it to be; or opinion as fact; or fact as so-called "fake news"; or fact as downright delusion.

For instance, the experience of mental health disability for one person may be seen by another as an unnecessary source of productivity loss, inconvenience, and expense. Previous chapters have already made the point that dilemmas that result from such diversity or disagreement may be reconcilable, or they may not. Perception, definition, and assurance are based on at least *five inter-related cognitive processes. These are listed as follow*, using the example given immediately above of mental health issues. A recent UK NHS Report indicates that psychiatric ill-health (such as anxiety, depression and stress-related conditions) is now the most common reason for people having to take time off work, ahead of back pain or other musculoskeletal problems.

Perception – in which a person becomes aware of, observes, or visualises an entity (or its attributes) using the mind or the senses, such that Knowledge is accumulated about this entity. *Example:* identifying the particular work behaviour of employees who may be suffering from severe stress or from mental health disorders (also described in Chapter 4). This Knowledge may then be subjected to the process of *conceptualisation*.

Conceptualisation – which involves the use of intellect, mental constructs, paradigms, or the imagination in order to categorise and to fit perceptions (and the Knowledge now associated with them) into a pattern, a classification, a codification, or a scheme of things so that as a concept it may be subjected to interpretation. *Example:* the category of mental health disability in the workplace as a construct separate from physical disability.

Interpretation – which involves submitting perceptions, concepts (and Knowledge) to the process of explanation, comment, opinion, inference or judgement. This may be done by making use of a relevant and perhaps pre-conditioned or learned Knowledge Base, and prevailing values, attitudes, or cultures in order to create meaning. *Example:* how mental health disability can be related to the demands of the work environment within the context of disability legislation.

The derivation or establishment of meaning – by which the interpretation and understanding of a developing or developed Knowledge take a particular form, significance, direction, or intention. *Example:* how to prepare policies for, or to manage people with mental health disabilities in the work environment.

Assurance – by which perception, conceptualisation, interpretation, Knowledge and the derivation of meaning are subjected to processes of:

❑ confirmation;
❑ comparison (for example with standard diagnostic categories, or with values and norms);

❏ evaluation;
❏ validation; *and*
❏ certification

such that a greater degree of certainty and confidence about the issue of concern is the result. *Example:* the medicolegal confirmation and certification of mental health disability, or post- traumatic stress disorder (PTSD), prior (i) to formulating treatment regimes; (ii) prior to the formulation of legislation; or (iii) prior to legal action at Employment Tribunal or court.

HERMENEUTICS
These processes of perception, definition, interpretation and assurance are sometimes categorised as "hermeneutic".

Hermeneutics are given detailed treatment in the Author's text *Equality, Diversity and Opportunity Management*, available from Bookpoint, Routledge, and Amazon; and cited in the Introduction.

THE KNOWLEDGE BASE AND KNOWLEDGE MANAGEMENT
A detailed and cutting-edge treatment of the subject of Knowledge Management is given in the Author's text *Principles of Strategic Management*, available from Bookpoint, Routledge, and Amazon; and also cited in the Introduction.

CASE EXAMPLE
Transcultural perceptions of terrorism – what are to us senseless criminal acts of so-called "terrorist" murder or familial violence might variously be perceived elsewhere by their proponents as being any or all of:

❏ acts of revenge for perceived past injustices;
❏ a consequence of an absolute or "fundamentalist" intolerance and rejection of the beliefs, values or way of life of others (to include the absolute denial of equal Human Rights to women or widows in the practice of certain religions, or rejection of any belief in the democratic process);

❑   the acts of a vengeful God; *or*
❑   acts of aggressive nationalism such as those perpetrated by the IRA in the UK, by so-called "Islamic State" in the Middle East, or by various ethnic minorities in Turkey and other parts of Asia.

DILEMMAS, PERCEPTION, AND TIMES OF CHANGE

The perception and definition of dilemmas, and the validation or assurance of that perception and definition, may be critical *at times of significant change*. Such times of change may be identified:

❑   from the Dilemma Sources being identified in Parts Two and Three of this Book; *and more generically*
❑   from the analysis of the "S" Curves, Technology Discontinuities, and Kondriatev Waves (such as those that might be experienced by the UK if it withdraws from the European Union; or instead caused by roboticisation) and described in more detail in the Author's text *Principles of Strategic Management*, available from Bookpoint, Routledge, and Amazon; and cited above.

There will be no guarantee that prevailing dilemma perceptions for example being described in this chapter will be in step (or congruent) with such changes and their implications. They may instead be out of date, obsolete, or out of step with these changes. Such lack of congruence (or Cognitive Dissonance) might be exhibited variously in the areas of:

❑   the attitudes of politicians towards the sentiments of voters and the wider electorate in a democracy;
❑   adherence to Human Rights and Equality issues;
❑   issues of religious tolerance and intolerance, the influence of Wahhabism, etc;
❑   attitudes towards the globalisation of economic activity; *and*
❑   attitudes towards the nature of (and remuneration for) jobs, roboticisation, entrepreneurship, or the payment by the state from taxation of a standard "living wage" and ultimate pension;
❑   healthcare realities, personal responsibility, and ownership of obligations (for instance as described in Chapter 10).

CASE EXAMPLE

Post 16 and post 18 education and training – significant controversy still surrounds perceptions about (i) the issues of, and (ii) priorities for post 16 and post 18 UK systems of education and training. The dilemmas associated with these issues are described at various points in this Book.

Vocationality has traditionally been seen in the UK (for instance as compared with Germany) as a "second class" entity in terms of *status* (Chapter 11). Parts of the (self-styled "elite") UK's educational establishment have long preferred not to equate the output of higher education with the reality of the country's Training and Human Capital needs. Which is why a plumber in London may earn considerably more than a university professor. Status and prestige (but not market needs for engineers, trained technicians, skilled craftsmen, nurses, bricklayers, etc) may still be predominant drivers of parental and student choices for post 16 and post 18 education.

No matter that questions are now raised as to the employability of many UK graduates. Some appear to know little or nothing of any direct vocational use. Others have very poor skills of written English. Many cannot communicate verbally at an acceptable or professional standard (even though many want to be lawyers, politicians, journalists, or instead "to go into the media"!). Many have poor or non-existent interpersonal skills (particularly if they have spent six hours per day, every day in their rooms playing computer games on their own). They are likely to struggle in a competitive interview or presentation situation, or in a teamwork exercise carried out at an assessment centre – "like", "sort of", "eh?", "you know what I mean", (etc).

Actually "it's huge", in fact "it's mega". And do I spit my chewing gum into your waste paper basket? Or on the pavement? Oh wow! OMG!

DILEMMAS, PERCEPTIONS, CONSTRUCTED REALITIES AND SEMIOSPHERES

The interpretation of Dilemmas, and any consequent decisions about how to deal with them may next be a function (i) of the perceptions and (ii) of the consequent behaviour patterns and decision choices that characterise what have emerged as *"constructed realities" or "semiospheres"*. Such entities will exercise some kind of influence on the reaction to Dilemmas on the part of people who "reside" in these constructed realities, or who for whatever reason see themselves as being associated with them.

A detailed account of the concept of constructed realities or semiospheres will be found in the Author's text *Equality, Diversity and Opportunity Management*, available from Bookpoint, Routledge, and Amazon; and also cited in the Introduction to this Book.

Constructed realities or semiospheres – may be characterised to *outsiders* by the possession of such features as:

❑   the choice of, and adherence to a particular set of ideologies, values, cultural variables, attitude, opinion and behaviour;

❑   some kind of dominant groupthink, exclusivity, or collective cohesiveness;

❑   a varying degree of openness to other thought patterns and cultures;

❑   a varying degree of behavioural neutrality or emotion, as described in Chapter 6;

❑   particular patterns and choice of language and communication variables, eg the party politician, the feminist, the Chartered Accountant, the Chief Executive, the teacher, the military, etc;

❑   the adherence to, or display of particular insignia or artifacts as cultural symbols that identify or differentiate the inhabitants of the semiosphere;

❑   a varying degree and strength of opinionation (or instead so-called "political correctness") as described in Chapter 8.

Semiospheric attitudes and behaviour are also likely to exercise an influence on issues of individualism and personal responsibility (Chapter 10); issues of status (Chapter 11); "Snowflake" behaviour (Chapter 12); and issues of risk and uncertainty (Chapters 17 and 18).

Any particular semiosphere may (i) be more or less open, or instead (ii) more or less resistant to external investigation or influence in respect of their adherence to ideologies, values, attitudes, opinions or behaviours. Similarly, the decision-making processes and behaviour (described in Parts Four and Five of this Book) to which they choose to adhere may be more or less transparent to the outsider, and thus relevant to the analysis of how they deal with the dilemmas in which they are involved.

Some examples of constructed realities or semiospheres – might include any of the following. These examples have been chosen simply on the basis that they may be judged as relevant, usable and useful to the purposes of this Book.

- ❏ families (eg see Chapters 2 and 6);
- ❏ full-time politicians or members of a political party or class;
- ❏ journalists and the media;
- ❏ members of special interest, campaigning or pressure groups; and / or
- ❏ inhabitants of the so-called "social media world"; *and / or*
- ❏ representatives of self-styled "victim groups" based (for example) on gender, race, age, sexual orientation (etc) active in the use of the media and social media;
- ❏ professional educationalists;
- ❏ members of well-established retail cultures;
- ❏ members of a business or institutional "corporate world" such as Chairpersons, Chief Executive Officers, Healthcare Officers, Trustees, senior members of the Uniformed Services;
- ❏ farmers and fisher folk;
- ❏ performing artists or sportspersons sometimes categorised by the media as "celebrities" or "celebs";
- ❏ members of the various layers of the prevailing class system; and / or
- ❏ members of the prevailing caste system (such as that of the Indian sub-continent, or more catastrophically at this time of writing in North Korea) in which the layers of hierarchy are more or less fixed and resistant to change or mobility amongst them;
- ❏ officially chartered, incorporated or certified professionals and functional specialists such as the legal, the medical, the

medicolegal, the accountancy, the uniformed services, or the civil and local government service (etc);

❏ stereotypical individualistic, self-centred, opinionated, materialistic or consumerist cultures, perhaps associated with areas of wealth and stable employment;

❏ members of well-established and influential *membership groups* such as Freemasons, Irish Orange Orders, the USA's "The Room", or the Knights of St John (who have periodically come into direct conflict with the Roman Catholic Church over medical issues associated with birth control, gynaecological practice, etc);

❏ religious adherents such as the Muslim Wahhabis or fundamentalist Christian, Jewish or Hindu groups (some for example highly antagonistic to other religions, or to the advancement of the Human Rights of women or the disabled). The inhabitants of such semiospheres may be very highly resistant to the views and attitudes of others, and may have to be categorised as being located at the most extreme end of any dilemma continuum.

The relationship between constructed realities or semiospheres – the relationship between (i) the occupants or inhabitants of a constructed reality or semiosphere, and (ii) those outside of it might be shown graphically as in **Figure 5**.

The relationship between the *dilemma perceptions* (i) of the occupants or inhabitants of a constructed reality or semiosphere, and (ii) those outside of it might instead be shown graphically as in **Figure 6**.

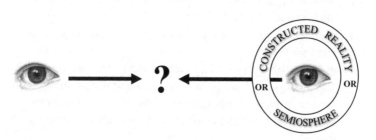

Figure 5

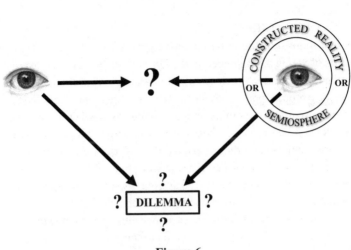

Figure 6

The identification, management, and assurance options of the dilemma shown in Figure 6 might in this case then have to be a function of *two processes*, not one, thus:

❏ the degree to which understanding and agreement can be established between the two parties about where each stands in relation to the other; *and*

❏ the degree to which understanding and agreement can be established by the two parties as to how to define and to deal with the dilemma itself.

CASE EXAMPLE

Female Genital Mutilation (FGM) – whilst the appalling practice of FGM remains widespread for instance in Africa, Asia and the Indian sub-Continent, recent prosecutions show that it is only recently being tackled in countries, such as the USA or Canada, which have very strict laws outlawing the practice as criminal. Investigators searching for evidence of wrong-doing may face a cultural wall of silence and denial not only from the parents of children subjected to mutilation, but worse from the local medical practitioners who carry out these acts of defilement (!).

CASE EXAMPLE

Good night out, then? [I] – major controversy has surrounded reports of young adult women in the UK who go out with the express intention of drinking themselves into a state of inebriation and incapacity, a process perhaps exacerbated by taking drugs. These women then present the authorities with a dilemma as to what to do or say about such behaviour (i) from the viewpoint of personal or victim security and safeguarding (Chapter 16), (ii) from the viewpoint of the justice system, and (iii) from the viewpoint of the resource costs imposed on the police, the courts (and the taxpayer) who have to deal with (and pay for) the consequences of such behaviour.

These young women have been shown either to be liable to attack by "predatory" men who perceive that their victims may not be in a fit state to resist an attack; or worse were actually subject to incidences of rape.

In two cases cited here (Toronto 2011 and Manchester 2017) reasonable comments were made by the authorities to the effect that heavy drinking and drug abuse were likely to increase the vulnerability of women to targeting by male attackers, and thereby increase the risk of rape. At the same time, Judge Lindsey Kushner (Manchester 2017) pointed out the likelihood that a woman might be less likely to report a rape attack because (i) she was drunk; (ii) she could not remember what had happened (with implications for the provision of *evidence* in the case), (iii) she felt too ashamed to report the attack, or (iv) assumed that because she was drunk at the time of the attack she would be less likely to be believed than if she had been sober and in full command of her senses.

The comments of the police and judicial authorities involved in these cases were however met with a chorus of public hostility and condemnation by various women's groups in both countries. These groups assert that the incidence of rape is a male crime, for which (from their viewpoint) female victims could not be defined in any way to bear responsibility (sources: *The Week* and *BBC News Online*). This Case Example is continued in Chapter 10.

CASE EXAMPLE

Embarrassing dads – UK advertising agencies appear to live in a robust, self-referential, strongly stereotyped, and impenetrable semiosphere. One of their recent Attention Economy-type strategies has been to use television advertisements to lampoon fathers (ie middle-aged or professional men) who are apparently unable (or just unwilling) to learn to operate a mobile phone or tablet like their offspring can. This lampooning may however be perceived to be an *open act of contempt* by such agencies for what is actually a critically important income source for telecommunication companies (the *Bank of Mum and Dad* usually pays for the costs of children's mobile phone and internet usage, which is now very substantial).

What advertising copywriters seem unconcerned about when (i) abusing older or professional men, or (ii) having a cheap laugh at their expense is the possibility that:

❏ such men do not wish to receive any unnecessary communications whatsoever; *and in particular*

❏ they wish to avoid encouraging their bosses to contact them by phone in order to see what they are doing, or what they are up to; *or*

❏ they have already had to deal with (perhaps) an hundred (written) e-mails at the beginning of their working day, before they actually started that day's work, and then had to attend endless meetings which further disrupt (or add to) their workload; *or*

❏ they are subject to formal communication protocols requiring them to answer (written) e-mails accessible at work, or via their portable computers (which they may have to carry with them – subject to GDPR), and possibly subject to specific policies about response times; *or*

❏ they are just tired, wish to switch off completely from everything, and rest!

The Author's text *Principles of Management*, to which reference is made in the Introduction to this Book, contains a detailed analysis of the types of Organisation Culture that may characterise certain types of constructed realities and semiospheres such as the advertising agency.

Chapter Ten
Individualism and Personal Responsibility

Selfie! Selfie!
OR INSTEAD
Leave your egos at the gate! – Burnley Football Club

Chapter 1 of this Book makes reference to the dilemmas created by the irresponsible and illegal use of mobile phones by drivers in the UK. A subsequent Report published by the RAC shows that matters have by now got worse. The Report states that nearly a half of drivers aged 25-34 admit to making or receiving calls with a hand-held phone whilst behind the wheel. About 30% of motorists aged 35-44 say that they use a phone to send texts, posts on social media, or to check e-mails while driving. Worst of all, the Department for Transport records that 43 people were killed and 135 were seriously injured in crashes on Britain's roads in 2017 in which a driver using a mobile phone was a contributory factor.

INDIVIDUALISM
Reference has been made in previous chapters to the phenomenon of Individualism and individualistic behaviour, such as using mobile phones whilst driving, or failing to maintain a reasonable personal health and weight.

CASE EXAMPLE
Abandoned pets – the Battersea Dogs & Cats Home, along with many other animal charities, reports that week in, week out, they receive, and care for abandoned animals. In one case, a litter of seven puppies were found abandoned in a basket by the side of a road during a winter's night. The puppies were traumatised, weak, hungry, cold, dirty and dehydrated. Charities like the Battersea Dogs & Cats

Home do their best to make up for **the irresponsible behaviour** of owners or breeders who are unable or unwilling properly to face up to their personal responsibilities in the matter of animal welfare.

Happily, these puppies were nursed back to full health and found new homes where they are loved and looked after.

INDIVIDUALISM DEFINED

The OED defines individualism in terms (i) of self-centredness or egoism as guiding principles of personal behaviour; or (ii) as placing an emphasis on freedom and independence of individual thought and action; or (iii) a focus on the self as the only real or knowable existence.

CASE EXAMPLE

Warlock brains – headlining a public dispute with the US media in which the actor Charlie Sheen had become embroiled during Spring 2011, *The Week* reported the views of a variety of US commentators. One noted Sheen's 'rants about his "warlock brains", his "tiger blood", and his "epic" adventures'. Another correspondent suggested that Sheen is 'cheerfully admitting to what we secretly suspect all stars think about themselves – that they are unique, enchanted, indestructible beings leading, in Sheen's formulation, "perfect, bitchin', rock-star lives". Deep down, said Alexandra Petri on *WashingtonPost.com*, we all think we're special, which is why Sheen's public display of unfiltered self-regard has so firmly "latched onto the public consciousness". Americans raised in the self-esteem movement secretly feel, as Sheen proclaims publicly, that our "genius is not adequately appreciated", [and] that we're being held back by "fools and trolls" who just don't get how wonderful we are'.

TWO DILEMMA MANAGEMENT CONSEQUENCES OF INDIVIDUALISM

A *first* consequence of Individualism may be *the direct causation of dilemmas*, such as in the road policing, healthcare or animal welfare examples given above, to which others will have to respond and for which resources may have to be made available. In this first case, the dilemma derives from attitudes or behaviours that result from the individual's own over-riding definition of their personal responsibility (or rather, *lack of responsibility*) towards the issue of concern.

A *second* consequence of Individualism stems from *individualistic perceptions of the nature of dilemmas* that have to be dealt with, irrespective of their source. In this second case, the perception of the dilemma will be a function of individual or semiospheric culture and mindset. In an individualistic or Snowflake society semiosphere this perception may not be consistent with that of other people, (or instead be a source of C.D.). In particular it may be inconsistent with the perceptions of those charged with the responsibility for the relevant Dilemma Management. The issues of dilemma perception and constructed realities were analysed in Chapter 9.

In either of these two cases, individualistic attitudes and behaviour are likely to affect the management, resolution, or non-resolution of dilemmas in which others (whether individuals themselves, or institutions) have become, or have to become involved, irrespective of their feelings or attitudes about the matter.

CASE EXAMPLE
Good night out, then? [II] – Chapter 9 described the controversy surrounding reports of young women who go out with the express intention of drinking themselves into a state of inebriation and incapacity, a process perhaps exacerbated by taking drugs. These young women were then shown either (i) to be liable to violence by "predatory" men who perceive that their victims may not be in a fit state to resist an attack; or worse (ii) were actually subject to incidences of rape by such men.

These women were described in Chapter 9 as presenting the authorities with a dilemma as to what to do or say about this behaviour from the viewpoint of personal or victim safety, from the viewpoint of the justice system, and from the viewpoint of the resource costs imposed on the police and the courts who have to deal with the consequences.

Subsequently, however, one rape victim waived her right to anonymity in order publicly to agree with the advice of Judge Kushner that women who deliberately put themselves "in harm's way" must bear some of the responsibility for what might happen to them. The Judge stated that she was duty bound to point out the realities of the situation, irrespective of the views expressed by women's groups in Chapter 9. She stated that it would have been remiss of her not to point out that a woman must bear some responsibility to protect herself from predatory men if she was deliberately intent on rendering herself incapable on a night out.

NATIONAL CULTURE EXPLANATIONS

National culture variables as dilemma sources were described in Chapter 6. Their impact on Individualism and on the definition of Personal Responsibility is illustrated by two examples, as follow.

Illustration One – some organisations may be characterised by *a very strongly centralised and individualised locus of power and control*. This may be evident in family businesses or businesses with powerful chief executives and / or majority shareholders; institutions run by autocrats or patriarchs who hold direct personal control of affairs; or kleptocracies characterised by endemic corruption and the wholesale theft of resources. These organisations or institutions may in National Culture terms be characterised by:

❏ very high Power Distance (perhaps associated with a low degree of transparency);
❏ very high levels of Masculinity;
❏ large Status inequalities; *probably associated with*
❏ a rigid and strong Hierarchy; *and*
❏ a very strong power base; *and maybe*
❏ an ability to circumvent or to corrupt the rules by which others have to live, profiting by the exceptions (such as uncontrolled executive pay, tax evasion, or money laundering) that they can create and enforce.

Illustration Two – organisations run by powerful individuals (and perhaps groups or semiospheres characterised by groupthink that is entirely congruent with that of the power source) may display dominant *uncertainty avoidance*. This uncertainty avoidance may shape proprietorial attitudes to risk and risk management (as in the case of 19th Century US capitalists such as Carnegie, JP Morgan or Rockefeller taking over or eliminating competitors, and forming cartels or monopolies in their place).

Alternatively, organisations run for instance (i) by ageing entre-preneurs, or (ii) by long-established political parties in government may develop an entrenched *inner-directedness* and *low trust* of oth-ers such that a powerful institutional resistance develops to entities and forces from outside (and which were "not invented here"). The entrepreneur may have become unwilling to accept the nature of ongoing technology dynamics which could render that person's once significant invention obsolete. And political parties and governments may lose touch with the views and concerns of the electorate, how-ever inconvenient these may be. Worse, the individual entrepreneur or political leader may mis- read the dilemmas with which they are faced such that they try to challenge them, with the potentially dis-astrous results of going out of business, losing power, or causing the financial losses described in Chapters 17 and 18.

PERSONAL CHARACTERISTICS

Individualism as a personal characteristic may be caused by, or be a function of a variety of factors. Some of these factors are described as follow.

Narcissism – which is defined by the OED in terms of self-love, self-admiration, or self-absorption on the part of an individual. Narcissism may derive from personal conditioning and cultural socialisation in a predominantly individualistic society like the UK or the USA. *Ultimately, the individual becomes his or her own semiosphere.* Latent or established Narcissism may then be strengthened by powerful Attention Economy-type consumerist and promotional pressures placing emphasis on individual gratification and fulfilment. Its implications may be particularly strong for young people whom earlier chapters described as feeling pressurised into an obsession with their physical appearance, and perhaps into some kind of competitive relationship with their peers. They may also become fearful of being out of touch with today's trends, or out of the thoughts of others, constantly peering into their mobile phones for the latest message, selfie, affirmation, or "reassurance" as described in Chapters 2 and 4. Life becomes an extended selfie.

Opinionation – which may be a key indicator of individualism or so-called "political correctness", as described in Chapter 8. Individualistic behaviour characterised by strong or determining opinion may be a feature of individuals, semiospheres, or groupthink cultures, already described in Illustration One above, that possess strong centralised control, the ability to bend or to manipulate the rules, etc.

Low levels of interpersonal sensitivity or emotional intelligence – in which the individual is, for whatever reason, unable or unwilling to empathise with, to understand, or accept the validity of the views of others. *This may be related to:*

The Snowflake Generation – described in detail in Chapter 12; *and to*:

"Type A" personalities – which tend to be associated with the national culture variable of Masculinity. "Type A" personalities may of course be either male or female. They are likely to be focussed and competitive, perhaps adept at getting things done or achieving results. But their behaviour towards those whom they perceive to be getting in their way, or not to be pulling their weight (eg because of their childcare responsibilities), being weak, or prone to illness may become aggressive or bullying in nature. "Type A" personalities may hold a view of themselves as being indispensable and indestructible (perhaps, for now at least, even immortal). Like Atlas, it is they who must carry the World on their own shoulders. Other people should be like them. If they are not, they must be failures.

Educational shortcomings – in which the formal education received by the individual displays a lack of congruence between (i) the prevailing educational paradigms, and (ii) a society or a country's

Human Capital needs, for instance in terms of vocational skills, competences, and required capability. A previous chapter has noted that some UK graduates, for instance, appear to be poorly equipped for the world of work. Others, for instance from prestigious universities, remain individually fixated on becoming a journalist, a lawyer, an actor or actress, or a politician – even if realistically there are few if any vacancies. This may be related to:

An outdated base of thinking, Knowledge and Competence – in which the degree of individualism and opinionation as a dilemma source affecting *Knowledge and Competence Management* is a function of:

❑ past cultural conditioning and socialisation associated with the development or encouragement of individual status and prestige;

❑ an adherence to outmoded class stratification, or perceptions of individual "social superiority" as compared with others (that is "snobbishness");

❑ the obsolescent education systems already described above which give inadequate priority for instance to Further Education, internationalisation, technology, skill and competence development, and vocationality. Such systems compare badly for instance at the Higher Education level with the German *fachhochschule* structure;

❑ the individual habitation in semiospheres characterised by powerful drives (i) to maintain groupthink and the status quo and (ii) to resist change. Resistance to change is dealt with in the next Section of this Chapter, below. This may be associated with:

❑ a lack (or denial of the need for) new or alternative experience and stimuli (as described in terms of the *genetic diversity* and *requisite variety* to which reference has already been made in this Book). Many (very highly individualistic and opinionated) UK journalists and media reporters are for instance stereotyped in the public mind to hover around the pubs of Fleet Street, frightened to go far from their London base. Indeed, media and political London-centricity was held to be one of the causes of a recent Government's failure to read the national mood running up to the 2016 Brexit Referendum. It seems that some people "don't get out much and especially not north of Watford!"

RESISTANCE TO CHANGE

Where *external* forces for change are for whatever reason rejected by a stronger *internal* personal resistance to change on the part of an individual or a semiosphere characterised by groupthink, then that change may not come about. This sets up a potential dilemma associated with that change where other parties are trying, or instead need to bring it about.

For example, attempts to make business or financial processes more transparent may be resisted by those:

❏   who do not see the change to be in their interest; *and / or*
❏   who have the power or influence to halt the change process, to distort it or to corrupt it.

Recent UK dilemma examples include taxation issues in corporations, football club player transfers, and apparent corruption in motor sport. *Also see:*

CASE EXAMPLE

CEO bonuses [I] – which have been a long running source of comment and argument. The calculation of CEO bonuses gives rise to a fundamental dilemma. Good performance in responsibly directing the affairs of an organisation should be rewarded. But at the same time:

❏   some CEOs are handsomely rewarded for poor performance or even failure; *and / or*
❏   the various (legal) accounting and taxation methodologies used to construct corporate financial reports, the possibility of the use of so-called "creative accounting", and the potential for significantly over-stating or under-stating results may mean that the level of bonus does not bear any real relationship with corporate performance, but still rewards the CEO.

CASE EXAMPLE

CEO bonuses [II] – the calculation of CEO bonuses may be a source of dilemmas where (i) the nature and requirements of executive responsibility are clearly prescribed (for example by politicians, funding agencies, trustee boards, football club owners, etc); but (ii) the level of resources, authority and control allocated by them to the CEO is either inadequate or inappropriate to the achievement of the results for which that CEO is being held responsible. This may happen for instance in healthcare or educational organisations, charities, police forces, or sporting organisations. Given the "no-win" situation faced by the Chief Executive, what does he or she do? Does the CEO abide by the requirements laid down (and possibly lose their job), or do they by whatever means necessary try to protect and to assure their own personal situation?

Dilemmas caused by direct individual or groupthink resistance to change – may be visible in the case of:

❑ individuals or semiospheres who actively feel challenged by change, or by the prospect of change. This change may be seen by them as an unwanted threat and an intrusion to, or a disturbance of the current status quo; and therefore to be resisted;

❑ *plateau'd professionals* who do not want to be bothered to adopt new knowledge, new paradigms, or new ways of working; *perhaps associated with*

❑ mental laziness and the loss of willpower and drive (for instance as in the case of the plateau'd professional) in which the individual or semiosphere feels comfortable with the status quo, and does not accept that new things should be learned or new skills learned. Quote "I did my learning at school!" This may also be associated with:-

❑ resistance to ongoing or continuing personal or professional development (CPD) giving rise to obsolescence of personal knowledge base, competence and capacity.

Issues of **Knowledge Management** and **Technology Dynamics** are given extensive treatment in the Author's text *Principles of Strategic Management*, to which reference is made at the beginning of this Book.

PERSONAL RESPONSIBILITY

The OED defines the word **responsible** as an adjective or an adverb in terms of a capacity and willingness (ie a capability) to fulfil an obligation, a charge, a trust or a duty; and being reliable or trustworthy in assuring that duty or reliability.

The OED defines the word **responsibility** as a noun in terms of that obligation, charge, trust or duty which is held by someone, and for which they are accountable to others for stewardship, care or achievement in respect of that responsibility.

INDIVIDUALISM, COLLECTIVISM, AND PERSONAL RESPONSIBILITY

Chapter 6 describes the National Cultural dilemma between *individualism* and *collectivism* as a concept which indicates the relative closeness of the relationship between one person (or a semiosphere as described in Chapter 9 characterised by groupthink) and other people in a society. It anticipates fundamental dilemmas associated with the nature of the role, place, and motivation of the individual in relation to their membership of families, clans, tribes, teams, groups, organisations, the neighbourhood or the community, and the wider collective that is society.

In *individualistic* societies, the demands and desires of individual persons or semiospheres take precedence. There may then be an expectation that the purpose of political, business and social institutions is to ensure that these demands can be met, for instance by the downplaying of the importance of social commitment or the importance of education in the development of a nation's Human Capital; or by the materialistic promotion of an officially relaxed attitude to the availability of consumer credit (and therefore to any resultant level of *personal indebtedness*), low interest rates, the effective discouragement of personal saving, and disinterest in investments in future pension prospects.

In *collectivist* societies, people are to some degree socialised into a collective orientation to life experience. In such a culture the responsibility is placed on the individual to put the collective or corporate interest first, ahead of individualistic priorities. The individualism

– collectivism dilemma is also found in strongly *familistic* societies, such as those of Italy, Spain, and the Indian sub-continent. Pressure is placed on each member to ensure that family interests take precedence over individual preferences. The Chinese State Social Credit System was described in Chapter 5.

Chapter 6 also contrasted *Low Trust* and *High Trust* societies. It noted that the leaders and decision-makers of societies, institutions and governments characterised by a *low degree of trust of others* may hold an attitude to the *uncertainty and unpredictability caused by individualistic behaviour* that takes the form of "fencing people in". This means controlling them with legalistic, bureaucratic, behavioural or hierarchical rules whose purpose is *to guarantee the compliance* of those with whom governments and organisations have to interact or to transact affairs. Transactional and behavioural requirements are pre-specified in codes, and backed up by law. Fukuyama suggested that individuals 'who do not trust one another will end up co-operating only under a system of formal rules and regulations, which have to be negotiated, agreed to, litigated, and enforced (if necessary by coercive means)'. He notes that such rules and laws impose their own dilemmas. The control that they imply costs money and resources. But they create little if any, positive benefit or added value.

Fukuyama then noted that the leaders and decision-makers of societies, governments and institutions that are instead characterised by a *high degree of collective trust of others* may not require extensive contractual or legal regulation of their relationships and architectures because an established and working consensus gives people a basis for *mutual trust*.

SOME DILEMMAS OF INDIVIDUALISM, COLLECTIVISM, AND PERSONAL RESPONSIBILITY MAPPED

A key implication of all this may be that, for whatever reasons, a variety of differing attitudes towards the personal responsibility of the individual to his or her employment, healthcare, community or society may occur. These variations are mapped in Figure 7, thus:

❏ **Map A** – in which the greater the priority of individualism or self-orientation, the less the individual perceives that he / she owes any duty of personal, social or collective responsibility to society; *and*

❏ **Map B** – the greater the degree of individualism and the lower the emphasis placed on personal responsibility to others and to society, the greater may be the likelihood of a generalised low trust of individuals in society ("l'enfer, c'est les autres"); *and*

❏ **Map C** – the greater the level of individualism, the lower may be the degree of personal or social self-control as perceived from the viewpoint of society; *and*

❏ **Map D** – the greater the individualism, the lower may be the priority placed by individuals on personally responsible behaviour, the greater may be the risk of amoral or immoral behaviour on the part of that individual, and the greater the potential for a socially corrosive *sense of impunity* as described in the text below; *and*

❏ **Map E** – the greater may be the risk, and the financial or resource cost to society of an individualistic orientation and behaviour.

ASSURANCE

Personal responsibility is a key component of the process of achieving the assurance described in Chapter 9. However, the lower is the degree to which the individual accepts the need to demonstrate personal responsibility on his or her part, for instance in a healthcare or customer service context, or instead playing for a Premier League football club, the greater will be the difficulty and cost of achieving the compliance required to achieve whatever is the level of assurance needed. Or is it a case of "don't ask me, mate … I only work here!"

CASE EXAMPLE

Betting in football – recent reports have revealed the extent in England and Scotland of betting by professional football players on league matches. One player, who has admitted to a severe gambling addition, even bet on his own team to lose matches. Matters are not, however, helped by the fact that leagues, clubs and even grounds receive substantial sponsorship from betting companies. Should the activities of these companies be taken as role models? And should individual players be categorised as irresponsible, or more significantly be banned from playing the game for doing what the sponsors want us all to do. That is to gamble, even though most people cannot afford it. They will in any case be unlikely to win, and may end up in debt as a result.

A SENSE OF IMPUNITY

Penultimately in this Chapter, the corruption of the concept of personal responsibility *may lead to a potentially amoral or immoral sense of individual impunity*. This was suggested in an earlier section above. An Italian, Michele Serra, commented that 'this is the real value of power, and what makes it irresistible, and at the same time ruinous. From a certain point it feels as if you have become a member of an elite which no longer abides by common rules, and which can instead create its own. You neither have the moral strength to withstand the climate of conceit in which you find yourself, nor may you even be aware that what you are doing is illegal and that you are riding roughshod over other people's rights'. If you *can* do it, you *will* do it, no matter whether right or wrong – *because you know you are likely to get away with it*.

DISCONNECT AND DYSTOPIA

Developing individualism and a widespread rejection of the need for the exercise of personal responsibility may ultimately lead to a world of *disconnect* and *dystopia*. These conditions may give rise to intractable and even impossible dilemmas affecting the very nature of society and its governance.

There will be a disconnect with requisite process, whether democratic, political, governmental, employment, social, judicial, healthcare (etc) upon which the proper functioning of society depends.

And the retreat of the individual or the semiosphere into the artificial worlds of virtual reality, the Snowflake, Twitter, "fake news", online gaming, so-called "reality shows" (such as the Jeremy Kyle Show), corporate control and all of the other creations of modern media and the Attention Economy may eventually lead people to embrace the kind of dysfunctional and dystopian life portrayed by such literature or films as Brave New World, Fahrenheit 451, 1984, A Clockwork Orange, Soylent Green, Blade Runner or The Matrix, (etc) to which reference has already been made in this Book. **The world may by then be approaching a destructive condition of *anomie*.**

CASE EXAMPLE

Oh No! – *The Week* recently reported that 'a nineteen year-old man contracted hypothermia after climbing Snowdon' (a very large mountain in Wales) 'in only a pair of Superman pants. Now, four hikers in their twenties have had to be helped off Scafell Pike, in the Lake District' (a very large mountain in England) 'after smoking so much cannabis en route that they could no longer walk. "Words fail us" said the local police'. The views of the (*volunteer and unpaid*) Mountain Rescue Teams involved were not forthcoming about these rescues, nor would they be likely to be printable?

MAP	DILEMMA VARIABLE	INDIVIDUAL ORIENTATION	COMPROMISE ?	PERCEPTIONS OF COLLECTIVE RESPONSIBILITY
A	RESPONSIBILITY	PRIORITY	DILEMMA ?	FEW OR NONE
B	SOCIAL SELF-CONTROL	LOW	DILEMMA ?	NOT APPLICABLE
C	RISK OF INDIVIDUAL AMORAL / IMMORAL BEHAVIOUR, OR SENSE OF PERSONAL IMPUNITY	HIGHEST	DILEMMA ?	LOWER
D	SOCIAL TRUST	LOW	DILEMMA ?	NONE
E	COST TO SOCIETY OF LOW TRUST	HIGHEST	DILEMMA ?	LOWEST

Figure 7
**Dilemmas of Individualism, Collectivism, and
Personal Responsibility**

Chapter Eleven
Status

The meek shall not inherit the Earth. At least not until
they have a good Agent (Anon)
"I'm rich and powerful – I know more than you do."
(The Week)

Status may be defined as *the standing or position of a person in society relative to others*. This chapter describes *three key social status dilemmas*. These are:

- ❏ **firstly**, decisions associated with *how status is allocated*, and the *criterion* by which this status may be assigned;
- ❏ **secondly**, the extent to which social status is a factor in determining whether a society is characterised by *a high or instead a low degree of mobility between social classes or segments*. This is often termed "social class mobility"; *and*
- ❏ **thirdly**, the potentially large differences in personal status and wealth associated with the development of the so-called "superstar culture", and with the advantages and disadvantages of this artificial phenomenon.

THE ALLOCATION OF STATUS

DILEMMAS OF ACHIEVED STATUS

Chapter 6 commented that decisions on the allocation of status (and any *reward* that is associated with this status) may be dependent upon the *achievement* of certain types of results directly associated with communal, institutional, governmental, political (etc) performance in an operational context. This might include the number of patients successfully treated; or marketplace results such as business success or the number of jobs created; or the reward for service to a community or to a political party.

Achieved status (and the dilemmas to which it may give rise) can therefore be defined as a status (and associated reward if any) that is dependent upon the achievement of certain types of results directly associated with the performance of task, work, service, neighbourhood, or communal activities (whether these be professional, commercial, political, or social). Ultimately, these results will be objective and measurable, be they represented by profit earned, enhancements made to healthcare, housing improvements, or the innovation and application of technological advancements (etc). Status will be dependent on the achievement of these objective and measurable outcomes, and not so much (if at all) on the nature or background of the person who has achieved them.

DILEMMAS OF ASCRIBED STATUS

The *ascription* of status and reward described in Chapter 6 may instead depend on the choice and application of some other characteristic (or characteristics) that is (or are) seen to be *culturally important*, and *whose demonstration those who make decisions on behalf of society wish to be seen to reward*. Such criteria might include age or seniority; social class; caste or tribal membership; wealth; gender; membership of a particular family or society; length of service; or type of education. It may correspond to some record of service to a political party, a military, a religion, or the state; or it may be associated with a prestigious type of occupation, business, or profession.

Ascribed status (and the dilemmas to which it may give rise) can therefore be defined in terms of a status that is associated (i) with reward for conformity associated with (ii) a commitment to values, behaviours, or traditions that are seen as important by the *dominant forces* in society. The greater the level of conformity and commitment, and the more the person exemplifies the value set of these dominant forces, the greater may be their ascribed status.

Such a value set *might* be strongly traditional or orthodox. Those people who cannot (for example for reason of social class, race, gender, poverty, caste, lack of educational or other opportunity, etc) demonstrate such conformity may find it difficult or even impossible to achieve any degree of status, particularly where for reasons of orthodoxy, hierarchy, familism, patriarchy, or high power distance any possibility of upward social mobility is blocked. The issue of social mobility is dealt with in a later section, below.

CASE EXAMPLE
Social Equality and Opportunity Agendas – where the ascription of status is well-entrenched and well-defended by the most powerful people in society, the promotion of Equality and Opportunity Agendas may at best be seen as an irrelevance, and at worst a direct threat to the *status quo* that must be protected at all costs. Such agendas may be subjected to aggressive counter- attack because they are perceived as unwanted, non-compliant, deviant and threatening forms of social change.

DILEMMAS OF ACHIEVED AND ASCRIBED STATUS
Any given society will need to determine the basis for allocating status and reward. This may place that society or its institutions in a dilemma. For instance, to whom should Knighthoods or CBEs be awarded in the UK, and for what reason? And what criteria should be in place to permit the removal of such rewards in the case (i) of subsequent lawbreaking by recipients, or instead (ii) apparent breaches of the spirit of the law and culturally expected behaviour by them?

The choice between these two bases for allocating prestige and reward depends upon what society, or those who control that society define to be important, and on what example it wishes to set to aspirants for such status. Such examples are criteria of fundamental importance, and may vary widely across any international perspective. They are likely to be a key source of cultural dilemmas, for instance at times of rapid social change.

SOCIAL CLASS MOBILITY

DILEMMAS OF HIGH OR LOW SOCIAL CLASS MOBILITY
Descriptions of *social class mobility*, and the identification of dilemmas associated with this mobility, may usefully be analysed by

making use of the National and Cross-cultural variables described in Chapter 6. Two generic and opposing propositions may then be identified and contrasted as fundamental sources of status dilemmas associated with high or low social class mobility.

HIGH SOCIAL CLASS MOBILITY

Equality of status and the potential for mobility between social classes or segments may occur where it is the case *that the lower (or the less entrenched) is the degree of*:

❏ power distance;
❏ orthodoxy or tradition;
❏ the relative difference between the strongest and the weakest social classes, or between the most privileged and the least privileged people in the society;
❏ uncertainty avoidance;
❏ the influence of familism / collectivism / communitarianism;
❏ masculinity;
❏ social class based discrimination;
❏ resistance to change;
❏ the enforcement of compliance with the status quo

and the higher the degree of:

❏ trust;
❏ the available opportunity for functional specialisation and professionalisation, and the development of competencies / Human Capital associated therewith;
❏ femininity;
❏ the achievement of status described in a previous section above

the more likely or the greater may be the potential for the incidence of:

❏ narrow or flat hierarchies of social class structure with relatively few strata or layers;
❏ the equality of social class status and influence;
❏ generally positive (or neutral) social class attitudes and values

towards (i) other classes, and (ii) towards issues of functional specialisation and professionalisation;
❏ accommodation or integration between the social classes;
❏ low thresholds of resistance to social class change; *and in consequence*
❏ weak limitations or resistance to upward social class mobility, and to the opportunities associated therewith.

LOW (RESTRICTED) SOCIAL CLASS MOBILITY

Status inequalities and restricted opportunities for mobility between social classes or segments may occur where it is the case *that the higher (or the more entrenched) is the degree of*:

❏ power distance;
❏ orthodoxy or tradition;
❏ the relative difference between the strongest and the weakest social classes, or between the most privileged and the least privileged people in the society;
❏ uncertainty avoidance;
❏ ascription of status described in a previous section above;
❏ rigidity in hierarchies of functional specialisation and professionalisation;
❏ the strength of the prevailing familism / collectivism / communitarianism;
❏ masculinity;
❏ resistance to change; *and*
❏ the enforcement of compliance with the status quo

and the lower the degree of trust, the greater may be the potential for the incidence of social class inequality, for instance evidenced by any or all of:

❏ tall or deep hierarchies of social class structure characterised by multiple and rigid strata or layers between which movement is difficult or actually "blocked",
❏ fixed and rigid social class attitudes and values, especially towards other classes or castes; and critically towards issues of

the "ownership" and control of functional specialisation and
professionalisation;

❏   the inequality of social class status and influence;

❏   social class discrimination;

❏   high thresholds of resistance to social class change;

❏   resistance to any process of accommodation or integration between social classes;

❏   the maintenance of impediments to social class change; *and
therefore*

❏   strong limitations (or resistance) to upward social class mobility
and the opportunities associated therewith.

CASE EXAMPLE

Grammar Schools: holy grail or a blast from the past? – controversy continues to surround government support for, or political
hostility towards grammar schools in the UK. Grammar schools are
seen by some as a valuable tool to encourage upward social mobility
and academic excellence. Others see them as bastions of middle
class privilege.

Grammar schools pose a number of dilemmas. For a start, is
the selection of pupils at 11 or 13 a matter of principle, or one of
expediency? How critical are considerations of the optimisation of
national Human Capital and Knowledge Management? What criteria
of knowledge transfer, functional specialisation, professionalisation,
and vocationality are now most relevant to these Human Capital and
Knowledge Management considerations, as well as to objectives
for academic excellence and social mobility? Where do the various
school types, Further Education and Higher Education systems now
fit in this respect, as compared, say, with the period 1940s to 1970s?

And are grammar schools the best means for the state sector
to be seen to provide competition with the many outstanding private schools in the country, thereby demonstrating a powerful
commitment to the encouragement of greater social mobility and
professionalisation?

The grammar school concept in the UK routinely faces the criticism that considerations of positive home study environment and

parental encouragement will favour candidates from middle class backgrounds. Such children are more likely to have been socialised and conditioned into the discipline of "tough study" and focus required by a high performing education environment. Proponents of grammar schools will counter that it is only state grammar schools (and not private schools) that can be used as sledgehammers to "level-up" the performance of comprehensive and academy schools in order to achieve necessary enhancements in national education performance (for instance in particular in key subjects such as mathematics, science and English).

Others will claim that the use (i) of *pupil streaming* and (ii) *strong and effective classroom discipline* by some comprehensive and academy schools have allowed them to match the quality of both grammar and private schools, thereby enhancing national Human Capital and social mobility.

Or does the matter come down to whichever sector can **in *performance measurement terms*** (i) ensure that **the psychological conditions of the study environment are fit for purpose, usable and favourable**; (ii) demonstrate **the maximisation of value addition**, particularly from homes and cultures not hitherto characterised by "study friendliness"; and (iii) prove excellence in evidential terms by the factual and objective results that they achieve?

SUPERSTAR CULTURE?

SUPERSTAR STATUS, SUPERSTAR CULTURE, AND DILEMMAS

Superstar Culture may be defined in terms of an artificial semiosphere or constructed reality (Chapter 9) in which any or all of individual:

❑ public esteem and adulation;
❑ media recognition, promotion, and exploitation;
❑ life of publicity "in the limelight";
❑ "stardom" or so-called "celebrity" status; *and*
❑ the possibility of amassing significant personal wealth

are seen by many people to confer status and power, and therefore to be worthy of emulation as personal role model.

The roots of this Superstar Culture appear to lie in any or all of the following circumstances:

❑ the development of the Attention Economy described in Chapter 5;

❑ the trend towards individualism and self-centredness described in Chapters 10 and12;

❑ the very significant development of the mass and social media as (i) sources of opinionation (Chapter 8) and influence, and (ii) as disseminators of fads, fashions, distractions from reality, fake news, ideas and values. This media includes the commercial tabloid press, so-called "celebrity magazines", cinema, television, electronic games based on the *superstar character* and the so-called "superhero" concept, and the widespread use of mobile telephone applications;

❑ the capitalistic globalising of culture into consumerist, materialistic, and self-centred behaviours which place priority on the short-term achievement of individual comfort and self- gratification;

❑ the development and reinforcement of this type of culture by the spread of the use of English (and particularly American English) as a global language; *together with*

❑ consistent and relentless global and local advertising driven by sophisticated and powerful advertising agencies serving the needs of the Attention Economy and Big Data; *also*

❑ the particular quality and influence of some visual advertising, with its ability to insert concepts, ideas, and phrases into the mindset and language of viewers.

The Superstar Culture is inhabited by the many examples of so- called "celebrities", whether from music, art, sport, film or business. These celebrities are created and kept alive by media and advertising companies so that there is always material to fill TV and radio programmes, newspapers and magazine columns (etc). One direct consequence of this has been the evolution of popular tabloid newspapers or magazines, whose content has become dominated by images of superstars and sports personalities, accompanied by articles analysing what are in reality totally insignificant details of their public and private lives. The high fees that these people earn come from lavish sponsorship deals, or from their contribution to testimonials in advertising campaigns. The same holds true for actors, singers and models whose success is seen in the Superstar Culture semiosphere *to entitle them* to popular recognition, esteem, wealth and popular envy.

THE SUPERSTAR CULTURE AS POSITIVE ROLE MODEL

The Superstar Culture may be capable of sending a strongly positive message if, and where the values, behaviours, and influence of so-called superstars are perceived to be beneficial to society in general, *for instance in terms of facilitating equality, opportunity and social mobility*. This may be illustrated (i) by the case of the empowerment to, and the enhancement of racial equality that has resulted from the success of black singers, performing artists and footballers; and (ii) by the effect of Paralympic success on the status of the disabled.

THE SUPERSTAR CULTURE AS NEGATIVE ROLE MODEL

The development of the Superstar Culture may have become an artificial and potentially insidious source of social class stereotyping, and as such could constitute a:

❏ a growing determinant of social inequality;
❏ a negative determinant of opportunity, mobility, and life chance; *and*
❏ a potential source and driver of discrimination.

This is because the development of the Superstar Culture may have *distorting consequences* for the development of social class equality and stability. It may have become a source of negative perceptions of, or actual discrimination against those (such as the disabled, or the working class) who, for whatever reasons, are artificially judged by some (for instance in an opinionated or London-centric media) to be "weak", to be an easy target for stereotypical derision, or to be "failures" in society's apparent scheme of things.

Superstars (and so-called "superheroes") may be perceived as *winners*. The rest (who by definition are not winners) may instead be seen as *losers*. For instance, "you do not win silver, you lose gold" – *Nike advertisement*. Winners (but not losers) should be emulated by others. They therefore become attractive role models compared, say, with school teachers who perform an absolutely essential but (in the UK at least) a difficult, demanding, and now sometimes impossible role for which they are paid a fraction of the wages received by some popular entertainers or footballers.

This issue is also dealt with in Chapter 19.

SOME NEGATIVE CONSEQUENCES OF THE SUPERSTAR CULTURE

Negative consequences of the development of the Superstar Culture include dilemmas associated with:

❏ *a misplacement of priorities* – again, consider the salary of an UK schoolteacher or FE college lecturer. This is likely to be a fraction of the salary of some TV presenters or Premier League football players. But at best a well-known TV presenter, for instance, cheers up viewers for a time. But that presenter does not have any long-lasting impact on people's opportunity or quality of life. Equally, society neither improves nor worsens as a result of the competitive level reached by the country's football leagues. On the other hand, society's development is strongly influenced by the quality of its teachers and educators. **The dilemma here lies in the correlation (i) between salary levels and (ii) the contribution that remunerated human activities or professions make to society's progress and welfare.** Should not a society make the most of the inventory of skills and talents of its Human Capital in any given period of time, thereby maximising the level of progress and ensuring the best quality of life for each member of society. If remuneration does not reflect the added value given to the good of that society, then progress will be hindered. Internal conflicts will then appear as a result of the artificial inequalities that will be perceived to have emerged;

❏ a growing global inequality between the wealth and prestige of the very rich and the rest of society; *accompanied by*

❏ an increasing concentration of wealth, influence, and power in the hands of a relatively few individuals (which may result in an increasing power distance and sense of hierarchy described elsewhere in this chapter);

❏ the creation and reinforcement of artificial social class divisions based on a manufactured form of inequality;

❏ the definition of opportunity in terms of something that is largely unobtainable for the majority; *or worse*

❏ the stereotyping of opportunity only in terms of extremes of success for the few, and failure for the many;

❏ the distortion or the actual downgrading of the values and work ethic associated with the opportunities and life chances that are really necessary to society. Try living without engineers, plumbers, bricklayers, electricians, steelworkers, carpenters, computer programmers, or vehicle mechanics;

❏ the belittling of those who, in their own way, are adding as much (or more) value to society than the superstar, but whose roles (such as nurses or retail employees) are seen as unattractive or "boring" by those who have come to perceive the superstar as the pinnacle of personal and communal achievement;

❏ the potential for discrimination against people who have for whatever reason become categorised by opinionated adherents to the Superstar Culture as "plebs", "second rate", "boring", "useless", "weak", or "losers". Worst of all they are "a waste of space" (BBC *The Apprentice Programme*).

CASE EXAMPLE
Let's value our binmen – writing to the *Guardian*, one correspondent lamented that there appeared to be a lack of 'political leaders or

media opinion-formers speaking for those who have not achieved lift-off to higher things. Someone is needed to clean the lavatory, empty the wheelie bins, deliver the post, answer the phone, etc. There is no one, it seems, shouting that we should value these people (who are most of us) much more highly. Instead they are implicitly branded as failures and expected to carry the austerity can for those who have escaped upwards' (Source: *The Week*).

Chapter Twelve
The Snowflake Generation

If you can't stand the heat, keep out of the kitchen

A DEFINITION

The term "Snowflake Generation" (or alternatively "Generation Snowflake" or "Snowflake Millenial") is given to a **stereotype** now fashionably used to describe present-day children, teenagers **(both Minors),** and young adults. This stereotype may be applied by parents and older people, sources of social influence, media pundits, or opinion-formers who believe that the stereotype has a degree of validity.

Whatever this validity (and the undoubtedly significant dilemmas to which it is giving rise), the term needs to be contextualised in comparison with preceding (and in particular post WWII) generations. This issue is dealt with at a later point in this chapter.

SOME CHARACTERISTICS OF THE SNOWFLAKE GENERATION

The "Snowflake Generation" stereotype is variously opined / described to be associated with:

❏ a perception of personal uniqueness – **every snowflake is different** – associated with an enhanced degree of narcissism (Chapter 10). In the end, each person becomes his or her own semiosphere or bubble (Chapter 9);

❏ a highly developed emotionalism, self-centredness, self-orientation, sense of self-esteem and sense of self-entitlement. In the specific case of most Minors, this sense of self-esteem and entitlement is not likely to be based on any particular tangible or meaningful achievement. It might instead stem from a cultural, parental or instead personal (self) ascription (Chapter 11), shaped and encouraged for instance (i) by consumer advertising,

(ii) by social media and Attention Economy pressures, (iii) by familial or peer group behaviour, (iv) by their associated patterns of self-indulgence, perhaps exacerbated for whatever reason (v) by a worrying adult or educational reluctance to say "No" to them or their demands;

❏ a perception by others of neurosis, anxiety, hypersensitivity, and weakened personal resilience – **snowflakes melt in the heat** – and an apparently declining threshold of risk tolerance. Failure of an internet connection or slow wi-fi speeds, (let alone Coronavirus) may give rise to a state of panic, hysteria or crisis. Thus, the stereotype's ability to cope with the new, the unexpected, the inconvenient, the challenging or the unwanted is questioned. In this respect the emergence of the erratic, un-predictable, intolerant, polarised, confrontational, fascistic or "no-platforming" behaviour of some university students is well documented. *This may be related to:-*

❏ a stated proneness (i) to taking offence at, or being unable to cope with ideas, events, facts or circumstances with which the stere-otype is unhappy or uncomfortable or by which it is challenged; and which (ii) appear to be inconsistent or non- consonant with the stereotype's (limited, inexperienced or personalised) attitude set or worldview. This may then become a source of Cognitive Dissonance;

❏ the presence of heightened (and potentially unrealistic) *expec-tations*. This is likely (i) to have been inherited from past gener-ations, and (ii) from external influences. For instance "I want it all and I want it now", "you can be whatever you want to be" or Coronavirus was most inconvenient. Such childish, unsustaina-ble statements or gratuitous self-indulgence must by definition contain an obvious potential (i) for subsequent disappointment, (ii) an eventual sense of failure, or worse (iii) an incidence of the mental health problems now increasingly being reported for this Generation and described below;

❏ the association of such heightened expectations with lowered (and potentially unsustainable) *boredom thresholds*, which may also be inconsistent with the prevailing reality and as such a source of CD; *and in which:-*

❏ *the effect of both variables on the Generation* may again be exacerbated by uncontrollable pressures variously from the Attention Economy, consumer advertising, and the relentless media pressures to which (i) this Generation is exposed; or (ii) chooses to expose itself; and (iii) which its parents do not necessarily understand (or want to understand); or (iv) of which at worst they are actually unaware, careless or non- responsible.

These characteristics might be further reinforced by any or all of the following:

❏ a strong *internal* protection, conditioning, reinforcement or "cocooning" by (and fear of litigation on the part of) parents, schools and the authorities. Whilst critics of the stereotype may use such epithets as "pampered", "spoilt", "little princesses", "little princes", "mollycoddling", "overprotection" or "infantilisation" to describe this syndrome, there is no doubt that external environments are not now safe in the way they were deemed to be, say in the 1940s when children played freely in the streets and wandered off on their own or with their friends. *This is related to:-*

❏ the perfectly reasonable syndrome by which activities such as some contact sports, playing outside, or talking to strangers (whether in reality or online) [etc] are now perceived to contain a significant degree of risk that must be monitored and managed, and young people safeguarded (protected) from them. The process of safeguarding, particular of Minors, is given various treatment throughout this Book. This syndrome (and the anxiety associated with it) has of course been created by concerned parents, schools, governmental bodies, the police, the legal profession and the wider society; *and may also be related to:-*

❏ the reported difficulties for universities and colleges, for instance in terms of their corporate reaction to such dilemmas as (i) to heavy alcohol or drug abuse by students, excessive gaming habits as displacement activity, sleep deprivation (etc); or instead (ii) naïve but very high risk research plans (such as investigating security policies and processes *in situ* the Middle East) by immature postgraduate students who (a) are by now adults responsible for their own actions, but (b) who may not have not developed any effective understanding of personal risk, its management or the seriousness of its potential consequences. To what extent should university authorities commit to active safeguarding policies and resource expenditures associated with such negative student behaviour? Or should they be obliged to provide expensive security capability empowered to dispense audience control and restraint for speakers who have been invited to give public lectures on subjects which some students dislike, find challenging or "offensive", and to which they might object (and with all of the implications for free speech)?

❏ an increasingly effective *external* conditioning by the various forces summarised in an earlier chapter to describe the "Attention Economy", as well as those of pressures from the media, social media, consumerist and advertising pressures. For instance, do your children insist on wearing Nike shoes or Diesel clothes (perhaps refusing to take "No" as an answer or even throwing a tantrum if denied), even though (i) they are the most expensive but (ii) in the case of shoes are only likely to last as long as other brands after the hacking about in the playground, on the bike, or the pavement to which they will be subject?

❏ the widely-held public opinion (to which reference is made in earlier chapters) now frequently reported that some of the responsible parents (?) of the stereotyped Snowflake Generation have failed effectively to monitor and control the internet-based interactions or computer gaming of their offspring as Minors; *given that:-*

❏ such parents may (i) be unaware of the nature and implications of some of these interactions or gaming activities; and may in any case (ii) not have the skill, patience, motivation, willpower, time or energy to control the total internet access and usage of their children. This point has been made in an earlier chapter.

❏ the suggestion that, probably like at least some of their parents, children and young people of the stereotype have become (or choose to be) conditioned to *celebrity worship*. Such admiration or emulation may for instance be (i) seen as a substitute for religion; (ii) as a vain search for alternative role models; and (iii) as a rejection of more basic or boring values such as those described in Chapter 11.

SOME SUGGESTED DILEMMAS ASSOCIATED WITH THE STEREOTYPE

Dilemmas could include any or all of the following.

[1] *reality* – to what extent are *the boundaries of the semiosphere* (or bubble) in which Generation Snowflake appears to reside made up by artificial social media, gaming and internet interactions, and the influence of (so-called) celebrities and TV soaps? What then is their reality if not virtual, self-constructed, self-indulgent and escapist / displacement-oriented? This issue has been dealt with at various points in the Book.

[2] *binary thinking* – the stereotype may have been artificially conditioned into a degree of binary thinking. Cognitive processes of over-simplification or polarisation may result from the use by Big Data of the concepts of "Like" (ie "Yes") and "Dislike" (ie "No", [or "Bullying"?]). Is there nothing between these extremes to qualify them or to add reality, and for instance being capable of mapping as described in Chapters 1 and 19?

Such binary thinking may pose limitations on the processes of perception (Chapter 9) and perceptual / cognitive development. It may contribute to the various dilemmas to which reference is being made in this chapter.

[3] *what measures of control or restraint* are available to parents, schools, the Police or the NHS? **And what does the word "No" actually mean? Is it to be perceived as a form of bullying?** There are for example undoubted reports from schools and the uniformed services that members of Generation Snowflake are unused to being told "No". Or they may be uncomfortable with, or resistant to *orders* which they must for whatever reason follow.

In particular, some younger children (Minors) may now have to be taught about the meaning of *instruction* and why (ultimately for their own health or safety) they must follow such instructions.

The specific and critical issue of classroom control and discipline is dealt with in detail in the Author's book "Equality, Diversity and Opportunity Management" to which reference is made in the Introduction.

Or are people and the authorities too nice and too indulgent in their dealings with Snowflakes? Is there a fear of the perceived bullying or conflict which might occur in attempting to provide a realistic and effective disciplinary framework for them? At what point in the day or evening do parents of Minors insist on switching off access to the internet and / or stop computer gaming activities? Do they then remove and secure tablets (etc) to enforce their will in the matter? Or instead do exhausted parents give up, leaving similarly exhausted teachers to lament their inability to exercise a necessary degree of attention or discipline in the classroom (and increasingly to contemplate leaving the professional role which they have done their best to fulfil).

[4] *emotionality and mental health issues* – the stereotype is reported to be associated with increases in the personal strength of emotional sentiment (Chapter 5), personal anxiety, hypersensitivity, depression and sleep disorders as (incipient) mental health issues. The reality, veracity and seriousness of these reports (and their UK and US causes) must **of course** depend on (be a function of) / be qualified by the proper and objective professional medicolegal validation of categorisation and duration issues, for instance under the ICD 10 Classification of Mental and Behavioural Disorders and the International Classification of Sleep Disorders (ICSD-2).

Certainly, the stereotype may be likely to have limited sympathy if, unlike their parents or grandparents, they are told to:-

❖ "grow up"
❖ "get a grip on yourself"
❖ "get real"
❖ "toughen up"
❖ "accept your proper responsibilities"
❖ "there is no alternative for you but **tough study** – so behave in class, get on with your school work and pass your exams"

Again, such exhortations or commands may be perceived by Snowflakes as a form of unjustified, unkind, hurtful, cruel, so- called "politically incorrect" or unwanted bullying by their source, who- ever this may be.

Reports of increases in the occurrence of mental health issues may be linked to the stated fragility of the stereotype already described above.

On the other hand, the Generation is hardly likely to be helped by external conditions affecting *the reality of future prospects* for UK employment, housing, or pension provision (etc) during the coming decades and ultimately during their life-time?

[5] *a sense of community* – critics of the Generation suggest that, whilst exhibiting a decreasing level of communal orientation and re- sponsibility, Snowflakes at the same time make increasing demands on what society and the economy should provide for them. It's their right? It's their entitlement? This point has already been made above. The issue was dealt with in Chapters 5, 8 and 10.

This could then raise the dilemma as to the degree to which parents, the education system and the relevant authorities (etc) in- sist on the promotion, financing and implementation *of community oriented activities*, particularly for Minors. These children may be seen as most vulnerable to the internal and external pressures being described in this chapter. Such activities might include:

❑ mandatory personality and aptitude testing (available from rep- utable commercial sources);
❑ team-based sports, activities and assessments;
❑ some kind of appropriate but mandatory community or entre- preneurial involvement;
❑ etc.

Older members of the Generation might instead be required:

❑ to undertake a significant and mandatory period of community service or entrepreneurial activity (say one year) post school or at 18, mirroring past UK experience of conscripted National

Military Service, France's "assistance technique" programme, or even Lord Sugar's present-day "The Apprentice (!);

❏ to be subjected on a voluntarily basis to officially controlled, validated and certified (or accredited) exercises ("power tests"), for instance financed by parents and run by carefully selected and trained members of the uniformed services in which young adults are deliberately exposed to difficult, stressful, challenging or emergency situations to which they must actively respond (eg Outward Bound type activities, Camp America, etc). Such activities would be structured to include a direct element of personal and team risk, to mandate communal interactions, to require the obeying of orders, to guarantee personal criticism by Instructors, and to include the frequent use of such phrases such as "No" or "you can't do it that way – it's not in the rules". No access to telephones or the internet (except for contextual operational purposes) would be permitted and a very high degree of isolation established for the duration of the event;

❏ etc.

STEREOTYPE OR CONTINUITY?

This chapter has described the concept of the Snowflake Generation as an ongoing societal development that (i) is undoubtedly dilemma-laden, and (ii) requires the implementation of some significant responses, for instance by parents, the educational authorities, and governmental action in respect of Big Data.

But an alternative view of the Generation must be that it represents the consequences of the development of a *post WWII continuum* in the UK (as well as elsewhere).The generation of so- called "baby boomers" born after the war, and the generations of their offspring have undoubtedly become more individualistic in outlook, more materialistic, more indulged and increasingly characterised by a sense of entitlement. Their grandparents had instead to put up with the privations of wartime and post war conditions, rationing, communal conditions, low expectations and a pre-war sense of place and position in a strongly class dominated UK. Complaints from children that they "were bored" met with very short shrift. They might be told to get on with their homework, read a book or find something else to do. Go and kick a ball about in the street or build a cart out of orange boxes and old pram wheels. TV was yet to come outside of the USA.

Subsequent generations had their TV and all of the other benefits of the modern consumer society, some ultimately being conditioned by the Attention Economy and internet dominance. The calamity of computer gaming, pressures from Big Data, severe problems of discipline and control in school, and high levels of turnover amongst teachers have all contributed to an increasingly individualised and dominant conditioning, driven by displacement activities which many young people cannot resist and which parents and schools are unable (or choose not) to control.

BUT MIGHT THEY GROW OLD (I)?

The prospect of growing older (and the possibility of having to take on responsibilities) *could* raise either of the following two dilemmas for Generation Snowflake.

[1] *managing the fear of the ageing process* – Snowflakes may be inherently *ageist*. They can view someone who for instance is aged 40 as "recidivist" (an inevitable traitor to the cause of eternal youth)? To be aged 50 years plus may mean that you are now of no value to anyone, anymore. Anybody over 60 is just "very old". Beyond that people are mere "wrinklies" or "crumblies", or even just a "waste of space" as NHS "bed-blockers".

In consequence, issues of the record of the scale of people's Income Tax payments, past subsidy of the BBC from already taxed earnings, personal investment in pension provision, insurance against funeral costs (etc) may be irrelevant. **Or even unthinkable**. *Death will never happen. The State ("they / them") will provide. Snowflakes are immortal?*

[2] *Snowflake parents* – consumer advertising in the UK appears to be developing a focus on the Snowflake parent. The *children* of Snowflake parents are therefore portrayed as designer accessories and consumer entities. They are there to show off (showcase) the parent (again as a stylish consumer).

This will inevitably raise the critical dilemma as to how parents and offspring (initially as Minors) will interact (or co- exist) when these offspring inevitably develop their own cognitions and personalities?

Might these children reject the crass, social media obsessed, and short-term materialism of their parents in favour of a more environmentally-friendly or climate-change orientation? *Equally important, will they be prepared to support their parents in the assuredly financially impoverished old age that by their own actions these parents will by then have brought upon themselves?*

Or might these children instead become even more entrenched as Snowflakes, reluctant voters and taxpayers, demonstrating a self-orientated and self-indulgent hostility to anything but the most essential features of the necessary community and governance (as represented by "they or them")? *And again, the State ("they / them") will have to provide.*

BUT MIGHT THEY GROW OLD (II) – THE SNOWFLAKE JOURNALIST?

Perhaps **the most dangerous** of all the developments described in this chapter is the emergence in a parliamentary democracy of the *Snowflake journalist or social media pundit*. Such (**unelected**) but skilled young media operators appear to the Author at this time of writing to be strongly characterised by any or all of:

❑ a very strongly London or metropolitan centricity; *and*
❑ an absence of any proper prior or accredited business, community-oriented, cultural or international work experience. This is made worse if the journalist comes (for whatever reason) as a graduate with a restricted (or "no- platformed") mindset straight from Oxbridge or a similar institution;
❑ a comfortable BBC, sofa, workstation, or Fleet Street tavern laptop-orientation (remembering the UK concept of "the armchair brigades" held in contempt in the past); *and*
❑ a complete dismissal of any value to be had from so-called "provincial interactions" (ie north of Watford; let alone from Wales, Scotland and Northern Ireland); *associated with*

❑   an *almost total metropolitan unawareness or acknowledgement* of (i) the existence of the agriculture and fishing industries as critical to the maintenance of UK foodstuffs supply and living standards; and (ii) critically in the case of farming, to the maintenance of the UK's *rural areas*;

❑   a pressure (imperative) to "file the story" – however good or bad ("fake") it might be; *at the same time demonstrating*

❑   an inability (or rather a deliberately imposed or binary choice to fail) to distinguish between fact and so-called "fake news", or an unwillingness to separate one from the other; *and at the same time accepting*

❑   a management imperative for the story to be characterised variously by immediacy, currency, sensation, anxiety or crisis attribution; or instead a deliberate trivialisation, dumbing down or (again) application of binary thinking;

❑   the use of overt and childish *emotionalism* to try to convince the audience. This is a strategy directly adopted from the US media and social media;

❑   a cynical, contemptuous, jealous, childish, immature and hostile attitude towards (i) people in authority such as elected politicians or appointed police officers (as Crown Servants) etc; or (ii) to the serious real-world issues of the day, such as Brexit, the abuse of Muslim women, or social care; *as well as*

❑   the characterisation as buffoons and ignorami of MPs and Crown Servants who are legitimate elected or appointed officials;

❑   the artificial syndrome of "everything is a game", "it's all a joke", "where's the fun?", "we're getting bored with the democratic process", etc, as described in earlier chapters; *and*

❑   a media assumption that it is the primary role of politicians, state institutions, corporations (etc) to provide a continuous flow of stories from which that media can benefit; *and*

❑   a media assumption of a right to demand corporate or personal influence without accepting any consequential electoral, financial or stakeholder responsibility.

SOME IMPLICATIONS FOR SOCIAL AND HUMAN CAPITAL

The development of Generation Snowflake may be a new evolution. Or it may instead derive and continue from already existing trends. Either way, each poses dilemmas associated with what the UK's Social and Human Capital needs are. Do trends towards individualism, cynicism, consumerism, factionalism or polarisation (driven by a powerful media, internet and social media orientation) serve to enhance the progress and welfare of community and society? Or do they constitute a risk that that this Capital may be damaged or diminished at a particularly critical (and possibly fateful) time for a post-imperial and potentially post-Brexit (?) Britain within the reality of its global context?

And is it a recipe for anomie?

Part Three

Some Dilemma Sources (II): Time, Finance, Security, and Risk

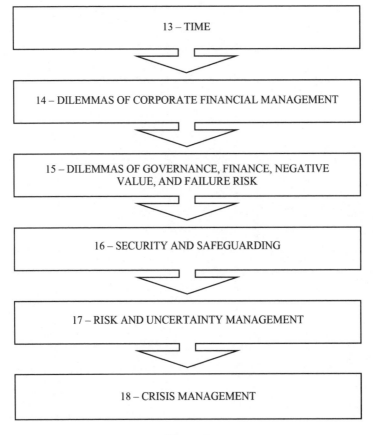

Figure 8

Chapter Thirteen
Time

RECAP

Chapter 3 described key reasons for the proactive management of dilemmas; and introduced the concept of the Management Dilemma as driver of events, action, or reaction.

Chapters 4 and 9 noted that the identification and resolution of dilemmas being described in this Book may depend on *specific* (**micro**) *cognitive and collective processes of perception, definition, value assessment and assurance.* Is everybody agreed about what the dilemma is and what its implications are?

The detailed process of identification, validation and assurance may have to rely on the nature of the characteristics of the *events* or the *concepts* which best represent the dilemma upon which focus is being brought to bear. These events or concepts may contain a variety or diversity of possible interpretations, about which agreement must be reached or disagreements overcome.

Event or concept characteristics described in Chapter 4 which may be *time-related* are recapped below:

absence or presence; ambiguity; change; complexity; entropy; equifinality; inconsistency; negotiability; novelty or innovation; originality, priority or urgency; stability, instability or pattern of relative stability; value implications; variety or diversity; volume.

Time-influenced dilemmas of security, safeguarding, risk, uncertainty and crisis are dealt with separately in Chapters 16 to 18; also in Part Four of this Book.

TIME AS RESOURCE

Time is a key *resource* for any and all types of organisation, irrespective of what these organisations do, or what sector they operate in. Western analysis does tend to assume that this *time as a resource is finite*. That is, time is perceived to be as limited as is any other resource used by enterprise or institutional management to implement its processes and procedures, and to carry out its business.

TIME AS CAPABILITY AND OPPORTUNITY COST

Time may be conceptualised in terms of *capability*. **Capability** is defined in a later chapter in terms *of what an organisation or institution is able, willing and motivated to do*. The enterprise can only achieve what its capability will permit given the amount of time that is available to it. Time, like all other resources, may therefore be seen to have its *opportunity cost*. Opportunity cost may in this case be described in terms of the "optimum return" that may be derived from the investment by the organisation of the time available to it, as compared with the potential alternative uses of that time. It is in the definition and resolution (or otherwise) of what is *the best use of that time* that capability dilemmas will reside.

TIME AS CRITICAL SUCCESS FACTOR (CSF)

Time may act as a *critical success factor* where decision-making or investment projects (such as in additional process capacity or infrastructure, new process development, or new product / service development) has to react to, or respond to external conditions such as apparent customer or voter demand as dilemma sources that are *time-dependent* or *time-limited*. For instance, public demand for improved surveillance or security facilities in the face of terrorist threat may have to be satisfied before people perceive that they are less likely to be under any further threat of attack.

Time may instead act as a CSF when the required outcome or output must be created *at an exact given moment*. The success of a restaurant, for example, depends on its ability consistently to deliver the exact selection of food from the menu to its customers, properly cooked, and served at the right temperature within an acceptable period of delay from the taking of orders. This implies an appropriate investment in catering expertise, cooking facilities, and staffing. That will especially be the case where the restaurant is catering simultaneously to a large number of diners (as in the hotel, wedding, or conference trade).

Time may also be a critical success factor where the provision of resources is *time sensitive*. For instance, dilemma resolution about the level of provision in any service-based activity will have to be based on an estimate of the maximum level of demand likely to occur at any particular time. For example, medical treatment needs to be available when it is required. Urgent or emergency treatment cases cannot be stored, nor placed in a queue until the appropriate level of resource becomes available to deal with them! Nor may a hospital be able to refuse to deal with a sudden epidemic on the grounds that the infection was unexpected!

TIME AS LIMITING FACTOR OR CONSTRAINT

Limiting factors may be defined as those influences that directly limit and constrain the nature of the choice of strategies and operations that are available to the organisation. The effect of such limits may be seen where the operational or management process is shaped *by known, fixed or predictable time horizons*. For instance:

❏ a school, college or university must teach and assess students within absolutely fixed (and known) time horizons, and produce an acceptable outcome (for instance in terms of statistically assured pass-rates or grades), at a given level of quality within that fixed time, irrespective of the character, capability, and motivation of any particular year's student cohort;

❏ a local government authority may instead have to manage its responsibilities within a fixed financial planning period of one year only, since decisions on taxation levels (and hence income) are continually subject to political pressure, and may formally be budgeted to vary from year to year.

TIME AS CONTINGENCY AND COMMITMENT

Time-related *commitments* may constitute a key example of a time-sensitive contingency. The organisation may be committed to courses of action (whether resulting from the making of past or present decisions) that are time-related or time-sensitive. Government decisions on investments in healthcare, pension, or social welfare provision will for instance be shaped by such contingencies as the time scales associated with the dynamics of the age structure and life expectancy of the population for which it must provide finance and benefits from the resources of taxpayers' money and the contracted private sector or insurance funding available to it. Past investment decisions, similarly, constrain an organisation's current and likely future strategic choices, since the enterprise will have to live with the present consequences of past resource commitments made by it. This is likely to be particularly critical where these resource commitments were long term in nature, for instance (i) as in the oil, steel, aviation, or petrochemical sectors; or (ii) in major infrastructure developments such as airports or rail networks.

The issue of commitment to decision-making is also dealt with in Chapter 26.

TIME AS A SOURCE OF ADVANTAGE AND COMPETITIVE DILEMMAS

Time may be used as a competitive weapon or source of comparative advantage. Commenting on his use of rapid movement and manoeuvre as a campaign strategy in order to make life difficult for his enemies, Ries and Trout noted of Napoleon that 'his troops, he claimed, could march two miles to the enemy's one. "I may lose a battle", said Napoleon, "but I shall never lose a minute"'.

The effective use of time may be a competitive source of dilemmas for others (as described in Chapters 3 and 23) for instance in the case of such activities as:

❏ the *reduction of cycle time* associated with operational or developmental activities. Reduced cycle time might for instance be associated with processes of manufacturing; supply chain management; the treatment of patients; teaching, learning, and assessment methods; or the management of working capital. Or the achievement of improvements in cycle time might instead be the objective of institutional programmes of lean / re- engineering, excellence, or Six Sigma described elsewhere in this Book.

❏ *new product development time* (or "time to market"). Competitive advantage will be gained by bringing effective new products or processes to the market or client more quickly than competitors, who may then be faced with a dilemma of how to respond.

❏ *on-time performance* within the quality and reliability parameters specified for product, service or policy delivery. On-time performance is for instance just as crucial to the provision of healthcare, government services, or the payment of benefits to dependent recipients as it is to systems of just- in-time supply, to running a railway or an airline service, or to delivering the right products on a mail order basis.

❏ *customer response*, in which competitive advantage may be gained by those organisations that respond most speedily to customer demand, or make them wait the shortest time for service. The timing of response to customer or client is again as much a key issue in the provision of healthcare, fire- fighting, security or police services as it is in the marketing of business or consumer ones.

TIME AND DILEMMAS OF SHAREHOLDER VALUE

Chapter 2 of this Book contained the Case Study "Private and Family Companies (II)". Chapter 4 contained the Case Study "Market Competition".

Both case studies made reference to the potential dilemmas which may be caused by the consistent and long-term need for companies to create *value for their shareholders*. Such dilemmas may arise where companies whose shares are publicly listed and openly traded on stock exchanges find that a large proportion of their shares are held by institutional investors such as insurance and investment companies, or pension funds. These large institutional shareholders are likely to require the management of the companies in which they hold shares to maximise returns in shareholder value terms on a short-term or an annual basis. This is needed so that these large investors may satisfy their own customers, for instance in terms of personal pension or investment income.

Such pressure for the continuous delivery of shareholder value will grow as the UK population ages, with (i) more and more people being dependent on institutional investment returns for their retirement income as (ii) governments struggle with the increasing and potentially unsustainable costs of the emerging Pension Crisis to which reference has already been made in this Book.

Chinese, Japanese, Swiss, and German companies may on the other hand be able to take a longer-term view of their business than for example their American, British, or Anglo-Saxon competitors. Companies in Japan, Germany, China or Switzerland are for a number of reasons under less pressure to maximise short- term shareholder value. Investment returns may instead be measured over a period of years, "taking one year with another". This may especially be the case where (as in the case of the examples given in Chapters 2 and 4) these companies are state or semi-state owned, family-owned, privately owned, or their shares are "close-held" or "cross-held" and therefore unavailable for purchase on the open market.

Dilemmas of corporate financial management are given further treatment in Chapters 14 and 15 of this Book.

NATIONAL CULTURE TIME DILEMMAS

Chapter 6 identified a variety of National Culture variables as source of dilemmas. This Section of Chapter 13 continues that analysis in terms of *time dilemmas*. Varying national culture concepts are associated with dilemmas that arise (i) from how a society chooses to perceive time and (ii) decides what it thinks is the best way to make use of it.

SHORT AND LONG-TERM ATTITUDES TO TIME

Hofstede notes the cultural difference between societies that take a *long-term* view of time and events, and societies that take a *short-term* view. The difference between short-termism and long-termism is of course a matter of degree; both are at opposite ends of a time continuum.

Oriental and South East Asian societies have tended to take a long-term view towards the evolution of society or the economy, for instance making long-term investments in technology development, education, infrastructure, competition strategy, or business development that may not pay off for many years to come.

Anglo-Saxon and some European societies, and the USA are instead characterised by a preference for short-term results and outcomes, for instance as a result of investments that have been made. *Impatience for results* may indeed be seen to be as much a virtue as patience, given the relentless drive of short-termist societies for rapid progress; continuous economic growth to meet individualistic, stock market and political expectations; continuous innovation; continuous novelty of experience; and media or Attention Economy-type stimulation.

Short-termist societies may however be vulnerable to dilemmas associated with issues that demand a long-term view, such as the future levels of personal pension provision to which reference was made above, or public spending on infrastructure provision, healthcare, social welfare support, or education and training.

Enterprises and institutions may therefore have to decide whether to take short-term or long-term orientations to time. This is likely to place them in a dilemma. Attitudes to time may depend upon the basic definition of the objective of the institution, and will be driven by the demands of stakeholders for results and returns. The point has already been made above that Chinese, Japanese, Swiss, and German companies may be able to take a longer-term view of their business than many of their American or British competitors. This may give them significant global market and technological advantages, for instance (i) in the development of new products or processes, or in business development; (ii) in the capacity to "pick winners" for the long- term; (iii) in the development of management process, leadership, and staff, and (iv) in the consequent accumulation of organisational capability, Knowledge and competence.

TIME AS SEQUENCE AND TIME AS SYNCHRONISATION

Hampden-Turner and Trompenaars suggest that societies and institutions may (for instance in *project management* terms) have to resolve the dilemma as to whether:

(i) to carry out individual processes or actions quickly, in the short-est possible sequence of time; *or instead*

(ii) to seek to achieve the synchronisation of events over time such that the achievement of those events is co-ordinated, and co-ordinates with other events which are related within a wider context, for instance on a "lean" basis to which reference is made below.

The enterprise might perceive an activity in terms of a single *linear sequence* of events that it has to carry out in order to achieve the objectives associated with that course of action. Matters will be conceptualised (i) in terms of the time consumed by any one single event; and (ii) in terms of the total duration of the sequence of events. This duration might be illustrated by the sequence that represents a *critical path in an activity or project network*. The enterprise may then conceptualise the process of the management of time in terms of concentrating its efforts and resources on finding the fastest way of completing that series of events, for instance by simplifying it by some process of reengineering, or by exploiting the value chain linkages of its relationship architecture. Time is then perceived in terms of a focus on carrying out individual activities as quickly as is feasible, which will result in the achievement of the shortest possible total sequence of time. Alternatively, the enterprise may perceive activity in terms of achieving the *synchronisation of events* (or of sequences of events) over time such that the completion of those events is co-ordinated coterminously (at the same time) or in parallel with other events that are related within a wider system or context. Hampden-Turner and Trompenaars give the example of Toyota's system of *kanban* and lean manufacturing. This is a flexible approach that depends for its success on the synchronisation of a coterminous series of procurement, supply, production, and quality management events rather than the speed of their individual execu-tion. Once this synchrony has been achieved, improvements in the required value outcomes may in any case follow, as in the case of just-in-time (JIT) processes where supply chain management, quality management, manufacturing, and cost management activities (etc) may all be optimised together on the basis of parallel processing. Such an approach characterised the completion of such mega UK projects as London Heathrow Airport's Terminal Five, or Transport for London's Cross-Rail "Elizabeth Line".

LINEAR AND CYCLICAL CONCEPTUALISATIONS OF TIME

The organisation may choose to perceive activity in terms of a linear sequence of events over time. Time-related processes of the analysis of perceptions, Knowledge, or event characteristics may be based on a *linear conceptualisation* of progress, moving forwards in a straight line into the future from the past and the present. This linear view of time for example underlies the marketer's idea of the dynamics of product management (which, confusingly is known as the "product life cycle"). Concepts based upon linearity are "logical" and "tidy" in the terms of deconstructionist Western analysis.

They may however (i) ignore the possibility that events may in reality at best only represent the status quo, or at worst (ii) show evidence of the retrogression that is described at various points in this Book. The use of such arbitrarily linear concepts may also (iii) be counterproductive to the development of the potentially more successful incremental, adaptive, and evolutionary approaches to the development of attitudes, values, knowledge, competences, technologies, resource applications and processes favoured for instance by the Japanese and the Germans. Western thinking may categorise an entity at a certain point on a linear sequence as being in "decline" or becoming "obsolete". The entity may be seen as having little or no future potential. This conceptualisation may blind the thinker to possible alternative cyclical views of the entity, for instance in terms of the "retro" associations of gleaming vinyl records displayed as prestige talking points in someone's living room.

Features of the entity may for instance comprise a resource to be recycled from the past or present into the future. It may be adapted and used within a wider and ongoing long-term context of reputation, capability, competence, tradition, or market management. For instance, see Figure 9. This illustrates Tatsumo's cyclical mandala of creativity, which demonstrates the Japanese belief in the evolutionary nature of society. Society is seen as being subject to *continuing change*. Society, and all of its works are seen as being amenable to improvement (*kaizen*), particularly as people accumulate experience, refine it, and hand it on over time across the generations.

The Japanese take a synchronous and long-term view of time rather than the linear, sequential and short-term approach of the West. The passage of time is associated with *cycles*. These cycles affect individuals, generations, entities, processes, and society. The present underpins the future, and lays its foundations. This is illustrated by the long-term and synchronous view taken towards technology and policy. Developments now will as progenitors yield generations of products and policies in the future. The development of technologies and policies may be synchronised over time to achieve "fusion". This may firstly take the form of the hybridisation for which Japan is famous. Secondly, it may take the form of newly synthesized processes and technologies, such as those based on telecommunication technologies, high-speed electro-diesel rail, dual-fuel cars, or the properties of the laser.

IMPOSE RULES OR ALLOW EXCEPTIONS

Chapter 6 noted that organisations, institutions and the wider society must of necessity formalise, standardise, or codify their basic policies and operations. There exists a minimum (*or "requisite"*) level of bureaucracy without which any activity (such as running a regulatory, a licencing, a military, or a healthcare institution) cannot be consistent or systematic. Policies, procedures, rules, and routines provide the basic framework for organised, legal, accountable, and assured work. This basic framework is a part of enterprise structure, technology, and relationship architecture.

At the same time, however, there will need to be a necessary recognition of time-related exceptions, changing circumstances, and the need for innovation. Relationships, policies, rules, operations, and technologies may need to be capable of:

❏ short-term adjustment (in order to deal with new or exceptional cases, new demands, or political readjustments); *or*

❏ the emergence of new threats, whether from criminal terrorism, cyber-attacks, unstable foreign governments, etc; *or*

❏ rapid and wholesale change (for instance when there is a sudden redefinition or shift in the Knowledge, technological, or market base, such as happened (i) with the development of computing, information, and telecommunications technologies; or (ii) in response to major shifts such as the UK decision to leave the European Union, or (iii) the emergence of China as a sophisticated world superpower); *or*

❏ long-term evolution, whatever form that takes.

DILEMMAS; AND TIME, EVENT AND CONCEPT CHARACTERISTICS

Time as a determinant variable described in this Chapter may have a direct effect on the perception, identification and potential for the resolution of dilemmas characterised or defined by the event or concept characteristics described in Chapter 4, and summarised at the beginning of this chapter. This may for example be the case whether:

❏ the dilemma is emerging as a contingency to be dealt with; *or*

❏ the dilemma has for whatever reason become a driving force, as in the case of dilemmas associated with the allocation of available taxpayer / public funds; or in the attempt to reconcile judicial / Human Rights with the continuing prosecution of criminal terrorism for instance deriving from fundamentalist religious extremism; *or*

❏ the dilemma has been deliberately created by others to discomfort rivals or opponents, for instance in a political context.

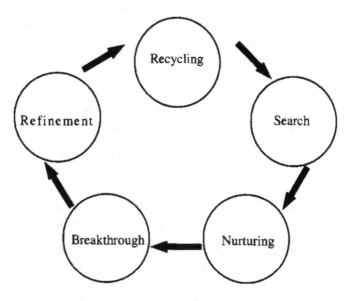

Figure 9
Tatsumo's Mandala of Creativity

Chapter Fourteen

Dilemmas of Corporate Financial Management

FINANCE AS A KEY RESOURCE AND CAPABILITY

Finance is a key *resource* of any organisation. The availability of finance is usually limited. It may constitute a *constraint* on, or a *limiting factor* for decision-making. ***The enterprise can only do what its available financial resources, and the quality of its financial management will permit it to do.***

Finance as a resource underpins the *operational capability and capacity* of the enterprise. *That is, it may determine what the enterprise is able to afford to do, and is therefore able to achieve. This is because the available funds will determine what kind of assets and people the enterprise can afford to use, and therefore what kind of output it can produce.* Wealthier football clubs for instance can afford to build bigger stadiums. These will be able to hold more paying customers. Such clubs may be able to pay the salaries of the best managers and the most expensive international players. These together should be able to win more games for the club, win championships, attract sponsorships, and bring in big crowds who will be prepared to pay higher entrance charges than anywhere else because they are watching the best and most successful teams in the land.

The *financial performance* of the organisation is crucial. *Financial performance is defined by **the financial results** achieved by the enterprise*, for instance in terms of profitability, cash flow, budgetary and cost management, dividends paid (and so on). Financial performance is a *critical success factor*, for example from the viewpoint of the providers of finance described in the next section below. Investors will expect a proper return on their investment. Banks will require interest and the repayment of loans. Family members will depend for their livelihoods on the financial performance of a family business. The state will expect public agencies, schools, or healthcare agencies to act as efficient stewards of the taxpayers' money they receive in order to meet their obligations.

FINANCIAL SOURCES

There is a variety of different sources of finance. Each has its own advantages and disadvantages. The use of each may be associated with different kinds of dilemma. Each also has its own risk profile. Issues of risk are dealt with in Chapter 17.

Advantages	Disadvantages
Personal capital: Availability, accessibility, control.	Risk of personal loss.
Joint personal or family capital: Increased available funds; may form private limited liability company status.	Introduces nature of relationship dynamic between partners, family members or private shareholders; potential loss of control for any one provider.
Equity capital: Increased available funds; benefit of limited liability; shareholders carry risk.	Loss of control; likely emphasis on achievement of shareholder value; emphasis on consistency of dividend flow and / or capital growth described in a later section below; possible short-termism in planning?

Creditors:

Temporary interest-free use of creditor resources prior to eventual payment; assists cash flow.

Eventual negative reaction of creditors to delay in receiving payment, particularly if they are large organisations; potential for legal action to obtain payment; creditor claims take priority in cases of bankruptcy (along with lenders).

Loan capital:

Access and availability (?); no commitment to remunerating shareholders; use for gearing or leveraging existing equity capital in order to boost performance

Commitment to pay interest and to repay loans which take preference over payment of dividends; loss of control; potential for gearing / leveraging to go into reverse and damage performance.

Retained earnings:

Availability, accessibility, control; may provide a buffer against trade downturns; may be used to buy back and cancel shares. Also facilitates innovation or acquisition (etc) as forms of business development.

Possible shareholder criticism (i) of returns received eg from low- interest investments, and (ii) of an apparent lack of management initiative in finding more profitable activities. A "cash-rich" company may also become an attractive acquisition target?

FINANCIAL PERFORMANCE EVALUATION METHODOLOGIES AND PARADIGMS

The nature of processes of evaluation or performance measurement is likely to be subject to specification according to chosen and / or regulatory *paradigms*. The choice (or imposition) of these paradigms, such as for taxation purposes, accounting for stock, or as used in formulating offer quotations, may give rise to dilemmas. Some of these performance measurement dilemmas are described in this section.

Volume or weight – the salt traders of North Africa once carried out their business on the basis of volume. They could not trust the accuracy of the weighing scales of the merchants who dealt in this precious commodity. Similarly, bales of cotton were once sold by weight and were kept in damp warehouses in Lancashire in order to stop them drying out too much prior to sale.

Unit to finance – the translation from unit values (such as specification, weight, volume, calorific value, etc) will inevitably require the application of financial values or paradigms. For example, fuel costs must be calculated (i) on the cost of production and distribution plus tax payable at a certain rate plus profit margin in conditions where (ii) cost is a function of supply and distribution considerations adjusted for currency values plus Government taxation policies (for instance no VAT or Sales Tax is levied on motor fuels in the USA, so motoring may be cheaper and large vehicle engines popular).

External Accounting Ratios – which evaluation methodologies are calculated variously on the basis of accounts published externally and mandatorily in the UK by shareholder corporations (but <u>not</u> by private companies). The results of ratio analysis are compared with certain established external norms, benchmarks, interfirm comparisons, or received wisdoms (such as those associated with solvency or indebtedness) for such as:

❏ operational performance, asset utilisation, and profitability;
❏ debt management;
❏ liquidity and solvency;

❏   cover (which is the degree to which the enterprise can meet its
    financial obligations);
❏   perceived financial strength;
❏   Stock Market requirements;
❏   comparative trends over time.

Published accounting data and ratio calculations are variously used
as an appraisal guide, to identify issues, and to provoke questions.
They augment and enhance the picture of the organisation being
built up in any process of corporate evaluation or appraisal.

REVENUES

Accountable revenues are likely to have to be declared *net* of such
costs as:

❏   VAT or Sales tax, especially where, as in the UK, the taxation
    system is effective and subject to little or no corruption;
❏   distributor or supply chain margins, as in the publishing industry.

Accountable revenues will in part be a function of:

❏   decisions associated with the necessary reaction to the level of
    market demand and competition; *and*
❏   the chosen pricing policies, for instance in respect of order vol-
    ume, or the offer of trade discounts;
❏   the use of *contribution* calculations (also described in a later
    section of this chapter) so as to cover such overhead costs as is
    consistent over the range of offer with meeting external price
    competition; *or*
❏   decisions on the use of adherence to techniques of *absorption
    costing* in which a proportion of fixed costs is allocated to cost
    structure. In this case, a specified or "standard" allocation is
    made of overhead costs to unit cost in order to establish sales
    price. This paradigm means that all products or services offered
    are priced to include an allocation of fixed costs, even if this
    results in an increase in offer price.
❏   the rate (speed) at which debtors pay their bills across the pe-
    riod of any one year. Price discounts may have to be offered

in order to encourage speedy payment and thereby to optimise cash flow. This may then reduce the need for borrowing on the working capital account to finance operations. Some large and powerful organisations will of course be able to benefit in both ways under this heading – debtors will (say) have to pay their bills after one working week of receipt of goods (ie seven days); the company will pay its bills on a monthly basis (ie 28 days). It will then have a positive cash balance and will be ruthless with slow payers. This is also a dilemma for companies supplying the UK public sector which has a mixed reputation for paying bills. Some Local Government Authorities may try to delay payment until threatened with legal action;

❏ forecasts or targets based on decisions as to what policies or paradigms define, or instead are likely to achieve a "requisite", "optimum", "shareholder acceptable" or so-called "maximum" revenue given the nature of operational, market and regulatory conditions.

COSTS

Costs are usually distinguised as being:

❏ *variable* as between differing levels of operation, to include raw materials and other consumables; *or*

❏ *fixed*, not varying with variations in levels of operation. Might include electric and other forms of fuel and power, also so-called "administrative costs" associated with the running of the organisation.

Costs of staffing or employment are often defined to be fixed, not calculated to vary on the short term with the level of operation. However, ethical and political controversy has arisen in the UK over the use of "zero-hour" or "gig economy" definitions of labour costs. These are deemed by some employers to vary directly with the level of operation or customer demand, and although legal at this time of writing may not meet the criteria of Minimum Wage requirements. The cost of capital is dealt with in a later section, below.

Decisions or judgements will have to be made about what is

perceived to be the best, optimum or most cost-effective ways of accessing or managing costs. This judgement may contain a variety of dilemmas such as:

❏ what cost-efficiency criteria might be chosen;
❏ where costs might be incurred, for instance on a global basis. For example, a call centre might be moved to India because wages are low there, but not your local hospital where wages are likely to be higher;
❏ whether to use forms of outsourcing, leasing or franchising which may be deemed (for instance by government agencies) to be more cost-effective than in-house operation;
❏ what taxation policies should be chosen by which (legally) an organisation's tax burden may be minimised.

CAPITAL EMPLOYED

Decisions will have to be made as to what is thought to be the best *single source* of finance or capital to be used, or instead what *mix of financial sources or capital* will be more appropriate to achieving enterprise objectives. Financial sources were described above. Decisions on the choice of financial source, and on the use of the capital it represents are likely to be associated with issues of Risk, which are analysed in Chapter 17.

Three capital source issues, and the dilemmas they represent, are dealt with here, as follow.

CAPITAL SOURCE EMPLOYED [I] – THE SERVICING OF LOAN FINANCE

The servicing of loan finance commitments represents a *fixed cost* to the business. Interest payments on loan finance, and capital repayments themselves, cannot normally be waived. Returns to preference shareholders and debenture holders also represent a fixed cost, as these too cannot be waived. Business loans and debentures would normally be secured against assets, which reduces the risk to the lender. Default on payment may allow the lender to take control of the company in order that funds can be recovered. And the higher the perceived risk, the higher may be the interest rate charged. On the other hand, loan capital does not carry any ownership rights *per se,* unlike equity capital. And interest payments may be *tax-deductible,* as in the UK.

The need to service loan finance commitments may present the enterprise (i) with a number of decision dilemmas, and (ii) with the need to make *trade-offs* or *compromises* between them. Interest payments and capital repayment absorb profit and cash flow. Where profit or cash flow fluctuate, there may be a "knock on" effect on the earnings available for reinvestment or the payment of dividends. Once interest payments have been made, the profit balance (or residue) could either (i) be shared in some proportion between returns to equity and reinvestment; or (ii) returns to equity may be stabilised to provide earnings consistency, leaving funds for reinvestment potentially subject to wide and unpredictable annual fluctuations.

This dilemma may also pose difficulties where the enterprise is committed to heavy and long term investments in business or technology development, innovation, or new product or process development, (etc). Additional sources of investment funds (which need to be financed by dividends or interest payments) may have to be obtained in order to maintain the continuity of innovation, new business development, and so on.

Strategic priority may, therefore, be given to *maintaining stable profit and cash flows.* This may in particular minimise the risk posed by the potential for wide variations in profit and cash flow, described above, in situations where extensive use is made of loan finance within the capital structure of an organisation based upon equity ownership.

At the same time this confirms the apparent advantage of structures of ownership and finance in which considerations of maximising short term returns to shareholders are displaced by the longer term objectives for competitive advantage, knowledge management, innovation, business development and market position that for instance characterise many German, Swiss, French, South Korean, Chinese, and Japanese businesses. Reference was made in this respect in earlier chapters to the grocery retailers Aldi and Lidl.

CAPITAL SOURCE EMPLOYED [II] – THE COST OF CAPITAL ("K")

Sizer comments of the *cost of capital* (or "K") that 'the minimum acceptable return from any project is the rate of interest which the firm is paying for the capital invested in it … a firm (may) draw capital from various sources and each has a different cost … the objective should be to develop a financing structure which minimises the firm's weighted average cost of capital'.

The variable "K" therefore represents *the notional cost of the capital invested in the organisation.* It is described above in terms of its *weighted average cost* or "WACC". This weighted average cost of capital is made up of a series of capital components, obtained from various sources, for each of which a *component cost* may be calculated. Weston and Brigham, for example, identify four such main component costs within the WACC of a business enterprise to be (i) any or all of preference shares or debentures; (ii) loan finance; (iii) retained earnings; and (iv) external equity. Weston and Brigham then calculate the company's weighted average cost of capital using the general formula:

$$K\% = \sum_{(t1)}^{(n)} w(i) \, k(i)$$

at time one *(t1)*, where *(n)* is the number of components, *w(i)* is the weight of the *i'th* type of capital component; and *k(i) is* the cost of the *i'th* component.

This weighted average cost of capital, together with the individual costs of debt and equity components, may for the purpose of illustration be plotted against the debt-equity ratio within the company's capital structure, as in **Figure 10.** *This shows an optimal point x at which the WACC is minimized.*

"K" and the return from capital investment – where the firm is carrying out an appraisal of possible capital investments, the minimum acceptable commercial return may be established as having to be equivalent to the firm's cost of capital. "K" is used in this case as an *appraisal hurdle* or *cut-off rate* against which forecast returns from the alternative investments are compared. Capital investment appraisal will then be based on either of the main methods of *discounted cash flow*.

In the simplest case, the forecasted revenue returns from the investment will be discounted to give their *net present value* or "NPV". The company's cost of capital K% is used as the minimum hurdle or threshold rate against which the expected returns are discounted. Where a positive NPV results, the return from the investment exceeds the cost of capital and the project may be viewed as commercially viable.

Where forecasted revenues can instead be discounted to calculate the *internal rate of return* ("IRR") from the investment alternatives available to the firm, the resultant IRR curve may conceptually be plotted against the curve representing the *marginal cost of capital* ("MCC") that would be required within the firm's capital budget to finance the investment alternatives proposed. This is shown in **Figure 11.**

Figure 10 shows that projects *m* to *n* would be undertaken. These projects equal or exceed the threshold cost of capital *a*% of a capital budget £b. Projects *n* to *q* would be rejected as their IRR would not cover K% as expressed in the MCC curve, given that *a*% is the hurdle rate below which investments are considered to be commercially unviable.

The relative level of "K" – where an investment opportunity exists and the potential returns can be forecast with any degree of relative accuracy, *the lower the cost of obtaining the capital required, the greater the profitability is likely to be.* Relative competitive advantage may be obtained where the enterprise is financially strong, or is in a good position to raise funds, or can obtain funding at the lowest possible cost. The lower the K% cost of adding the value represented by the investment, the more profitable may be the opportunity.

CAPITAL SOURCE EMPLOYED [III] –ISSUES OF OWNERSHIP, CAPITAL STRUCTURE AND DEBT MANAGEMENT

Published accounts are required to show information about capital structure, which comprises the various sources of finance used in a business. Funds may come from shareholders, institutional investors or trusts, banks, or the state. The process of financial analysis examines the relative importance of, or balance between these different sources, and how the expectations of their providers can be met.

$$\text{Gearing ratio} = \frac{\text{Short} + \text{long term debt ('borrowings')}}{\text{Capital employed}}$$

$$\text{Long term debt ratio} = \frac{\text{Long term debt}}{\text{Capital employed}}$$

The analysis of ownership and debt management is an important element of the appraisal process. Shareholders will expect dividends and capital growth. The use of debt and credit entails fixed obligations. Interest must be paid. Debt must be repaid.

Companies borrow money at a given interest rate and invest it in their business. They hope that it will yield a return greater than the cost of the interest. This process may "gear up" or "leverage" the business activity. It *may* increase the return to shareholders if a positive differential between the cost and the return results from the investment.

Such a form of financing, however, contains a significant risk. The process can go into reverse. Increasing competition, declining returns from the business activity, increasing interest rates, or recession may lower returns to shareholders. This may have the effect of lowering share valuations as well as dividends. And the greater the debt burden, the less profit there is to distribute to shareholders in the form of dividends, and the less attractive the shares become to investors. A downward spiral or "vicious circle" may be the result, leading to the loss of confidence or potential for hostile acquisition or takeover.

SOLVENCY AND LIQUIDITY

Indicators of solvency and liquidity show whether the enterprise can pay its suppliers (creditors) for goods and services received. They show whether it is in a position to pay dividends, to pay interest on loan finance, or to repay loan capital. They show whether it has adequate working capital upon which to base its current or planned level of business activity. And they indicate whether the enterprise is generating its own funds which may be used for investment and business development.

Financial analysis under this heading may also be used to identify management actions that would overstretch the organisation's finances and lead it into conditions of "overtrading". *Overtrading means trying to operate a level of business activity that exceeds the financial capacity of the organisation to sustain that level of business*. Any business or service organisation must ensure that it has adequate cash resources by which to pay its way, and a proper cash flow on which to base its operations. The relationship between overtrading and *the risk of corporate failure* is dealt with in Chapter 15.

Two critical accounting ratios are used to indicate the degree to which the enterprise can finance its operations and pay its debts. These are the:

$$\text{Current ratio} = \frac{\text{Current assets}}{\text{Current liabilities}}$$

$$\text{Acid test} = \frac{\text{Liquid assets (cash + debtors)}}{\text{Current liabilities}}$$

Where the acid test indicates that liquid assets do not cover the cash debts implicit in the figures for current liabilities, any appraisal process should seek some kind of compensating factor, such as a high level of cash sales (as in retailing or the fast moving consumer goods sectors). Otherwise, the appraisal process may have to look closely at the organisation in case there is any risk of insolvency and failure.

TAXATION

Interest on loan finance is for example tax deductible in the UK. Therefore its use may be preferred to that of additional equity finance (on which the payment of dividends is not tax deductible) within the capital structure *if its cost is calculated net of the tax that would otherwise have been paid if dividends to equity finance had been incurred.*

More generally, and depending upon national tax laws, taxation strategy may in part be directed towards minimising or offsetting the level of company or corporation tax that would otherwise be payable on declared profits. Certain types of investment may instead be made because they attract investment allowances against tax. Or additional expenditures may be made on employee welfare, contributions to pension funds, etc, which are tax deductible, or increase goodwill and help the enterprise to attract better employees.

In the private and SME sector, the objective of financial strategy is often to minimise the level of profit declared, rather than to maximise it. Directors may take advantage of company taxation laws that permit allowances against tax for company cars, perquisites, etc. Or they may deliberately undertake additional investments in marketing, market share enhancement, operational, or new product development activities that are calculated to have the effect of eliminating much of the taxation liability that would otherwise have to be financed. They might even purchase potentially loss-making activities like professional football clubs for reasons of prestige or personal ambition.

PROFIT ISSUES

Profit may be initially be defined as the difference (or surplus) between net sales revenue and net costs, to include payment of interest and the repayment of loans. Corporation tax may then be payable on this figure to give a net profit figure. However, different *accounting ratios* may be used to give different interpretations of the meaning of profit calculations. These accounting ratios are listed as a block below, with comments following.

$$\text{Profit margin} = \frac{\text{Net profit before tax}}{\text{Sales}}$$

$$\text{Return on net assets (RONA)} = \frac{\text{Net profit before tax}}{\text{Net assets}}$$

$$\text{Profit per employee} = \frac{\text{Net profit before tax}}{\text{Total number of employees}}$$

$$\text{Asset turnover} = \frac{\text{Sales}}{\text{Net assets}}$$

$$\text{Stock turnover} = \frac{\text{Sales}}{\text{Stock}}$$

$$\text{Debtor turnover} = \frac{\text{Sales}}{\text{Debtors}}$$

$$\text{Average collection period} = \frac{\text{Debtors}}{\text{Average daily sales}}$$

$$\text{Effectiveness of administration} = \frac{\text{Cost of administration}}{\text{Sales}}$$

$$\text{Return on capital employed (ROCE)} = \frac{\text{Net profit after tax}}{\text{Capital employed}}$$

$$\text{Return on equity (ROE) or Return on shareholder capital (ROSC)} = \frac{\text{Net profit after tax}}{\text{Shareholders' equity or shareholder capital}}$$

Profit margin – shows the relative profitability of individual lines or services, and the cumulative total. Such calculations may be combined with the Internal Appraisal Viewpoints described in a later section, below, in order to manage the performance of these lines or services, and to identify their competitive or market standing.

Return on net assets (RONA) – which may be used to identify the relative efficiency of the enterprise in using its assets to generate the necessary profit. This calculation may be augmented by the six ratios that follow, thus:

❑ Profit per employee
❑ Asset turnover
❑ Stock turnover
❑ Debtor turnover
❑ Average collection period
❑ Effectiveness of administration

These ratios indicate the level of return being generated by the assets and people being employed by the organisation. They show how fixed assets are used to generate profit, and how working capital is used in the process of generating sales and cash flow. They also show the speed and efficiency with which the business completes its transactions with customers.

Return on capital employed (ROCE) – which shows how efficient the business has been in generating profit from the totality of its capital, including the loan capital it may be using to gear up its equity capital and cash.

Return on equity (ROE) or Return on shareholder capital (ROSC) – which calculations focus solely on how enterprise management has created profitability and shareholder value using equity capital. This excludes borrowings of loan finance which are seen merely as a cost to the business; and ideally not to be used at all in order to reduce risk and to maximise value generation.

EXTERNAL ACCOUNTING RATIO APPRAISAL VIEWPOINTS

The *interpretation* placed upon externally published financial information and accounting ratios derived therefrom, trends over time, and interfirm or benchmarking comparisons may depend on the particular viewpoint of the person carrying out the appraisal. For instance:

❑ *the investor* and the *Stock Market* may focus on trends in annual or short-term performance and profitability, share and asset valuation, cash flow, and growth potential. Stock Market requirements are also dealt with in the next section below;

❑ *the supplier as creditor* is interested in short-term cash flow, the ability pay debts, long term enterprise viability, and evidence of the systematic avoidance of conditions of overtrading;

❑ *the potential acquirer* monitors trends in relative performance, efficiency and profitability (for instance against industry benchmarks), potential for efficiency, growth and profitability gains, and share valuation (especially if the present stock market valuation is perceived to be too high or too low). So- called "asset strippers" will instead be looking for undervalued assets whose real value they think they can realise at a profit if they can acquire them;

❑ *management and employees* are concerned with short and long-term viability and performance, cash flow, comparisons with competitors and benchmark companies in the sector, and with the potential for unwelcome or hostile takeover bids;

❑ *the state* will be concerned with supplier performance and status where it has concerns about cost over-runs or delivery delays, such as those characterising investments in weapon systems, naval ships, nuclear power stations, or large construction projects which are putting suppliers or contractors under pressure or risk of failure, (etc.).

STOCK MARKET REQUIREMENTS

Stock Market assessment of a company's trading performance and its profitability will be based on an interpretation of the trends over time of the following ratios:

$$\text{Earnings per share (EPS)} = \frac{\text{Profit after tax}}{\text{Number of ordinary shares issued}}$$

$$\text{Price / earnings ratio (PE)} = \frac{\text{Market price per share}}{\text{Earnings per share}}$$

$$\text{Dividend yield} = \frac{\text{Dividend per share}}{\text{Market price per share}}$$

$$\text{Dividend payout} = \frac{\text{Dividends paid}}{\text{Profit after tax}}$$

Analysis of these four ratios is used, among other things, to indicate:

❑ stock market evaluation and acceptance of the company as an investment;

❑ the relationship between earnings retained in the business, and dividends paid to investors;

❑ the degree to which retained earnings are being used to provide funds by which to finance the business. A low payout from a healthy firm may indicate that earnings are being reinvested for growth, or that the business wishes to minimise its dependence on other sources of capital such as new share issues or borrowing.

Cover – the analysis of cover deals with the adequacy of the margin of profit over and above a required rate of dividend payment, or the ability to pay interest on loan finance, thus:

$$\text{Dividend cover} = \frac{\text{Earnings per share}}{\text{Dividend per share}}$$

$$\text{Interest cover} = \frac{\text{Profit before tax}}{\text{Loan interest}}$$

In this case, the appraisal process looks at the capacity of the organisation to meet its immediate commitments to shareholders and lenders.

The analysis of cover may also be extended to the capacity of the organisation to repay the capital of the loan by the due date. At the same time, banks and institutional investors (such as pension funds and insurance companies) are interested in the value of the assets against which a loan may be secured. This is a particular issue for the small to medium sized enterprise (the SME), the private company, or for the riskier venture.

Financial strength and capability – the profitability analysis of the enterprise may reveal clues about the strength of its financial capability and capacity. For instance, it may indicate the degree to which it already possesses funds for use in the business; or is instead likely to be able to obtain new monies, from whichever source. It may indicate how easy (or otherwise) it would be to obtain these additional funds. The analysis of financial strength may therefore demonstrate such features of capability and capacity as:

❑ the capacity of the organisation to self-finance itself, without the need for additional share issues or external borrowing, whilst at the same time meeting shareholder dividend expectations, debt service commitments (etc); *and*

❏ the feasibility of growth or development strategies, since the availability of finance is essential to their implementation.

INTERNAL APPRAISAL VIEWPOINTS
Internal forms of evaluation include calculations of:

❏ *Contribution* – where **Contribution = Net Sales Revenue minus Variable Costs**. This allows the enterprise to relate the level of sales income (and the prices it charges) to the Fixed Costs that need to be covered, particularly in competitive markets where Absorption Costing is deemed to be unviable; *and*

❏ *Break-Even* – where **Fixed Costs are multiplied by the ratio of Sales to Contribution** so as *to indicate the point at which the enterprise is at least covering its Fixed Costs; and*

❏ *Margin of Safety* – which is represented by **the level of sales revenue in excess of the Break-Even Point**. Calculations of Margin of Safety are used to identify the degree to which a company is more or less vulnerable to a decline in sales, for instance back down to, or below Break Even point (where losses will be incurred);

❏ *Zero Based Budgeting (ZBB)* – as described in the following section below.

Such internal appraisal viewpoints would not normally be made available on a public basis because of their commercial confidentiality.

THE MANAGEMENT OF PUBLIC SECTOR COSTS
As an example, the annual cost of Local Government services (for instance to Council Tax Paying electorates) may in part be a function of such uncontrollable factors as:

❏ the gross level of finance being allocated by Central Government, and the basis of the budgetary time scales it has chosen to use;

❏ Central Government decisions on the preferred efficiency measurement paradigms it wishes to impose on Local Government authorities. This might mean taking such forms as lowest cost, value for money or Best Value (however defined), lean, or Six Sigma, (etc.).

The state will also be concerned with the *effectiveness and efficiency* with which public sector organisations use the financial resources that they have been allocated, relative to the objectives set. For instance, in recent years in the UK this has meant a requirement to demonstrate the achievement of "Best Value" type performance against pre-established service targets, performance benchmarks, and Performance Indicators (PI's). It has also meant adapting (i) to rigorous government policies of the "resource stretch and leverage" (or "doing more with less") process in conditions of resource reductions; or (ii) equally to conditions in which public sector operations are prioritised simply on the basis of the money made available to them (if any?).

Dilemmas associated with considerations of performance and efficiency in such sectors as healthcare, education, and the uniformed services have at this time of writing become very highly sensitive and politicised in the UK.

The Reader might therefore at this point care to ponder the cost and dilemma consequences of a future decision imposed by the UK Department of Health to force the National Health Service to make use of Zero Based Budgeting (ZBB, described below) to require regional acute mega-hospitals to implement and to assure Six Sigma standards of patient / client care and infection control.

THE STEWARDSHIP OF GRANT OR CHARITABLE FUNDS

The stewardship of public and / or charitable funds, for instance allocated in *grant form* may pose a potentially risky Management Dilemma. Such funds are made available to external and / or charitable organisations in order that they may carry out their functions, whatever these may be. The organisations in receipt of such funds are then legally obliged to demonstrate accountability for the use of funds at their disposal, for instance in the form of their proper performance management and control. This stewardship must then be assured by means of a formal annual audit and the submission of a valid Annual Report.

However, the effectiveness of such assurance may be function of the degree to which the organisation has an adequate performance management capability and willpower. Can the members of a charity, for example, or its Trustee Board prove that they have the requisite skills in order to demonstrate trustworthiness and credibility (i) to the providers of finance (such as a central or local government authority, or donors from the general public); and also (ii) to those members of the media, pressure groups or the wider community who for whatever reason have taken an interest in its affairs.

It is of course a responsibility of the Trustees to ensure that there is no misuse, theft or misappropriation of funds; that no fraudulent or criminal acts are undertaken in the name of the charity; and that there is transparent evidence of a proper, accounted, and legal disbursement of the monies available to it, whatever their source.

Issues of Performance Measurement and Performance Management are dealt with in Chapter 24. Reference is also made in that chapter to the **Nolan Principles** for public and charitable conduct.

ZERO BASED BUDGETING (ZBB)

Zero Based Budgeting (ZBB) is a formalised system for reviewing the process of adjusting or setting budgets for the activities of an organisation. Its use may lead to the identification of significant strategic, financial, or political dilemmas associated with the resource allocation processes in use.

Zero Based Budgeting examines each activity as if it were being performed for the first time, that is, from a "zero base". A number of alternative levels of provision for each activity may be identified, mapped (Ch.19), costed, and evaluated in terms of the benefits to be obtained from them. Zero Based Budgeting is sometimes also called "priority-based budgeting".

ZBB may be used because it is based on the policy *that management should be required to justify <u>existing activities and existing</u>*

resource allocations in exactly the same way as *new proposals*. The appraisal process will compare established activities with alternative potential applications of the resources that are to be committed during the planning period in view. Implicit in ZBB, therefore, are the concepts of:

❑ *opportunity cost* – how may the available resources **now best be used**?
❑ *priority* – do past and current commitments of resources reflect or match present strategic, business or political priorities?

Business organisations and public sector institutions may have habitually made use of *incremental budgeting* over time. Budgetary planning is based on current or immediate past practice. Existing budgets are updated for the planning period ahead for instance by applying expected price, volume, inflation or operational changes. The main justification for next year's expenditure is last year's expenditure. The fact of the allocation of resources to each activity is effectively taken for granted. It is assumed that the activity will continue its right to a claim on resource allocation *because it is already there*.

The use of ZBB within the process of financial management *challenges these assumptions*. It may be used to question the implied right of existing activities to receive a continuing allocation of resources. It may be used to ask such questions as:

❑ what are the current objectives of the activity being appraised?
❑ what are the current resources and operational processes invested in the achievement of these objectives?
❑ are there now alternative or more efficient ways of achieving these same objectives, for instance by reengineering or outsourcing (etc) the processes involved in it?
❑ are any of these alternatives now more appropriate or more cost-effective, for instance because the Government is making cuts to annual public sector financial allocations?
❑ in any case, how relevant are these objectives to today's circumstances?
❑ is the activity actually now really necessary?

❑ what would be the consequences *in terms of costs and benefits* if the activity were now to be reengineered, outsourced or actually discontinued?
❑ what would be the consequences of *not funding* the activity at all?

WORKSHOP
Think of your own ZBB example, and take ownership of it, even if you don't like it!

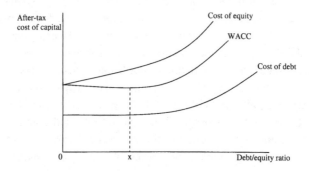

Figure 10
The Weighted Average Cost of Capital (WACC)

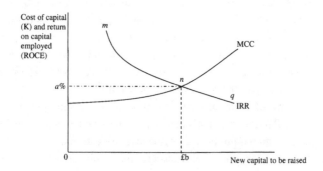

Figure 11
IRR and Capital Investment Appraisal

Chapter Fifteen

Dilemmas of Governance, Finance, Negative Value, and Failure Risk

Subsequent to the collapse of Carillion, the UK's National Audit Office (NAO) commented that the Government and its Civil Servants must "better understand the financial health of its major suppliers and avoid creating relationships with those that are already weakened." Reference to Carillion is made as a Case Example at a later point in this Chapter.

THE PROVIDERS OF FINANCE AS KEY STAKEHOLDERS

Individuals, families, institutions, or the state provide the financing of the enterprise. The capital provided may take the form of equity, overdrafts, credit, loans, or funds made available from the public purse. The providers of this finance are *key stakeholders* in the organisation. These providers expect an appropriate return on their investment; or the proper payment of interest and the repayment of capital; or clear evidence of the effective use of monies provided by the state for the public good, however this effectiveness is measured.

COMPANY STRUCTURE

Decisions may be made to structure organisations in any of the following ways:

- ❏ the sole tradership (perhaps categorised as a "Small to Medium sized Enterprise" or **SME**);
- ❏ the partnership (whether SME in status or larger, as in the case of limited liability professional partnerships in legal or accountancy practice);
- ❏ the family business (which may or may not be of SME status);
- ❏ the private business with limited liability (such Walmart, or the retailers Aldi and Lidl to which reference has been made in earlier chapters);

❑ the private business whose ownership may be characterised by dominant and / or close-held or cross-held shareholdings (such as the *chaebol* of South Korea);

❑ the publicly quoted business whose ownership is characterised by dominant or close-held shareholdings (such as ABB Asea Brown Boveri, Fiat, or Electrolux);

❑ the shareholder corporation with limited liability status;

❑ companies working directly with State involvement as "semi-state" enterprises;

❑ companies or organisations *owned wholly by the state but directly involved in business activities* such as running public utility services; or whose security status (for instance in the development of weapon or cyber systems) instead requires direct government control;

❑ the co-operative;

❑ the charitable, community, or philanthropic trust;

❑ the community interest company.

Each has its advantages and disadvantages.

MEETING SHAREHOLDER EXPECTATIONS

Shareholders as stakeholders may, in particular, expect:

❑ consistency and reliability of dividend flows over time;

❑ growth in the real value of these income flows over time;

❑ growth in the capital value of the shareholding that may arise from increasing company profitability and business value.

These were described in Chapter 14 in terms of:

❑ earnings per share;

❑ price-earnings ratio;

❑ dividend yield;

❑ dividend payout.

ABB Asea Brown Boveri states, for example, that *the maximising of shareholder value* is one of its primary objectives, and shapes its corporate governance, financial strategy, and financial management accordingly. ABB believes that many companies fail to maximise shareholder value, and as a result under-perform as far as shareholders are concerned. The company also believes that such under-performing companies make good acquisition targets for its own business development because once they are purchased, effective leadership and competent management can be put in place to increase the level of shareholder value yielded by the investment.

Shareholders may include individuals, families, investment trusts, holding companies, banks, insurance companies, pension funds, financial institutions, and the state.

Shareholders may expect the enterprise to provide a return *that they deem to be appropriate* to their investment. Enterprise management has therefore to judge what shareholders perceive to be appropriate by using:

❏ past performance trends;
❏ interfirm comparisons and benchmarks;
❏ current market expectations;
❏ knowledge of alternative investments and opportunity cost.

At the same time, shareholders may have expectations about the *quality of earnings* that they should receive. Quality of earnings means the *dependability of dividend income streams*. The more dependable the income, and the lower the risk, the more desirable will be the investment. The resulting share price "premium" may protect the company from the threat of takeover, if it is publicly quoted, but places management under pressure to provide consistent dividends, year in and year out (irrespective of fluctuations in trading conditions or the emergence of recession). Major institutional investors, such as pension funds and insurance companies, seek dependable earnings above all else so that they can satisfy the demands of their own customers and investors.

Shareholders may also be concerned about the *asset backing* of their investment. Assets provide a buffer for share price in the event of the enterprise running into trouble. Ideally, these assets should be easily realisable (encashable; like stock, or investments in valuable subsidiaries) and unencumbered by securities on loan finance. In this case, the enterprise can realise some of its finance and reassure its shareholders that there is no risk to their investment, thereby lessening the chance of a fall in share price and company valuation.

Shareholders are concerned with *enterprise cash flow*. A shortfall in cash flow may make it difficult to pay dividends. Dividend and interest payments, loan repayments, payments to creditors (etc) may have to be financed through further borrowing or the issue of additional equity capital, which will exacerbate the difficulty. At the same time, a shortfall in cash flow may bring about a drop in company valuation, since the enterprise may have to sell off productive assets or investments in order to make good the cash shortage.

Strong cash flow, on the other hand, makes the enterprise attractive to investors. Cash is available to fund competence building, innovation, business development, and so on. The payment of dividends and interest are likely to be perceived to present few problems. The capacity to *internally finance* the chosen development strategies also means that the enterprise can seek additional funds from outside investors at competitive rates, since little risk is likely to be involved. And the quality of the investment may discourage shareholders from trading their investment. Share values are high and any potential takeover threat may be so prohibitively expensive as to be unlikely.

Shareholders may also favour a company that has strong *institutional* backing. Large institutional investors, such as insurance companies, pension funds, investment trusts, or unit trusts are often reluctant to withdraw their support for the enterprise. They may view their investment as long term, provided that they receive an appropriate quality of earnings taken one year with another. The presence of key institutional investors may "keep management on its toes", since a fundamental purpose of financial strategy and financial management will be to keep these large investors happy.

Managing returns to equity – earnings per share (EPS) are maximised when the enterprise achieves the greatest possible *sustainable* return over time on the capital employed in the business. EPS can be improved (i) by increasing the return from existing assets; (ii) by new investments, new acquisitions, or innovation; or (iii) by reducing capital employed but maintaining earnings.

The reduction of capital or assets employed may imply the strategy of *divesting* activities that are no longer considered to be able to meet the minimum target for earnings quality or return on investment. Company management may feel on grounds of opportunity cost that such activities contain no further useful potential for earnings improvement, so wish to invest the funds they represent in a more profitable line of business. Effective, consistent and long term performance in terms of EPS may have the effect of boosting share prices and keeping share valuations high. This (i) encourages existing shareholders to hold on to their investment; (ii) makes the enterprise less vulnerable to takeover; and (iii) makes it easier for the enterprise to raise additional equity.

Dividend policy and retained earnings – dividends (and therefore the EPS they represent) may be reduced if profits are low. They may also be reduced if there is a pressing need *to retain funds in the business* for investment in new business development, acquisition or innovation, etc. These *retained earnings* are a widely used source of working capital and investment finance.

Policy decisions therefore need to be taken on the *relative distribution* of available cash and profit to (i) dividend payment or (ii) retention in the business. Dividend policy, in consequence, has two interrelated objectives:

❏ optimising or maximising returns to shareholders in the short and the long term; *and*

❏ maintaining the investment that will generate these returns to shareholders within the time scales appropriate to the sector.

The need to provide a consistent quality of earnings, but at the same time to fund competence development, innovation, new product or process development, acquisition or new business development poses decision makers with a significant dilemma. They might (i) choose the most appropriate *trade-off* between paying out, or retaining profits. They might instead (ii) take a short term view of the business, abandoning longer term investments in innovation, research and development, business development (etc), despite the likelihood that their competitors will gain competitive advantage from such activities. Or (iii) they may use a *mix* of investment funds, including long term loans and income from cash flows, to attempt to satisfy a wide range of strategic, product market and business development objectives, whether short or long term.

Managing risk and return – Chapter 14 referred to the following *risk-related* appraisal calculations:

❏   current ratio and acid test as indicators of solvency and liquidity;
❏   gearing ratio and long term debt ratio as indicators of debt management;
❏   dividend cover and interest cover as indicators of ability to meet the requirements of key financial stakeholders;
❏   margin of safety.

Issues of risk management are analysed in a later section below, and in Chapter 17.

Risk and returns to equity capital – shareholders may (i) expect a return on their equity capital that is at least above a minimum threshold figure described as "K" in Chapter 14. Otherwise they might invest their money in risk free fixed interest bonds or deposit accounts (etc).

Shareholders may also (ii) have expectations of growth in the capital value of their investment, taken over some "reasonable" period of time. They may therefore be prepared to make some kind of *trade-off* between these two expectations, for instance favouring lower dividends for greater capital growth.

Thereafter, the degree to which any particular equity shareholding *meets owner expectations* may determine:

❏   investor attitude to the relative desirability of the investment;
❏   investor willingness to make further investments in the company;
❏   company valuation and share price;
❏   incidence of trading of these shares;
❏   the degree to which acquisition by others might be seen to be a viable and profitable course of action; *and*

❏ hence perceptions of, and attitudes towards the potential threat of hostile takeover by a predator or asset stripper (etc.).

Shareholders may therefore seek investments that at the same time:

❏ contain a minimal risk of achieving a poor rate of return;
❏ maximise the chance of obtaining a satisfactory rate of return;
❏ yield a consistent and dependable quality of earnings;
❏ "optimise" share values – whatever this means in trading terms.

Such expectations may have to shape the choice of business and financial strategies pursued by the enterprise. They may constrain the strategic choice that is perceived to be available where equity capital is a key constituent of the capital structure. These expectations may play an important part in the formulation of management decisions for instance about the nature and direction of the competition, product-market, and business development strategies to be pursued.

The level of risk inherent in the strategic decisions made by the enterprise must therefore, to an appropriate degree, be consistent with the prevailing expectations and experience of equity shareholders.

Company risk management – perceptions of business risk, shareholder expectations, and investor confidence in the enterprise may all be interrelated features of dilemmas associated with *company risk management.*

This interrelationship between (i) decisions on enterprise risk management strategies and (ii) the maintenance of *investor confidence* is of particular importance in the case of activity proposals *that contain higher than usual risk, or whose outcome may prove unpredictable.* High risk business development; innovation; new product, service, or process development (and so on) must be capable of attracting funds from investors. In such cases, investors might expect that their shareholding:

❏ stands a "reasonable chance" of yielding a high rate of return;
❏ has an "acceptable chance" of achieving a satisfactory rate of return;

❏ contains the minimum acceptable risk of an unsatisfactory rate of return, or an actual *loss of value* as described in Chapter 17.

The formulation of enterprise financial strategy may therefore have to accommodate to the potential dilemma of investors formulating their own *risk return trade-offs*. These investor preferences may depend upon:

❏ the level of risk perceived by existing or potential investors (or by their financial advisers);
❏ the effectiveness of corporate communications, and the capacity of the ***investor relations activity*** (i) to create understanding about the investment proposal and (ii) to generate favourable external attitudes towards it;
❏ the perceived risk posed to the overall sustainability and valuation of the business in total that is inherent in the consequences of any particular investment proposal. This issue is dealt with in a later section below, and also in Chapter 26.

Management decisions about the choice of strategy may ultimately have to accord with the performance expectations and risk tolerance of existing and potential investors. The choice of business, product market, and development strategies (etc) may therefore, of necessity, have to be informed and constrained by these key investor parameters. This is particularly true in the case of the traditional UK and US public company, quoted on the Stock Exchange, dependent on shareholder funding and investor attitude, and potentially vulnerable to the threat of takeover by competitors, predators, corporate raiders, or asset strippers.

CORPORATE GOVERNANCE

The concept of "corporate governance" may be dated back to the time in the 18th and 19th centuries when the incorporation of business companies with limited liability became available. *A corporation is a legal entity*. It is separate and distinct from its owners and managers. Governance issues arise when such a corporation acquires a life of its own, that is, whenever ownership of the entity

is separated from its management and control. A change in ownership structure for instance from family or private to public company
status (with the opportunity to raise capital through the external sale
of stock), separates the owner from the functions of leadership and
management. The role of owner may ultimately change from active
participant to passive observer.

Thus, one major issue or dilemma of corporate governance is
the separation in business companies of equity holders and owners
from those who lead and control these business enterprises. The
separation of ownership from control, and the wide dispersion of
equity ownership amongst shareholders implies that the latter may
no longer be able to control the leadership and direction of the corporation of which they are the owners. Control shifts to the hands
of executives responsible as "agents" or "stewards" for the assets
of the shareholders. The rise of professional directors and managers
acquiring wide powers in shaping the future strategic direction of the
corporation then means that there may be a large body of shareholders who exercise little or no control over the wealth of the enterprise
that they own.

Definitions of corporate governance – the Organisation for
Economic Co-operation and Development (OECD) defines corporate governance in business organisations as 'the system by which
business corporations are directed and controlled. The corporate
governance structure specifies the distribution of rights and responsibilities among different participants in the corporation ... and spells
out the rules and procedures for making decisions on corporate affairs. By doing this it provides the structure through which the company objectives are set, and the means of attaining those objectives
and monitoring performance'.

*Corporate governance may therefore be defined as a process
whose purpose is to shape, to direct, and to supervise the actions of
an organisation, to include:*

❏   the setting of strategic intent, purpose, and direction;
❏   the selection, development, and compensation of senior
    management;

❏   the supervision of leadership and managerial action, for instance in the strategic management and decision-making process;

❏   the evaluation of the capability, competence, and leadership record of decision-makers and managers;

❏   the creation and guarantee of corporate accountability variously to primary beneficiaries such as owners, the providers of finance described in Chapter 14, or other key stakeholders so that the interests of all are properly safeguarded.

The governance role is not concerned directly with the operations of the organisation, but instead focuses (i) on the process by which directors or governors (etc) give leadership and direction; (ii) on overseeing and controlling the executive actions of management in achieving enterprise objectives; and (iii) on satisfying the legitimate expectations of shareholders, stakeholders, or other interests, within or beyond the boundaries of the corporation, for regulation, account-ability, adherance to the Nolan Principles (Ch.24), etc.

Corporate governance may in this sense be regarded as a means of (i) safeguarding the interests of, and (ii) balancing the relation-ships between the corporation's constituents, namely shareholders, banks, other sources of finance, or the representatives of taxpayers; directors, governors, and management; suppliers and creditors; em-ployees; customers, clients, or patients (etc); and other stakeholders including the state, the community and the general public.

In addition, the need for the proper *co-ordination and integration* of the affairs of the organisation is seen as a further reason for the presence of an accountable authority and control. Corporate govern-ance may be concerned to ensure that this necessary co-ordination takes place in order to prevent fragmentation and the risk of loss of shareholder or stakeholder value it may represent. This risk might be illustrated by events in the UK financial services sector when man-agement failures led to unco-ordinated, ill-advised and uncontrolled lending that resulted in serious institutional crises, some requiring government support or bail-out.

Corporate governance and the shareholder corporation – cor-porate governance in this case is rooted in the concept of profit optimisation or maximisation for shareholders. Corporate governance in a shareholder corporation may therefore be defined in terms of strategic decision-making that is based on the relationship between the investor, the board of directors of a company, and the management team. Decision-making is founded on the requirement for an accountability towards shareholders that requires the enterprise to focus primarily on maximising shareholder welfare or utility.

This implies the implementation of a model of managerial discipline in which the single most important responsibility of company directors is to ensure that managerial behaviour conforms to the wishes of the company's shareholders. Shareholder value is defined in terms of company earnings, dividend payments, and share price. These issues were also dealt with in Chapter 14.

It may also mean that directors could be discouraged from forestalling a takeover from which shareholders as owners would benefit financially. This may then provide a major dilemma for employees and the local communities affected.

Governance in a shareholder corporation ultimately deals with the ways in which shareholders as the providers of finance assure themselves of getting a "proper" return on their investment.

Corporate governance and the stakeholder corporation – the concept of the stakeholder organisation or stakeholder corporation is instead defined to provide for, and to balance the interests of a spectrum of stakeholders as beneficiaries. These beneficiaries may include owners, taxpayers or their representatives, or shareholders; the relevant sources of finance; suppliers and creditors; appointed officials, decision-makers, or the management of the organisation; employees; customers, clients, patients, or voters; the state, and / or the wider community or its environment (etc). The governance of the public, the educational, and in some cases the healthcare sectors in any one country may be characterised by the use of such stakeholder-oriented institutions. The success of such institutions in achieving their objectives may then be judged by the degree to which the required service outcomes can be achieved whilst harmonising or balancing stakeholder interests within the relevant financial and time-related constraints dealt with in other chapters of this Book.

REGULATORY INTERVENTION

The process of corporate governance and financial management will take place within the prevailing context of *regulatory intervention*. This regulatory intervention may, as an event characteristic (Chapter 4) add complexity and constitute an additional source of dilemmas. The process of regulatory intervention may include any or all of the following:

❑ direct intervention by such Regulatory Authorities as competition watchdogs; agencies such as the UK OFGEM and OFWAT; or the state in the case of banks and financial service institutions, (etc.);

❑ the specific legislation and regulation associated with company structure and governance, for instance as laid down by the German *grundgesetz* and *handelsgesetzbuch* and their European equivalents;

❑ legislation associated with personal and corporate liability for the use of funds, and any restrictions thereon as in the case of limited liability;

❑ the regulation of the company stewardship of investor and / or pension funds;

❑ the establishment of methodologies and paradigms for financial performance evaluation, reporting, and calculation of taxation obligations;

❑ regulation associated with the incidence of corporate failure, to include processes of bankruptcy and administration, and the protection of lenders and creditors;

❑ the scrutiny of public sector expenditure and efficiency;

❑ the relevant general or generic dilemma sources, whether external or internal described in Chapter 4;

❑ the relative influence of the *Voices* of stakeholders; voters; taxpayers; customers, clients or patients; employees; families and householders; benefits claimants (etc) as described in Chapter 4;

❑ the generic application of the event and concept characteristics described in Chapter 4 to include value implications, change, ambiguity, patterns of relative stability, (etc).

LOW AND HIGH NEGATIVE VALUE DILEMMAS
Chapters 14 and 15 describe a variety of management dilemmas associated with the application of finance as a critical resource, and of the need to monitor and to control that use. Some of these dilemmas may have a *low (or even zero) negative value potential*, for instance where a company has strong liquidity or a premium share price. *Such low negative value dilemmas may therefore be characterised by a low degree of risk*, for instance as described in Chapter 17.

Other financial management dilemmas may have a *much higher potential negative value (and therefore increased risk) as dilemmas*, for instance where:

❏ liquidity is poor;
❏ borrowing, for instance to finance gearing, has become unsustainable, or worse, now refused by lenders;
❏ stock market sentiment has become negative or, worse, hostile;
❏ there is an external perception of failure risk; *or*
❏ a government is badly in deficit and dependent on borrowing to finance its spending programme; as well as heavily committed to disbursing a significant proportion of taxpayer funds simply to service the debt; *or*
❏ a charity's funding at best remains static (for instance as a result (i) of falling donations, or (ii) because of central government pressures on funding allocations to local authorities from which grants are made) at the same time as efficiency gains (if available) cannot compensate for rising costs such as staff salaries, property costs, rising costs of GDPR, etc.

BUSINESS SURVIVAL AND CORPORATE FAILURE
Ultimately, the emergence of risk associated with the identification of high negative value dilemmas described above may force the enterprise to take urgent steps (i) to ensure its long term corporate survival, and (ii) above all to identify and remedy potential causes of *corporate failure*.

[1] Classic symptoms of corporate failure – there are *three classic symptoms* of corporate failure. These are:

❏ low profitability;
❏ high gearing;
❏ low liquidity.

Each of these three symptoms may be indicated by trends in the company's accounts. The relevant ratios were described in Chapter 14. The symptoms are interrelated, and are shown in Figure 12.

A classic path to corporate failure starts with the company experiencing *low profitability*. This may be indicated by trends in the ratios for:

❏ profit margin;
❏ return on capital employed;
❏ return on net assets.

A downward trend in profitability will raise the issue of whether, and for how long the enterprise can tolerate a return on capital that is *below* its cost of capital "K". If profitability problems become entrenched, a failing company might seek additional funds and working capital by *increasing its borrowings*, whether in the form of short term or long term debt. This increases the company's gearing, since the higher the proportion of borrowed funds, the higher the gearing within the capital structure. The increased debt burden this represents may then have the effect of exacerbating the situation, particularly if the causes of the decreased profitability have not (or worse, cannot) be resolved.

The worsening profit situation must now be used to finance an increased burden of interest and capital repayments. In the case of a publicly quoted company this means that fewer and fewer funds will be available to finance working capital or dividend payments. It may then become impossible to obtain external credit or to raise further equity funds. Confidence in the company as an investment may wither away, leaving the share price to collapse. If however the company is basically sound, for instance, but **ineptly managed**, the best that can be hoped for is a takeover bid for what may be now a significantly *undervalued investment.*

The company may at this point not be beyond redemption but a rescue attempt might not occur or be sought. This may be because the company's management does not recognise the seriousness of the situation; or is by now too heavily committed or too frightened to admit the truth to its stakeholders; or is instead simply "living on borrowed time" before it must face the inevitable. Then, when the next round of refinancing (or attempted refinancing) occurs and profits fail to cover interest payments or capital repayments a *cash-flow crisis* occurs. Effectively the *liquidity position* has become desperate but no more money can be borrowed nor equity issued. Creditors are then likely to withdraw their support and seek to obtain the payment of outstanding debts, thereby hastening the final outcome.

Company solvency and liquidity, as indicated by the current ratio and acid test, now indicate the desperate nature of the situation faced by the business. The patience and goodwill of lenders and creditors becomes exhausted. Stakeholders will be concerned to limit their own losses, and they will petition for the company's *administration, receivership* or *liquidation*. This step may be forced upon the company, or it may seek the end gracefully by voluntary means.

Thus, the forms of financial analysis described in Chapters 14 (and also Ch.26) may find a critical application in the prediction and avoidance of corporate failure. Rescue attempts may fail because the processes of governance or financial management did not recognise the symptoms of potential failure early enough to do anything about the causes.

Worse, shareholders, stakeholders, the Stock Market, or external analysts may be the first to recognise the impending potential for failure. The apparent absence of recognition by management of the existence of this potential for failure, or an apparent unwillingness to remedy the causes may itself spark off a loss of confidence amongst stakeholders that may make the eventual failure all the more likely.

[2] Argenti's overtrading and large project failure model – Argenti suggests that corporate failure may instead result from any (or a combination) of:

❏   high gearing;
❏   overtrading;
❏   investment in very large projects.

The risks of excessive borrowing and *high gearing* have been described in the previous section, above. *Overtrading* describes a situation in which the enterprise attempts to finance a given or increasing level of operational activity on the basis of inadequate working capital. Where the working capital base is inadequate, the enterprise runs the risk of becoming over reliant on short term financing from banks and trade creditors. An increasing reliance upon such funds may eventually lead to a situation in which there is a significant excess of current liabilities over current assets, and the threat of the withdrawal of bank and creditor support.

Large projects instead pose a threat to the financial viability of the organisation where the investment they represent:

❏   has the effect of decreasing company profitability below an acceptable level, or over an unacceptable time scale;
❏   is financed by excessive borrowing, thereby increasing gearing beyond what is regarded as a safe level;
❏   is the cause of overtrading, for instance (i) in the case of the SME which is trying to expand into larger or more competitive market segments than those with which it has hitherto had experience; or (ii) in the case of the unsustainable commitments described in Chapter 26.

CASE EXAMPLE

Carillion plc – Carillion plc was a large international UK company diversified in to three broad market segments. These were (i) construction, (ii) the building and servicing of rail infrastructure (including the UK's HS2), and (iii) the provision of business services, in particular to the UK Government. It held about 450 government contracts with the ministries for education, health, justice, transport and defence. It was a significant sub- contractor to Network Rail, and also to the Canadian Government. Its collapse in early 2018 resulted in part from:

❏   very significant delivery delays, *costs of poor quality (COPQ)* including necessary remedial work associated with structural faults, and various other cost overruns on some of its largest construction projects; *resulting in*

❏ losses and consequent write-offs totalling £1 billion incurred on what had proved to be unprofitable contracts; *and*

❏ the accumulation of an unsustainable level of debt; exacerbated by

❏ delays in receiving payment from international customers; *and also by*

❏ its apparently extensive use of (expensive) reverse factoring (getting banks to pay its bills direct to creditors): *and*

❏ ineffective pricing and risk analysis; *associated with*

❏ what the BBC described as a "desperate" search for new contracts, and a consequential under-pricing of bids to try to ensure future business and incoming cash flow; *and*

❏ the low profit margins (and high break-even points) that characterise contracts in the highly competitive markets served by the company.

Commentators suggested that the company had over-reached itself at a time when market demand was slackening. It issued profit warnings in 2017 (even after which it was awarded further railway contracts valued at £1.53 billion by the Government). It suffered a share price collapse in the July. The BBC then commented that the company eventually "buckled under the weight of a massive £1.5 billion debt pile", exacerbated additionally by a £587 million pension deficit. Subsequent negotiations between the company, its lenders (including Santander, HSBC, and Barclays) and the UK Government achieved nothing and the company was put into administration. But by then it owed £1 billion to the many (maybe 30,000) firms in its supply chain. Estimates suggest that some of these creditors may get less than a penny back for every pound they are owed by Carillion.

The company only had £29 million in cash before going bankrupt. Its bosses had already been criticised for paying enhanced dividends to shareholders even as its pension deficit grew. In the meantime the UK Government has had to underwrite the cost of Carillion's public sector contracts in order to ensure the continuation of vital services.

The cost of Carillion – according to a 2018 report issued by the National Audit Office (NAO) the collapse of Carillion may have cost the UK taxpayer in excess of £150 million *(as value losses)*. The NAO, a key government spending watchdog, criticised the Government Cabinet Office's response to the collapse, suggesting that that the Cabinet Office was unprepared despite the July 2017 profit warning, and continued to make deals with the company worth more than £1 billion. The NAO warned that the Government and its Civil Servants must better "understand the financial health of its major suppliers and avoid creating relationships with those which are already weakened". It is estimated that Carillion's collapse has resulted in the loss of 2300 jobs **(Source: The Week)**.

"Carillion carrion" – to make matters worse, **The Week** reported that in amongst the soul-searching surrounding the collapse of Carillion, 'several large speculators are quietly toasting their foresight in "shorting" (betting against) the company's shares. City hedge funds have made "tens of millions" gambling that Carillion would hit the rocks, with bets reaching "a peak" [in July 2017] just before a profit warning signalled the scale of the group's problems. According to the analysis firm IHS Markit, 18 funds made £80 million from the initial share slump ... but much more is "likely to have been banked since then, after further steep falls."'

The Week concludes that it is 'a pity that the hedgies' suspicions took so long to filter through to politicians and the public'.

LEADERSHIP AND FINANCIAL MANAGEMENT
The use of finance as a key resource, and the governance and control issues associated with that use, are all likely to give rise to dilemmas. *As such, they will constitute critical dilemma sources.* The institution will have no choice but to attempt to manage these dilemmas, and to manage the negative value possibilities that they contain and the risks to which they will give rise. This means:

❏ that skills of financial dilemma management will be an essential part of the Dilemma Management process being described in this Book; *and therefore*

❏ such skills must be a necessary part of the process of enterprise leadership, for instance as described in Chapters 21 and 26.

That is, business, enterprise and community leaders; politicians; charity trustees; and others in positions of financial responsibility need at the very least to be comfortable (if not skilled) around money as the key measure of resource use, scrutiny, control, accountability and assurance.

COMMITMENTS TO DECISIONS

The issue of Dilemmas that result from the making of significant financial commitments to decisions are also dealt with in detail in Chapter 26 of this Book.

Financial Strategy and Management

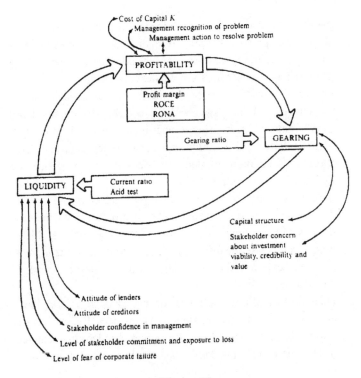

Figure 12
The Corporate Failure Cycle

Chapter Sixteen
Security and Safeguarding

Estimates of fraud in the NHS now exceed £1 billion per year.

SOME SECURITY OBJECTIVES

Decisions about security objectives, and any dilemmas associated with them, are firstly predicated on the question "who or what is the organisation trying to secure?" The answer to this question might include any or all of:

❏ **people** – whose security or safeguarding should (in theory) always take priority. People's Human Rights and personal privacies are based on the most basic assumption that they will be protected against harm – from whatever quarter;

❏ **locations** – which may be specified and managed to secure the integrity of the assets and the people who are in them. This might include housing or apartments, hospitals at the risk of potentially fatal infection, nuclear or defence installations, sports or entertainments stadia, transportation hubs frequented by large volumes of travellers, etc;

❏ **processes** – such as the industrial, political or transportation. The dynamic or extended nature of such processes may increase the risk of harm, increase the probability of operational dilemmas, and increase the difficulty of security. Witness the increasing time scale of delays associated with securing the work of airports and airline companies;

❏ **events** – such as popular music concerts characterised by large, enclosed (and potentially emotional) audiences. Recent security failures (perhaps caused by cost-cutting?) under circumstances of terrorist attack have led to catastrophic human losses in the UK;

❏ **property** – UK law has historically placed significant emphasis on securing property, in part because of the significant political and economic influence of property owners, and the emphasis on the stewardship of assets described in Chapters 14 and 15; *and which is related to the securing of*

❏ **assets** – as a specific categorisation of property, now exemplified for instance by the compilation and maintenance of asset registers used (i) for security purposes and (ii) for the performance measurement described in various chapters; *this category is likely to be augmented by a separate category of*

❏ **data and information (cybersecurity)** – whose value, whether for personal, business, political, defence, intelligence- seeking purposes, (etc) has become critical. The need to secure such data and intelligence from the threat of hacking, theft or damage now takes a high priority. One result is the organisational identification of *information asset holders* who are officially charged with the responsibility of managing information and ensuring its confidentiality and security;

❏ **money** – whose theft remains a target for all manner of physical or electronic criminality, and whose security remains an specialised, expensive and potentially dangerous proposition;

❏ **other items defined as "valuable" or "valuables"** – to include jewellery and art works whose size, portability and value may make them an attractive target for specialised criminal activity. Disposing of such items provides the criminal with significant and risky dilemmas, perhaps making apprehending thieves more probable than the actual recovery of what was stolen. The bulk industrial theft of uninsured jewellery stock-in-trade from protective vaults in London's Hatton Garden showed how determined criminals may become in testing established security under this heading.

SPECIFIC SECURITY RISK

Such security objectives may have to be further refined where an entity is categorised as being "at specific risk". The level of complexity as an event or concept characteristic, and the risk of dilemmas needing to be managed may be enhanced for instance where:

❏ there is a risk to children as Minors, or to those categorised in any way as "protected" (also see below);

❏ there is a risk to the public from terrorist attacks whose probability of occurrence may to some degree be predicted from intelligence-gathering sources;

❏ there is highly sensitive or confidential data, to whose cybersecurity reference was made above;

❏ criminality may be explained by drug distribution, patterns of inter-gang dynamics, or cultural hostility (etc.);

❏ the incidence of football hooliganism will have to be planned for by the police, and decisions made as to who will pay for the cost of its deterrence;

❏ the likely incidence of specific security events may require hospital Accident & Emergency departments to maintain expensive contingency plans which imply the diverting of resources from apparently more desirable alternative uses. This is an opportunity cost dilemma;

❏ bio-security processes aimed at maintaining plant stock integrity against pests and diseases;

❏ certain art works are at risk of theft, for instance by the criminal agents of wealthy private collectors.

SAFEGUARDING

Certain categories of people are deemed to be at such specific security risk that, for example in the UK, their *vulnerability* is deemed to justify the implementation of official *safeguarding*. These categories include:

❏ children (Minors) or young people judged to be *vulnerable*, for instance to such risks as female genital mutilation (FGM, to which reference has been made in earlier chapters, and in the Author's two Equality books); physical, sexual or psychological harassment and abuse; cultural brainwashing as extreme form of social conditioning; forced under-age marriage; cyberbullying; internet corruption, pornography, violence, perversion, or damaging of personal capacity; or "so- called "modern slavery", etc;

❏ temporary or casual workers contracted to work in environments (i) where (perhaps unknown to them in advance) their Health &

Safety or Equality Rights cannot be (or are not), for whatever reason guaranteed and secured beforehand; and (ii) in which they subsequently find themselves (and their personal safety and / or dignity) to be in what proves to be an unsafe or unfit place of work;

❏ elderly sufferers of incurable or terminal illnesses, people with dementia, or those at risk of abuse in care homes, etc; *and more specifically*

❏ those people subject to **UK Deprivation of Liberty Safeguards**, who are deemed (i) to lack personal capacity, (ii) not to be capable of responsibility for their own actions, (iii) potentially to constitute a danger to themselves and others, and (iv) to require external advocacy services in order to protect their interests; *or*

❏ the mentally afflicted, for instance restrained under Sectioning Orders of the UK Mental Health Act 1986, and specifically Section 136.

WHY SECURE OR SAFEGUARD?

There are a large number of reasons as to why the processes of security or safeguarding are necessary to the management of the dilemmas to which events or concepts affecting them give rise. These might include any or all of the following:

❏ the assurance of Human Rights and established ethical paradigms;

❏ the assurance of the Rule of Law, and the Judicial management of criminality;

❏ Health & Safety and Duty of Care requirements, freedom from avoidable incidents;

❏ the need to plan for the potential scale of human, material, and non-material losses, for instance in terms of replacement, compensation, insurance, prestige or reputation;

❏ the signalling of intent or sentiment, for example through political, media or investor relations processes;

❏ the demonstration of assurance or reassurance eg to the public, to voters, to stakeholders or shareholders, to quality assurance agencies (etc);

❑ the countering of negative or hostile political, institutional or media comment; *associated with*

❑ the specific need for crisis management described in Chapter 18.

SOME SECURITY DILEMMAS

Examples of dilemmas associated with security and safeguarding issues or events might include:

❑ the definition and level of stakeholder risk tolerance in general;

❑ the making of decisions about institutional or political budgetary priorities in conditions of a constrained availability of resources; *or*

❑ the use (or requisite use) of Management by Exception and Pareto's 80% – 20% Rule by which the use of resources is concentrated only on the 20% of intelligence leads that are deemed to identify the 80% of the most potentially likely or serious incidents or events, and for which there will be a low tolerance of risk. The remaining 80% of leads are deemed to have only a 20% chance of occurrence and risk tolerance of them will (perhaps unavoidably) have to be higher;

❑ use of Zero Based Budgeting (ZBB) as described in Chapter 14 and as applied in Chapter 19, especially in circumstances characterised by changing security needs or developing miscreant innovation;

❑ dealing with sensitive communities and religions such as Muslims from whom critical intelligence may sometimes have to be collected in the UK under potential conditions of cultural hostility and / or racist attitudes on the part of the wider community;

❑ protecting lives or assets even where this "gives away" intelligence expensively gained (for instance as in the case of the WWII bombing of Coventry which was known about before the event), or vice-versa?

❑ making decisions about the number of agencies to be directly or indirectly involved in security matters, with the concomitant risk of secret or confidential information "leaking out". Are all agencies "singing from the same hymn sheet"? What is the likelihood of occurrence of negatively serendipitous events such as people walking down Whitehall with open files, or loss of laptop computers, or officials who "mis-spoke" (etc?);

❏ the specific management of public (and equally important, media) reaction to terrorist atrocities;

❏ the specific management of public (and equally important) media reaction to perceived failures of institutional management (eg fires in tower blocks) or security (eg on London Underground). UK media reaction may now be highly sensationalised, febrile or hysterical – perhaps in order (for competitive, ideological, or whatever other reason) to create or to enhance the crises to be described in Chapter 18.

POLICY DECISIONS TO DEAL WITH LIKELY DILEMMAS

Decisions about how to deal with dilemmas that arise from perceived security and safeguarding needs may have to be based on policies associated with:

❏ what resources are deemed to be desirable or required; *and*
❏ perceptions of the various opportunity costs of those resources;
❏ the definition of what form the concept of "deterrence" might take;
❏ a definition of the required level of crisis management capability and validation;
❏ the nature of the necessary communication and relationship architecture with other relevant agencies;
❏ perception (as dealt with in Chapter 9);
❏ the collecting of intelligence;
❏ establishing norms or paradigms of what is, or is not deemed to be "predictable" as an event characteristic;
❏ the available or chosen patterns of response;
❏ the available or chosen methods of containment;
❏ the available or chosen methods of prevention;

❏ the available or chosen methods of assurance and reassurance eg to the UK Government Home Office, politicians, stakeholders, the general public, etc;

❏ the available or chosen punishment paradigms, which might range from attempted terrorist rehabilitation through to execution, and even the payment of "blood money";

❏ methodologies for accumulating required *experience*, with processes for review, Knowledge Management, and the subsequent training of those tasked with intelligence seeking, implementing security policies, legal prosecution, etc.

THE RULES OF EVIDENCE

The judicial management or resolution of security and safeguarding dilemma analysis may ultimately have to be consistent with the *Rules of Evidence*. These will require the demonstration by the prosecution of:

❏ intent;
❏ motive;
❏ risk posed to others;
❏ means;
❏ opportunity;
❏ probability.

SECURITY, SAFEGUARDING AND LATER CHAPTERS OF THIS BOOK

Dilemmas of security and safeguarding may then be subject to:

❏ the process of the analysis of risk and uncertainty described in Chapter 17;

❏ the process of crisis analysis and management described in Chapter 18;

❏ the process of mapping described in Chapter 19;

❏ processes of strategic management and dilemma leadership described in Chapters 20 and 21;

❏ other processes of making dilemma decisions described in Parts Four and Five.

Chapter Seventeen
Risk and Uncertainty Management

This chapter analyses the potential for *Risk and Uncertainty* associated with dilemmas and the Dilemma Management process in societies and their institutions. Reference to Risk and Uncertainty has already been made at various points in previous chapters of this Book.

DILEMMA RISK AND UNCERTAINTY DEFINED
The process of risk assessment and risk management has two components. Each is summarised below.

Risk defined – the concept of dilemma risk may be defined for the purpose of this chapter in terms of decision-making that is to some degree characterised (i) by a knowledge of the *alternative solutions* available to the decision-maker; and (ii) by some knowledge of the *probability* of occurrence of these various alternative outcomes. That is, the likelihood of achieving any one of the available options may at least be estimated, or a forecast for it created.

Uncertainty defined – the concept of dilemma uncertainty may be defined in terms of decision-making that is characterised (i) by a lack of knowledge of the likely alternative resolutions or outcomes available to the decision-maker; and (ii) by a lack of knowledge of the probability of occurrence of the alternative outcomes that might be identified. That is, the likelihood of attaining any one of the potential alternative resolutions, outcomes or non-resolutions may be difficult or even impossible to predict or to forecast.

SOME TYPES OF DILEMMA RISK AND UNCERTAINTY
Types of dilemma risk and uncertainty may usefully be categorised as follow:

❑ those associated with the potential for *direct damage*; *and*
❑ those associated with the potential for *resource and value loss*.

DILEMMAS AND DIRECT DAMAGE

The process of dilemma identification and Dilemma Management may firstly identify and categorise types of risk and uncertainty which are associated with *the potential for causing direct damage*. Direct damage could take any of a number of forms. These are summarised below on a scale from *macro* (broad categories) to *micro* (specific categories).

❏   generic damage resulting from a failure to diagnose, understand or acknowledge the Dilemma Sources as described in this Book;

❏   political damage, for instance associated with an over-reliance on ideology or journalistic opinionation, or with a failure to hear and to learn from the Voice of the Voter, the Voice of the Taxpayer, or the Voice of the Victim. The potential consequences of the UK's 2016 "Brexit" Referendum were described in such contexts in earlier chapters;

❏   direct financial, economic and asset damage, for instance as described in the next Section below under the heading of loss of resource value;

❏   legal damage, such as that self-inflicted by the BBC in its attempt to justify so-called "public interest disclosure" in the case of the claimed invasion of the personal privacy of Sir Cliff Richard;

❏   damage resulting from failures of regulatory compliance; or from breaches of Health And Safety at Work (HASAWA), Data Management and GDPR, General Duty, or Duty of Care regulations (etc). Issues of litigation are dealt with in Chapter 18;

❏   reputational damage, such as in the UK Ratner Jewellery, Saatchi & Saatchi, local authority childcare and child abuse cases, NHS Stafford Hospital, etc;

Direct (micro) personal injury risks (whether fatal, physical or mental) – for instance arising (i) from the *security or safeguarding issues* described in Chapter 16; or (ii) such as those inflicted on the *armed and uniformed services* as a result of Human Rights, Duty of Care, Health and Safety, or equipment shortcomings; or failures adequately to arm police at key moments; or political indecision, vacillation or so-called "political correctness" (e.g. see Chapters 8 and Part Five); and (iii) other failures of leadership, policy or decision-making (etc) resulting from an ineffective Dilemma Management process.

DILEMMAS, RESOURCE AND VALUE LOSS
The risk of value loss – where the implementation of any particular chosen strategy involves the combination and use of the *resources of the enterprise or the institution*, the objectives may include:

❏ *the generation or adding of value* as a result of the combination and use of resources or assets in the relevant value chain, value chains, or relationship architectures such that a *positive return* may be obtained from the investment in these resources over the time during which they are in use. This return may be measured in outcome terms such as patient treatment success rates or improvements in public health; enhanced voter satisfaction; improvements in neighbourhood, childcare or community management; reduced household indebtedness; positive financial contribution earned, profit margin, return on investment, payback, net present value (NPV) or internal rate of return (IRR); and so on; *and*

❏ *the maintenance of the real value of the resource or assets* invested in the implementation of the chosen strategy. *Example:* if you have an investment in shares or unit trusts, are they worth more or less than last year? Similarly, how quickly are service pressures and healthcare dilemmas contributing to the wearing out of staff and operational facilities in the national healthcare system? For how long will any particular hospital infrastructure or regime of infection control be viable before expensive re-organisation and renewal in the face of changing pressures becomes essential? How does a government keep its military security capability from deteriorating in (unknown and unpredictable) conditions where they may suddenly be called upon to deal with an highly motivated, desperate, dangerous and well-equipped adversary?

In evaluating the choice of strategies and the preferred modes of implementation, institutions will need to remain aware that any investment of resources *may give rise to the risk that those resources or assets lose some of their value or even disappear altogether*. The potential for loss of value *may firstly* occur as a result of such *internal sources* of dilemma risk and uncertainty as:

❑ ineffective or inadequate dilemma identification and management process capability on the part of the responsible staff;

❑ issues with diagnostic and decision-making capacity described in later chapters of this Book;

❑ the direct loss of relevant staff competence (for instance through retirement; through the "poaching" or "head-hunting" of key managerial staff, technologists, engineers, specialist professionals, or experienced decision-makers; or instead the failure to identify and to train new and appropriately skilled staff);

❑ ineffective governance or leadership, leadership naïvete, or the exhaustion/erosion of leadership motivation and willpower.

The potential for loss of value *may secondly* occur as a result of such *external sources* of dilemma risk and uncertainty as:

❑ shifts in the external environment or market;

❑ sudden or drastic changes in demand pattern or volumes, such as have in the past affected international sales of grass-fed British beef;

❑ the impact of technological change (the Boeing 707 killed off the transatlantic ocean liner at a stroke); *or*

❑ the interaction of innovation dynamics; new product, process or service development; and product or process obsolescence as described at various points in this Book;

❑ the impact of powerful government, environmental, or environmentalist influences on demand (for instance on the attitude towards the consumption of cigarettes; alcoholic, sugary or stimulant drinks; diesel fuel; or on operational process (eg the generation of electricity by means of the use of nuclear or wind power, or the burning of fossil or biomass fuels);

❏ the "wearing out" of state institutions and infrastructures (such as roads or prisons) as a result of usage rates for which such entities or assets were not specified when put in place;

❏ the likelihood of (maybe unprovable?) political corruption, or instead "cronyism";

❏ the emergence of powerful criminal, mafia, or terrorist influences.

Risk and the level of resource commitment – the risk of value loss may be related to *the proportion of total available resources or assets being committed to any one venture*. This is an "eggs in the basket" argument. Do you put all your eggs in one basket? What then happens if you drop the basket?! The greater the proportion of its resources that the institution commits to the implementation of any one strategy, the more pronounced may be the consequences if the strategy is unsuccessful for instance because of its failure to properly understand and to manage the potential dilemmas involved in the project. This lack of success may be clearly demonstrated in terms of losses to taxpayers, stakeholders and investors; in terms of a loss of institutional credibility accompanied by reputational damage; and in the form of criticism (or replacement) of enterprise leadership.

Risk and time scale – the risk of value or asset loss, or of negative financial or fiscal return may be a function of the *duration* and *time scale* of the resource commitment. For instance:

❏ the longer the time scale, the more possible it is that the institution will suffer exposure to the dilemma risk and uncertainty being described in this chapter;

❏ the longer the time scale, *the less certain may be any of* (i) the generation of the requisite voter, taxpayer, patient, stakeholder, customer or client value; or (ii) the generation of added value, and the return on the investment of stakeholders; or (iii) the maintenance of the real value of the assets involved; or even (iv) the actual survival of those assets, *but*

❏ the longer the time scale, *the proportionately greater may be the eventual requirement* for the generation of value, and for the return on the resources invested by stakeholders. Long term investments, for instance in health or social care, neighbourhood management, or high-speed rail infrastructure may raise the dilemma that (i) obtaining a return on investment may be uncertain and unpredictable over such a long time frame; whilst (ii) at the same time it may become increasingly difficult to convince voters as taxpayers, stakeholders, or alternatively shareholders of the viability of the strategy being proposed, and to persuade them to continue to fund the necessary investment in it. This syndrome was demonstrated by the failure of expensive past UK investments in high-tech weapons systems (such as "Blue Streak", or surveillance systems such as "Nimrod"), and their partial replacement by proven international suppliers such as the USA's Lockheed Martin, Northrop Grumman, or Boeing.

DILEMMA RISK MANAGEMENT LIMITATIONS

The types of risk and uncertainty with which the process of dilemma identification and Dilemma Management may be associated, whether for instance (i) having the potential for *direct damage*; or (ii) with the potential for *resource and value loss* may be characterised by significant risk management limitations. Earlier chapters have noted that dilemmas may present as events, concepts, circumstances or contingencies which have an substantial influence or impact. These events, concepts, circumstances or contingencies *may not however respond to standard processes of risk assessment and risk management* such as those routinely used in the UK business, public and security sectors. Earlier chapters noted for instance that dilemma properties might include any of:

- ❏ a lack of precedence or consistency;
- ❏ value dilemmas;
- ❏ the existence of "unknown unknowns";
- ❏ a lack of agreement about definition, or indeed actual conflict amongst stakeholders as to how to proceed (as for example in the political, healthcare, local government, charitable, and public sector contexts; retail management, or in the professional football industry);

❏ directly conflicting ideologies, (e.g. such as in international relations);

❏ features of mutual exclusivity, such as incompatible expectations or Voices;

❏ constituting a source of complexity or instability, (e.g. again as in international relations);

❏ significant negative issues associated with the possibility of reconciliation or resolution;

❏ irreconcilable opinionation.

MESSY, WICKED, AND WICKED MESS RISK

Risk management limitations may then be exacerbated (made worse) where the dilemmas that are the basis of events, concepts, circumstances or contingencies might be categorised by **David Hancock** (2010) as being *messy, wicked, or wicked mess* in character.

Messy Risk – which Hancock describes as having 'high levels of *system* (or structural) *complexity* and comprise clusters of interrelated or interdependent' issues, paradigms, problems or threats. Messy Risk dilemmas may have to be resolved by agreed *and* co-ordinated or "joined up" thinking by the parties to them. *The application of fragmented or single-discipline based thinking may be insufficient or counter-productive*, for instance where a number of agencies as stakeholders operating with different systems and different cultures, capabilities, or ideologies are dealing with issues of indebtedness, health or social care in the community, security issues, or with marginalised groups (having a low Voice of the Victim) that "fall differentially below the collective radar";

Wicked Risk – which may be described as being characterised by high levels of *cultural, attitudinal and behavioural complexity* in which there are inconsistencies, disagreements and conflicts in ideologies, 'opinions, assumptions, beliefs and perspectives. Under conditions of high behavioural complexity it is difficult to get people to agree on what should be done because they see the world differently and because they have different preferences and goals'. It may (i) be difficult to conceptualise dilemmas (for instance associated with the assurance of Human Rights in respect of the care of the vulnerable young, the elderly or the disabled), or (ii) to achieve stakeholder agreement on definitions, objectives, financial involvement, or modes of implementation and validation.

Wicked Mess Risk – which Hancock describes as an *ultimate condition* in which both system and behavioural complexity co-exist and interact. Dilemmas to which this interaction gives rise may be resolvable, or they may not. Hancock notes that systems complexity requires a capacity for a high level of conceptual thinking, whilst behavioural complexity requires a high level of relationship and negotiative skill in terms of architecture management.

Case Example: dilemmas associated with the implementation, assurance and validation of people's *Human Rights* cannot be resolved if there is no agreement or likelihood of compromise amongst the parties involved as to how to deal with them, or how to facilitate any resolution process. This syndrome, whatever form it has morphed into at any given time, has remained for many decades an unfortunate feature of political and social policy in the national and regional governance of the United States. Rights issues in the US are a Devil's Brew of conflicting ideologies, religions, perceptions and attitudes; discrimination against blacks, First Nation peoples, and women; and made worse by easy access to firearms that can be used to promote individual grievances, or instead to give a lethal edge to mental illness in a community which has (by European standards) only a restricted access to free on-demand healthcare.

CASE EXAMPLE
Uncertainty Avoidance and security issues – security agencies may face dilemmas based on varying perceptions of the Uncertainty Avoidance described in Chapter 6. They may have to decide whether it is judged to be preferable to be seen to be doing something in the face of an apparent security threat (for example putting armed police or troops onto the streets) irrespective of the relevance of such an action (i) to the resolution of the dilemma involved; or rather (ii) to the apparent or perceived desirability of resolving that dilemma under

the prevailing circumstances; or instead (iii) incurring the risk of communicating warnings for instance to terrorist organisations that intelligence gathering about them is ongoing (and thereby causing them to change the plans and personnel about which that intelligence gathering is currently focussed).

Chapter Eighteen
Crisis Management

DILEMMAS AND CRISIS

Processes of Security and Safeguarding (Chapter 16), and Risk and Uncertainty Management (Chapter 17) may be further complicated where the dilemmas which are the basis of events, circumstances or contingencies they describe result in the emergence or creation of *crises*.

RECAP

Relevant dilemmas of opinionation were described in Chapter 8. Issues of perception were described in Chapter 9. The potential effects of excessive individualism, individual focus, and reluctance to consider the need for personal responsibility were identified in Chapter 10.

Reference has also been made in this Book to the effects of the *febrile and unpredictable behaviour* of pressure groups and the media (including social media) as (i) sources of, or (ii) exploiters of dilemmas. This chapter shows how they themselves may become the drivers of crises.

CRISIS DEFINED

A crisis may firstly be defined *as a set of events or conditions that could pose a serious threat (i) to the basic structures, and (ii) to the fundamental norms and values of any technological, social, political, management, information, or administrative system.*

Secondly, Borodzicz defines a crisis as a potentially negative or dangerous situation requiring an urgent diagnosis and response, but in which the risks for decision makers may be difficult to define owing to the uncertainty and lack of clarity of that situation. It may also be the case in such situations that the effect of any response is likely to be unclear, controversial, or indeed the source of further dilemmas.

Borodzicz describes a general category of crisis events which arise out of dilemmas associated with a lack of congruence (that is, a mis-match) between management processes associated (i) with operational or technological systems, and (ii) with human and information systems within (iii) the context of the social architecture described by Hancock in Chapter 17 (and in Figure 13 at the end of this chapter). This lack of congruence or mis- match may arise for example from the existence of any of the following:

❏ interdependency amongst variables;
❏ vulnerability to disturbance, unplanned events, or external intervention;
❏ complexity;
❏ potential for system failure;
❏ excessive pressures for profit generation, cost reduction or fiscal rectitude which have had the unplanned consequence of taking operational activities below a critical threshold, for instance in terms of prevailing health and safety or security criteria. Controversial examples in the UK railway industry have (i) been crashes resulting in loss of life, which *inter alia* were caused by ineffective track maintenance, or (ii) disputes over the responsibility of train guards in supervising passenger safety;
❏ a failure to match positions of leadership and operational responsibility with the requisite personal intellectual capacity and competence (for instance as described in Chapters 20 and 21); *perhaps exacerbated by*
❏ the exercise by senior staff or influential role holders of excessive personal brashness, aggression, individualism, greed, cronyism, incompetence, or uncontrolled public opinionation.

Worse, the emergence of a crisis *may not be immediately apparent* to decision makers who would be responsible for dealing with it. Borodzicz suggests that crises are ill-structured situations in terms of technical, social and cultural contexts. The greater the degree of ill-structure, the more difficult the incident becomes for recognition and management; the more may be the number of agencies that become involved, and the more agendas that may become juxtaposed. Such a spiral can lead to disaster.

Regester & Larkin add that a crisis may then become an event which causes an institution or an organisation to become the subject of widespread, and potentially unfavourable attention from the national and international media and other stakeholder groups such as voters, customers, shareholders, employees and their families, politicians, trade unionists, patients, and environmental pressure groups (etc) who, for one reason or another, have an interest in the ongoing activities of that institution or organisation.

INDUCED CATASTROPHE

Nudell & Antokol define an induced catastrophe as a category of crisis that results directly from the *intentional activities* of individuals or groups who are able to exploit conditions to which emergent or unresolved dilemmas have given rise. Two types of induced catastrophe are identified under this heading.

A non-security catastrophe – is any form of ecological, human, social, political, financial, corporate, or business crisis that result from the incidence of dilemmas which have become associated with negative or hostile *external* conditions or event characteristics; and/ or instead result from dilemmas which have revealed such *internal* features as ineffective leadership, personal or political misjudgement, precipitate action, mismanagement, ineffective government policy, greed, incompetence, corruption, maladministration, or anti-social, unethical or illegal practice.

A security type catastrophe – is any kind of crisis that is associated with such illegal features as extortion, fraud, corruption, the tampering with or contamination of product or process, sabotage, arson, kidnapping, bombing or other forms of violent attack, terrorist activity, etc. Such catastrophes have bedevilled Europe in recent years, culminating for instance in fatal terrorist attacks on civilians in London, Paris, Barcelona and Nice (and to which reference is made at various points of this Book).

Case Example: **"total crap"** – in 1991 the UK entrepreneur Gerald Ratner described his products as "total crap" in a speech to the UK Institute of Directors. Regester & Larkin comment that Ratner's 'upmarket audience thought the joke was funny and true. It was next day's tabloids, notably the *Sun*, which devoted five pages to the story which tore Ratner apart for his mocking insincerity towards the customers who had made him his fortune'.

HOW TO CREATE A CRISIS

Institutional or governmental crises and catastrophes may be created or exacerbated by *pressure groups,* or by *the media* in all its various forms. **This process may be deliberate** (particularly if it will make good copy). It would be undertaken in order to further some particular objective or purpose espoused by that pressure group, media or social media.

Or the process might be opportunistic. Pressure groups and the media may be highly skilled at rapidly exploiting the sudden emergence of dilemmas as "trigger" events for creating *a story* to be associated with external perceptions of the developing crisis or calamity. This point has been made in earlier chapters of this Book (and also in Chapter 26). Curtin *et al* suggest some characteristics of such a *manufactured or created crisis*. These might include any or all of the following.

Simplicity of concept – a crisis may be created if the dilemma can be defined in very simple or unequivocal terms. Curtin *et al* comment that 'this allows sides to be taken, particularly by the media. So, genetically modified (GM) foods are bad…organic foods are good'. Some so-called "celebrities" have recently claimed that gluten (as well as many other perfectly acceptable foodstuffs) are bad, and should be avoided by everyone. They offer no scientific proof but rely on people's gullibility when reading what is actually something (*a fad*) a jobbing actress thinks, but who has no necessary (nutritional) qualifications to say so. Quite apart from the potential for the malnutrition of the children of said gullibles! Have you had your Vitamin D today?

Scientifically complex – like nutrition and paradoxically, the science surrounding the dilemma 'must be complex and impenetrable to the ordinary person. This is essential because otherwise people would be able to make reasoned decisions on what is right and what is wrong'. This syndrome was clearly illustrated in the disastrous UK agricultural cases (i) of BSE in cattle (and the fears of its potential connection with CJD in humans); and (ii) in the later incidence of foot and mouth disease. These calamities resulted from massive governmental, farming, and food industry failures to accept and to deal with policy and cost dilemmas associated with slaughtering and food supply; with the allocation of associated subsidies and the application of compensation schemes; with some incidence of fraud; and in the case of BSE the failure to differentiate and "ring-fence" grass-fed (Aberdeen Angus) cattle who were never at risk of contamination in the first place.

Data rich – governmental and corporate environments in Anglo-Saxon countries are characterised by a large variety, diversity, and volume of information that is openly available to anyone who wishes to access it, and who can use it to create external perceptions (or "spin") about issues or events in which they have an interest. Curtin *et al* comment that in this respect 'there is no truth, only *data*. From this data one can manufacture information, perspectives and assumptions which may be accepted by other people as *Knowledge*' (for example as in the case of gluten, to which reference is made above).

The law of the absolute – scientifically complex and data rich events make ideal dilemma controversies. There has, by definition, to be an element of uncertainty and doubt within any controversy about events or circumstances associated with such dilemmas. The more people think they know about something, the less they might actually know. This is the "law of the absolute". As science advances, it throws new light but also shows up the imperfection of existing understanding. As a result, anything may be categorised as potentially unsafe or dangerous if someone wishes to make such a case, even if the risks are actually miniscule. Curtin *et al* for instance comment of the Perrier Water case that 'to the question "can you categorically assure me that drinking mineral water with tiny traces of benzene in it will never harm me?" the categorical answer "no" is not available'.

Slogan-ability – people should be able to summarise or to encapsulate the crisis and its meaning in a few succinct words. For instance, genetically modified crops may be used to manufacture "Frankenstein foods"! Curtin *et al* comment that 'slogans like this are hard to argue with – generally because they have enough truth in them to make them credible, and they have no "small print" to qualify them For the media there is no choice: the words to be used are those that are the most understandable or those that shock the most'.

THE WORKING OF MURPHY'S LAW

The triggering of a crisis or catastrophe may be made harder to identify, or more difficult to deal with where Murphy's Law comes into play. Murphy's Law states that *if something can go wrong, it will go wrong*. For instance, in the case of apparent dilemmas that as trigger events could lead to the development of a crisis:

❏   the necessary people will not be in the right place at the right time to deal with unfolding events;
❏   the crisis will happen late at night, on Friday, during the weekend, or during a public holiday;
❏   the unpredictable will happen;
❏   people and systems that normally operate to the highest efficiency will suddenly or inexplicably fail;
❏   things will get worse before there is any chance of them getting better.

Curtin *et al* comment that 'it is uncanny that when a crisis strikes, it always seems to be at the time of holidays, weekends or when people are not prepared'. They suggest that the media or pressure groups who are responding to, creating, or developing a crisis are likely to use this syndrome to good effect, choosing 'their timing with deadly accuracy'.

CASE EXAMPLE

Saatchi & Saatchi – the (then) (male) Chairman of the Saatchi & Saatchi advertising agency commented in 2016 that "the debate on gender bias in the advertising industry is all over" and that he did not think that "the lack of women in leadership roles was a problem". These opinions were published on a Friday. During the weekend that followed, the press and social media reported the critical reaction of the parent company (Groupe Publicis). The Chairman's views were then rebutted on the following Monday morning's UK BBC Radio Four by another (this time female) senior executive of the Saatchi Company, and by Wednesday the Chairman had submitted his resignation. But by then the damage had been done. All and sundry had had a field day at Saatchi & Saatchi's expense. The massive and on-going dilemma associated with the promotion of women to positions of responsibility, in this case in a notoriously masculine-oriented, opinionated and sexist global industry, had claimed yet another individual victim, who will as a result have wrecked his own (lucrative) career. It will have in addition inflicted significant *reputational damage* on the company. What price advertising contracts now with clients who have female CEOs?

Regester & Larkin comment in respect of such occurrences that 'in our experience, some executives have difficulty admitting that their companies could face a crisis because in doing so they would have to question the excellence of their company and, in some cases their own professionalism. Others subscribe to the fallacy that well-managed companies simply do not have crises'.

LITIGATION

Ultimately, Nudell & Antokol note that *the risk of litigation* and *the response to it may* have to be a critical factor in governmental or institutional response to crises or induced catastrophes to which unresolved or unresolvable dilemmas have given rise. Litigation for instance has become an over-riding feature of the aftermath of the UK Hillsborough football disaster, or of child care abuse cases.

Nudell & Antokol comment that 'regardless of the type of emergency, organisations that neglect advance preparations (for dilemmas and crises) run the risk of becoming targets for lawsuits. And, should the emergency prove to have been avoidable or, if unavoidable, mishandled, then the ramifications of such lawsuits, coupled with adverse publicity may trouble the organisation for years after the event'.

DIRECT THREAT

Finally here, the failure (i) to diagnose the risk or uncertainty associated with any particular dilemma, or (ii) to deal with crises or litigation that result from that failure may result in the emergence of a *direct threat* to the institution. This threat could take any or all of such forms as:

❑ the direct damage described in Chapter 17;
❑ the resource, asset or value loss also described in Chapter 17;
❑ the evident failure of any risk assessment and risk management strategies that might have been put in place, resulting in the likelihood of public or stakeholder perceptions of mismanagement, incompetence, or a loss of institutional control;
❑ the development of unresolvable messy, wicked, and wicked mess risk as described in Chapter 17, also resulting in a loss of control.

Ultimately, the *continued existence, credibility, or viability of the institution* itself may be threatened. Governments may fall. Political parties may unravel, disintegrating into factional in- fighting or power plays associated with unresolvable ideological dilemmas. Local government authority departments, such as those associated with child welfare or housing, may be disbanded and placed under the control of external commissioners. Hospitals or care homes may be closed because their operational standards have become unacceptable. Police forces may be merged. And so on.

AN ILLUSTRATIVE DILEMMA RISK SUMMARY

Figure 13 shows a diagrammatic summary of one potential interaction between the Risk, Uncertainty, and Crisis variables described in Chapters 17 and 18. The dilemma continuum is based in this case on *Hancock's risk categories* (a, b, c) to the left; a category of *manageable risk* (described by Hancock) as "tame" (d) and a category of *managed risk* (e) to the right. The degree of Dilemma Risk is plotted as curve "x". The likelihood of successful Dilemma Resolution is plotted as curve "y". The curves "x" and "y" intersect at point "z". It will only be at this point, and to the right of it, that Dilemma Risk may be most effectively managed, and the likelihood of successful Dilemma Resolution maximised.

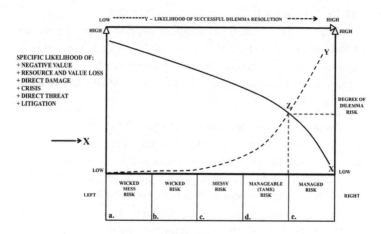

Figure 13
An illustrative dilemma risk

Grenfell Tower – crisis and catastrophe

Part Four

A Dilemma Management Process

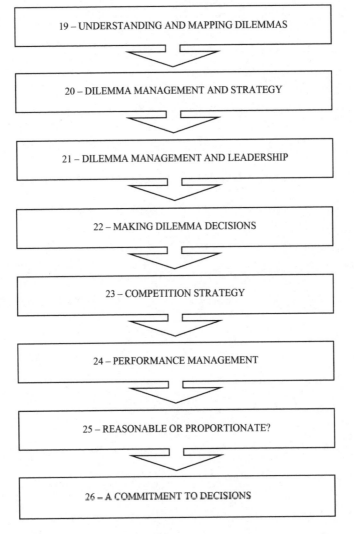

19 – UNDERSTANDING AND MAPPING DILEMMAS

20 – DILEMMA MANAGEMENT AND STRATEGY

21 – DILEMMA MANAGEMENT AND LEADERSHIP

22 – MAKING DILEMMA DECISIONS

23 – COMPETITION STRATEGY

24 – PERFORMANCE MANAGEMENT

25 – REASONABLE OR PROPORTIONATE?

26 – A COMMITMENT TO DECISIONS

Figure 14

Chapter Nineteen

Understanding and Mapping Dilemmas

MANAGEMENT DILEMMAS RECAPPED

Management Dilemmas were defined in Chapter One as a contingency or a set of circumstances in which a choice may, might, or must have to be made between decision alternatives which are at the same time any or all of:

❏ favourable or unfavourable to the decision-maker; *and / or*
❏ likely to put the decision-maker into a position of doubt or uncertainty as to the resolution or resolutions that might be possible; *and / or*
❏ may or may not be resolvable to the complete satisfaction of all parties affected by the dilemma; *and / or*
❏ were created by others whose motives may or may not coincide with those of the decision-maker, or indeed be actively competitive or hostile to them

and in which:

❏ the identification or fixing of the occasion for decision may be unclear or not agreed; *and / or*
❏ the choice between making the decision, or not making it may be unclear or not agreed by the parties to the dilemma.

Chapter One gave as example the existence of two or more variables which must be taken as determinants of diagnosis, policy choice, decision or action; but at the same time:

❏ which may, or may not be congruent, coterminous or conflicting; *and also*
❏ whose interaction may, or may not be congruent or conflicting; *or*
❏ whose interaction may preclude certain other actions, or increase the level of risk associated with such other actions;

❏ *but* whose inter-disciplinarity and need for co-ordination are essential features in policy-making, decision-making, assurance and practice (for instance as in the cases of child safeguarding, mental health care in the community, policing and security matters, or the integrated concept of "Social Care")

and which (i) will act as drivers of the choice of options or outcomes from which diagnoses, decision choices or modes of implementation may have to be made; but (ii) to which the relevant stakeholders may be more or less attached in their scale of priorities; and (iii) whose necessary identification or solution may be associated with varying perceptions of:

❏ what "should (or should not) be done" as compared with "what could (or could not) be done"; *or*
❏ what is politically possible; *or*
❏ what is consistent with available leadership resources, capability and willpower; *or*
❏ prevailing and alternative views based on the concept of opportunity cost (such as those of the Best Value, Lean, Six Sigma, or Public Value type approaches to public expenditure); *and*
❏ which render non-professional, amateurish, subject simplistic, specialist, single interest, micro-local, high power distance, emotional, or what some people term "politically correct" approaches to finding, implementing or assuring solutions as undesirable, invalid, ineffective, or unsustainable **may give rise to Dilemmas.**

UNDERSTANDING MANAGEMENT DILEMMAS

Any generation of options for dealing with dilemmas is dependent on the existence and effective operation *of institutional processes of identification, diagnosis, analysis and mapping*. This applies whether the dilemma is faced by a government, a political party, a charity, a healthcare or social welfare organisation, a company or an entrepreneur, (etc). Previous chapters of this Book have already dealt with:

❏   the issue of the need to manage dilemmas (Chapter 3);
❏   the necessary identification of sources of dilemmas (and the values or ideologies attaching to them) in order to be able to facilitate their resolution (Parts Two and Three); *and specifically for example to include*
❏   issues of time, governance and corporate financial management (Chapters 13 to 15); *and*
❏   issues of security, risk, uncertainty, crisis, litigation and threat (Chapters 16 to 18).

Deciding on the occasion for decision – the Author describes the occasion for decision elsewhere as *a response in time and in current circumstances* to the requirement to undertake some form of positive leadership or management action in respect of that time and circumstance. Examples were described in Parts One and Two. Issues of Leadership are dealt with in Parts Four and Five of this Book. The process of resolving dilemmas will at some stage call (i) for the making of decisions or (ii) for the avoidance of such decision-making. If the former, then the dilemma may be subject to the decision-making and evaluation processes described in the following sections of this chapter, and in later chapters.

Indecision may instead mean leaving the dilemma unresolved, whether deliberately or as a matter of serendipity. This indecision may be a function (i) of some particular prevailing discretion in the organisation; or (ii) of a perception that (for whatever reason) a decision should be put off; or (iii) of a lack of the relevant institutional competence, capability or willpower to deal with it (as described in Part Five). This indecision may be sharpened by perceptions of the risk attaching to any decision-making processes, or by a significant personal or cultural aversion to uncertainty or conflict.

GENERATING DECISION ALTERNATIVES
E.R.Alexander suggests that the range and quality of decision alternatives generated by an institution may be a function of *two inter-related features* of the process by which such alternatives are identified and analysed. **Figure 15 refers.**

The **first variable** of Alexander's model is *the degree to which the search process is systematic and creative in character.* This is shown on the vertical axis of Figure 15 as "search-type, creativity mix". Alexander suggests that decision search processes have two dimensions. The first is the *level of creativity* inherent in the process. The second is the *type of search*, which may range between:

❏ the *systematic* – which search process is structured, ordered, and comprehensive. It "leaves no stone unturned";

❏ the *pragmatic* or *heuristic* – which search process is satisfactory or effective in terms of "common sense" or "practicality". People do what appears to them to be "reasonable" or "sensible" under the circumstances;

❏ being based on *precedent* – which search process is carried out in the manner by which it has always been done. It does not appear to matter to decision-makers that this process might now be out of date, or that it is instead likely to miss new or critical developments that have never been considered before;

❏ being *reactive* or *passive* – which search process lacks any form of pro-activity or creativity, instead for instance simply reacting on a crisis basis to events or threats as they unfold.

The **second variable** of Alexander's model is *the degree to which the search process is pre-empted or "closed".* This is shown on the horizontal axis of Figure 15. This variable indicates the extent to which the process of generating decision alternatives (for instance using the *event or concept characteristics* described in Chapter 4) is an open or instead a restricted one in the institution.

Classic sources of closure (*restrictions* on the type, range, or novelty of the alternatives generated) include:

❏ a restricted focus, restricted values, or an intellectually limited mindset (or "small minds", "closed minds" or "Snowflake" mindsets; and the "detail obsessed" described in earlier chapters and in Part Five); *or*

❏ strongly established but out-dated values and opinions, verging on the dogmatic as described in Chapters 6, 8 and 12; *or*

❑ the fear of new ideas or fear of the need for change;

❑ a high degree of power distance, authoritarianism, and the cen-tralisation of power as described in Chapter 6; *and*

❑ a low degree of trust of other people and ideas, or a high degree of uncertainty avoidance (also described in Chapter 6); *and*

❑ the "not invented here" syndrome in which concepts not orig-inated by the leader or the organisation are rejected precisely because they were not generated internally; *and*

❑ the "we have nothing to learn from them" syndrome, in which "foreign" ideas are rejected precisely because they are foreign, or derive from a source which is not judged as being worthy of being taken seriously. Hence the initial dismissal by European and North American car manufacturers of imported Japanese cars such as the Datsun or the Toyota, with their quality finish and all-inclusive price, because long established car-makers saw no serious competitive threat from them. Such manufac-turers had not even learned the lesson from the earlier post-war Japanese success in dominating the global motor cycle market;

❑ negative value judgements or negative cultural features, in which ideas are rejected because they do not accord with enter-prise value set or culture. For instance, private sector ideas are often rejected by public sector cultures that face a requirement to become more efficient, more responsive to public expecta-tions or client demand, or to meet the Best Value, Lean, or Six Sigma (etc) performance indicators set by the state for the use of taxpayers' money;

❑ strong or hostile professional, political, or ideological forces, which make it difficult to accept new ideas about how things should be done. For instance, should a country's railway sys-tem be (i) nationalised, or (ii) privatised in order to improve its service quality, cost and safety? Should that railway system be expected to make profits, or are subsidies acceptable as a funding solution, for instance to reduce costs to commuters? Do you think that nationalised SNCF (France) with its reputation for operating safety but variable customer service, or instead Union Pacific (USA) as a profit-orientated freight transportation corporation should be allowed to run part (or all) of your country's railway system on a franchise or licence basis, or indeed, China Rail?;

❏ a high level of risk aversion, such that risky but potentially effective or financially viable ideas are automatically rejected if they contain more than a certain degree of risk of loss or failure;

❏ complacency, inertia, and the desire to maintain the status quo; perhaps allied to

❏ an excessive degree of indulgence in the debate, dialectic, and opinionation described in earlier Chapters;

❏ short-termism ("will the decision pay back in two years?").

Alexander suggests that the "best case" is located at the upper left quadrant of the matrix shown in Figure 15. Here there is a minimum of pre-emption, coupled with a systematic and creative search process. Alexander suggests that the "worst case" is located at the bottom right quadrant of the matrix. Here there are severe constraints on the type or range of alternatives that it is permissible to identify. At the same time, the search process is reactive or passive, and is characterised by a lack of creativity.

MAPPING A DILEMMA

A dilemma was conceptualised and shown in Chapter One, Figure 3 as a continuum between two polar extremes. The decision options that comprise the dilemma may most simply be mapped at various points between these extremes. For the specific purposes of Chapter One the extent of the dilemma was shown as most negative on the left and most positive on the right. **If the reader finds this distribution ideologically or "politically incorrect" then the positive may be shown on the** left and the negative on the right.

The meaning of the extreme ends of the continuum may then be categorised and intermediate points interpolated between them in terms of their relative desirability to the decision-maker. In the case of two currently controversial UK cases, the BBC and the NHS, the options might for example be shown using Figure 3 as varying between:

❏ at one end, leave entirely alone and maximise state funding, however this is achieved; *or*

❏ in the middle, resource allocation and funding would be decided by incremental negotiation or compromise over time between the stakeholders involved, almost certainly influenced by powerful individuals, and by media, political, pressure, and trade union groups who will have involved themselves in the matter; *or*

❏ at the other end, break up or franchise / privatise some or all parts of these institutions, offering subsequent but highly targeted financial support (eg to assist the development of cutting edge technologies, drugs, or Six Sigma infection control; world class radio, film and television programming; or the care of the mentally ill, the disabled and the elderly) but insisting on much increased public or user contribution from those deemed able to pay. After all, what is more important: (i) paying for your fags and your new car or (ii) taking proper personal responsibility for your health and your healthcare? This of course assumes that you cannot have both without someone else (ie taxpayers who behave in a more responsible manner than you) having to pay something to subsidise your healthcare – a dilemma indeed!

The dilemma continuum might for the sake of argument have three or five compartments, as shown in Figure 3. Either way, the continuum needs to have a centre compartment. This means that the number of compartments will always be odd (3 or 5 or 7, and so on).

Multiple alternatives – where the process of identifying decision alternatives (described in detail in following Sections of this Chapter) indicates a variety of options attaching to any one compartment, these may be mapped at an angle of 90 degrees to the dilemma continuum, as shown in **Figure 16**. Where the options are positive to, or congruent with, or reinforcing of the *meaning or values* of that compartment, they will be shown *above the continuum*. Options which are deemed undesirable, negative to, incongruent or incompatible with the values of that compartment will be shown *below the continuum*.

MAPPING AND DECISION CRITERIA

The Introduction described a purpose of this Book to be *relevant, usable and useful*. This is the **first set of criteria** upon which the mapping of dilemmas could be based. **Two further types of criteria** are described here, as follow.

These criteria will be applied within whatever form of budgetary management, prioritisation or resource allocation methodology is being applied to the dilemma.

Single value criteria may include any of the following:

❏ units (such as the number of Olympic Gold Medals won, as described in the final Section, below);

❏ time;

❏ financial, such as cost, break-even or profit;

❏ direct measurement of customer or client benefit (eg customer satisfaction, benefit payment effect, or patient treatment success);

❏ direct stakeholder satisfaction;

❏ direct voter and / or taxpayer satisfaction (eg as evidenced by electoral success or failure).

Composite value criteria, including:

❏ unit values converted, including into financial measurements (eg cost per Olympic Gold Medal won);

❏ performance relative to budgetary and project management targets;

❏ financial measurements to include Payback, Net Present Value (NPV), Internal Rate of Return (IRR);

❏ generic economic benefit (however defined);

❏ the *individual*, the *public*, and the *fiscal benefit* of the allocation of taxpayer and other government resources;

❏ efficiency criteria, including Best Value ("economy, efficiency, effectiveness"), Lean, Stretch & Leverage (eg "doing more with less"), Six Sigma, Public Value;

❏ institutional or enterprise performance comparison, treatment success rates, benchmarking leagues; etc.

❏   the efficiency and effectiveness of subsidy, eg state benefit payments, training of 16 to 21 year old "NEETS", railway and transport infrastructures, state investment banks.

Reference has already been made to some of these mapping and decision criteria in earlier chapters of this Book. Other specific dilemma issues of **Performance Measurement and Performance Management** are dealt with separately in Chapter 24.

CASE EXAMPLE

The National Funding of UK Olympic Sports – the UK Olympic Team Great Britain ("Team GB") has in recent years taken a successful *Zero Based Budgeting* (*ZBB*) approach to the *opportunity cost* dilemma associated with resource allocation in support of Team GB's Olympic efforts, as follows.

The dilemma continuum is shown in **Figure 16** as compartments "A", "B" and "C" from left to right. Team GB's preferred option has clearly been compartment "C" on the right. *This is characterised by a self-imposed requirement to maximise the medal tally won, and in particular the winning of gold medals.* Current attitudes appear to favour a "winning orientation" in which competitive sport carries a very high national as well as international priority. A country's reputation may in part be defined by its sporting success. After all, according to Nike, "you do not win silver, you lose gold". Such values separate competitive from community sport. Each should have its own funding, for instance to ensure that future national winners have the opportunity to develop through from the community base.

Compartment "A" – in which "fairness" for all in funding is seen as most desirable. The differentiation between community and competitive sport may be blurred by some, and the issue of equality of sporting opportunity for all may be raised by others. Compartment "A" may be characterised by a high degree of risk- aversion.

Compartment "B" – in which funding allocations are decided on a negotiated and compromise basis, for instance dependent on the views of the most powerful influences (whoever these are) and the media. Resource allocation might be shifted in favour of potentially better performing disciplines? It may have to be accepted that there will be winners and losers in such a process, and that the arguments involved could be driven by status issues amongst the various sports. Decisions made about funding allocation may or may not be relevant to the actual process of winning medals.

Compartment "C" – in which the sole concern is to maximise the number of medals won, as described above. This means an emphasis in resource allocation on achieving gold medals because these determine the final national league listings. This in turn implies developing and playing to the capabilities that are most likely to succeed. Winners do not play to their weaknesses but to their strengths and willpower. Compartment "C" may also be characterised by a high degree of risk tolerance on the part of the decision-makers involved.

The alternative values for each of these compartments are listed below, prefixed by the compartment letter. Their location is shown in Figure 16 as *either positive to the values of the compartment (above), or negative to them (below),* thus:

[A1] everyone gets the same piece of the action; characterised (i) by "niceness", (ii) by principled perceptions of equality and opportunity, (iii) by fear or rejection of concept of "elites", plus (iv) some desire to avoid conflict (this Book notes that many middle-class Britons – and politicians – have a personal horror of conflict, for which they are not personally culturally adapted. They may be likely quickly to give way to aggression towards them by others). "Everybody gets a prize" in this case. May also be so-called "politically correct" in some quarters?

[A2] dissatisfies the performers who know that they would be more likely to win medals in their discipline.

[A3] performance may be seen to be sub-optimised, or the strategy seen as a recipe for national mediocrity.

[A4] effectively no target to act as driver for community sport achievement leading to national excellence?

[A5] contains no guarantees of winning any medals. An invalid strategy if other countries are pursuing Strategy "C"?

[B1] may keep some peace between the sporting disciplines, and sooth the ruffled feathers of those most likely to win medals who perceive that they have the most to lose in the resource allocation process in this compartment?

[B2] a form of satisficing behaviour, which is as good (or as bad) as the results it produces. An invalid strategy if other countries are pursuing Strategy "C"?

[B3] may produce a "lowest common denominator" compromise which satisfies no-one?

[B4] *and still* contains no guarantees of winning any medals.

[C1] places emphasis on driving competitive success and on winning. Only the most successful get a prize, which they have to earn on merit.

[C2] may maximise Olympic medal tally.

[C3] creates national success stories; maximises media benefit.

[C4] makes no apologies for so-called "elitism"; puts pressure on low-performing sports disciplines to get their act together and to demonstrate improvement prior to the next round of Olympic resource allocation (eg for 2020, 2022, 2024, and 2026) including paralympic equivalents.

[C5] maximises risk of low medal tally if chosen sports do not deliver.

[C6] maximises risk for underperforming disciplines who may as a consequence lose their funding at the next round of resource allocation.

[C7] seen by some people as "not a nice strategy", "brutal", "politically incorrect", or potentially characterised by conflict. Oh dear! Shock horror!

HERE ARE SOME FOR YOU TO TRY

Try mapping any of the following dilemmas, and establish / apply whatever decision criteria you think are best associated with them:

- ❏   UK Brexit.
- ❏   The Snowflake syndrome (Chapter 12).
- ❏   UK Childhood obesity, soft drinks; *and / or*

❑   UK Adult obesity.

❑   The UK treatment of (self-induced) sports injuries.

❑   The UK treatment of (self-induced) conditions based upon poor diet, smoking, alcohol and drug abuse.

❑   The treatment of "non-curable" conditions associated with the ageing process (eg balance issues / Menieres Disease; or Alzheimers / Dementia) etc.

❑   The establishment of local Medical or Triage Centres, or the reinstatement of "cottage hospitals" (i) to treat low level acute disorders, accidents and emergencies, (ii) to free up beds in regional centres, and (iii) to deal with localised shortages of qualified medical practitioners.

❑   The UK response to mental health issues, however and wherever these are defined.

❑   The UK response to individual personal isolation and associated depression.

❑   UK housing.

❑   The negative impact of so-called "celebrity culture".

❑   The negative UK impact of so-called "political correctness" (for instance as analysed in Chapter 8).

❑   The performance management, success or failure of your favourite professional football or rugby club (etc) financially involved in player transfers. Also see previous chapters, and Chapter 24.

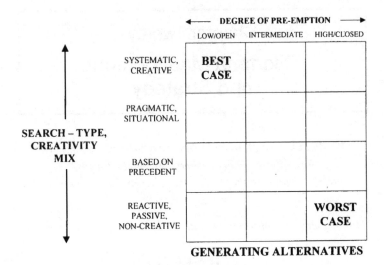

Figure 15
Alexander's Matrix

+VE   A1   B1   C1
                                       C2
                                       C3
       | A | B | C4   +VE

       | A | B | C |

-VE   A2   B2   C5   -VE
       A3   B3   C6
       A4   B4   C7
       A5

Figure 16
UK Olympic Sports Funding

Chapter Twenty

Dilemma Management and Strategy

"We don't have a plan, and when we do discover people who have plans, we take vehemently against them"
Roger Scruton on the British character and its preference for amateurism.

"Don't let your failure to plan ahead become my crisis"– Anon

STRATEGY

[1.1] THE CONCEPT OF STRATEGY

Strategies may be defined as the means by which an enterprise or an institution achieves its objectives across the chosen time horizons or the time spans of control to which it is working. Time dilemmas were described in Chapters 13 and 15. The concept of time span of control is identified in Chapter 21. Strategies act as "ground-rules", "plans of campaign", "paths to goal", or "routes to achievement". These concepts are used to determine the nature and occasion of the decisions needed to achieve objectives or goals. Strategies have their time scale and their risk.

Concept and event characteristics were described in Chapter Four. Part One of this Book defined the concept of the Management Dilemma, which will have a determinant influence on strategic choice and implementation. Parts Two and Three of this Book have identified a variety of dilemma variables which the process of strategic management must take into account in formulating (or not formulating) decisions.

Strategic management as a key component of the management process in organisations and institutions is described in

the Author's *Principles of Strategic Management,* as listed in the Introduction to this Book, and described in his website www.prin-ciplesofmanagement.com

[1.2] DILEMMAS OF CAPABILITY, CHOICE AND FIT

Strategic choice or decisions made by an institution in response to dilemmas will have to be consistent with, or "fit" its *capability.* Otherwise the implementation process will be unviable from the start. The enterprise will be unable to do what it has set out to do.

Capability is defined in this Book as *comprising two variables*, as follow.

Capacity – which includes necessary *resources* such as tangible and intangible assets (including reputation or brand), *time, finance, Human Capital* (to include expertise, competence and skill sets), *requisite bureaucracy* (defined in terms of operational systems and process, relationship architecture, responsibility allocation, account-ability, and performance measurement), *management process*, and *leadership*. Issues of leadership within a Dilemma Management context are dealt with in Chapter 21.

Willpower – by which plans and purpose are actively implemented by the enterprise on the basis of *a clarity of governance purpose* and *an appropriate stakeholder drive*. In the context of this Book such willpower and motivation will be proactively applied (i) to the identification and definition of dilemmas, and (ii) to the making of decisions about how to deal with them.

The effectiveness of the Dilemma Management process, whether in the process of identification, mapping, decision, or resolution must then depend to a significant degree on the relationship or *fit* between:

❑   the available capability (being capacity plus willpower as de-scribed above); *and*
❑   the particular requirements or potential consequences asso-ciated with the dilemma under consideration as (i) contingent

variables with (ii) their potential impact on the outcome or the organisation.

CASE EXAMPLE

A towering inferno: the catastrophic destruction by fire of a West London multi-occupancy residential tower block during 2017 revealed a set of critical dilemmas faced by the (apparently cash-strapped?) leaders of UK public housing authorities in a variety of polyglot locations, in some cases inhabited by concentrations of migrant workers.

The specific location in this case, the London Borough of Kensington and Chelsea, is characterised by extremes of both (i) very high levels of residential owner wealth, and (ii) very significant urban poverty. The fiery calamity appears to have raised such matters as:

❏ emerging dilemmas associated with the nature and application of UK building regulations, for instance in respect of (i) exterior cladding (whose unexpected flammability caused the fire that killed so many tenants) and (ii) the installation of such basic protective devices as fire doors and sprinklers;

❏ the nature of the validation, assurance, and certification of building specification and testing in the UK;

❏ the accountability of the construction companies involved (who may be interpreted to have sufficiently "deep pockets" to deal with issues of accountability and legality of specification and practice);

❏ the risk of corruption in such disastrous circumstances, however this might occur and whomsoever it might involve, in particular where charges of corporate manslaughter might ultimately be pursued by the courts (?);

❏ the issue of identifying residents, some of whom may be illegal immigrants and subject to exploitation by the notional tenants of the accommodation who (illegally) claim benefits on their behalf (etc!?);

❏ reinforcing and ensuring resident responsibility for, and conformance with UK rules of health and safety (such as no smoking, or a ban on the use of gaseous or liquid fuel based cooking to avoid paying electricity bills; or the removal of batteries from smoke alarms) with which some will be ignorant, resistant, or directly hostile as being alien to their experience;

❏ the need for a minimum level of understanding of written English by residents (again, as in the example of smoking or dangerous methods of cooking or storage).

Equality issues associated with such calamities are dealt with in detail in the Author's two Equality Books published by Routledge, and described in his website www.equalityrisk.com

The *circumstances of this catastrophic event very clearly fit the dilemma conditions described as wicked mess risk* as analysed in Chapter 17, and *those characterised by crisis* as analysed in Chapter 18.

[1.3] THE BASIS OF STRATEGY FORMULATION

Strategies were described above as being formulated to determine how the organisation intends to carry out its activities during the time horizons, or time spans of control to which it is working in order to use its capability to achieve its purpose.

However, strategies do not just exist of their own accord; nor may there necessarily be any "recipe books" by which to find and implement them in the context of Dilemma Management? Individual, institutional, corporate or governance decisions will have to be made about what strategies should be pursued and how they should be implemented in a Dilemma Management context. This section of Chapter 20 suggests that the character of such decisions, and their outcomes, may in part depend on the *nature of the basis and process of strategy formulation* used by the enterprise or institution. This process is described by Mintzberg as comprising *four bases of strategy formulation.*

Forced – the choice (or non-choice) of strategy may be forced (or imposed) on the organisation where its Dilemma Management capability (i) is poor or non-existent, and where (ii) it is unwilling or unable to identify the dilemmas which are having a direct impact upon it.

Incremental – in which strategic choice and decision-making follows some kind of iterative (but most likely) reactive definition over time of dilemmas and their impact. This may imply that the institution responds to events when or after they have occurred.

Proactive – by which the choice of strategies to be pursued is based on a proactive process of dilemma identification, definition or forecasting. Decision-making is informed by the nature of events and (to the extent possible) is ahead of them. Such proactivity may be reinforced where the enterprise and its leadership are aware of, and implement the *time span of discretion* concept described in Chapter 21.

Emergent or opportunistic – in which a proactive stance to the management of dilemmas and their impact is augmented by an ability and willingness to make strategic decisions that exploit or take advantage of the conditions to which dilemmas have given rise. The example of private and family companies was for instance given in Chapter 2. The creation of dilemmas by others was described in a variety of chapters.

Chapter Twenty One
Dilemma Management and Leadership

THE CONCEPT OF LEADERSHIP

Dilemma decision-making or resolution success is likely to be a function of the presence of an appropriate **leadership process**, as described below.

The leadership process defined – leadership may be defined in the context of this Book as a process in which people in an enterprise or an organisation (whether in governance, management, or otherwise) *make a motivated, responsible, appropriate and congruent use of the available capability and willpower to achieve the desired dilemma outcomes.* This in turn calls for the purposive and organised inter-action of individuals, groups and stakeholders in an organisation or a community, for instance in the decision-making and Dilemma Management processes described in Part Four. *The greater the de-gree of "fit" or congruence between stakeholder demands, decision variables, willpower, leadership, and the available capability, the greater may be the likelihood of the resolution of dilemmas with which decision-makers are faced.*

The need for effective leadership – this Book emphasises the need for the identification, location, and allocation of responsibility for Dilemma Management, decision-making, accountability, and reso-lution (whether this is individual or collective). Performance relative to this responsibility, and for the resource allocation and use implicit in it, should then be monitored and controlled by the use of formal Governance and Performance Management systems, such as those described in subsequent chapters of Part Four.

Where (in addition) such an emphasis might conventionally have been perceived to be mechanistic, formulaic, bureaucratic, or administrative; or instead does not take place in a strongly hierarchical and high power distance context (as described in Chapter 6), *current received wisdom states that there will be a need for the effective leadership of the Dilemma Management process*. This leadership may be governance, individual, group or collective in its basis.

LEADERSHIP AND DILEMMAS

This chapter now moves on to a variety of leadership issues. It firstly describes some *sources* of leadership influence and control. It then goes on to identify *various approaches* to the implementation of leadership in a Dilemma Management context.

Leadership as a key strategic component in organisations is described in both of the Author's *Principles of Management* and *Principles of Strategic Management*, as listed in the Introduction to this Book and described in his website www.principlesofmanagement.com

SOME SOURCES OF LEADERSHIP INFLUENCE

The exercise of leadership involves the use of *influence*. This is concerned with how the leader affects or motivates followers, and is in turn affected or motivated by them. *There are a variety of sources of leadership influence, power, or authority.* These include:

Tradition – historically, traditional leaders derived authority from their inheritance by birth or kinship. Kings, queens, and clan or tribal leaders were born to lead the people over whom they would be expected to hold sway. There may be similar leadership expectations (for instance in France, Spain, Italy, or South Korea) of those who as offspring (i) inherit from their parents or predecessors the assets of the private or family businesses described in earlier chapters; or (ii) instead (or as well as) the allegiance of political parties.

Office – leaders in this case derive their authority from the *offices they hold*. These offices or positions may be associated with political and economic power to act on behalf of others, and may be backed up by sufficient authority or force to ensure compliance. For instance, countries such as France and Russia have long histories of powerful (or "absolutist") leadership that to this day influence attitudes to leadership in these countries. One consequence of this approach may be *the perception or expectation that hierarchical position and leadership are correlated*. Organisational rank, the right to exercise influence and authority, the expectation of leadership responsibility, and the expectation of compliance from subordinates may all be seen as components of senior management roles. This may similarly be expressed in terms of the exercise of:-

Legitimate power – which derives from the authority formally vested in a hierarchical position or office held within the organisation, the necessary exercise of which by the leader is recognised by subordinates as appropriate and proper.

Reward power – which derives from the authority to decide and to make the allocation of rewards to others. Such rewards may take the tangible form of pay increases, bonuses, or promotion; or the intangible form of recognition, congratulation or praise.

Coercive power – which describes the authority to recommend or impose punishment. The exercise of coercive power might take the form of the threatened or actual withdrawal of custom or contracts; personal or public criticism; the denial or withdrawal of optional conditions or rewards of employment (such as bonuses); staff demotion or dismissal; or some form of actual restraint.

Expert power – which derives from the leader's special knowledge or professional skill. Subordinates will comply with the leader's decisions and actions because they perceive him or her to know better, or to be more experienced, or to be more effectively equipped to deal with dilemma situations characterised by the conditions of complexity, novelty, uncertainty, or risk (etc) described throughout this Book.

Referent power or personal "charisma" – which derives from features of the personality or character of the leader, and which might be used to command the respect, admiration, or compliance of others. Followers might even wish to identify with the leader, to whom they could refer as a desirable role model or example. The special case of the concept of "charisma" as a source of leadership influence and power is dealt with in a later section of this chapter.

IMPLEMENTING LEADERSHIP

[1] PERSONAL TRAITS AND QUALITIES

Some studies of leadership have focused on *personal traits or qualities as sources of influence* that appear to be correlated with people's perceptions of effective leadership. Such studies identified such personal traits and qualities as:

Intelligence – as for instance indicated by apparent evidence of effective perception, reasoning, judgement, communication, and decision-making skills relative to the needs of the situation and the group.

Self-confidence – by which the individual appears to others to be self-assured about his or her own capability and competence, and certain and comfortable in the application of this capability in the leadership situation.

Sociability and emotional intelligence – in which leaders who demonstrate sociability are perceived by others to be friendly, outgoing, courteous, tactful and diplomatic. They are sensitive to others' needs and show concern for their well-being. Sociable leaders have good interpersonal and social skills and may be able to create co-operative relationships with their followers and others in the relevant internal and external architectures. As such, they are likely to possess a high degree of emotional intelligence.

Determination – which may be described in terms of a strong personal desire to get the job done. It includes characteristics such as initiative, persistence, enthusiasm, and drive. Individuals with determination may be willing to assert themselves, they are proactive, and they have the capacity to persevere in the face of obstacles. Being determined includes showing dominance at times and in situations where followers need to be organised and directed.

Integrity – which indicates personal characteristics of honesty and trustworthiness. Individuals who adhere to a strong set of values and principles, and take responsibility for their actions are likely to be perceived to be exhibiting integrity. Leaders with integrity may inspire confidence in others because they can be trusted to do what they say they are going to do.

The "helicopter factor" – the possession of which describes the ability of the leader to rise above the detail of a situation and to see it as a whole entity within its wider context.

Other personal traits and qualities might include:

- ❏ robust personal health and the ability to cope with pressure and stress;
- ❏ the possession of above average personal competence; *perhaps combined with*
- ❏ a validated depth of personal professional or technical knowledge, experience and expertise; *combined with*
- ❏ effective professional judgement; *and*
- ❏ professional prestige; *but at the same time*
- ❏ being able and willing to accept the professional or political views (etc) of others;
- ❏ an ability to deal or work with a wide variety of different kinds of people and attitudes;
- ❏ an originality or creativity of thought and action; *and*
- ❏ an ability to think laterally or to act unconventionally, as circumstances require; *and*
- ❏ an ability to think and to respond quickly, also as circumstances require;
- ❏ communication fluency and effectiveness; *associated with*
- ❏ effective or persuasive self-presentation; *and*
- ❏ decisiveness.

Proponents of trait models of leadership are likely as a caveat to have to accept that the application of personal traits and qualities to the leadership situation must be *appropriate to the situation and decision-making* to which they are being applied.

Thus, for example, an individual might be expected to exhibit decisiveness and self-confidence in a dilemma crisis situation (for instance as described in Chapter 18) where others will expect clear leadership.

But where there is a need to make a complex technical judgement in an uncertain or ill-defined dilemma situation whose outcome may be dependent on the exercise of a wide range of expert judgement (and perhaps a degree of serendipity), then (i) the leader's professional credibility and prestige, and (ii) his or her ability to maintain or manage close and participative working relationships with and between other informed sources, stakeholders or professionals may instead be seen to be the test of leadership competence. This issue is also dealt with in the later section of this chapter, below.

[2] TRANSACTIONAL LEADERSHIP AND DILEMMA MANAGEMENT

The components of a transactional approach to the Dilemma Management process are summarised as follows, and illustrated in Figure 17. The recognised leader, leaders, and / or those involved collectively in the leadership process need, in this case within any particular Dilemma Management context, to specify and to ensure the appropriate implementation of:

❏ an awareness of, and an adaptation to the situation or dilemma as a critical contingency; *and*

❏ the resultant purpose, task, and path to achievement defined for them or by them; *and*

❏ the operational capability and motivation of the people involved in dealing with the task or dilemma, whether as individuals, groups or collectives; *as well as*

❏ appropriate relationship architectures, whether or both internal or external.

At the same time, the leader or the leadership process will, again within the context of the significance of the dilemma issue being dealt with, have to attempt to:

❏ ensure the establishment of an effective and legitimate *structure* (or *requisite bureaucracy* as described in a later section of this chapter) to shape, to formalise, to control, and to assure the Dilemma Management process; *and*

❏ ensure the implementation of motivational drives and responses to keep people focussed on purpose and task, whilst at the same time meeting such needs as are relevant to empowering these people in the circumstances in which events and decisions have placed them; *and*

❏ ensure the provision of necessary assistance in dealing with such complexities or inconsistencies as event or concept characteristics that are associated with the Dilemma Management process, for instance as described in earlier chapters of this Book, and in Parts Four and Five; *and*

❏ ensuring the *paying of attention to detail*, whereby leaders may have to be seen to be comfortable with detail as well as with broad issues. This is demonstrated (i) by their ability to perform the detailed tasks that they require their subordinates to carry out; or at least to show an understanding of the relevance of these tasks. This is *leadership by example*. It is also demonstrated (ii) by their identification and empathy with, and respect for the expertise and routines of their subordinates. Leaders who downgrade the importance of detail, or who appear contemptuous of day-to-day routines, may be perceived by subordinates as incompetent and arrogant. Such behaviour may be perceived to be highly inappropriate to the requirements of effective leadership.

The Transactional Leadership Style, Effort Justification, and Vroom and Lawler's Expectancy Theory – Expectancy Theory was developed by V H Vroom and E E Lawler. Vroom and Lawler start from the premise that an individual's work behaviour is a function of that individual's perception (or the cognitions described in Chapter 7) of the realities of the situation (or the transactions) in which he or she finds himself or herself involved. The core of expectancy theory relates to how the individual perceives the transactional relationship between effort, performance, and reward. This is the *effort justification* described in Chapter 7. The individual will expend effort where he or she wishes to produce an effective performance as the result of that effort. This level of performance will, in turn, be perceived to be worthwhile because it will eventually lead to rewards that are seen as attractive. In other words, effort and performance are motivated (justified) by the perception of the desirability of the eventual reward. The individual's perception of the available rewards, and his or her view of the likelihood (or probability) that they will be achieved, is crucial to the individual expectancies (or expectations) that are seen as the key motivating force. The available rewards may be *intrinsic or extrinsic*, or both.

Intrinsic rewards will have the effect of fulfilling personal needs such as for status, self-esteem or personal development. The individual may perceive that he or she has some degree of control over this kind of need satisfaction.

Extrinsic rewards include pay, conditions of work, the quality of supervision, and promotion prospects. The individual is more likely to perceive that the allocation of these kinds of reward is outwith his or her control. The failure of work performance to secure such extrinsic rewards may, in consequence, constitute a particularly strong source of individual dissatisfaction, Cognitive Dissonance and de-motivation.

The relationship between effort, performance and reward will then be complicated by the issue of *capacity*. The individual must perceive that he or she is capable of achieving the levels of performance that they perceive to be likely to result in the eventual reward. That is, the individual will have to have the *competence* to put in the requisite effort. He or she may also feel that an appropriately defined role (or job) specification is needed, as is a supportive supervisor or organisational structure.

If however these contextual features are perceived to be inappropriate or unsympathetic, then the performance (while desirable in principle because of the potential reward) may not in transactional terms be forthcoming. The individual may not put in the effort because he or she will perceive that there is unlikely to be an ultimate benefit.

It will be the task of the leader in transactional terms, therefore, to try to understand individual perceptions, to understand the prevailing competence and contextual factors, and to understand the effect of the reward systems on the work behaviour of subordinates. The leader will have to attempt to shape (i) the determinant variables of employee cognitions and expectancy, and (ii) the interrelationship between these variables, such that (iii) subordinates perceive (a) that it is worthwhile to put in a maximum effort; (b) that effective performance is valued; and (c) that the appropriate rewards will be eventually forthcoming.

[3] CHARISMATIC LEADERSHIP

The term "charisma" can be used in a leadership sense to describe characteristics that enable particular individuals to exercise influence over others by force of personality, reference, or charm. Such charismatic people may be capable of demonstrating significant powers or, with the help of their followers, being able to achieve extraordinary accomplishments. Charisma could be described as "a fire that ignites followers' energy and commitment, producing results above and beyond the call of duty". The charismatic leader may be able to inspire and to motivate people to do more than they would otherwise do, in spite of the obstacles to progress that all may face, and despite the potential need for some degree of personal sacrifice. Followers may over-ride their own self-interest for the sake of the leader, the purpose, the cause, the organisation or the department (etc).

In order for this charisma to be effective, it must (for the purpose of this Book) be recognised and accepted as *valid* by followers in order for them to accept the leader's influence.

Charismatic leaders may be able to transform the self-perceptions, values, and ideologies of followers into those that they themselves hold or promote. In the case of organisations or political bodies (etc), this may mean forging a strong correlation between (i) the individual identity of the followers, and (ii) the collective identity of the institution led by the charismatic leader. Followers internalise and take ownership of the values and ideologies of the enterprise and its leaders, identifying with them in preference to alternatives (such as the individualism or personal self-actualisation described in Chapters 10, 11 and 12) that might otherwise be available to them.

Charismatic leaders themselves may however pose a dilemma. *They may be unpredictable*. Their personalised style of leadership behaviour may be associated with a higher degree of variation, risk and uncertainty than the other types or bases of leadership being analysed in this chapter. Their behaviour may become self- referential, self-centred and self-absorbed, restrictively focused, obssessive and unreasoning. It may become incapable of adapting to changing circumstances or ideas that do not conform to the leader's mind-set, wishes, or values. This is sometimes a problem in entrepreneurial businesses where the founder is committed to his or her ideas or inventions, and is unable to adapt to external change affecting these ideas. It may also become a key issue in political parties, trade unions, the media, charities and organisations whose purpose is ideological.

Charismatic leadership may achieve positive outcomes from which individuals or the organisation may benefit. But it may also be used to achieve the leader's self-serving or corrupt purposes of the deception, manipulation, and exploitation of others, ultimately resulting in the evil done by the likes of so-called charismatic leaders such as Adolf Hitler, Idi Amin, Benito Mussolini, or the current North Korean family dictatorship.

One key difficulty with charismatic leadership is that it may be the case that few people are likely to possess the exceptional qualities required to transform all around them into willing followers. Nor may it be possible to acquire or develop these qualities by any form of training or developmental activity.

Another key difficulty within the context of this Book is the potential for the charismatic leader to face significant difficulties in the process of making dilemma decisions, as described in Parts Four and Five.

CASE EXAMPLE
Put not your trust in these ersatz princes – a correspondent from the *Guardian* newspaper commented that 'one of the malign ... effects of our celebrity culture is that we've come to think the only way to get things done is to entrust projects to "turbo- powered" leaders blessed with awesome "knowledge, drive and networking prowess". Not that we should discourage "audacity in the pursuit of the public good": but without adequate oversight it soon morphs into recklessness and arrogance.' This commentator then gave some examples (which the Author cannot reproduce here), concluding that people should not put too much faith in charismatic individuals. 'We have

grown scornful of the mundanities of democracy', he writes, which 'may slow things down, but the dull, traditional, sometimes tortuous structures – with checks and balances, and inquests and punishments – [does exist] for a reason' (**The Week**).

[4] TRANSFORMATIONAL LEADERSHIP

The concept of *transformational leadership* is based on a process of accessing the needs and motives of followers as well as those of leaders in order better to achieve the purpose of the organisation and hence the goals of the leader. This implies that the leader engages in a dynamic with subordinates that may create an increased motivation and performance through a positive change (transformation) in the values, attitudes, and willpower of those followers.

CASE EXAMPLE

Sun Tzu – unite your own people in purpose and commitment – reference is made to Sun Tzu in Chapter 23. Sun Tzu was a skilled military adviser to the Chinese Emperor Wu. One of Sun Tzu's principles was that people who are in broad agreement with their ruler are more likely to be willing to accept the hazards of conflict than those who are in disagreement. For instance, in a competitive business situation, enterprise leadership may have to attempt to create meaningful and shared corporate goals 'so that all in the company come to view themselves as members of the group crossing the river in the same boat. They would be more likely to consider company affairs as their own and be willing to make personal sacrifices when needed…as Sun Tzu said, "he whose ranks are united in purpose will win"' (**Source:** Min Chen, in Principles of Strategic Management).

CASE EXAMPLE
Jack Welch (GE Corp) on leadership

❑   control your destiny, or someone else will;
❑   face reality as it is, not as it was or as you wish it were;
❑   be candid with everyone;
❑   change before you have to;

❏ don't manage, lead; *and*
❏ if you don't have a competitive advantage, don't compete.

Transformational leaders may not rely solely on tangible rules and incentives in order to manage their dealings (transactions) with followers. They also focus on intangible qualities such as vision, shared values, and ideas to build relationships, give larger meaning to activities, and find common ground to enlist followers in the creation of enhanced capability (defined in this Book as capacity plus willpower).

The transformational approach to leadership attempts to motivate followers to do more than the expected by raising followers' level of consciousness about the relative priority or importance of the goals (such as customer service excellence, innovation, patient care, or zero defect manufacturing) with which they are being presented by the leader and the organisation. It is the leader's responsibility to persuade followers to transcend their own self-interest for the sake of the team or the organisation. In return, the leader will attempt to facilitate a move towards satisfaction of the higher order personal needs of followers, for instance in terms of feelings of self-worth or esteem; the accomplishment of challenging tasks from which experience may be gained; or occupational self-actualization or gains in personal value.

Strategies used to implement transformational leadership might include any of the following:

The creation and communication of a vision that others can believe in and adopt as their own – "vision" is defined in this sense as an imagined or perceived pattern of communal possibilities to which others can be drawn into commitment. This vision must derive from the needs of the organisation as well as the leader, and those involved in the work of this organisation must be empowered to take ownership of such needs. As a result, the vision might have to be desirable, realistic, and credible to all concerned. It might have to be simple, understandable, and obviously beneficial. It would also have to be capable of releasing willpower, and creating motivation amongst the people involved.

The use of concepts of relationship architecture – by which the leader actively influences or shapes the nature of internal relationships, trust, and structure; values, culture, social norms, and accepted patterns of behaviour; and perceptions of purpose and identity.

The creation of a high degree of trust within the organisation – which may be achieved by the clear demonstration of leadership integrity, and by a relationship architecture characterised by open and honest exchange within the enterprise. Ultimately, all parties to any communication relationship must feel able, at least from their own point of view, to speak as they think best, to talk about things as they see them, and to know that criticism will be constructively given and positively received. Issues of high trust were described in Chapter 6.

The creative application of leadership competence – by which leaders demonstrate and prove their capability in furthering the purposes of the organisation and the goals of the people associated with it. Leaders are strongly identified with their work, and their competence and confidence "cascades" down to their subordinates, who demonstrate their own feelings of confidence and self-worth on a reciprocal basis.

Idealised influence – which describes a leadership capability to act as an influential role model for followers, and to command their respect. Such leaders are seen "to do the right thing" and to represent appropriate values or ethics. Such leaders may use this capability to communicate, to instil, and to empower both vision and mission into the group and the organisation (for instance to be number one in the sector; to be the best hospital or university; to eliminate the incidence of pupil exclusion from schools, or to offer social progress to an electorate, etc). Such a leadership style aims to create a high level of trust, or to operate in a high trust context, again as described in Chapter 6.

Inspirational motivation – which describes a leadership capacity to articulate and to communicate high performance expectations to followers, inspiring them to share and to become committed to the achievement of the vision and mission of the organisation, thereby creating a total effort that goes beyond self-interest. The transformational leader may function as a "synergising force", releasing and combining capabilities and energies amongst those they lead. Ultimately, the leader may develop the ability to create a state of achievement far beyond what individuals, teams and organisations might otherwise think possible.

Intellectual stimulation – which describes a leadership capability that stimulates positive values of creativity or innovation within the organisation, and permits the analysis and challenge of received wisdom or established mindsets. The leader is able to create a high trust environment in which the fear of experimentation and failure are eliminated, and in which mistakes are categorised as "learning experiences".

Individual consideration – which describes a leadership capability to create a supportive climate within which colleagues can operate at their best. Leaders might use the maximum delegation of responsibility and authority to empower those subordinates and groups who seek autonomy, advising or coaching them in their work in order to develop their capabilities. Other staff might instead prefer clear direction and structure, or exact guidance on how to fulfil their responsibilities. At the same time, the leader may be required to negotiate resolutions to interpersonal or inter-group conflicts that arise, or to be seen sympathetically to attempt to heal any wounds that may have been inflicted by change.

LEADERSHIP VISIBILITY

A key Dilemma Management issue must be that of the level of leadership visibility (or presence) thought to be most appropriate. This part of Chapter 21 summarises the issue in dilemma format, using Figure 3 with three compartments, thus:

❖ right compartment = **high levels of visibility**;
❖ centre compartment = **intermediate levels of visibility**;
❖ left compartment = **low levels of visibility**.

Each is summarised as follows.

High levels of visibility – this choice may be a function of any of the following variables where:

❑ there is a manageable or concentrated scale of activity eg in a SME, at the level of core governance, in a specialist or family organisation, in a charity where success is seen to result from the leader's personal activities, or in a political party;

❑ there is a deliberate adoption of a strategy of Management By Wandering Around (MBWA) as routine and repeated activity by the leader, or instead belief in the need to lead by example and / or from the front;

❑ the leader perceives that his or her needs (for whatever reason) are paramount;

❑ there is an application of such national and cross-cultural features (Chapter 6) as (i) high power distance, strong hierarchy; (ii) a high level of uncertainty or risk avoidance; (iii) low trust (for instance associated with a Theory X style of management); (iv) a familistic / clan emphasis;

❑ there is a refusal or inability of the leader to delegate to others lower in the hierarchy;

❑ for whatever reason (secrecy, security, paranoia, the protection of proprietary knowledge, etc) the leader is effectively the only person who knows the whole picture. Subordinates work in deliberately segmented areas that contribute only partially to the desired outcome; and / or

❑ there is a belief in the desirability of charismatic leadership as described in an earlier section of this chapter.

Intermediate levels of visibility – this choice may be a function of variables where:

❑ the scale and diversity of activities may render a high level of leadership visibility unviable;

❑ leadership may be conceptualised as a process – it does not have to be individualised or personalised;

❏   this leadership process may be conceptualised in functional, rule-driven, or operational terms, as in the uniformed services;

❏   issues of leadership, style of management, location, performance management (etc) are perceived as issues of capability. Focus is placed on role, work, communication and on the organisation thereof; *and / or*

❏   there is a perception that the application of a transactional style of leadership may result in the creation of effective capability and responsibility through the internalisation by managers, teams and subordinates of rules, obligations and performance management requirements in return for corporate guarantees about terms and conditions, the availability of CPD and / or career advancement patterns (etc). That is, the role of the leadership process is (i) to facilitate and to make everything work in return (ii) for being seen to keep to its side of the bargain. This echoes the Expectancy Theory described in an earlier part of this chapter;

❏   the need for compromise may be accepted. Thus, the delegation of the leadership role (for instance on a collective basis) may be seen as sensible, as well as being dependent on the scale of operations; *and*

❏   there may also be some belief in the application of a leadership role in promoting mission and values whilst maintaining focus, motivation and discipline. This may or may not be associated with corporate scepticism about the concepts of collective type responsibility, as described below.

Low levels of visibility – this choice may be a function of variables where:

❏   the scale and diversity of activities may again render a high level of leadership visibility unviable;

❏   neither the needs or direction of the leader, nor the leadership process itself are seen as being of over-riding importance; *and perhaps at the same time*

❏   there is a dependence on high levels of professional and technical skill. Influence may be in the hands of the people who apply these skills because they are core to organisational capacity and willpower (capability) – and hence the critical leadership need *to keep these people updated and motivated* rather than succumb to plateauing or the effects of the Peter Principle (etc);

❏ there is an application of such national and cross-cultural features (Chapter 6) as (i) low levels of hierarchical influence; (ii) low levels of uncertainty avoidance and a high level of risk tolerance; (iii) low power distance; and (iv) high trust (eg application of Theory Y or Theory Z, etc);

❏ where an application of transformational or values-based processes may achieve the internalisation of corporate values, imperatives or ideologies (etc); *and maybe*

❏ there is a belief in the attainability of collective-type responsibility as well as personal responsibility.

LEADERSHIP AND THE TIME SPAN OF DISCRETION CONCEPT

Elliot Jaques' concept of the *time span of discretion* is based on the premise that *a critical feature of the implementation of leadership capability is the willingness and the capacity to look and to think far ahead in time. Long-term time orientation is seen as an indicator of a high level of leadership capacity and status.* Time dilemmas were analysed in Chapter 13 of this Book.

Time span of discretion is a feature of the *requisite bureaucracy* described by Jaques. According to Jaques, the proper functioning of any kind of institution depends (that is, *contingent upon*) its having at the same time (i) an appropriate organisational and administrative structure, to include relationship architecture; and (ii) the right people to fulfil the roles to which these structures give rise. Only in this way will the objectives, strategies, and tasks of the organisation be achieved. This is because (in contingent terms) differing conditions (such as those that are dilemma- defined) will require different structures and different kinds of leadership in order to deal with them. This point is also made in the description of Hancock's tame, messy and wicked risk conditions contained in Chapter 17.

Jaques contends that organisational structures or heirarchies contain a range of increasingly complicated levels or "strata", each carrying out different levels or complexities of work. Jaques' conceptualisation of "level of work" is defined in terms of *the time span for which people are required to exercise discretion* (that is the time span for which they carry personal and / or collective governance, strategic or decision-making responsibility).

These *hierarchical strata* are differentiated by time spans of discretion that range from a few weeks, to three or six months, to a year or two, and to the medium or long term. Jaques defines *seven* such hierarchical strata. These are the:

❑ *immediate* – being day-to-day and reactive to immediate events;
❑ *supervisory* – being responsible for monitoring and controlling operational activities (for instance as described in Chapter 24), and ensuring a proper response to events for instance as they occur on a day-to day or short-term basis;
❑ *planning* – being responsible for anticipating and ordering operational events from the present into the future time scales of the organisation;
❑ *business management* – being responsible for decision-making associated with the achievement of purposes and objectives established in the planning process, and for maintaining the health and viability of organisational and administrative structures as it does so. Business management may be characterised by the need for processes of negotiation at any number of levels, both within the enterprise and external to it. The capability of the available relationship architecture and its management become critical at this level;
❑ *strategic management* – being responsible for charting the course and decision-making of the enterprise into the medium to long-term; and ensuring that the organisation has the necessary governance, resources, capability, and competence to achieve its purposes over that time span;
❑ *environmental management* – being responsible for dealing or negotiating with wider political, economic, social, and cultural

environments external to the institution, and as necessary being capable of exercising influence over them;

❏ *visionary management* – being responsible for rethinking, re-conceptualising, or transforming the purposes and capabilities of the enterprise so as to secure or strengthen its long-term position (or survival) within the external, political, legislative, regulatory, customer, or market environments it is likely to face.

Dilemmas may occur at any of these levels, and are likely to become increasingly significant the longer is the time span associated with them.

Hierarchical strata – are seen by Jaques as structural or architectural variables requisite to the complexity of the task in hand. The complexity of the task will be determined by the number, diversity, duration, rate of change, novelty, uncertainty, risk, and degree of interdependency of the variables and / or concept and event characteristics that characterise that task.

Jaques contends that these hierarchical strata reflect in organisations the (statistically predictable) existence of stratification and discontinuity in the nature of human capacity (i) to operate or manage through increasingly intellectual and abstract concepts; and (ii) to deal with increasingly complex circumstances, such as those involving severe dilemma risk. Thus:

❏ each category of task, interpersonal, and situational complexity is seen to call for a corresponding category of *cognitive capability* (intelligence and competence) in human beings; *and therefore*

❏ complexity in leadership and work behaviour are of necessity likely to have to be matched with an appropriate level of cognitive capability in people in the organisational layer in which that leadership and work requirement occurs.

Leadership aptitude and capability is therefore seen by Jaques to be a function of, or contingent upon:

❏ personal cognitive capacity and intelligence that is appropriate (or requisite) to mastering the level and degree of complexity to which the prevailing circumstances give rise;

❏ the possession of the necessary professional value sets, conditioning, training and individual motivation that are consistent with the willingness to deal routinely, flexibly and in a sustained manner over time with complex *(and also potentially exhausting and stressful)* situations;

❏ the personal capacity and willingness to make appropriately skilled use of the available accumulated knowledge and experience *as are relevant to the circumstances*, even if this knowledge is novel, risky, or uncertain;

❏ a highly developed personal wisdom about, and experience of dealing with people and entities. (This might however provide a significant problem for the aggressive and self-centred "Type A" personality described in Chapters 2 and 11; or the "charismatic" leaders described in an earlier section of this chapter above; or the under-competent plateaued leaders described by the Peter Principle in Chapter 2 and recapped in the next section below);

❏ a natural and relaxed interpersonal style of behaviour. (This might also pose a problem for the "Type A", charismatic, or under-competent plateaued personality described immediately above); *and*

❏ an absence of serious individual defects in personality or temperament. These defects might include an unstable or unpredictable temper; the inability to interact appropriately with people who reasonably question or criticise the received organisational wisdom; poor judgement; inconsistent behaviour; a lack of proper objectivity; an unwillingness to properly share information with others or to delegate; or an inability to work with people from another gender, nationality, persuasion, or ethnic group. Such defects are likely seriously to damage the leadership credibility of such people in the eyes of colleagues, subordinates, or stakeholders. They are also likely to hamper or obstruct the necessary achievement of task or purpose, and may impede the decision-making or governance process.

Jaques suggests that the greater and more effective is the training or development of a person's professional capacity, capability and aptitude, the greater may be the number of variables and the greater the situational complexity that the person can cope with. In consequence, the greater may be that person's time horizon and the greater his or her time span of discretion. *And the greater, therefore, may be his or her leadership potential.*

Jaques comments that the development of personal cognitive capacity may be *evolutionary*. Some people reach a final plateau of personal and leadership competence. Others develop an on- going capacity to manage increasing levels of complexity and longer time spans of discretion. As people learn, mature, and develop competence and experience, they may progress through a variety of developmental stages, moving from one level of capacity to the next more complex one until they reach their cognitive (or preferred) limit. This evolutionary pattern may be matched by the increasing levels of necessary complexity to be found in the strata that make up the governance, strategic decision-making, leadership and management levels within the hierarchy.

TWO REALITY CHECKS

[1] MANAGEMENT RECRUITMENT AND THE PETER PRINCIPLE

Reference to the *Peter Principle* was made in Chapter 2. In the context of this chapter, the workings of the Peter Principle may give rise to dilemmas which affect the appointment, promotion or management of staff who are to be employed in governance, organisational, or line roles characterised by a responsibility and accountability for Dilemma Management, decision-making, staff management, resource usage and stewardship, or departmental supervision; leadership requirements, (etc); and the wider processes of time span and strategic management described in this chapter and in Parts Four and Five.

A judgement will for example have to be made that appointees or promotees will be able to fulfil role performance expectations (for instance, see the case of **Bill** in the Introduction). The success of this judgement might for example be dependent on:

❏ the influence, competence, motivation, relationships (and personal friendships) of people at governance level who are to be involved in the making of senior appointments;

❏ the degree to which the control of senior management on the recruitment and selection process is *inward-looking, strongly influenced by membership group affiliation and groupthink;* or characterised by the workings of the Peter Principle as described in Chapter 2; *and / or*

❏ the degree to which the control of senior management on the recruitment and selection process is a function of determinant cultural variables such as power distance, uncertainty avoidance, low trust, entrenched familism, or collective / party control (etc) as described in Chapter 6;

❏ the degree to which institutional bases of thinking are entrenched; or instead amenable to change (for instance (i) in the promotion of women to senior posts; or (ii) in the acceptance of the need to bring new technologies or new paradigms into play – with the implication that outsiders may have to be brought directly into senior posts); *and*

❏ the prevailing cultural reluctance or instead enthusiasm with which outsiders are to be considered for appointment to internal managerial, stewardship, leadership or corporate posts; *and*

❏ the effectiveness of "head hunters" in identifying suitable external candidates; *and*

❏ the likely effectiveness (or otherwise) of (internal or external) management and leadership development programmes, Continuing Professional Development (etc).

CASE EXAMPLE
Spend and go bust (or where did that money go?) – it might be argued that in Dilemma Management terms the workings of the Peter Principle (as well as other principles described in this chapter)

can usefully (and potentially ruinously) be illustrated at this time of writing (i) by the "merry go-round" of (apparently desperate) high-profile and expensive appointments of UK Premier and Championship League Football Club managers and coaches; and (ii) by their subsequent (and often rapid) sacking; and (iii) by the subsequent / expensive remuneration as contractual payoff?

It may also however be argued that such dynamics result as much from corporate shortcomings at the level of ownership (and its vanity), governance and leadership which are characterised by unrealistic expectations, confused objectives, fear of failure and negative publicity, the manipulation of the state's corporate taxation system, and the gross and yearly exploitation of club fans and season ticket holders. Or worst of all, of fantastical thoughts of glory over the horizon but always just beyond the Club's reach?

[2] A POLITICAL LEADER'S DILEMMA; AND THE CONTINGENCY APPROACH TO LEADERSHIP AS SOLUTION?

The *Contingency approach to leadership* (for instance as summarised in the Author's text *Principles of Management*) is conceptualised on the basis of "leadership-match" or "leadership congruence". It analyses leadership choices, leadership behaviour, and leadership effectiveness **within the equifinal context** *of the degree of "appropriateness" to the situation or dilemma in which that leadership occurs.*

In order to understand leadership performance, contingency theorists believe it is necessary to diagnose and understand the situations and dilemmas in which leadership (such as critically those with which politicians must engage) occurs. Leadership in this sense is seen as "contingent" because the approach suggests that leadership effectiveness will depend on how well the leader's style fits the context in which leadership choices and behaviour are to occur. Effective leadership is seen to be contingent (*dependent upon*) on matching, or securing an appropriate degree of congruence between leadership style and the needs of the dilemma or situation.

This section looks at two different contingency models of leadership, namely:

❏ **F.E.Fiedler's leadership contingency model;** *and*
❏ **C.B.Handy's "Best Fit" approach**

F.E.Fiedler's leadership contingency model – F.E.Fiedler's leadership contingency model and its subsequent development was based on the study of the styles and effectiveness of many different leaders working in a variety of different contexts.

Fiedler combined *task motivation* and *relationship orientation* variables, with a *position power* variable in order to describe the effectiveness of leadership style in particular situations or contingencies. Any particular dilemma leadership situation is therefore described by Fiedler as (equifinally) comprising *three inter-related variables*, namely:

1. *Leader-member relationships* – which describe the degree of confidence, trust, liking, loyalty, preference and commitment shown by individuals and the group towards the leader. This may indicate a positive ("good") or negative ("poor") degree of relationship orientation.

2. *Task structure* – which refers to the degree to which the requirements of the dilemma or task are clearly defined (or definable). Dilemmas or tasks that are completely structured are seen to give more control to the leader; whilst vague or unclear dilemmas or tasks are seen to lessen the leader's influence and control. Routine tasks associated with (say) political, legal and departmental administration, or transaction processing are *structured*. Creative or innovative tasks instead associated (say) with dealing with difficult political, security, or sales negotiations; managing difficult media, communities, ethnicities, customers, pressure groups, or clients; carrying out new surgical procedures or new product or process development; lecturing part-time Masters or MBA level vocational university students, or writing a professional book like this one are *unstructured. By definition there is no one best way of fulfilling such tasks, nor*

any way of guaranteeing a successful outcome. The approach to these dilemmas or tasks must by definition be equifinal in nature.

3. *Position power* – which refers to the degree of authority or influence possessed by the leader to carry out transactional and motivational activities associated with task accomplishment, reward, sanction or punishment. This chapter has already noted that position power may for instance include:-

    • the power individuals acquire from the position they hold in the organisation;

    • the power that individuals possess because of their demonstrated knowledge, expertise or experience ("expert or professional power");

    • power that is associated with personal traits such as charisma (already described in an earlier section of this chapter); or the intelligence, self-confidence, determination, energy and perseverance, personal integrity, and sociability also described in an earlier section above.

Taken together, the three contingent variables described above are held to determine the "relative favourableness" of various dilemma leadership situations. Fiedler conceptualises *the degree of "favourableness"* as follows:

❏ "very favourable" situations, which are those circumstances that have any combination of good interpersonal leader- follower relationships, well defined tasks, or strong leader position power. These situations are shown as scores 1, 2 and 3 on **Figure 18.**

❏ "least favourable" situations, which are those circumstances that have any combination of poor inter-personal leader- follower relationships, unstructured tasks, or weak leader position power.

❏ "moderately favourable" situations, which fall between the first two polar positions described immediately above. These will be located within the area of the scores 1, 2 and 3 on the diagram, but do not represent such ideal conditions.

❏ the potentially "favourable" situation shown as score 8 on the diagram, which is characterised by any combination of relatively weak leader-follower relationships, poor or uncertain task structure, and weak leader position power. In this situation, leadership may be effective if (i) a consultative or participative approach is taken to leader-follower relationships or to the task; and (ii) subordinates are encouraged to take responsibility for the situation. Individuals or the group may be more competent than the leader (for instance through their possession of the relevant expert power) to deal with the situation and the task. And in any case, individual members or the group may hold the competence or expertise of the leader in low esteem, and may have low expectations of his or her capacity to deal with the conditions that all of them face.

Fiedler's findings therefore indicate that different leadership styles may be appropriate to, or effective in different situations. For instance:

a. individuals who are task orientated may be effective in very favourable or very unfavourable situations, such as:-
    • those that are proceeding very smoothly and successfully; *or instead*
    • those circumstances in which events are getting out of hand or showing signs of failure, *or*
    • those conditions that are so much out of control that everyone is forced to accept drastic and urgent leadership decisions to remedy or turn-around the affairs of the organisation.
b. individuals who are more relationship-oriented may be effective in moderately favourable situations in which there is some degree of certainty but events are never completely under control. This for instance characterises many political, customer service, relationship marketing, social or public service situations; or tasks characterised by creativity, innovation, risk or change.

Fiedler's findings also indicate that if the leader's approach or style is not in any way adequately matched or appropriate to the dilemma or circumstances that he or she faces, then that leader's decisions and actions may be entirely ineffective. Or indeed they may prove to be negatively counter-productive, potentially making the situation worse – not better.

C.B.Handy's "Best Fit" approach to leadership – C.B.Handy comments instead that his *Best Fit* approach to leadership is based on the equifinal assumption that there can be no such thing as a "right style" of leadership. Leadership may only be effective when there is *congruence* between *the various needs of all of:*

❑ the dilemma, the situation, or the circumstances as contingencies; *and*
❑ the leader, and his or her objectives; *and*
❑ the task or operational requirement; *and*
❑ the capability, commitment or expectations of governance, managers, the team, or subordinates.

A failure to achieve a degree of "fit" or harmony between these four variables may lead to dilemmas in which leadership choices or behaviour might be rendered ineffective. *Or the mismatch between them may instead be so significant that leadership outcomes may prove to be negative and counterproductive.* This syndrome (and its potentially disastrous consequences) is for example described in Chapter 26 as well as in Part Five.

For example, there may be hierarchical disagreements within the institution, organisation, or political party about the interpretation of the character and dynamics of current political, equality, security, or risk conditions (etc); or conditions of external change faced by an enterprise, whether in markets, High Streets, technologies, informatics, competition policy, globalisation, employment prospects, or the stability of international environments.

Such conditions of change, uncertainty and risk may (i) be interpreted by some people in the organisation to require increasingly varied, flexible and *decentralised management* processes in which individuals are locally empowered to drive processes of adaptation and adjustment.

Others may however (ii) interpret the threats implied by these conditions to give rise to a need for *aggressive re-centralisation*, the rigid structuring and control of strategies, priorities and tasks, and determined prescription by senior politicians, administrators, or management as to what must be done.

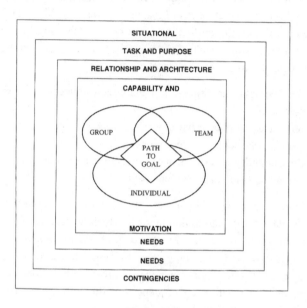

Figure 17
The Layers of Transactional Leadership

LEADER – MEMBER RELATIONS	POSITIVE				NEGATIVE			
TASK STRUCTURE	HIGH STRUCTURE		LOW STRUCTURE		HIGH STRUCTURE		LOW STRUCTURE	
POSITION POWER	STRONG POWER	WEAK POWER	STRONG POWER	WEAK POWER	STRONG POWER	WEAK POWER	STRONG POWER	WEAK POWER
	1	2	3	4	5	6	7	8
RELATIVE FAVOURABLENESS OF LEADERSHIP SITUATION	← MORE FAVOURABLE →				← LESS FAVOURABLE →			MORE FAVOURABLE

Figure 18
Fiedler's Leadership Model

Chapter Twenty Two
Making Dilemma Decisions

A correspondent to the **Daily Telegraph** *wrote that she 'recently heard yet another interviewee, in a publicly funded organisation, describe a problem as "systemic". In other words – "not my responsibility"'.*

Chapter 22 focuses on issues of authority, responsibility, and decision-making practice.

THE RESPONSIBILITY FOR MAKING DECISIONS

Where the operating environment of the institution or organisation is characterised by the presence of dilemmas as event categories or contingencies, as described throughout this Book, **then it will be necessary for those people directly charged with the responsibility for governance and strategic direction to ensure that clear lines of accountability for the process of Dilemma Management and dilemma resolution are laid down.**

There will be a need to ensure that the processes of managing dilemmas and dilemma decision-making correlate with the locus or loci of responsibility and authority (i) in the organisation; and / or (ii) within the relevant relationship architecture. Individual, governance, or corporate roles; and levels of hierarchy will have to be clearly designated as accountable for Dilemma Management and for its consequences.

Clarity of responsibility becomes increasingly important the more that the dilemmas involved (such as those at the level of government or national institutions which deal with health and social care, security, the allocation of international aid, immigration, etc) for example possess:

❑ characteristics of scale, importance, visibility, urgency or prestige;

❏ complexity;
❏ a need for the *prioritisation of response* according to *varying urgency and risk criteria* amongst multiple and potentially conflicting demands, for instance in the inter or multi-agency provision of policing, security, overseas aid, healthcare or ambulance services; *or instead*
❏ in the negotiation of very large scale defence, aviation or construction contracts with foreign governments or companies;
❏ significant levels and timescale of resource commitment (for instance in education, or in the construction of airports and runways, infrastructure, mega-hospitals, or mega-prisons, etc); *and*
❏ the likelihood of public, electoral, stakeholder or donor response to decisions made;
❏ potential or actual risk or threat to the institution.

Multi-Agency Relationship Architectures – issues of decision-making responsibility may be brought into sharp focus where the direct fulfilment of leadership, role and task will have to be based on a *multiple agency relationship architecture*, for instance in the provision of mental health triage, alcoholic drunk-tank, or social / child care services in the community. Similarly, the solution to dilemmas occurring as a result of investments in very large infrastructure or defence projects are likely to have to depend on the interaction of a whole series of independent agencies or sub-contractors. Some of these issues have been dealt with in earlier chapters.

CENTRALISATION AND THE LOCUS OF AUTHORITY
The locus of authority to make decisions about the resolution of dilemmas (or instead to put the matter off until another day) may be described in terms of the concept of *centralisation*. The more that the authority to make decisions is restricted to a small number of roles or individuals at the top of a hierarchy (and the higher is the degree of power distance involved), the more centralised is that organisation, and vice versa.

Take for example the case of the UK's (former) General Electric Company (GEC), described below.

A CASE EXAMPLE OF PERSONAL RESPONSIBILITY

The UK General Electric and English Electric Companies merged during 1968. The purpose of the merger was to create an electrical engineering company that could compete on an international basis. This was seen by the then British government as a critically important development for the UK economy and for its export activity. Electrical Engineering is an absolutely critical sector in any industrialised country.

The two constituent companies had very different styles of operating. The new GEC Company very quickly decided that it had urgently to reconcile management processes and architectures as well as product lines. Following the merger, the new Company Managing Director Arnold (later Sir Arnold) Weinstock wrote as follows to all Unit MDs, outlining his requirements for the new Company's management. He stated that 'at HQ, the management directors and I are responsible to Lord Nelson as (Company Chairman) for the performance of the business overall. Kenneth Bond (joint deputy managing director), Sandy Riddell (joint deputy managing director) and I are helped and prodded by ... you will hear from all of them in due course. *But the real success of our new Company depends on the individual managing directors of our many product units.* Our help (or lack of it) from HQ does not relieve you in the least of the responsibility for that part of the business which is in your charge. You will, of course, see that your sub-managers are given well defined, specific objectives and tasks and then discharge their duties effectively.

Our philosophy of *personal responsibility* makes it completely unnecessary for you to spend time at meetings of subsidiary boards or standing committees. Therefore, all standing committees are by this direction disbanded and subsidiary boards will not need to meet again.

You will be held personally accountable for any decision taken that affects your operating unit ... incidentally, on this matter of personal responsibility, prior permission from HQ is required for any proposal to employ management consultants.'

DECISION MAKING PROCESSES

Decisions about dilemma diagnosis, resolution, or delay may be made by the responsible people using any of the following means:

❑ **by prescription or command** – in which the decision-making process is centralised to the locus of dominant power or authority in the institution, for instance in the case of companies, governments, or hierarchies characterised by high power distance;

❑ **in consultation with others** – for instance by taking expert advice (such as in legal or medicolegal matters), seeking trade or public opinion, employing scientific advisers, or using management consultants (where this is permitted in order to compensate for an acknowledged lack of in-house capability) in order to identify and specify options and alternatives;

❑ **with the participation of others** – by which any or all of politicians, civil or state servants, stakeholder or trade union representatives, directors, managers, employees, customer or patient representatives, members of the public, advisers (etc) are to some degree involved in the process of dilemma diagnosis and resolution. This might assume a high level of enterprise openness and a low degree of closure, a low power distance, a low degree of uncertainty avoidance, high levels of trust, open communication networks, and a high level of risk tolerance. These issues were described in earlier chapters, including Chapter 10. Decision-makers would have culturally to be prepared to have their decisions questioned and criticised; and perceived "mistakes" openly discussed and challenged by others;

❑ **by negotiation** – in which Dilemma Management is based on the outcome of negotiation amongst stakeholders and the relevant sources of power within or external to the government, agency, or institution;

❑ **by compromise** – in which decisions result from the dynamic of an (architectural relationship) interaction between the perspectives, positioning, parameters, and values upon which most, some, or instead none of the participants can agree. Compromise outcomes may in particular be characteristic of the Dilemma

Management process in political, public sector and not-for-profit organisations. Any resultant compromise **may (or instead may not)** be relevant to dealing with dilemmas, or instead only to delaying their resolution. The possibility of such outcomes is illustrated in various chapters of this Book;

❏ **by vote or quasi-democracy** – in which the process of dilemma resolution is determined (or not) by processes which are more or less democratic in form. Such processes may be subject to negotiation or compromise as above; *or may instead be subject to:-*

❏ **lobbying and "persuasion"** – by which processes of dilemma resolution are subject to politicised pressures from "interested parties" such as industry representatives or business companies, trade unions, political and single-interest ("pressure") groups, the media, "social media" campaigners for instance using mass petitions, and others who have a particular interest in shaping the outcome of the resolution process. In the UK, for instance, ongoing dilemmas associated (i) with Brexit; (ii) with the nature and source of essential foodstuffs (as well as the sugar content of soft drinks), and the critical implication for the UK of the high environmental costs of imported foods and the need for agricultural import substitution; (iii) with the funding and performance of the NHS; (iv) with the constitution of the BBC; (v) with wind and nuclear power generation; (vi) with national / border security and defence; (vii) with the arming of police officers; (viii) with the relevance of vocational and non-vocational education; and (ix) with the nature of the taxation and benefits system are all subject to massive pressures of lobbying and influence. This may make dilemma resolution difficult (or even impossible). It may also reflect the degree to which the processes of debate and dialectics, reinforced by opinionation and the power of the media and social media in the UK may run counter to the reality of responsible governments or institutions having actually to get things done within the time, the resources and capability available to them (eg see Chapters 24 and 28) – however imperfectly they may do so.

COLLECTIVE RESPONSIBILITY

Forms of collective decision-making responsibility are evident in governmental-type institutions, for instance using "cabinet" systems. Once all of the relevant information is to hand, cabinet members will come to an agreement (or instead a failure to agree) on the basis of any of the decision-making processes listed above. Critically, decision-makers may take the advice of civil servants, lawyers, chief officers, special advisers, or departmental directors about the issue to hand. But once an agreement is reached and a decision is made, then all members of the collective *are supposed to be committed* to that decision and are responsible for it to the electorate. Such decisions might be subject to mechanisms of scrutiny prior to finalisation. But they may then only be overturned by successful legal challenges (for instance to planning decisions); or by more senior state representatives. The latter has been the case in child welfare or educational shortcomings where government commissioners may be put in place as overseers, or an entire function withdrawn from the authority's control.

MINTZBERG'S FOUR DECISION ROLES

Henry Mintzberg identifies *four key decision roles*. These roles may have to be used no matter what kind of decision-making process, as described above, is applied by the institution. Mintzberg is well-known as a North American management academic and business adviser to the Canadian Government.

The disturbance handler role – Mintzberg describes this role as being responsible for identifying and formulating strategies or protocols for dealing with dilemmas as *unexpected, involuntary, unwanted, unavoidable or unpredictable events and crises* whose origin and timing are to some degree beyond the control of the enterprise, and which are likely to be a significant source of disturbance or risk to its equilibrium or status quo. These events are judged to require decision-making and action, for instance in terms of:

- ❏ an enforced need to change strategies, plans, or positioning;
- ❏ the need (i) to make additional use of available power or (ii) to

commit more resources, for instance in conditions of parliamentary democracy where the application of such power is open to scrutiny and challenge;

❏ engaging in the lobbying behaviour as described above.

Case Example: the management of the likely dilemmas, delays and cost issues associated with the construction and commissioning of new nuclear power stations seen from (i) a potential future scenario of electricity shortages, and (ii) the possibility of Chinese involvement as trading partner.

Case Example: at a recent meeting 'the chief executives of sixty NHS Trusts were forced to join in a chant of **"we can do this"** by a senior NHS official, who told them that it would help them to improve their A & E treatment targets in advance of what was predicted to be a tough winter for the NHS. The hospital bosses described the exercise as "bullying", "humiliating", and "unhelpful" ... others called it "Bob the Builder for NHS leaders"' (source – **The Week**).

The negotiator role – the Dilemma Management process may mean that the institution finds itself involved in major, non-routine negotiations with powerful individuals, governments, stakeholders, and other organisations. Such negotiations might for instance result in the signing of major commercial contracts associated with building construction developments or defence systems; or establishing new industry, educational or vocational standards. The negotiator roles may be required to:

❏ act as representative and spokesperson;
❏ provide information and expertise relevant to the negotiation;
❏ add "weight", credibility, and prestige to the negotiating position of the enterprise;
❏ persuade, to sell, and otherwise to make an appropriate use of interpersonal skills and power in attempting to shape the outcome of the negotiation in the interests of the enterprise; *and then (maybe)*
❏ "sell the deal" to the institution and its stakeholders, thereby creating commitment to it.

The negotiator role is likely to involve the use of power, lobbying and political behaviour in order to facilitate the decision-making process.

Case Example: negotiations between pharmaceutical companies, and the National Health Service as the primary buyer of prescription drugs in the UK, as to what should (and should not) be on the list of drugs from which practitioners may choose when prescribing to patients. Are "on patent" drugs to be made available, or are such drugs to be deemed to be too expensive for normal patient prescription? What happens when the media gets wind of someone suffering when a new (but unavailable) patented drug could work a miracle cure?

The entrepreneurial role – which is responsible for specifying and initiating action or change as a result of the resolution (or otherwise) of the dilemma. This might mean the positive search for developing opportunities which the institution can use its resources or its competitive advantage to exploit in its own interest. Such a strategy is described as key to the eventual disengagement of the UK from the European Union.

Case Example: Alan Sugar's decision to create the UK market for home and small business personal computers (PCs), thereby presenting existing computer manufacturers with a concept dilemma. The emerging small business market was largely ignored during the 1980s by market incumbents, who were at that time fixated (in the case of IBM to a disastrous degree) on supplying large and medium scale business machines. It also caught the manufacturers of typewriters unawares. IBM's electro-mechanical "golf ball" typewriters for instance cost in excess of £3000 each at the time. Office word processors cost £10,000 each. Very soon Amstrad's low-cost computers and word processors (introduced at prices between £500 and £1000 each) had established a position of market leadership. Typewriters rapidly became obsolete. And the many proprietors of small businesses had reorganised their paperwork around an Amstrad system and cost-efficient accounting packages (such as Sage or QuickBooks), giving them more control and less work to do.

The resource allocator role – as resource allocator, the decision-maker has the authority *to commit the resources of the enterprise* as a consequence of the need for dilemma resolution. This role must therefore hold a corresponding responsibility for the proper use of those resources, for whose *performance measurement and performance management* (Chapter 24) they may be held to account. The resource allocator may *inter alia* be responsible for ensuring that:

❑ the necessary resource base and capability is put in place (whatever this is judged to be), on the best available terms and conditions;

❑ resource allocation priorities are established, so as to make the best use of those resources for instance in terms of opportunity cost, capital budgeting, or the Zero Based Budgeting (ZBB) to which reference was made in earlier chapters;

❑ any resource disbursement is properly authorised (and the potential for misuse or corruption eliminated entirely);

❑ time as a critical success factor and limiting factor is managed appropriately (for instance in co-ordinating and minimising travel disturbance associated with motorway refurbishment or the installation of urban tramway systems) This may include *project management type* controls on the scheduling of work and the programming of tasks and achievement;

❑ monitoring and controlling enterprise activity;

❑ presenting *performance-based evidence* to stakeholders or suppliers of finance of the results of resource investment and use. This has for instance become a critical requirement for agencies or charities (such as those involved in community welfare or the provision of social benefits) in receipt of UK **grant type funding** from local and central government in order to carry out their functions.

Case Example: funding dilemmas associated with decisions about the allocation of hospital budgets in the current resource- constrained context in which the UK National Health Service (NHS) operates. Who is to get what money (and for how long)?

Should large sums be committed to regional "super" or "mega" hospitals dedicated to achieving rigorous acute treatment and research standards but implying that certain patients will have to travel long distances for certain types of access? And how will such establishments *guarantee* Six Sigma performance in the consistent eradication of infection? What types of patient conditions are / will in future be excluded from NHS treatment? What will happen to services involved in Accident & Emergency, mental health assurance, or aggressive alcoholism, all of which must of necessity be rooted on a multi-agency basis in the local community, (etc)?

Chapter Twenty Three
Competition Strategy

"I don't like the lust for failure in Britain. The only reason we don't have the death penalty … is you're gone too quick – you can't jab people through the bars when they're dead".
Billy Connolly

INTRODUCTION

This chapter analyses competition strategy. Decisions about how, why and where to compete will provide critical dilemmas for any organisation (or indeed region or country) which (i) has to operate in a competitive environment, or (ii) has more specifically to deal with any form of competing institutions (such as in the internal public sector process of bidding for state funds, in education, or in the healthcare system).

The chapter summarises a variety of competitive positions. It then describes alternative *competition strategies* ranging from the proactive and the aggressive through the defensive to co-operation and partnership.

The nature of enterprise competition strategy will in part be determined by the prevailing competition policy or competition laws of the country in which the organisation is operating. A generic reference was made to these kind of Big Picture macro or regulations in Chapter 4.

COMPETITIVE POSITIONING

An enterprise, institution or country may select, work towards achieving, or instead have forced upon it any of the competitive positions described immediately below. This *competitive position* will depend upon the relative strength of the enterprise or region within its *competitive environment*, on its capability, and on its sources of *competitive advantage* to which this capability may allow access.

Dominance – in which the enterprise or country is the outright leader. Its strategy is deliberately to maintain its position and to shape the nature of the trading environment in its own interest. Du Pont is for example often quoted as being dominant in a number of global chemical markets. Germany is a world leader in the manufacture and export of high quality engineering products. Ultimately, dominance may take the form of oligopoly or monopoly if the prevailing competition laws will permit such a position in the sector or industry.

Leadership – in which the enterprise is "number one" in the perception of customer and trade alike. The leader acts as a benchmark for the sector. Leadership is likely to be based upon the possession and exploitation of very significant sources of capability and competitive advantage. A leadership position may, or may not be associated with a significant market share.

Seeking parity – where the enterprise or country attempts to maintain equality with its main rivals, ideally so that the emergence of any dominant or leading player is inhibited or discouraged. The enterprise however takes the nature of the competitive "game" as given. It plays the "same game" as its rivals. It is not likely to be in a strong enough position to shape or redefine the nature of that game. This strategy is for instance characteristic of mature markets for fast-moving consumer or electronic goods in which companies (or countries) are forced to compete for *relative market share*.

Followership – where the enterprise, institution or country follows the dominant or leading competitors, playing the required game by the rules that these dominant or leading players have laid down. Followers may be forced to introduce "me too" products or campaigns that imitate the strategies of market leaders; or may instead be forced to calculate their price or national taxation position relative to the leader's benchmark.

Low profile – in which the enterprise actively seeks to avoid the attentions of the main players in the market, thereby minimising the risk of a head-on confrontation which would inevitably be damaging to the weaker party.

Complementarity – where the existence of the enterprise is complementary to the competitive position of other organisations. For instance, markets characterised by an oligopoly situation based upon a small number of very powerful large players may also contain a range of mid-sized companies. The continued existence of these smaller companies is essential to their more powerful rivals in order to avoid statutory investigation or interference that could lead to an enforced increase in the number of significant competitive players.

Alternatively, the enterprise may supply its customers with products or services which those customers need, but which they do not wish to provide for themselves. This was the case for the development and manufacture of printers for the computer industry. The work of such companies as Canon and Hewlett- Packard is complementary to that of computer manufacturers, to the providers of microprocessors such as Intel, and to the providers of software such as Microsoft or Sage.

ATTACKING STRATEGIES

PROACTIVE, OFFENSIVE OR ATTACKING COMPETITION STRATEGIES

Proactive, offensive, or attacking strategies are predicated upon an aggressive determination *to shape the nature of the competitive environment in the interest of the enterprise, institution or country*; and where possible to disadvantage competitors. The enterprise "plays to win". Others may therefore lose.

The enterprise may attempt to shape the rules of the game (and the conditions in which it is played) in its own interest. Competitors will have to play the game by its rules, and not by their own. A classic example is for enterprise management to use political, relationship architecture, and reputation advantages to ensure that *standards* are set (either or both by official standards institutions, or by market perceptions of benchmark quality and desirability):

❑ such that few, if any rivals can match these standards; *and*
❑ such that these standards constitute powerful barriers to entry; *and*
❑ such that the exit of weaker players is encouraged.

First mover advantage – where the enterprise is in a position to redefine the nature of the market or competition, or to establish a "new game", it will have the advantage of both (i) being able to be the first to move, and (ii) being free to choose the direction of that movement. This "first mover" advantage may then be used to establish leadership or dominance, since rivals will be placed in a position where as followers they may always be trying to catch up. The nature of the competitive game, and the strategy will both be forced upon them by the leader.

Picking winners – the ability of the enterprise to pursue proactive, attacking, or first-mover strategies may be strengthened where it has developed the long-term ability successfully to identify, invest in, bring to market, and exploit "winners". Its track record in *picking winners* may variously depend on:

❑ the depth and continuity of its leadership focus and competence, and the management skill of the institution;

❑ the strength of its capability and sources of competitive advantage;

❑ its ability financially to sustain consistent long term investment in new technologies, new institutions, new processes, and new products or services.

Establishing outright market leadership – the objective of this strategy is to establish leadership in a new market or sector created or developed by the enterprise. The new market, and the leadership of that market are likely to be based on the possession and exploitation of some significant capability, or other source of competitive advantage.

The strategy aims to create new demands, new customers, and new markets which the originator then dominates. Examples include:

❑ the acquisition and development of the first vitamin patents by Hoffman LaRoche during the 1920s; and that company's subsequent development and patenting of the tranquillisers Librium and Valium during the 1950s. Both developments established large new markets;

❏ the development and marketing of the synthetic fibres nylon and
polyester.

Segment-specific attack – this form of strategy may (i) be described
in terms of "hitting the competition where it isn't". Alternatively,
(ii) it may take the form of an attack on market segments or market niches that have been under-exploited or neglected by existing
suppliers.

Products or services may be introduced that provide satisfaction
within customer or client usage contexts not already adequately covered by existing suppliers. Or instead products or services may be
introduced that outperform what is already available but perceived
by customers to be unsatisfactory. Examples include the introduction by Sony of small, portable transistor radios; the development by
Amstrad and Apple of efficient but relatively low cost word processors; or the replacement of steam traction by diesel-electric railway
locomotive technology during the 1940s and 1950s.

The enterprise looks for market, process or service opportunities
not yet recognised nor properly provided for by existing suppliers.
This was the case in the development of industrial scale computing,
mobile telephony and data services. Newcomers can use this route
because the barriers to entry may not be high. Defensive tactics by
existing suppliers may prove ineffective if the market is unsatisfied
and the newcomer provides the value or satisfaction being sought by
customers, clients or institutions.

Flanking attack – a segment-specific strategy may also be used as
a form of flanking attack on existing suppliers. The enterprise or
institution concentrates at first on those parts of the market or its
environment that are ineffectively provided for. But eventually the
newcomer may be able to use its evolving and strengthening position
to mount a wider or more general attack on the segment strongholds
of existing suppliers, particularly where (i) these suppliers have
become complacent; (ii) these suppliers have stopped investing in
innovation in order to maximise short term shareholder returns; or
(iii) naïvely dismiss the newcomer as insignificant and unimportant.
Thus was the market dominance of National Cash Register (NCR)

in the field of electro- mechanical measuring and office equipment destroyed by electronics based newcomers such as Burroughs' Machines; and Imperial whose manual and electric typewriters were made obsolete almost overnight by computer-based technologies.

The Prospector – "prospectors" are organisations that regularly search for new market opportunities, and experiment with potential responses to emerging trends within the technological, regulatory or market environment. Prospectors are creators of change and uncertainty to which their competitors must respond. They conceptualise their environment and the event characteristics within it as being characterised by dynamism. They believe that the parameters of that environment can be shaped in a deliberate and opportunistic manner in the interests of the enterprise.

Copying and creative imitation – creative imitation implies the copying or the improvement of a product, process, or service previously introduced by a competitor. The creative imitator copies or develops the competitor's offering, perhaps improving its specification or introducing it at a lower price level than the original. Examples include:

❏ the copying and development by Japanese manufacturers in the 1950s of British and American motor cycles; and the subsequent Japanese dominance of the world market;
❏ Seiko's adaptation of Swiss electronic quartz digital watch technology and its introduction into the mass watch market.

The strategy of creative imitation may contain less risk than that of innovation. It may also contain less risk than the strategy of attempting to establish outright market leadership already described above. The innovator or the originator of the product carries the burden and uncertainty (i) of developing the "new"; (ii) of familiarising people with it; and (iii) of creating the market. The creative imitator can avoid these costs of origination and market creation; make improvements or cost reductions; and capitalise on the efforts of others.

Skilful imitators may be capable of rapid copying and fast seconding to the market. They are never far behind the leader in exploiting the market it is creating. The mass international toy market is characterised by a continuous cycle of new product introductions, market development, short product life cycles, imitation, and fast seconding.

THE STRATEGIC THINKING OF SUN TZU

Sun Tzu was an adviser to the Chinese Emperor Wu. His political dexterity and strategic ruthlessness helped his employer overwhelm the state of Chu, with whom the Emperor was in conflict. His teachings, compiled around 500 BC, are based on historical Chinese experience of fighting wars and handling the frequent conflicts that characterised the times.

Sun Tzu's book *The Art of War* describes effective and ineffective strategies by which to fight wars or defeat opponents. The Chinese ideogram for "strategy" is the same as that for "war", so it is natural for the Chinese to perceive the two concepts in the same light. As a result, South East Asians tend to perceive the marketplace as a *battlefield*. The success or failure of a business or an economy directly affects the survival and well-being of the family or the nation. Strategies for waging war have therefore been applied to strategies for *waging business*. In competitive terms these strategies are summarized as follows.

Defeat your opponents by strategy and flexibility – the objective here should be to conquer the opponent by strategy not conflict. Conflict may ultimately benefit no-one. Defeating the opponent by strategy implies 'careful and detailed planning', that is, clear business strategy and proper strategic management. At the same time, given Sun Tzu's reminder that 'no plan survives contact with the enemy', enterprise strategy must be flexible and opportunistic according to the circumstances that present themselves.

Use competitive information – in order to win by strategy the enterprise needs to be well informed about its business environment and about its competitors. The manager needs to be in possession of the 'total picture of the situation'. Min Chen (in *Principles of Strategic Management*) suggests that 'to be competitive, an enterprise…needs the information of its competitors, such as the development plan of its new products, operational plans and financial situation'. Its rivals, meanwhile, would be well advised to put systems and incentives in place to ensure that such commercially sensitive information is kept secure and inaccessible!

Divide your opponents – divided or fragmented opponents may provide the least resistance to your competition strategies. An unified opposition may instead be a force to be reckoned with. Hence, for instance, the individualism of western societies and a prevailing ethic of "going it alone" has in the past made difficult the establishment of the co-operation and partnership between companies. South East Asian companies, but especially the Japanese and South Koreans, have found it relatively easy to "pick off" industries (such as consumer electronics, heavy engineering, shipbuilding, or automotive) which were characterised (i) by intense and divisive national competition between fragmented and inward-looking companies, or (ii) restrictive competition laws as in the USA.

Use climate and conditions to your advantage – a good general knows how to exploit to his or her own advantage the uncontrollable elements of geographical conditions and climate in which his army finds itself. Thus did the Russian General Kutusov defeat Napoleon's troops with the help of the severe Russian winter. Similarly, the choice of business strategy needs to be appropriate to such prevailing environmental features of economic climate and business culture as:

❑   the prevailing political situation;
❑   demographic, social and cultural factors;
❑   on-going changes in consumer tastes and attitudes;
❑   economic conditions and trade cycles;
❑   the prevailing investment climate.

Better still, of course, if the enterprise can shape its environment in its own interest, for instance through controlling distribution outlets (as in the movie or alcoholic spirits markets); or through the effective political lobbying and persuasion of such institutions as national governments, international standards bodies, the World Trade Organization (WTO), European Union (EU), or North American Free Trade Association (NAFTA), etc.

Play to your capabilities and strengths – like the general deploying his troops in battle order, the leader and his or her managers should concentrate personal and organisational capability, willpower, and enterprise experience where it is likely to prove most advantageous. At the same time, the enterprise will have to recognize the strengths of its rivals and avoid meeting them head on. It could lose such a confrontation.

Play to the weaknesses of competitors – at the same time the leader, like the general, should position enterprise strengths and capability against the weakest points of the competition. Thus, such was the difference in perceived quality between mass- produced Japanese cars and those made in the west during the 1970s and 1980s that Japanese manufacturers were able to capture a major slice of markets there.

THE EXPERIENCE EFFECT

The experience effect as a competitive concept assumes that increases in the scale at which an activity is carried out may yield both of:

❏ a build-up of *experience*, the accumulation of which may be used to lower unit cost; *and*

❏ a proportionate decrease in the unit cost of production or provision that results from accessing *economies of scale*.

The concept postulates a relationship between total unit cost and the cumulative volume of units produced. For instance, in a manufacturing company, this states that:

production or provision + marketing / branding +
distribution + capital cost

may decrease at a certain rate each time the volume of total output is increased or doubled.

The rate at which this unit cost decreases may decline as cumulative volume increases, and might eventually reach a zero value.

The concept can be illustrated by a simple example of an experience curve, shown in Figure 19.

Sources of the Experience Effect – there are three likely sources of the experience effect. These are listed as follows.

[1] *Benefits of accumulated experience, for instance demonstrated by increments in value-added* – including:-

❑ *increases in labour productivity* resulting from downward movements on the learning curve. The more that an organisation carries out its tasks, the more efficient it is likely to become at accomplishing them, and the greater is the productivity that may be achieved;

❑ *resource specialisation*, for example in staff competence and professionalisation, manufacturing equipment, physical distribution systems, Information Systems, and so on;

❑ *new operational processes and improved methods.* For example the introduction of the "Chorleywood" process permitted the large scale baking of bread on a continuous flow basis, speeding up the manufacturing process, ending the need to leave large quantities of dough (working capital) waiting to prove and rise, and reducing the need for expensive climate- controlled working space;

❑ *product and process standardisation*, the effects of which are widely visible in car manufacture, where many parts are standardised and interchangeable between models and ranges, and between different manufacturers;

❑ *substitution in the product*, whereby cheaper but equally effective materials or processes are used to replace more expensive ones. Why use a bolt to secure a nut when a cheaper spring clip or a self-tapping screw will perform equally as well?

❑ *product redesign*, yielding cost decreases or value-added gains. Compare the wordprocessor with the complex and now obsolete heavy electro-mechanical typewriters. The electro- mechanical typewriter had reached its ultimate point of development, and was expensive to purchase and maintain. Technological changes have increased the capacity and options of text preparation, but very significantly decreased its relative cost. Developments in simpler electric technologies may have the same effect in replacing expensive internal combustion engines for instance specified for the urban use of passenger cars.

[2] *Benefits of accumulated experience resulting for example from process re-engineering and the application of Six Sigma to the performance measurement process described elsewhere in this Book –* and by which core operational business processes are redesigned or re configured to yield more value, or decrease costs, or both.

[3] *Economies of scale –* which yield proportionate decreases in the unit cost of production or provision as the scale of activity is increased. There are many examples, including (i) increases in the physical size, scale and volume of operation; (ii) the absorption of fixed costs over a greater volume of output, thereby reducing the contribution required from each unit sold to pay for these fixed costs; and (iii) the benefits of mass and time-consistent branding and advertising applied to ranges or families of products or services such in consumer goods or financial services.

Exploiting the Experience Effect: the potential competitive volume, cost and market share relationship – the experience effect concept may for example be applied to competitive conditions *in which the products and services being supplied are broadly similar, or cannot be fully or effectively differentiated from each other.* Ultimately this may mean conditions where products or services are of a *commodity* nature. These cannot effectively be differentiated.

Such conditions may then be characterised by the massive scale of expenditure on branding and advertising support described immediately above. Such support may be needed to retain shelf-space in retail outlets or to maintain online representation.

Commodity type products include standard raw materials such as wool or cotton; fresh and processed foodstuffs; basic housewares such as cleansers, detergents and polishes; standard bread lines; bulk industrial purchases of paint, steel and consumable items;

standardised telecommunications services, standardised technical services, standardised financial services; standardised / mass houseware or electrical brands, and so on.

The experience effect concept suggests that the manufacturer or supplier who is able to produce more units than its competitors may, given (i) the similarity between available products, (ii) a strong marketing support, and (iii) any particular level of market demand, *become the market share leader. This is because the supplier with the greatest volume of output is furthest down the industry's experience curve.* It has the lowest cost per unit, and can therefore enjoy a cost and price advantage.

The reasoning then becomes cyclical. The greater the supplier's volume of output, the lower the unit cost. The lower the unit cost, *the lower can be the price per unit* at which the product or service is offered for sale. The lower the price, the larger will be the sales and the greater will be the market share. The greater the market share, the greater the volume of manufacture or supply; and so on.

In theory, at least, the market share leader should then be able to steadily increase its market share at the expense of those competitors whose unit costs for producing a similar product are higher. This kind of pattern can be illustrated by the following examples:

❏ the UK bakery industry, which is dominated by two major companies;

❏ the global telephony and telecommunications market, dominated by "Big Data" to which reference has been made elsewhere in this Book;

❏ the manufacture only of standard alcoholic products (beer, manufactured spirits such as vodka, etc) which is carried out by a very small number of very large multinational companies;

❏ the manufacture and supply of standardised artificial fabric fibres such as nylon or polyester which is dominated in the West by the brands of such companies as Du Pont;

❏ the mass manufacture, branding and distribution support of electronic timepieces, for instance by Japanese companies such as Seiko.

DEFENSIVE STRATEGIES

DEFENSIVE (OR REACTIVE) COMPETITION STRATEGIES

Defensive or reactive strategies are used to defend enterprise or institutional position in the sector or market against the threat of competition from rivals, and in particular against the proactive, offensive or attacking strategies described above; or against strategies of creative imitation.

The enterprise will attempt to maintain its position, for instance by developing, reinforcing, exploiting, and protecting its various sources of capability, incumbency and competitive advantage. At the same time, it will attempt to block or neutralise attacking moves by competitors. Ries and Trout for instance commented that a well-entrenched market or brand position, effectively reinforced and subject to continuous innovation and improvement, may be very difficult for a competitor to dislodge. Effective defenders include Unilever and Procter & Gamble's washing powder and cleaning products businesses; Du Pont, Coca-Cola, Guinness; Mercedes Benz automotive; and British Airways.

Segment protection – a basic defensive strategy is that of *protecting existing segment provision*. The enterprise or region attempts to monitor threats to its position within the market segments from which it draws its business. It may choose to:

❑ defend and enhance its presence in that market segment, for instance by undertaking activities that strengthen product, reputation and brand value, increase trade, customer or voter loyalty, and so on.

❑ make entry harder or more expensive for would-be entrants or attackers, even where they may have achieved some initial platform of competitive or political advantage.

The potential for entrepreneurial or innovatory pressures from competitors is likely to make it sensible for the enterprise to undertake periodic reviews of its current segment provision. This may help to ensure that there is little or no potential "virgin territory" close to the business or institution that a newcomer could use as the base for a later attack on the wider range of segments within which the enterprise operates.

Case Example: a classic case of failure to protect existing segment provision was demonstrated by the wholesale change in the information technology and telephony markets brought about by the first minicomputer and microcomputer manufacturers, and software houses such as Sage. The innovations they introduced (and their concept of distributed processing) were initially ignored or rejected (for instance because of the working of the "not- invented here" syndrome) by the manufacturers of mainframe computers. Companies such as IBM eventually awoke to find that these mini and microcomputer manufacturers and producers of software had entered a variety of market segments; taken away much corporate business; and changed the entire direction in which the market was to develop.

The Defender – "defenders" are entrepreneurs, institutions and organisations who consciously and deliberately impose on themselves a restricted product-market mission or capability. They might be specialists in their field. They might instead take a limited view of what they do and how this fits within the external environment. The enterprise and its staff may be expert in a limited field of operation, and may be highly effective in the knowledge and technology management that this expertise calls for. But enterprise management does not tend to search outside for new opportunities. They instead concentrate their efforts upon improving the efficiency and effectiveness of their existing operations.

Defenders are careful to protect their existing market segment provision and market share. They pursue strategies of innovation, resource stretch, and continuous improvement in order to maintain their leadership of a specialist area of operation.

But such organisations may have to rely on the continuing stability of their market and external conditions. The potential for major change in these external parameters (such as caused by "S" curve and technology discontinuities described elsewhere by this Author) may pose a significant threat for which they could be ill- prepared. Such was the threat to the Zeiss business when (i) national governments started to rein in public spending, affecting its high-cost research and healthcare instrument businesses at (ii) the same time as cheaper Japanese products became available (of which some were undoubtedly copied from Zeiss).

COUNTER-ATTACK STRATEGIES

COUNTER-ATTACK STRATEGIES

An attack by one competitor on the market position of another may provoke a competitive response in the form of a *counter- attack*. Ries and Trout suggested that counter-attack strategies are particularly likely to be used where a position of established market dominance is under threat from an attacker. The defender of that market position necessarily sees the need for a counter-attack as a forced or self-imposed strategic response. It considers that it is left with little choice but to commit such resources as are necessary to defend its market position. The resulting counter- attack may be based on any of:

❏   *head-hunting* (or poaching) key personnel currently employed by attackers;

❏   *exploiting competitor weaknesses* revealed during the attacking process. These weaknesses might include the technological or operational shortcomings of new capabilities, processes or products (such as the failures of the UK's Comet programme which were subsequently and ruthlessly exploited by Boeing, who were to demonstrate the robustness of its pioneering 707 aircraft being flown upside-down); emergent shortages of finance; mismanagement, or overtrading (etc);

❏   *embroiling the attacker in litigation* which, apart from the expense, may damage the attacker's corporate, brand and market reputation. This strategy was successfully used by Polaroid against Kodak when its rival attempted to introduce its own brand of instant photographic film on to the market;

❏ *using copying, creative imitation and fast seconding* in order rapidly to introduce better versions of the products, processes, or services introduced by competitors as the basis for the original attack;

❏ *outspending the attacker*. Ries and Trout suggest that the defender may be prepared to expend more resources in order to protect the position it holds than the attacker may be willing (or able) to commit to the attack. This may eventually place the attacker in a vulnerable or even unsustainable position.

❏ *leapfrogging the attacker*, for instance by introducing better innovations, better processes, or moving further down the relevant experience curve. This may have the effect of undermining or negating the advantage upon which the attack was originally based. If this strategy is combined with outspending (described immediately above), the result could potentially be highly damaging or even fatal to the original attacker.

OTHER FORMS OF COMPETITION STRATEGY

MIXED COMPETITION STRATEGIES AND THE ANALYSER

"Analysers" are those organisations, institutions or regions that operate in two types of product-market. One type of product- market is relatively stable; the other is changing. In their stable markets, these organisations function as defenders, protecting their existing segment provision and seeking operational efficiency. In the more turbulent sectors, the enterprise monitors the performance of competitors (but especially the "prospectors" described above) and looks out for evidence of successful experimentation and innovation. They then adopt, copy or creatively imitate on an opportunistic basis those new ideas that appear to them to be proven and the most promising, perhaps using their operational efficiency or ability to "fast second".

THE REACTOR

"Reactors" are those organisations or regions (etc) whose owners, senior managers, or stakeholders *do* perceive change and uncertainty occurring within the external, political or market environment, but which are unable to make any effective response to it. The only "strategy" of which such organisations *may* be capable would be adjustments made as a result of irresistible external and environmental pressures. Reactors may be at the mercy of rivals once they have reached or exceeded their limited (and often self-imposed) capacity for response.

Reactors might also be characterised by some kind of powerful influence from Webbists, the political believers in so-called "disinterested experts" and entrenched state control, Snowflakes, and entrenched defenders of the eggshell divides described at various point in this Book.

GOING IT ALONE

Competition strategy in this case may be based upon the maintenance of total independence of enterprise strategy formulation and implementation. This was once the basic strategy of IBM and Eastman Kodak. This "go it alone" independence is likely to have been entrepreneurially and culturally self-imposed. This strategy may be predicated upon an basic ideology and value set of *aggression* towards rivals who compete in the same market or sector. Behaviour towards these competitors may be attacking or defensive as described above. It may be predatory where the prevailing competition laws permit. Or it may be focused on acquisition or take over as a prime business development strategy.

CO-OPERATION AND PARTNERSHIP

Strategy in this case is based upon the premise that the enterprise may benefit from the voluntary sharing with others of the risks and burdens of operations, politics or business, for instance:

❏ by achieving the *synergy* that results from the combination and interaction of a variety and scale of resources that are unavailable to any one company. *Synergy is a concept of joint effect*;

❏ by being better able to compete with giant global corporations by jointly achieving a greater scope and scale of operation than that which could be achieved by any one individual player.

A CAVEAT

Strategies of co-operation and partnership may also be predicated upon a dilemma-based assumption that ongoing competition between rivals, institutions or countries is <u>not always</u> or necessarily a good thing. John Kay, for instance, contended that there may not be any guarantee that a maximisation of competitive conditions results in the maximisation of utility for the consumer, of welfare for the citizen or voter, or even of profitability for the enterprises in the sector. Co-operation and partnership that reduces (or "takes out") what may be perceived as unnecessary, unwanted or destructive competition may be an attractive strategic option to players, regulators and politicians in the field.

Competition strategy and the working of the Experience Effect are described in more detail in the Author's *Principles of Strategic Management*, to which reference is made in the Introduction to this Book.

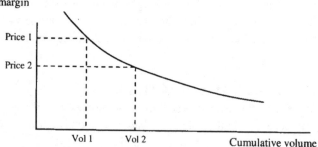

Figure 19
An experience curve

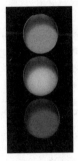

This Chapter analyses Dilemma Decisions associated with the processes of *Performance Measurement and Performance Management*. It does this on the basis of three main Headings, being:

❏ Determinant Variables
❏ Decision Dilemmas
❏ Six Sigma Performance Measurement Dilemmas

DETERMINANT VARIABLES

FOUR DETERMINANT VARIABLES

The first part of this chapter is based on the process interaction between four determinant (or contingent) variables that are likely to shape critical *decision dilemmas associated with the processes of performance measurement and performance management* . These four variables are listed immediately below, and illustrated in Figure 20. They are:

❏ **Purpose**
❏ **Techniques**
❏ **Measurement Criteria**
❏ **Performance Standards**

Each of these variables is presented here in the form of a *selective summary* (or checklist) as necessarily befits the comprehensive scale of the subject. Issues of performance measurement and management are given very extensive treatment in all of the Author's existing books, as listed in the Introduction.

PURPOSE

The purpose of procedures of performance measurement and performance management may be most simply described in terms of the achievement of management process control and feedback to comprise:

❑ the establishment of performance objectives and requirements;
❑ performance monitoring;
❑ comparison with plan, standard or budget;
❑ the communication of feedback;
❑ the analysis and interpretation of variances or deviations;
❑ the undertaking of corrective action.

Other purposes – may include any or all of:

❑ assuring the process of *Hearing the Voice of the Customer (VOC)* and the Voice of the Stakeholder as described throughout this Book;
❑ the fulfilment of statutory (etc) governance-level obligations for the provision of proper evidence of stewardship; audit, accountability and responsibility; the payment of taxes; and the avoidance of corruption or malpractice;
❑ the proper implementation of processes of assurance and certification, whether (i) of efficiency, quality, on-time provision, patient recovery; or (ii) the proper use of government, charitable or donor funds, (etc), as dealt with in other chapters of this Book;
❑ and otherwise the fulfilment of specific requirements for *transparency* as may be laid down;
❑ assuring the process of Hearing Voices for instance as described in Chapter 4 (and also in the Author's two Equality books to which reference is made in the Introduction);

❑   assuring processes of security and safeguarding (Chapter 16);
❑   assuring processes of risk management (Chapter 17);
❑   the avoidance of crises (Chapter 18).

Activity basis – the process of performance measurement and management may of necessity have to be based on feedback about changes in *activity level*. Targets or budgets may be re-assessed and reset. Operations may be rebalanced in the light of changes in market, operational or financial circumstances.

Case Example: at this time of writing the UK motor trade was having to adjust (i) to significant uncertainties about the volume of future sales of diesel cars relative to petrol; as well as (ii) to ongoing concern about the run-time viability of electric cars, and the dangers of the silence of their running to pedestrians, cyclists (etc) around them.

TECHNIQUES
Selected techniques of performance measurement and performance management are listed as follow.

The Financial Health Check – for instance as described in Chapters 14 and 15.

Budgetary planning and control – this technique may encompass the control of any or all of:

❑   cost;
❑   efficiency;
❑   cash flow;
❑   returns by way of profit;
❑   divisional / unit / asset performance;
❑   matrix structures operating for instance on the basis of internal markets;
❑   investment returns.

Processes of budgetary planning may be fixed on an annual basis; or instead be rolling; activity based; or zero-based (ZBB). They are likely to be associated with *formalised standards* and *variance assessments from the desired norm*.

Techniques of Operations Management – to include:

- ❏ project management;
- ❏ network analysis;
- ❏ Programme Evaluation Review (PERT) and PERT-Cost;
- ❏ reengineering;
- ❏ lean;
- ❏ Six Sigma.

Case example – rail track (or railroad) capacity. Long-established paradigms of (lengthy) block working and signalling are used deliberately to limit the capacity of a railway network safely to schedule the passage of high speed trains (with their very long braking distances). The use of GPS positioning may however be used to increase the frequency of running of such trains, each of which will occupy a smaller track length integrated on a computer-controlled flow basis, thereby increasing the utilisation of track and reducing the need for new (and expensive) pathways such as HS2.

Value (non-public sector) – variously to include the value proposition, value generation or addition, and value management, for example based on:

- ❏ Best Value, or Best Value Generation given the prevailing Critical Success Factors and Limiting Factors such as supply limitations; retail floor space available; warehouse capacity; supply logistics relative to demand patterns;
- ❏ Business Model Canvas;
- ❏ Operating Model Canvas.

Public sector techniques – to include any or all of:

- ❏ fixed annual financial budget covering income and expenditure;
- ❏ rolling annual financial budgets with year-end adjustments;
- ❏ Best Value, defined for instance as comprising Effectiveness, Efficiency, and Economy characteristics; *and in the UK associated with*
- ❏ benchmark comparisons, for instance based on the relative performance of groupings of similar organisations, local authorities, etc;

❑   the use of pre-established benchmarks of *required compliance*, as in healthcare and in the treatment of safeguarded or protected categories, and for instance widely applied by the Care Quality Commission (CQC).

The provision of Public Good – an alternative public sector performance management technique focuses on the conceptual (or theoretical?) provision of so-called "Public Good". This concept is for example described by Moore; and Benington & Moore. Public Good *might* be defined:

❑   as a "necessary" utility or value, such as healthcare on the NHS, whose specified and formalised availability is not (or should not?) be reduced (or be likely to be reduced?) by the consumption over time of those who are entitled to access it (**but see** *qualifying risk issues* associated with the potential for reduction or "wearing out" in *asset capability* as described in Chapter 17); *and*

❑   as a utility or a value from the access to which no-one (voters, taxpayers, protected or safeguarded categories, etc) can (or should?) be excluded.

The effectiveness of the provision of Public Good might *in practical and dilemma terms* have to be measured by the technique of the assessment of *Public Value Outcomes*, as described in the next main section of this chapter, below.

MEASUREMENT CRITERIA

Selected measurement criteria are summarised as follow:

❑   unit eg the number of patients treated, or patient recovery / death statistics;

❑   financial value eg the cost of purchasing components, or employing staff;

❑   unit to financial value eg the cost of treating patients, for instance in comparison to other healthcare providers or treatment regimes; the cost of providing private sector residential care for the elderly or the incapacitated;

❑ costs as compared with benefits;

❑ cash-flow eg the relationship between credits and debits;

❑ profit and loss;

❑ asset utilisation eg in respect of transportation and logistics, manufacturing process, hospital bed occupancy;

❑ performance relative to assuring the achievement of the required specification or fitness for purpose eg food safety and hygiene, generic quality and reliability, on-time service, safeguarding and security, data protection (GDPR, etc);

❑ the application of operational, comparative or statistical techniques eg in process control;

❑ Cost Of Poor Quality (COPQ), "Hidden Factory" costs;

❑ value dynamics eg value added, management of the value proposition, indications of value loss described in previous chapters;

❑ what is reasonable or proportionate (Chapter 25);

❑ attitude or satisfaction, however measured eg on the part of customers, clients, patients, voters, stakeholders, donors, distributors, creditors, auditors (etc);

❑ reputational enhancements or damage;

❑ degrees of required compliance eg in dealing with people in protected categories; adherence to proper building standards;

❑ educational exit performance (also see value dynamics above).

❑ the use of number order, "excellent" to "unacceptable", or "traffic light" indicator ranges (green, amber, red; or green, yellow, amber, red) for *performance rating* – as used in healthcare provision, the charitable use of taxpayer funds, food hygiene ratings, disability access, (etc).

Case Example: charity / Third Sector liquidity – accurate indicators of cash-flow and liquidity are essential to the proper running of a charity or a Third Sector organisation. Sufficient cash reserves are needed to ensure that salaries, rents or bills can be paid as required even when the pattern of cash incomes (eg from donations, government or local government agencies, philanthropic trusts as funding sources (etc)) are uncertain or suffer delay. The necessary figure for *cash reserves* may be calculated on the basis of monthly budgeted, or likely estimates of operational expenditure. A figure of (say) three to five months might be regarded as an illustrative minimum value. The performance measurement process may therefore need to look out for:

❏ any sudden or significant reductions in the figure for cash reserves, since this may indicate an unacceptable level of risk eg of payment default (particularly if the charity has no tangible assets as such);

❏ the holding of excessive cash reserves, which might indicate (i) that the charity is not properly spending its money in order to achieve its stated objectives: and also (ii) lead sources of finance to decide that the organisation already has sufficient funds for its purposes and at this time should not be given any more.

Public Value Outcomes – the previous Techniques section suggests that the effectiveness of the provision of Public Good might in practical and dilemma terms have to be monitored, measured, and managed by the technique of the assessment of specified *Public Value Outcomes*, as follow. Public Value Outcomes:

❏ might be measured in generic terms by enhancements to a society's *Human Capital*. Reference is made to the concept of Human Capital in earlier chapters of this Book. Indicators of Human Capital enhancements might be identified by productivity gains, national comparative advantage, Gross Domestic Product (GDP), increased social mobility, and politico-social stability;

❏ may be identified by the value that results from the delivery of specific benefits to persons or groups in a society;

❏ may be identified by evidence of the making of the best use (however defined) of politico-fiscal arrangements by government. This might include the balancing of taxation income with borrowing, the payment of interest on those borrowings, and loan repayments (for instance as a form of gearing and leveraging described in Chapters 14 and 15); *and* /or

❏ may be identified by the value that results directly from improvements to government and the governmental process, as (what should be?) a key asset to a society;

❏ might instead (and perhaps controversially) be indicated by the value or values that result from the specific application and disbursement of taxpayer monies *as determined by direct surveys of taxpayers themselves*, and potentially separate from the political process. The latter would then be expected to comply (to whatever degree) with such direct taxpayer preferences. In this case, Public Value Outcomes are indicated and measured by "Taxpayer Value" type models, for instance as applied in the USA.

The Voice of the Customer (VOC) – Voice of the Customer methodology can be used in the Six Sigma process to specify and to measure the most critical service requirements of the client or customer (for instance as in the case of the Public Value Outcomes or Taxpayer Value models described immediately above). The parameters and constraints of these critical requirements are then used to define the necessary outcomes or outputs of service provision, thus:

The quality or fitness for purpose of these outputs may be stated in customer service terms by the formula
$$Q \times A = E \text{ where}$$
the quality of the solution (Q) x the acceptability of that solution (A)
= the effectiveness of that solution (E)

The achievement of optimal customer service at the level of quality of $+4\sigma$ (95.46%) or $+6\sigma$ (99.73%) may be illustrated by the national variations apparent in the treatment given to elderly patients and the mentally afflicted (*perhaps also voters and former taxpayers with a very weak Voice of the Victim*) in the UK's health and social care sectors. At this time of writing, this very serious Cost Of Poor Quality (COPQ) issue remains controversial in the UK's National Health Service, for instance where for whatever historical, organisational or cultural reasons the *customer service priorities* of NHS managers, nurses, and staff appear to remain below what might (*or as a matter of human dignity and respect ought to be*) expected in respect of society's elders.

PERFORMANCE STANDARDS / STANDARDS OF PERFORMANCE

Performance standards may be any of:

❏ at worst the unplanned, the "shambolic", the amateur, the un-scrutinised or the uncontrolled, the crony-based, the non- ethical or the non-legal; *or marginally better as being*

❏ based on the practice of "muddling through" or a lack of professionalism (also see Chapter 32);

❏ at least (or to some degree) being reactive to events;

❏ *incremental*, in which the organisation (i) manages to learn from its ongoing experience, and ideally (ii) incorporates this learning into its Knowledge base, process, procedure and strategy;

❏ the satisfactory, the satisficing, or the meeting of criteria of fitness for purpose;

❏ specified on the basis of *strict strategic priority* to meet the requirements of, and / or the limitations of contingencies, constraints and Critical Success Factors (CSFs) such as maximising value propositions, meeting demands for shareholder or donor value, optimising patient care, or maximising educational exit performance (etc);

❏ specified instead to optimise stakeholder requirements (as described immediately above) based on the best use of capability, and on the exercise (and financial reward) of the best available leadership quality;

❏ in addition, being subject to the application of processes of stretch and leverage; *and / or*

❏ specified to meet standards of World Class, Excellence or Six Sigma, with organisational capability and leadership determined by the requirements of such standards.

Case example: this Book has made repeated reference to the need for Six Sigma standards of infection control in certain parts of the acute sector of the UK's NHS. This requirement will become even more critical (i) as certain treatment pathways that are dependent on the capability only available from very scarce, very expensive (and as a result highly mobile) skilled staff resources are (ii) concentrated into fewer and fewer regional or mega-hospitals, at the same time as (iii) the future effectiveness of antibiotic drugs may diminish.

Compliance – the degree of compliance with expected standards has become a key performance requirement for instance in the public, charitable / Third Sector, security, safeguarding, and healthcare sectors in the UK. This is also the case for adherence to Equality standards, and the need for the protection of specific categories (who, unless they are Minors, are at the same time voters and taxpayers) from discrimination, exploitation and abuse (and as dealt with elsewhere in detail by this Author).

The Nolan Principles – which describe the formal requirement of the UK Public Standards Committee that people engaged in *public service* should display / comply with the following behaviours:

❑ *selflessness* – acting solely in the public interest;
❑ *integrity* – in the honest and transparent performance of public duties, and in the avoidance and as necessary the exposure of cronyism, malpractice, or corruption;
❑ *objectivity* – in which actions are made on the basis of what is deemed to be best for the state or the organisation, not personally for the decision-maker;
❑ *accountability* – in which responsibility is accepted, and the process of scrutiny or audit becomes an accepted part of the decision-making process or the making of commitments;
❑ *openness* – restricting information about decisions and actions only when it is officially and formally judged to be in the public interest;
❑ *honesty* – for instance (i) admitting mistakes; or (ii) in declaring potential conflicts between personal or corporate interests, and those of the state to which they in whatever capacity are obliged or dependent;
❑ *leadership* – by which holders of public office should support and promote these behaviours by their example and by their leadership.

DECISION DILEMMAS

DECISION DILEMMAS ASSOCIATED WITH THE PROCESSES OF PERFORMANCE MEASUREMENT AND PERFORMANCE MANAGEMENT

Selected decision dilemmas associated with the processes of performance measurement and performance management are listed as follows. Checklist form is again used because of the need usably to summarise a large variety of relevant items in the relatively limited space available in a Book structured as this.

Basic Performance Measurement and Management Dilemmas may include any or all of:

❏ what is being measured, what is the need for this measurement, and why is this the case?

❏ what are the evaluation and assurance criteria for the fitness of purpose of the performance measurement and management process?

❏ what is the base or starting point? For instance is it to be break-even or profit over a given time scale? Or increments in educational value addition for instance (i) in the case of the poorest child in a tough inner-city school, or (ii) in the case of a public school or grammar school entrant in a wealthy area?

❏ what are the relevant time scales to be applied?

❏ who is / are the person or persons accountable and responsible for the process? *And*

❏ where is this, or where are these persons? For example are they remotely situated in a multinational company somewhere else in the world? Or are they agents of central / federal government, region or state, or local / provincial government (etc) responsible for funding activities to other organisations?

❏ what decision-making techniques are to be used (as dealt with at various points in this Book)?

❏ what are deemed to be the impact of the concept and event characteristics described in Chapter 4?

❏ what are deemed to be the impact of the relevant Critical Success Factors, limiting factors, contingencies and constraints to which reference is made throughout this Book?

Strategic dilemmas – may be based on the decision criteria of:

❏ appropriateness;
❏ "fit" with organisational purpose, objectives, capability, culture, leadership process (etc);
❏ desirability;
❏ feasibility;
❏ facilitating comparison, identifying relativities;
❏ facilitating the achievement of comparative or competitive advantage eg in the case of manufacturing or service quality;
❏ the demonstration of the achievement of the requisite level of compliance;
❏ the demonstration of what is deemed to be reasonable or proportionate (Chapter 25) eg in the case of rewards by way of bonus payments to CEOs or CFOs, or the financial returns required from private sector care homes.

Measurement intensity – which may be indicated by Management Dilemmas associated with any or all of the following:

❏ does an apparently *inadequate* degree of monitoring and measurement imply a risk of loss of control, eg in the case of funding allocated to charities who for whatever reason are later judged to have displayed a serious lack of effective trustee board oversight of operational management or financial disbursements?
❏ is there instead evidence of *over-measurement and over control?* Control procedures (or an obsession with control) may overwhelm and distort operational processes or stifle the necessary intrapreneurship. The management process may instead be reduced to the "ticking" of arbitrary boxes, or a fixation on the achievement of certain publicly declared targets only (eg waiting times in a hospital, or the on-time arrival of trains or flights in which external conditions are not under the complete control of operators). Such over-measurement and control may

create excessive bureaucracy; *and indicate a professional lack of awareness of:-*

❏ the degree to which techniques of *management by exception* or the *Pareto Principle* (the 80 – 20 rule) should be used to reduce the incidence of unnecessary or cost-ineffective monitoring and control, for instance in the case of dealing with specified levels of variances from the norm.

Dilemmas of management style and / or installed bases of thinking – might for instance include the impact on performance measurement and performance management of:

❏ the high power distance and lack of trust described in Chapter 6, perhaps characterised by strongly autocratic, centralised, hierarchical, and "top-down" styles of control-obsessed management process. Techniques of management by exception may be an anathema to the proponents of such an uncertainty avoidance style. *But* in Dilemma Management terms they may have instead to be symptomatic of the behaviour of state agencies who are disbursing taxpayer funds (*other people's money*) for which absolute account must be made and any possibility of corruption eliminated on a Six Sigma basis at source;

❏ "closed", "plateau'd" or just "stale" leadership, governance or organisational cultures possessed at best (i) of a limited willingness or ability to adapt to changing external circumstances, or (ii) are instead fixated on the status quo.

Dilemmas, Public Value Outcomes and the provision of Public Good – Moore, and Benington & Moore comment that the provision of Public Value Outcomes may be dependent on two variables which are inherently dilemma-laden. These variables are (i) the nature of the *authorising environment*, and (ii) the provision of the necessary *capability*, thus:

❏ the nature of the authorising environment, by which value outcomes are a function of decisions made by people in positions of responsibility who are empowered and willing (*or for whatever reason unable or unwilling*) to sanction the disbursement of public funds, when, and for whatever intended policy or purpose. For instance, are Public Value Outcomes seen as best served by public sector suppliers, private sector, or charitable / NGO suppliers as sub-contractors, or jointly between them? To what extent should borrowed money, with loan interest and re-payment commitments, be used to finance the public purse? And to what extent should failed private sector contractors (such as Carillion or Interserve) be rescued or bailed out with taxpayer funds?

❑ and consequently, what is the nature of the capability required to create this public value? Should this comprise a full operational capacity (such as in the case of a nationalised railway network), or instead a high degree of sub-contract provision with state agencies acting (i) as policy-makers and (ii) as honest auditors, scrutineers, assurers and certifiers of quality and fitness for purpose?

The proper provision of Public Value Outcomes and the provision of Public Good described above may also (and critically) depend on how the stewards of public finance are able and willing to deal with (manage):

❑ the key dilemma associated with the decision as to whether or not an activity to be funded by public money is essential to, or integral with *the purpose and reputation of government itself* (such as (i) defence, but not necessarily defence research which may be available from key sub-contractors; or (ii) running a railway network such as the UK's Railtrack or Network Rail; or (iii) channelling overseas aid?);

❑ the efficiency, fitness for purpose and cost-effectiveness of state enterprises (such as the UK's National Health Service) funded by taxpayers' money;

❑ the failure of state-sponsored and state funded projects or ventures;

❑ the pressure for the making of (non-legal and non-accountable) "commission payments" or "kick-backs" in the award of gov-ernment, local government or public sector contracts, arms sales, etc; *and*

❑   the wider potential for the corruption described in an earlier chapter that is sometimes associated with the control and disbursement of the public purse.

SIX SIGMA PERFORMANCE MEASUREMENT DILEMMAS

SIX SIGMA METHODOLOGY

Six Sigma defined – Sigma (σ) represents the *standard deviation*, which is a measure of the variation within a population or number set around the *mean* value of that statistic.

Six Sigma represents the population or number set that falls within plus or minus six standard deviations from the norm. *That is, a normal distribution is described as having six deviations positive to the mean, and six deviations negative to it.* Six Sigma therefore accounts for more than 99% of all potential eventualities, whether these be positive or negative.

A figure of $+6\sigma$ must for instance be the minimum performance standard required:

❑   for safety-dominated industries such as air transportation, nuclear power generation, or the handling of dangerous or toxic materials;

❑   for the formal audit of an organisation's financial affairs, relative (i) to the regulatory criteria for which its governance body is liable and accountable, and (ii) to assure that there is no fraud, malpractice, cronyism or corruption;

❑   in crowd-handling (eg after the Hillsborough tragedy) or crowd security;

❑   for any and all matters of the safeguarding of, and advocacy for people who are Minors, or categorised as being protected under Equality legislation, or in any way not capable (ie "lacking capacity") of looking after their own affairs, (etc).

Plus Six Sigma therefore describes one end of a service continuum represented by its normal distribution.

Six Sigma in service provision and community management
– Albeanu *et al* (in Morden "Equality, Diversity and Opportunity Management") note that 'one of the key differences between manufacturing environments and services is that in manufacturing the products are tangible and can be stored and inspected for quality assurance before they reach the client. However, [intangible] services are delivered in real time and cannot be stored or inspected before they reach the client.

Therefore, it becomes imperative that the process by which the service is delivered is designed and tested before it is rolled out to customers. Service processes must be made robust and foolproof. Six Sigma methodologies and a process-focused approach to service design are ... tools for achieving this goal.

The role of the individual involved in delivering the service is ... critical to the success or failure of the outcome ... any process whose output is largely dependent on human performance is a process that runs a high risk of having a significant variance, which means that it [may be hard to predict and to control]. The human element cannot be eliminated from most service delivery processes, but these processes can be engineered [or re- engineered] in such a way as to maximise performance. Some common ways to do this include:

❏ automating as much of the process as possible, using automated workflows, [pre-specified but non-discriminatory protocols and algorithms], validation procedures and other service automation solutions. A process that is backed up by technology can also support the individuals involved to perform better;

❏ eliminating inefficient, non value-adding steps in a process. Opportunities for defects are directly proportional to the number of steps in [a] process;

❏ eliminating bottlenecks within [a] process;

❏ using well-defined procedures and processes, and training the staff who perform these activities to a very competent level; facilitating a good flow of information between all parties involved in the process (clients, stakeholders, employees, and so on);

❏ standardising the process so that the same way of delivering service is achieved in different locations by different [people]'.

CASE EXAMPLE

Six Sigma and the implementation of an Equality Agenda – Six Sigma methodology may be applied to the understanding, implementation, and management of an *Equality Agenda* where for instance the current status of:

❏ generically specified variations from a standard or norm;
❏ customer or client service satisfaction ratings;
❏ the degree of access to service providers, for instance at the edge or limits of service provision to what are sometimes described as "hard to reach" or marginalised groups;
❏ opportunity ratings, whether educational, employment, healthcare or service-oriented (etc); *or*
❏ the actual incidence of Discrimination against people, or failures of compliance

may be driven by the performance management process from, say, $+2\sigma$ (68.26%) acceptable towards an ultimate goal of $+6\sigma$ (99.73%), at which point virtually all unacceptable types of performance variations (and therefore Costs Of Poor Quality) will have been "squeezed out" of the employment record or service provision (etc) of the entity or the organisation.

Given the sensitivity, risk, and potential cost associated with the formulation and implementation of an Equality Agenda, it is perfectly reasonable to incorporate Six Sigma methodologies into the process of improving (i) employment or service practices; (ii) educational and healthcare provision; and (iii) neighbourhood / community management. Such improvements include the reduction (or elimination) of costs and disturbance (as Costs of Poor Quality) associated with incidences of discrimination and below-standard service delivery, failures of compliance, ill-health, legal action, the loss of franchise or licence, problems of social exclusion or marginalisation, and the distorted use of management ("Hidden Factory") time that will be incurred.

Six Sigma Equality performance measurements – could include any of the following:

1. The *mean*, which may for instance be defined by:-
    *   assessments made of an actual or forecast incidence and cost of events (such as harassment, discrimination, compensation payments, litigation, or requirements for remedial action); *or*
    *   assessments of event characteristics (Chapter 4) as demonstrated on a histogram basis; *or*
    *   assessments based on minimum prescribed standards to which all without exception must adhere (as in social care or healthcare); *or*
    *   assessments of standards of provision made on the basis of expert judgement (such as those made in respect of housing; the policing of inner-cities and multicultural suburbs; or the treatment in the protective care of the elderly or the disabled;); *or*
    *   assessments of standard of provision made on the basis (i) of internal monitoring and review, and (ii) external feedback or rating, as in the case of features of community management such as the available state of access and opportunity.

2. *Performance variations positive to the mean (up to +6σ)* for example associated with positive client ratings, performance enhancements achieved, the receipt of performance or quality awards, enhanced access, cost savings and efficiency gains, reputation enhancements, additional contracts, funds, or work attracted, etc.

3. *Performance variations negative to the mean (up to -6σ)* for example associated with failures of compliance, negative ratings or regulatory assessments, past litigation record, compensation payments, incidences of public disturbance and injury (such as in the form of riots), etc. Such negative performance variations are likely to be associated with the incidence of Costs of Poor Quality (COPC).

4. *Critical Characteristics* (or Critical Success Factors, or Event Characteristics) comprising variables:-

- critical to process;
- critical to quality – for instance as identified by required standards associated with health, social, and adult care, safeguarding, or child protection;
- critical to cost – for instance in achieving outcomes which can be defended as reasonable or proportionate (Chapter 25) under conditions of resource constraint.

5. *Indicators of process capability* – which is defined by Albeanu *et al* as 'a measure of how well a process that is in control performs within its specification limits. [This] capability can be measured using capability ratios [such as] *Cp* [which is the] ratio of the allowed variation of the process (variation within technical specifications) and its real variation. This shows how close the variation of the process is to the desired variation.' Albeanu *et al* describe three alternatives in their Figure 3.23, **reproduced below as Figure 21 with permission**. These are:-
   - Cp<1 in which the process creates outputs that lie outside of the specification limits. This is an unacceptable situation in performance or compliance management terms. It is described as "incapable";
   - Cp=1 in which process outputs occur exactly within the specification limits. This means that sometimes the output is equal to, or close to the specification limits. Whilst this may be categorised as a "capable" process, it suffers the risk that, given the slightest drift, the outputs will fall outside of the specification limits, for instance into non-compliance;
   - Cp>1 in which all process outputs fall within the specification limits and there is a gap (i) between the highest and lowest output and (ii) the upper and lower specification limits respectively. In this case, the robustness of the capability means that even in the case of drift there is enough space to keep the outputs within the specification limits laid down.

6. *The Hidden Factory* – to which reference has already been made above, and in which for example resources and management time are consumed on a Cost of Poor Quality (COPC) basis by (i) the need to enforce compliance under internal or external

conditions of uncertainty and unpredictability, (ii) by the need for remedial or restorative activities, or (iii) by the management of the crises described in Chapters 15 and 18. **The concept of the Hidden Factory implies the incurring of unnecessary costs and inefficiencies, and represents sub-optimal or non-compliant conditions.**

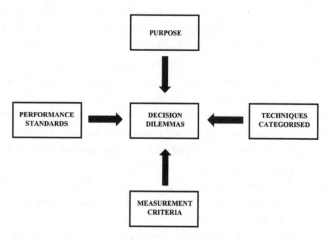

Figure 20
Performance Measurement and Performance Management

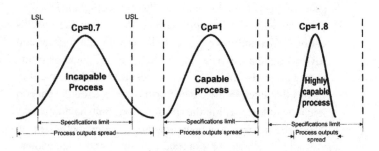

Figure 21
Six Sigma

Chapter Twenty Five
Reasonable or Proportionate

This chapter focuses on issues of definitions of what are judged to be *reasonable* or *proportionate* outcomes of the Dilemma Management decision-making process. Such considerations are of particular relevance to decision-making in the UK associated with the public sector, social and healthcare, security and policing, etc.

WHAT IS REASONABLE?
The OED defines the concept of reasonableness in such contingent terms as being 'of such an amount, size, number (etc) as is judged to be appropriate or suitable to the circumstances or purpose ... possessed of sound judgement ... sensible, sane ... agreeable to reason; not irrational, absurd or ridiculous ... not going beyond the limit assigned by reason; not extravagant or excessive ... moderated'.

WHAT IS PROPORTIONATE?
The OED defines the concept of proportionality in contingent terms as being 'adjusted in due proportion, measure or relationship to something else' (or some kind of standard).

RECAP
The example of specific dilemmas inherent in the use of *drunk- tanks* was raised in Chapter 2 of this Book.

INPUTS AND OUTPUTS
In the relationship between (i) a desired purpose or outcome (such as some kind of dilemma resolution); and (ii) the proposed use of a particular resource, time, capability or willpower (etc) as input whose application is intended to achieve this desired outcome, it may be the case (iii) that the *following criteria* (inter alia as described in Chapter 24) may have to come into play:

❑ the degree of *desirability* (or perceived desirability) from the viewpoint of the relevant stakeholders, electorates, etc;

❑ the degree of *appropriateness* to the relevant Critical Success Factors (CSFs) involved eg cost implications of resource use; efficiency and effectiveness; outcome quality and assurance; stakeholder satisfaction, etc;

❑ relevance to *concept and event characteristics*, and Knowledge base;

❑ the degree of *feasibility*;

❑ the degree of *viability*;

❑ the degree of *fit, compatibility and congruence* between the variables involved.

Issues of this relationship, for the specific purposes of this Book, may also be described to depend for their reasonableness or proportionality on matters of perception (Chapter 9) and other sources of influence / drivers described in Parts Two and Three.

CASE EXAMPLE – A REASONABLE USE OF POLICE FORCE

[1] What is a reasonable use of police force? – UK police officers are routinely required to deal with dilemma and risk-based situations in which there are (i) potentially direct, obvious and irrefutable threats of violence towards their persons or others; and / or (ii) alternatively they have an "honestly held belief" that there is a likely incidence of violence towards themselves and others.

Such circumstances may arise as a result of the police discovery of, and disturbance to any kind of criminal or terrorist activity; violent street drunkenness; drug distribution or drug- taking; inter-communal aggression (all police officers in Northern Ireland are routinely armed); the illegal use of knives and firearms; domestic violence; or transcultural infringements such as violence towards, or robbery from wives dealt with at various points in this Book.

All of these contingencies pose a direct threat to the Human Rights of police officers as Crown (ie state) Servants. They similarly pose a direct threat to the Health & Safety Rights owed to police officers as public sector employees. In dealing with such contingencies, police officers are empowered as Constables in the UK to "use as much force *as is reasonable in the circumstances*" to deal with any threat made towards them. Common Law states that "an officer does not have to wait for the first blow to be struck before using any necessary force to defend himself, herself or another".

[2] The UK Home Office – rules that police officers may deal with work-related threats to themselves and / or the public by the use of any of the following strategies:

- ❑ *officer presence* – in which the appearance of uniformed officers may have the effect of calming a situation containing a potential for developing into one characterised by aggression or violence (etc);
- ❑ officers attempting to discuss the circumstances, or calmly to reason with the people involved;
- ❑ police officer communication of (or warnings about) the potential options available to them to deal with the situation as they perceive it. The drawing of a baton, a threat to use a police dog, the use of officially sanctioned methods of control and restraint, the threat of arrest, or the likelihood of the establishment of a personal Criminal Record may be enough to bring a confrontation to a close *without the actual use of force;*
- ❑ the actual use of the options available to them to deal with a developing or deteriorating situation as they see to be appropriate. This includes any or all of officer presence, talking to people, issuing warnings, the use of procedures of physical control and restraint and / or arrest;
- ❑ the employment in a worsening scenario of threats to use; or actually to make use of batons, dogs, incapacitant sprays such as pepper, aggressive physical restraint ("laying hands" on those resisting arrest, etc), public order (riot) tactics, or Taser (etc);
- ❑ the direct, potentially lethal but *officially sanctioned and controlled* use of firearms in confrontations. Such firearms may vary from handguns through to high velocity rapid fire automatic weapons (essentially hand-held machine guns).

[3] **The Taser** – a current received wisdom in the UK is that the *officially sanctioned and controlled* use of (or more likely the threat to use) high-voltage electro conductive *taser devices* to disable assailants represents a reasonable and proportionate response to very high risk incidents in which (i) the police have to become involved; and (ii) where there may have been threats of, or instead actual evidence of violence giving rise to circumstances where the use of force by police officers is now perceived by them or their controllers to be necessary in order to resolve the situation.

Police forces in other countries might in contrast be much more likely to deal with such threats by drawing, and as necessary using firearms – potentially leading to fatal outcomes.

The threat to employ a taser has instead been shown to be a highly effective deterrent in the UK. The threat of its use is often enough to bring the situation under control. However, if actually used (and currently only at most in 20% of the UK cases in which they have been deployed) the firing of a taser device protects the police officer (as a public servant to whom a statutory Duty of Care is owed), and is statistically likely to be much less damaging to the recipient than the use of firearms.

[4] **Other countries** – which may in contrast deal with threats to police officers by the use of any of the following (*and arguably much less reasonable*) strategies:

❏ deterrence by the direct or culturally established creation and reinforcement of fear and threat of violence by police or paramilitary forces on the scene, whatever form this threat of violence or oppression might take; *or more specifically*

❏ deterrence by the direct use of physical violence by police or paramilitary forces, whatever form this violence might take;

❏ the direct use of chemical agents such as CS gas to incapacitate assailants;

❏ the dispersal of people or rioters by the use of water cannon and / or infantry and cavalry-type charges;

❏ the (potentially lethal) firing of rubber or plastic bullets (attenuated energy projectiles or AEP) at assailants or crowds.

The use of such tactics in Northern Ireland created a very severe negative public reaction. *Such methods are no longer used in the UK*;

❏ the direct and potentially lethal use of firearms in confrontations, as in the USA and many countries elsewhere. Such firearms may vary from handguns through to high velocity rapid fire automatic weapons.

CASE EXAMPLE – MENTAL HEALTH RESTRAINT
The use of restraint in a mental health context – judgements may have to be made by UK police and emergency paramedic officers as to what is the most reasonable or proportionate response that they can make in dealing with incidences of mental health crises that are occurring on the street, in the community, or in a person's home. Local mental health triage or police response teams, perhaps acting in last resort, may have to be prepared in Dilemma Management terms (i) to deal with any violence directed at themselves; or (ii) to make the decision to return the client to their own home on the understanding (?) that a GP will subsequently become involved in their care; or (iii) to take the person to an Accident & Emergency Hospital (whose staff may be unable, unwilling or even hostile to the need to treat the client, particularly if they are a persistent repeat offender); or (iv) to take the person to a "place of safety" – which may have to be a police cell for which no specialist medical capability is likely to be available; or (v) to a properly designated "place of safety" within a hospital or mental health facility – *if* such a capability exists or is available at that particular time.

An alternative is to *section* the client under the Mental Health Act Paragraph 136, an action which may cost the authorities up to £2000 per occasion.

REASONABLE OR PROPORTIONATE FURTHER ILLUSTRATED: SOME EQUALITY (EDOD) IMPLEMENTATION DILEMMAS

The analysis of what might be deemed reasonable or proportionate contained in this chapter may further be illustrated by the issues of *Equality, Diversity, Opportunity, and anti-Discrimination ("EDOD")*. UK (and North American) policy on these major dilemma issues is shaped *by a critical need to be seen to implement policies that people (i) can perceive to be fair, but (ii) whose implementation has to be judged to incur what may be defined in real-world terms as a "reasonable" commitment to resource and time obligations.*

The Author has drawn on his own medicolegal experience as a person categorised under UK Equality Legislation in writing this part of Chapter 25, and as attributed in the Introduction to this Book.

Talk, exhort, debate, "have a conversation" – or instead act? – a variety of media, political and pressure groups comment routinely and copiously about the ongoing dilemmas faced by the UK government and its agencies in the promotion of *Equality and fairness*.

On the one hand there must be an *Equality (or EDOD) Agenda* based on the protection of Human Rights and the promotion of justice, Opportunity, and fairness, **for instance as described in ground-breaking detail elsewhere by this Author.**

On the other hand *there has to be a reasonable implementation strategy available in order to get things done.* **But talk and argument are cheap and easy.** This is a "windbag" syndrome? It is one of the contentions of this Book that in Dilemma Management terms the UK is now overly subject to indulgence in the negative distractions (i) of excessive, unnecessary and febrile theorising, debate, dialectics and a negative self-serving media coverage (Chapter 4); (ii) entrenched opinionation as a form of influence without responsibility (Chapter 8); and (iii) a serious corporate failure to accept role or positional accountability for events, and yet for which (maybe) a very large salary is being paid, that slow things down and impede real progress for the people caught up in *genuine* poverty, inequality, domestic vulnerability, the need for access to emergency services, etc.

Some dilemmas of implementing the Equality Agenda – an Equality implementation strategy may in practical terms have to be based on a comparison of the *relevant costs and benefits of the Equality Agenda*, in which a *pragmatic* (or equally a "business-friendly"?) view is taken at any particular time of the utility to be obtained from policies associated with Equality, Opportunity, Diversity, and the countering of Discrimination. In such a case, and in order to calculate any realistic order of short-term priority, (i) the incidence of economic and financial cost and / or disturbance, plus the requisite demands of mandatory performance management (for instance associated with the disbursement of public funds as described in Chapter 24) may have to be weighed (ii) against the social and human benefits to be gained.

Case Example: a college or university may have to make judgements in respect of disability legislation about the level of investment it must make in upgrading its buildings and facilities to an appropriate level of "wheelchair or disability friendliness" without at the same time knowing in advance how many disabled students it will actually recruit each year. So, *it might reasonably choose to prioritise its expenditures on a cost-benefit basis*, concentrating wheelchair access, disability capability, and related safety investments in teaching buildings, Information Technology resources, libraries, pathways, and student facilities. It would then provide disability-trained staff to take the walking disabled and students in wheelchairs to other locations, such as laboratories, which they are less likely to have a frequent need to visit, or require to visit only on specific or timetabled occasions.

Reasonable, proportionate, pragmatic, cost-beneficial and performance managed – the process of the Dilemma Management of the Equality, Diversity, Opportunity, and anti- Discrimination Agenda might therefore have to be informed by a pragmatic, cost-beneficial and performance measured view of what are considered to be reasonable or proportionate outcomes in political, organisational or resource terms, and in the varying time scales described at different points in this Book.

For instance, there may be a need to streamline, to optimise, or to simplify processes of validation, action, monitoring, reporting, review and assurance of EDOD implementation in order to avoid creating an excessive bureaucracy that becomes a cause of negative organisational and public perceptions of the Equality and Opportunity Agenda. Advice to UK schools for example suggests steps that may be taken by educational institutions in order '*to minimise the additional work required* to demonstrate they are meeting their legal obligations in respect of equal opportunities ... there is a duty to assess and to monitor the impact of policies on pupils, staff and parents, in particular the attainment levels of pupils from different racial groups. Such steps *as are reasonably practicable* should be taken to publish annually the results of the monitoring.' Another way of achieving this lies in the creation of "Single Equality Schemes". Advice to UK schools suggests that in order to minimise the burden created by the need to comply with the various statutory duties 'we recommend that schools produce a Single Equality Plan' covering all of the stated requirements.

Available resources – the process of the management of EDOD Dilemmas is also likely to be described in terms of the *absolute and relative level of resources available*. The larger the organisation, or the greater the level of resources and capability deemed to be available to it, the lower may be the threshold at which a full and comprehensive level of compliance will be required, and the greater may be the expectations of its performance. Certainly, public sector organisations in the UK are now expected to demonstrate consistent levels of the achievement of EDOD excellence or best practice, and on occasion have been severely punished for failing so to do.

Default decisions – the argument described immediately above is however complicated by the issue of "fair shares for all". Not everyone works for large and well-funded organisations. Nor is everybody aware of their rights and entitlements under the law, nor are they necessarily able to fight for them.

Ultimately, therefore, a decision as to what is defined to be a reasonable level of resource allocation to the EDOD Agenda, or instead a proportionate course of action can be taken on the basis of *default*. This may mean the interpretation by lawyers of the relevance of case law and legal precedent to the situation at hand. The outcome of such a form of external enforcement may then be complicated by issues of status and bargaining power, by the behaviour of Employment Tribunals and law courts, and by the values and objectives of the legal profession.

CASE EXAMPLE

Making "Reasonable Adjustment" – the concept of reasonable adjustment is in particular associated with disability Discrimination. Both of UK and US law require employers to provide some kind of *reasonable adjustment* or *reasonable accommodation* for applicants and employees with a disability. The US Equal Employment Opportunity Commission defines reasonable accommodation as "any change in the work environment (or in the way in which things are usually done) to help a person with a disability to apply for a job, to perform the duties of a job, or to enjoy the benefits of employment".

The UK Disability Discrimination Act (DDA) 1995 notes (Part II Section 6 Paragraphs 1 to 3) that:

1. 'where (a) any arrangements made by or on behalf of an employer, or (b) any physical features of premises occupied by the employer place the disabled person concerned at a substantial disadvantage in comparison with persons who are not disabled, it is the duty of the employer to take such steps as it is reasonable, in all the circumstances of the case, for him to have to take in order to prevent the arrangements or feature having that effect.

2. subsection 1(a) applies to arrangements for determining to whom employment should be offered; *and* any term, condition or arrangements on which employment, promotion, a transfer, training or any other benefit is offered or afforded.

3. the following are examples of steps which an employer may have to take in relation to a disabled person in order to comply with subsection (1.) *above*:
   a. making adjustments to premises;
   b. allocating some of the disabled person's duties to another person;

 c. transferring him to fill an existing vacancy;

 d. altering his working hours;

 e. assigning him to a different place of work;

 f. allowing him to be absent during working hours for rehabilitation, assessment or treatment; giving him ... training;

 g. acquiring or modifying equipment;

 h. modifying instructions or reference manuals;

 i. modifying procedures for testing or assessment;

 j. providing supervision.

 k. providing a reader or interpreter.'

What is then considered to be a reasonable form of adjustment in the UK may be a function of statutory regulation, case law, or Code of Practice.

Alternatively, decision-makers will have to make their own judgement on a contingency basis as to what would be considered reasonable or proportionate *under the particular circumstances.* For example, in the potentially difficult, medicolegal, and possibly contentious issue of the management of mental health disability given extensive treatment in this Book, employers know that whatever judgement they make in the UK could be tested at Employment Tribunal and, if found wanting, a different resolution enforced by due legal process. This is because the onus may be placed on the employer (or subsequently a service provider) to show that their actions were reasonable, or were instead a proportionate means to achieving an objective and legitimate aim.

In the US, a reasonable accommodation is required unless its provision would cause significant difficulty or expense for the employer. Such "undue hardship" is defined to mean that the reasonable accommodation would be too difficult or too expensive to provide (i) in the light of the size and financial resources of the business, or (ii) in terms of its operational needs. Similarly, the UK Disability Discrimination Act (DDA) 1995 notes (Part II Section 6 Paragraph 4) that in determining whether it is reasonable for an employer to have to take a particular step in order to comply with its obligation to make reasonable adjustment, regard shall in particular be had to:

a. the extent to which taking the step would prevent the effect in question;

b. the extent to which it is practicable for the employer to take the step;

c. the financial and other costs which would be incurred by the employer in taking the step and the extent to which taking it would disrupt any of his activities;

d. the extent of the employer's financial and other resources;

e. the availability to the employer of financial or other assistance with respect to taking the step'.

The Equality Act 2010 strengthens UK legislation by requiring the employer to demonstrate that its actions are, in some kind of objective sense, *motivated by the need to achieve a legitimate aim or purpose* associated with the management or operations of the organisation.

CASE EXAMPLE
What should be the language of the UK's National Health Service (NHS)? – a 2012 report commented that at the time the NHS spent £64,000 per day on translation services. The *Daily Mail* (6.02.2012) had noted that 'the cost to the [British] taxpayer has risen by 17 per cent since 2007, with more than £23 million spent' in 2011. Experts had stated that 'some [healthcare] trusts translated material into 120 languages' and that 'huge sums could be saved if hospitals and GP surgeries pooled resources, [warning] that translating information for those who do not speak English could encourage segregation'.

Julia Manning of 2020 Health, the think-tank that conducted the research, gave her opinion that 'the costs involved are truly staggering in an age of austerity, and [are] incredible when taken in the context of [the need for] efficiency savings across the' NHS. The report did however highlight the strategy of healthcare trusts that refused to provide translation services, instead producing (multicultural) documents in "easy to read" English, for instance suitable for patients learning the language.

Chapter Twenty Six
A Commitment to Decisions

Chapter 26 focuses on the potential impact on Dilemma Management of organisational commitments to major or even "bet- the-company" / "bet-the-government" type decisions associated with large scale infrastructure or information technology developments; the development of weapons or cybersecurity systems; significant policy matters involving military interventions, border security, or wholesale reorganisation of state agencies such as the NHS or local government; or the attempted re-positioning of political parties; (etc).

STAW & ROSS – COMMITMENT TO A DECISION DESCRIBED

Staw & Ross undertook a series of investigations over a number of years into what they termed *commitment to a decision* by an organisation or a government. They published a number of propositions and conclusions about what may happen over the time span associated with any particular commitments made, whether it be by a business organisation; a government, public sector or healthcare body; a political party; a utility company, a military or a security service (etc).

This work has been adapted in a summary form for the purposes of this chapter. Staw & Ross' ideas are illustrated in Figure 22, using a *Lewin-type change or force-field model*. This figure has *three main components*, described as follow. Lewin's change model is described in the Author's Routledge text *Principles of Management*, to which reference is made in the Introduction to this Book.

[1] a commitment to a course of action – (*middle level*) – whether this be an initiative, a project, a campaign, a reorganisation or an investment. By definition, this course of action:

❏ may result from the identification or definition of a dilemma, as described in Chapter 1, for instance in terms of an attempt to find a resolution to a pressing policy issue or need for competitive market response as described at various points in this Book; *and / or*

❏ may instead result from the development (Staw & Ross use the term "escalation") of this course of action into a dilemma in its own right. This may clearly be illustrated by the dilemma affecting housing policy in the UK at this time of writing. Such policy is complicated by (perhaps at least five potentially *wicked mess risk laden*) issues (i) of access to suitable land (and the existence of so-called "land banks"); (ii) the role of local government authorities in granting the necessary planning permissions, particularly where (iii) the construction of low-cost housing will be electorally unpopular; and (iv) there is an *a priori* reluctance to build low-cost housing which yields a low level of property tax, (relatively) low levels of rent in revenue, and commits housing associations to expensive long-term maintenance programmes. The waters in this case may further be muddied (v) where construction company executives are in receipt of enormous bonuses earned by completing contracts which contain an element of "right to buy"?

[2] the determinants of commitment – (*lower level*) – which comprise the following variables:

❏ the degree to which (i) the nature of the *event or concept characteristics* (Chapter 4), and (ii) other relevant contingencies are (for whatever reason) perceived at a particular time to be compelling;

❏ a perceived *strategic or leadership* imperative, for instance as described in Chapters 20 and 21 of this Book;

❏ a *project* imperative, to include the employment of the necessary resources, capability, specialisms, motivation and willpower. The organisation will need to reassure itself (and its stakeholders) that it can deliver on the new commitment over the relevant time span (which might be decades in the case of major infrastructure or defence projects);

❏ *behavioural dynamics*, to include the level of investment of personal and professional identification with, and emotional attachment of senior managers to the course of action. Perhaps it will become a "life's work"? Perhaps its completion may yield significant financial reward or public recognition in the form of a Knighthood or a CBE?

❏ the attitudes and authority of the *governance body*, and its ultimate ability or willingness to become involved in risk assessment or ongoing managerial activities;

❏ the existence over time (or otherwise) of an effective process of monitoring and review, backed as necessary by authority at a governance level and to include some kind of mapping process as described in Chapter 19;

❏ contextual, stakeholder and environmental forces that might in any way affect the commitment.

[3] escalation and potential endgame – (*upper level*) – which if it should develop into a worst case, bet-the-company, or bet-the-government scenario could contain *five increasingly negative and risk-laden outcome stages as the commitment develops over time.* The characteristics of these five stages are listed in a temporal (time-linear) order, thus:

❏ *Phase One* – initial enthusiasm about the forecasted benefits of the commitment, maybe artificially boosted by cost under-estimates and / or expensive Advertising, Public or Investor Relations activities;

❏ *Phase Two* – appearance of initial criticism about original forecasts and assumptions, exacerbated by the emergence of objective evidence of directly questionable or risky outcomes. It may be at this point that the first sign of *reinforcement behaviours* emerge (as described in the next section of this chapter), encouraging continuing internal and stakeholder commitment to the chosen course of action;

❏ *Phase Three* – development of significant criticism and comment; and receipt of undoubted and objective evidence of potentially negative outcomes as time has passed. Reinforcement behaviours may now be stepped up;

❏ *Phase Four* – receipt at governance and senior management levels of incontestable evidence of potentially highly risky or negative outcomes, perhaps taking the form of very serious dilemmas requiring urgent resolution (and perhaps including the possibility of corporate failure described in Chapter 15);

❏ *Phase Five* – **endgame**, in which a decision has to be made as to whether (i) to continue with the commitment, and / or (ii) to continue to reinforce it, or (iii) to now contemplate abandoning it (with the loss of face involved and the likelihood of governance intervention in removing Chief Executives and other senior staff conspicuously involved in continuing the course of action in spite of what may now be perceived as a near certainty of failure and significant value / resource loss to the organisation).

SOME DYNAMICS OF ESCALATION AND ENDGAME

The circumstances of escalation and the potential for an endgame may be again be described by the application of Lewin's force field analysis, as shown in Figure 22.

FORCES OR DRIVERS REINFORCING / ESCALATING COMMITMENT TO A DECISION

Such *reinforcing / escalating drivers* may be listed as follows:

❏ an increasing leadership or personal investment in commitment, energy, motivation, the development of specific skills sets, technical and professional knowledge and experience (for instance such as the "installed base of thinking" that characterised the continuing development of IBM mainframe computers in the 1970's and 1980's at the time when the first distributed, mini, and microcomputers – such as those marketed by Alan Sugar under the Amstrad brand – were making their mark);

❏ the application of the "sunk cost" argument, in which there is a corporate perception that *too much value* has by now been invested to justify withdrawal from the project. Closure would mean an unacceptable loss of the resources that have already been committed;

❑ the subsequent filtering and / or distortion of corporate information flows about progress, project risk, and emergent criticisms as the commitment is escalated. This information control may be carried out on behalf of CEO's, COO's, CFO's and other corporate leaders, project controllers, PR specialists (etc). *This might at this stage be associated with*

❑ attempts to keep Boards of non-executive directors or other governance bodies uninformed, misled, or "out of the loop"; *at the same time as*

❑ potentially escalating corporate demands for (i) compliance with, and / or (ii) stakeholder and staff loyalty to the "party line" in support of the commitment or decision, and with the escalating reinforcement or groupthink about it; *perhaps associated with*

❑ a progressive downgrading or failure of the risk management process. The process of risk management was described in Chapter 17 of this Book;

❑ attempts to reinforce (or to "up the ante") associated with the authority, indispensability, personality and irreplaceability of such people as the CEO, the CFO and the COO. The project or commitment has by now become synonymous with such people. The prospect of sacking them is at this point an option that few if any stakeholders wish to be seen to be associated with, or to contemplate. *This may be associated with*

❑ an ongoing defence of the responsible CEO, CFO or COO by the governance body, which by now is becoming increasingly involved in the dilemma posed by the commitment or project; *and*

❑ by a fear of, or resistance to the dismissal by this body of CEO, CFO, COO or project managers for fear (i) of personal loss of face, (ii) the questioning of corporate competence, or (iii) tangential features of personal / social / cultural / membership group relationships, and personal or trust financial investment in the project, etc;

❑ the emergence of powerful exogenous forces such as clients, government, unions and other key stakeholders who now reaffirm their commitment to continue backing and / or financing the commitment. This was the case in past investments in the development of weapons systems in the UK to which reference has already been made in this Book. The concept of any endgame is not yet something that can realistically or publicly be considered;

❏ the development of a significant fear of a crisis occurring, as described in Chapter 18, and a growing realisation that the dynamics of such a crisis may neither be containable nor manageable; *perhaps coupled with*

❏ a reluctance to contemplate, or even worse to conceptualise an endgame as a potential outcome; *now associated with*

❏ an escalating and by now an internally substantiated fear of negative value and corporate failure (as per Chapter 15) leading to thoughts about, or actual planning for an endgame to be put off, or put back as constituting an unresolvable dilemma (Chapter 1);

❏ a final or "last-gasp" belief that (i) the commitment or project remains essential to the scheme of things; and (ii) that the commitment is too valuable to terminate; and (iii) that financial backers, the state or other key stakeholders will continue their support come what may; *that is that*

❏ a negative endgame outcome would be unacceptable or even inconceivable. Staw & Ross suggested that this form of reinforcement behaviour characterised US thinking during the Vietnam War, in which the possibility of military defeat by the Vietnamese had come to be unthinkable. It is of course quite possible at this time of writing that such a syndrome has re-emerged, now instead associated with political and military events in the Middle East?

FORCES OR DRIVERS WEAKENING COMMITMENT TO A DECISION, AND POTENTIALLY REINFORCING MOVES TOWARDS ENDGAME OR ABANDONMENT.

Such *reinforcing / escalating drivers* may be listed as follows:

❏ a developing dynamic over time of the nature of critical performance measurement and performance management information flows (for instance as described in Chapters 14, 15 and 24). This dynamic may be accompanied by a *waning of the strength* of internal corporate denial, information filtering, and proactive requirement for compliance. A point is then reached that represents a critical *threshold* where corporate silence on the developing scenario can no longer be maintained, for example because fears are beginning to emerge that the commitment could lead to a potentially fatal bet-the- company or bet-the government value / reputation loss scenario;

❑ this may lead to the emergence of increasingly powerful *internal* pressures (eg from CFOs) pointing to the escalation of the project risk, possibly reinforced by influential *external* warnings eg from financial commentators or the financial press;

❑ the emergence of internal fears that the "lid" may no longer be kept on events as they escalate; *and*

❑ the emergence of internal fears and external opinions that governance or scrutiny bodies will soon have to involve themselves in events (whether they like it or not); *particularly if it now appears that*

❑ there are obvious signs of disapproval, distress, or panic on the part of stakeholders, financial sources, suppliers or creditors described in Chapter 15;

❑ backers of last resort such as the state, government or international funding agencies (etc) now making it clear to all that they will not rescue the project or compensate for any value loss. It may next become obvious to all concerned that somewhere or somehow external preparations are being made (or will have to be made) for the collapse of the commitment, bringing about an endgame and a conclusion one step closer;

❑ and in the meantime Staw & Ross point to the potentially inevitable *staff movements*. Rats will try to leave the sinking ship in order to save their skins or their careers. Significant "staff adjustments" will be made at senior management level. This might start with a purge of middle level employees, for instance directly involved in the project's management. But ultimately decisions at a governance level will remove the most senior staff associated with the commitment, whether they are CEOs, COOs, CFOs, Hospital or Educational Directors, Civil Servants, Local Government or senior officers in the military and the uniformed services (etc); *and*

❏ and an endgame has been reached. At this point there may be some kind of corporate collapse; a strategic withdrawal or acceptance of defeat; a large loss of value; the failure of a government or political party; or (and instead) at best the emergence of conditions in which the fate of the organisation passes into the control of others.

A FEW SOURCES OF COMMITMENT RISK OR FAILURE

Sources of project failure associated with such variables as groupthink in semiospheres, investment in large projects, failures of risk and crisis management (etc) have all been dealt with in earlier chapters of this Book. Other failure sources might include:

❏ the misreading of (or failure to understand) knowledge and / or technology dynamics, for instance as described in the Author's texts *Principles of Management* and *Principles of Strategic Management* to which reference is made in the Introduction to this Book;

❏ failure to understand and to apply change management processes, also described in the texts listed above;

❏ an obsolescence or actual failure of intellectual or professional paradigms to which people associated with the commitment process are habituated, and which prove to be flawed in their application to the particular context of the decision and its consequences;

❏ a progressive and fearful "freezing" of the thought processes of people whose fate is bound up with the commitment as they come to confront an increasing liklihood of personal career wreckage. They may "redouble their efforts" in the hope that a reinforcement of their commitment to the project will see them justified and rewarded. Perhaps everything will come right on the night?

Ultimately, the endgame (and the damage it causes) may come down to ineffective leadership and a failure to implement the proper process of Dilemma Management as described throughout this Book.

Author's Note: The Reader may choose, if he or she so wishes, to apply the contents of this Chapter 26 to the UK's Brexit process?

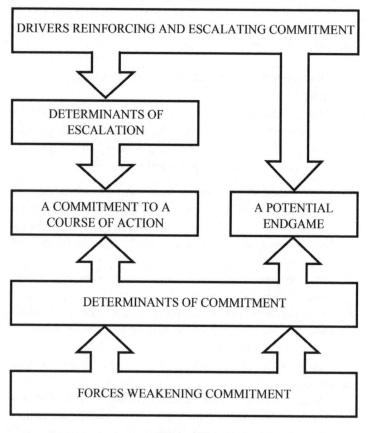

Figure 22
Staw & Ross – commitment to a decision

Part Five

Endgame: Some Final Dilemma Management Issues

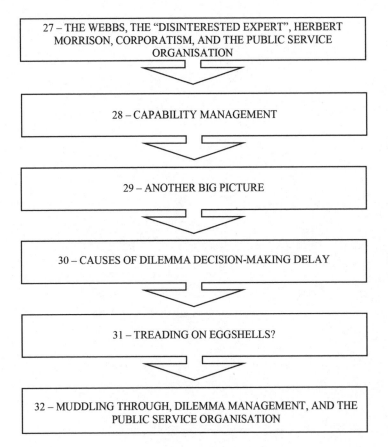

27 – THE WEBBS, THE "DISINTERESTED EXPERT", HERBERT MORRISON, CORPORATISM, AND THE PUBLIC SERVICE ORGANISATION

28 – CAPABILITY MANAGEMENT

29 – ANOTHER BIG PICTURE

30 – CAUSES OF DILEMMA DECISION-MAKING DELAY

31 – TREADING ON EGGSHELLS?

32 – MUDDLING THROUGH, DILEMMA MANAGEMENT, AND THE PUBLIC SERVICE ORGANISATION

Figure 23

Chapter Twenty Seven

The Webbs, the "Disinterested Expert", Herbert Morrison, Corporatism, and the Public Service Organisation

[27.1] May the Author welcome you in this Chapter to what he describes as the <u>world</u> of the (well-paid) amateur UK professional, *with (i) all of its dilemmas and calamitous lack of real work experience, (ii) its undoubtedly questionable capability issues and (iii) its naïve over-dependence on the (horrendously expensive) services of (hard-selling) management consultants paid for by the taxpayer (ie me and you) in order to try to mask its operational shortcomings.*
Also see Chapters 22 and 24 of this Book.

[27.2] A Bureaucrats' refrain (I):
"We don't apologise and we don't explain".

[27.3] A Bureaucrats' Refrain (II):
"I hear what you say
I read what you write

But your views ain't mine
I <u>know</u> they're not right

However for getting in touch
I thank you so much

The Webbs, Herbert Morrison, and their intellectual, ideological and political followers have become associated in Dilemma Management terms with the UK State, Nationalised or Public Service Corporation, and the Public Service Administrative Organisation.

These organisations may for the purposes of this chapter include any or all of:

❑ nationalised concerns such as Railtrack;
❑ the National Health Service (NHS);
❑ state corporations such as the BBC;
❑ the Civil Service and its agencies (such as the Cabinet Office);
❑ local government and its agencies such as the uniformed services, Transport for London;
❑ state QUANGOs.

These are either:

❑ state run organisations; *or*
❑ organisations in which the state is the sole or dominant stakeholder; *and in which*
❑ state / taxpayer funding is predominant, and shapes / (should shape?) whatever paradigms of performance management are in place. Also see Chapter 24.

This chapter is divided into various components. These examine *some* of the legacies of **Sidney Webb** (1859 – 1947) and **Herbert Morrison** (1888 – 1963) specifically in relation to the relevance of their contribution to the contents of this Book. These two gentlemen worked from the Edwardian era onwards to the mid twentieth century.

This chapter is based on a description of certain aspects of their work as it was when they promulgated it. There is no direct attempt by this Author to judge their work by the standards of today. **Nor should there be.** The development, nature and consequences of their work were strictly products of their time and circumstances.

However, their work has undoubtedly had a subsequent, significant and continuing influence <u>beyond</u> the times and ideologies which generated it. This continuing influence is relevant to the concepts of Dilemma Management and management process as these concepts now relate to today's circumstances. It is entirely acceptable to evaluate the consequences of this influence <u>outside</u> of its original time and circumstances. New ideas and paradigms will inevitably bring about change, taking the place of their predecessors, however worthy and relevant these predecessors were in their time and in their own historical perspective.

SIDNEY WEBB AND "WEBBISM"

Sidney Webb and his wife Beatrice (1858 – 1943) were amongst the most influential British thinkers of their day. They:

❑ became involved in the establishment of the variant of socialist thought known as "Fabianism";

❑ believed in a gradual, incremental and pragmatic but nevertheless a cumulative approach to bringing about change and improvement in civil society;

❑ were keen proponents of a form of industrial democracy based on the development of self-governing voluntary social movements such as Trade Unions and the consumer co- operative movement. They did not believe in the more revolutionary concept of worker co-operatives, soviets and the like; *and they*

❑ established the "New Statesman", a publication that remains influential to this day.

An key exposition of their thought, *Industrial Democracy* (1897) combined (i) democratic themes with (ii) what has been widely described as an elitist view of the *functional indispensability of the disinterested expert*. Never entirely reconciled, this paradigm dichotomy was to represent a continuing line of tension or dilemma in their work.

The phrase "Webbism" later emerged to become known as being synonomous with big, intrusive and controlling government. This was to be accompanied by a belief in the education and state employment of the *disinterested expert* described immediately above. This belief was exemplified by the establishment by the Webbs in 1895 of the London School of Economics (the "LSE").

WEBBISM

The concept of Webbism thus describes Sidney Webb's attachment to statist and technocratic perspectives.

Big government – the political support for the development of big and intrusive government was designed as a catalyst for, and driver of *social and economic change* (for instance developing out of Chamberlain's earlier "gas and water socialism"). Belief in the state as an agent for, or driver of social betterment was evident in the Webb's ground-breaking campaign for the overhaul and rationalisation of the Poor Law. Belief in the necessity of big government was also exemplified by the support of the Webbs for the needs of Empire, and in their links with social imperialists in Parliament and in the Indian and colonial services.

Implementing change – the implementation of social and economic change *was to be achieved by what was at the time conceptualised as the capability and motivation contributed by the disinterested expert or professional.* Such people would fulfil roles (i) in the civil and government service, (ii) in the colonial and Indian service (for instance as described by Kipling), and (iii) subsequently in industries that were nationalised (for instance by Herbert Morrison) in the 1930's and 1940's.

The LSE was of course to make its contribution (for instance in the continuing form of its suites of Public Administration courses).

But there were no UK equivalents to the technological / vocational Grandes Ecoles of the French pattern. Nor were there enough universities and wealthy research-savvy companies in the UK for instance to match those in the USA who were prepared (i) to abandon comfortable academic complacency and (ii) to embrace the reality of financial, technological or professional *risk* in developing engineering, aviation, management, agricultural, financial, information technology / computing, efficiency, experience-effect, performance management and customer service / marketing agendas.

Thus, the technological needs of WWI, WWII (and the subsequent Cold War) were for instance critically accommodated (i) by the development of computing as it is now understood by the code-breaking work of Bletchley Park (outside of the UK university system), and Browning's incorporation of computer- aided guidance of weapon systems for US bombers, or (ii) the experience-effect (Chapter 23) based building programmes for Abram's tanks or Liberty ships.

Such issues (like Whittle's fortuitous development of jet propulsion for aircraft) might instead be left on the basis of serendipity or the "old-boy network" to individual entrepreneurs in the UK (who had to convince sometimes uncomprehending civil servants or academics of the validity or relevance of their work), or instead to the military (who had the same problem).

And the final years of WWI cannot be properly understood without acknowledging the influence on the UK Government, Earl Haig (as Commander-in-Chief) and the British Army of the two Empire Field Commanders Monash (Australia) and Currie (Canada).

It was almost inevitable therefore that given the circumstances of the time the technocrats, disinterested experts, colonial administrators, military commanders, etc; and also the "mandarins" and "eggheads" (terms still used today by the popular media) would be likely above all to have come from the educated upper and middle class output of elite public schools and universities. This might mean the Haileybury and Imperial Service College (for the colonial service), Marlborough (for the Army), or Eton and Harrow (preferred by the Foreign and Diplomatic Service). And of course Oxford and Cambridge.

At the time the UK possessed limited alternative resources for high level education and training outside of the internal resources of government departments, the military or the colonial service. Indeed, the Webbs were active in encouraging the establishment (often by business benefactors or philanthropists) of local trade and night schools, vocational colleges (etc) whose task was train and certify the craft skills of technicians, industrial apprentices, etc. Such institutions eventually became involved in the UK's first tentative (and academically highly unpopular) steps towards the proper establishment of the paradigms and protocols of the management process applied in this Book and referred to in the Introduction.

SOME DILEMMA MANAGEMENT CONSEQUENCES OF THE WORK OF THE WEBBS

The Webbist framework of state intervention and control in "the public interest", as described above, appears to have had a particular Dilemma Management consequence, as outlined below.

CULTURAL DILEMMAS

It is the contention of this Book that (i) *at this time of writing* and (ii) in Dilemma Management terms, Sidney Webb's concept of the disinterested administrator, "mandarin" or technocrat in the UK's government, public and healthcare services has come to be associated with such controversial features as:

❏ an established and continuing dominance by a restricted, highly amateuristic, managerially unqualified, and "semi- detached" (ie self-centred) upper or middle class elite; *characterised by:-*

❏ a significant failure to acknowledge, to accept, or to update management and performance management processes *as would elsewhere* now be widely understood and accepted as *requisite* frameworks and paradigms (as described in Part Four); *and*

❏ significant unawareness or ignorance of the relevant concepts and paradigms of the management and performance management process as they have been developed in the UK, North America and Europe during the twentieth and twenty- first centuries; *as well as:-*

❏ *very strong institutional hostility* to the development and application of the modern management and performance management process as described here and in the Introduction; *associated with:-*

❏ *the residues of covert hostility* in **Opportunity Management** terms to the recruitment of the non-Oxbridge and non-Upper / Middle Class or polyglot type candidate who hold **vocational qualifications** in technology, financial management / accountancy, agriculture, or business management (etc). Also in computing and ICT. Indeed, the UK Government spends enormous sums of taxpayer money on the employment of external consultants of all kinds. This would appear to indicate a calamitous lack of internal capability and willpower; Human Resource planning, staff development and CPD; and a gross irresponsibility towards the state and its sources of funding; *as well as an associated:-*

❏ recidivist and grudging attitude towards the vocational graduate and polyglot products of the opportunity-led UK Polytechnics and their successors in the form of the Modern Universities.

This Book argues that as far as the management process is concerned in the UK's public, governmental and healthcare service organisations, these developments have become associated with any or all of the following:

❏ a developing intellectual and cognitive obsolescence, Cognitive Dissonance and outdatedness; *associated with*
❏ the unjustifiable expenditure of large sums of taxpayer monies on the services of external consultants, to which reference was made above; *and*
❏ the syndrome of a lack of incoming requisite variety and genetic diversity of knowledge, staff and system inputs; *and*
❏ the calamitous workings of the Peter Principle;
❏ an expensive and long-established inability to manage / performance-manage large government projects or assisted investments (such as the Brabazon aircraft, the Groundnut Scheme, Blue Streak, Nimrod, Crossrail, HS2, Carillion plc, the SmartMeters programme, Heathrow Airport, NHS Information and Communication Technology programmes, and even the apparent excessive use of antibiotic medications, etc etc);
❏ issues of upper and middle-class "niceness" and fear of conflict (eg during the Brexit negotiations) dealt with at various points in this Book; *associated with*
❏ a failure assertively to confront and to deal with what to the tax-payer are dilemma-laden, emotional (but costly) issues (i) of un-believable catastrophies resulting in the death or traumatisation of British Minors caused directly by the influence of so-called "social media" and Big Data; (ii) mental health problems, (iii)

escalating crime; (iv) the effects of smoking, alcoholism and drug abuse; (v) snowflake behaviour or "semi" detachment from society; etc.

HERBERT MORRISON, CORPORATISM AND NATIONALISATION

HERBERT MORRISON (1888 – 1965)

Herbert Morrison was a British Labour politician who held a variety of positions in government and in the London County Council (LCC). Morrison developed some of his social views from his work in local government politics with the LCC, of which he was at some time Leader. He was at pains (like many others at the time) to place an emphasis on the importance of public works as a strategy to maintain the level and quality of employment.

Morrison, like the Webbs, had no sympathy with the ideology of establishing democratic or worker control by the employees of state institutions.

Morrison oversaw the nationalisation programme of the 1945 – 1951 Labour Government. His views on nationalisation were shaped by the establishment of the London Passenger Transport Board ("London Transport") in 1933. This unified bus, tram and trolleybus services with the London Underground and Metropolitan commuter railways. His views on nationalisation had also been influenced by the setting up of the British Broadcasting Corporation (BBC) in 1927.

Morrison's supervision of the major post 1945 programme of nationalising large sectors of industry and infrastructure followed this LPTB and BBC type model. The owners of corporate stock were given government bonds, and the government in turn took full ownership of the enterprise, consolidating all of the affected establishments into national monopolies such as British Railways, BOAC, British Steel, British Waterways, British Road Services, and the National Coal Board (NCB), etc. Boards of Executive Management would be appointed to run these nationalised monopolies in the public interest.

Operational managements remained in situ, once the necessary consolidation and rationalisation (as in the railways and in coal- mining) had taken place. But effectively senior managements became public servants working on behalf of the government. For Morrison and the Labour Government, state ownership was a strategy to consolidate post-war national planning, control and economic management into government hands. Agendas of improvement, modernisation, increasing efficiency or organisational restructuring were of a lower significance, or instead took place at institutional level. *Example:* British Railways invested in new steam locomotive technology (whilst by then effectively obsolete, this was also cheap and well understood) rather than diesel (i) because of government concerns about the wider currency implications of any increased need for imported oil fuel; and (ii) because railway electrification outside of the big cities was seen to be of low priority as compared with the post-war reconstruction of housing, the development of the new National Health Service (NHS), etc.

SOME DILEMMA MANAGEMENT CONSEQUENCES OF THE WORK OF HERBERT MORRISON

Morrison's concept of the state, nationalised or public service administrative corporation, established as a monopoly within a Webbist framework of intervention and control in the public interest appears to have had a number of Dilemma Management consequences, as follow.

[1] PLANNING STYLE (AND "CORPORATE PLANNING")

An initial consequence derived from the choice of *planning style*, a critical potential source of dilemmas as well as a part of the Dilemma Management process. **This planning style is described in detail by the Author in his book *Principles of Strategic Management*, to which reference was made in the Introduction.**

The Strategic Management concept of planning style may have been perceived historically as a part of the process of so-called "Corporate Planning".

Top down or planning down – a *top down or planning down style* describes a *centralised* approach to strategy formulation in which the responsible politicians, civil servants and Chief Executive (CE) / Chief Executive Officer (CEO) of the organisation, and the CE / CEO's Board or senior colleagues at the "corporate centre" determine that this corporate centre or head office is to be absolutely predominant. The corporate centre decides mission, business model, objectives and strategies for the organisation as a whole, and for all of its parts. It formulates strategy for operating units, irrespective of whether or not they are notionally established as companies or divisions. Unit managers are seen as mere implementers of pre-specified corporate strategies.

Planning down in the organisations being considered here made use of *rationalistic, deliberate,* and *universalistic* forms of *strategy formulation*. These are described in the next section below.

[2] STRATEGY FORMULATION (AND "CORPORATE PLANNING")

A second consequence lay in *the chosen pattern of strategy formulation*, again a critical potential source of dilemmas as well as a part of the Dilemma Management process. The process of strategy formulation may also have been perceived as a part of the process of so-called "Corporate Planning".

Rationalistic approaches to strategy formulation – strategy formulation would have been assumed to be a *rationalistic process* (also see Chapter 6). Rationalistic strategy formulation implies a systematic, planned, and centralised approach in which:

❑ the responsible politicians, civil servants and Chief Executive (CE) / Chief Executive Officer (CEO) of the organisation, and the CE / CEO's colleagues at the corporate centre are central and dominant forces in decision-making; *and*

❑ strategic, corporate and business plans are "handed down" (or "thrown over the wall") from the corporate centre to subordinates for implementation. Subordinates *may* be consulted but their lack of status, accountability and lack of access to relevant information precluded them from detailed participation in the process of strategy formulation and strategic decision-making.

Deliberate approaches to strategy formulation – strategy formulation would also have been assumed to be a *deliberate process*. Under this approach to strategy formulation there is an attempt to realise strategies exactly as intended because the responsible politicians, civil servants and Chief Executive (CE) / Chief Executive Officer (CEO) of the organisation, and the CE / CEO's colleagues at the corporate centre perceive (or believe) that:

❑ the enterprise can formulate precise intentions and unambiguous objectives;

❑ organisational staff and resources (*capability*) can be shaped exactly to "fit" what is needed to realise these objectives (that is, this capability can be administered / managed so as to be totally congruent with them); *and*

❑ external political, environmental or competitive forces are not considered likely to be able to distort any of the processes of strategy formulation, implementation, and realisation. Nor indeed may they necessarily have even been taken into consideration in a political, state-owned and controlled institution. This syndrome may have characterised the Brexit process?

Universalistic approaches to strategy formulation – which are defined here as being characterised by:

❑ a paradigm based on centralised prescription, codification, formalisation, standardisation, and regulation. Rules are to be universally applied in order to standardise decision-making; individual discretion is to be prescribed or limited. Again, subordinates are seen by their bosses as mere implementers;

❑ a strong belief in management by written role description, formal hierarchy, and "mechanistic" (requisite, regulated, programmed or prescribed) interaction; *and*

❑ a strongly prescriptive style of leadership, perhaps reinforced by the extensive post 1945 recruitment of former military officers into the nationalised and public service organisations being discussed in this chapter.

[3] ORGANISATION STRUCTURE AND STYLE OF MANAGEMENT

A third consequence of the analysis of planning style and strategy formulation being dealt with here is the correlation with features of *organisation structure* as means of implementing strategy and decisions in state or nationalised corporations and public service administrative organisations. Some of these features are described below.

Organisation structure – state or nationalised corporations and public service administrative organisations are usually characterised by *a responsibility to accountable individuals* who hold official positions as government ministers, elected officials, elected mayors, and so on. Behaviour is likely to be driven by the performance management need for the control of, and accountability (i) for the flow of public funds that is implicit in achieving objectives, and (ii) the quality and reliability of operational activity.

This is likely to be strongly linked to a high degree of centralisation. This point has already been made above. The greater the degree of political or external control of an organisation, the more centralised and formalised *(rationalistic, deliberate and universalistic)* will be its management process and behaviour. External or politicised authority will then:-

❑   hold the Governance body, executive committee, or CE / CEO responsible for the detailed process of objective setting, strategy formulation, strategy implementation, and the achievement of results within operational and budgetary constraints;

❑   impose requisite core values and standards which must underpin strategy formulation, implementation, and performance evaluation; *and*

❑   establish a strong control culture and mentality amongst decision-makers and managers within the organisation; *but also potentially*

❑   create a "closed" environment, groupthink or semiosphere. This may be resistant to unwanted and unwelcome incoming information flows, and have difficulties with uncertain conditions characterised by change that is internally perceived to be threatening to the status quo. This point is again made in a later section below.

State or nationalised corporations and public service administrative organisations would be set up in the form of classical hierarchical mechanistic structures or "machine bureaucracies". These are characterised by a hierarchy of management roles and offices, embodying the scalar chain. The Author notes in his Principles of Management that 'the scalar chain is used to establish a "top down" unity of command in which instructions flow down and feedback on results achieved flows back up the hierarchy. Communication and control processes are vertical. Decision-making will be centralised, that is carried out at the "top" or "apex" of the organisation'.

Classical hierarchical mechanistic structures are again characterised by a *rationalistic, deliberate,* and *universalistic* approach to strategy formulation and decision making in which it is assumed that rational and logical plans, policies, rules, regulations and procedures can be effectively used (i) to implement strategic decisions; (ii) to ensure "fit" between strategy, structure, leadership, capability and resources; and (iii) to deal with exceptions that arise.

It may also be assumed by decision-makers that sufficiently robust and comprehensive rationalistic, deliberate, and universalistic procedures of planning can be put in place by the corporate centre (or by its functionally specialised corporate or strategic planners and advisers) such that any exceptional, unpredictable, novel, high risk, or ambiguous events and contingencies (for instance associated with conditions of external change and uncertainty) could in the main be legislated for *in advance*.

Structural variants characterised by divisionalisation might instead be characterised by "controlled" or "co-ordinated" decentralisation in which strong direction from the corporate centre remains.

[4] STYLE OF MANAGEMENT

A fourth consequence of the analysis of planning style and strategy formulation being dealt with here is the correlation with features of *style of management* as means of implementing strategy and decisions in state or nationalised corporations and public service administrative organisations. Some of these features are described below.

Style of management – might be characterised by some or all of dilemmas associated with:

❑ high executive power distance; *associated with*
❑ an emphasis on the use of hierarchical power cultures;
❑ an emphasis on the use of highly detailed written role descriptions and personnel specifications in procedures of recruitment, staff appraisal, discipline and dismissal;
❑ a high degree of uncertainty avoidance, correlated with universalism, centralisation, closure, and the strong control mentality described above. It will be assumed that the responsible politicians, CE / CEOs or civil servants should not tolerate things going wrong (such as massive cost-overruns, project delays or project failures, the emergence of crises, etc);
❑ low trust and / or Theory X (McGregor);
❑ a restricted awareness or concern for issues of client or customer service (as remains in the UK's NHS) – the institution is classically specified to be production or operations orientated.

Again, these features were strengthened by the recruitment of former military officers post 1945.

SOME OTHER DILEMMA MANAGEMENT CONSEQUENCES OF THE WEBBIST AND MORRISON MODELS

The state corporations and the other agencies of big government such as the Local, Civil and Healthcare Services have over the years (for instance in their dealings with political masters or the general public) shown a closure-based tendency (i) to be unaware of, (ii) to refuse to acknowledge, or (iii) even deliberately to dismiss relevant incoming information influences or information which:

- ❏ signifies unavoidable change; *and / or*
- ❏ demonstrates an unavoidable content of requisite variety and genetic diversity; *or*
- ❏ results in a residual and sometimes immovable Cognitive Dissonance (CD); *or*
- ❏ implies the workings of the Peter Principle eg in terms of leadership, capability, value generation, or CPD, etc;
- ❏ is associated with the potential impact of events likely directly to present government, stakeholders or the public with unavoidable performance management crises (such as Oxfam; Carillion; the Groundnut Scheme; failures of BOAC's Comet jet programme; or weapon systems failures affecting TSR2, the Nimrod Programme, and British troops during the Gulf War); *or*
- ❏ demonstrates the dilemma associated with attempts to define, explain and enforce the nature of responsibility in an *executive committee* (also see Chapter 22);
- ❏ may indicate the potential for, or actual incidence of internal cronyism, fraud or corruption, for instance in the transaction of sensitive international trade deals, the award of civic honours (especially knighthoods), in the negotiation of construction contracts by local government, or in the failure of NHS properly to control and to manage professional clinical staff;
- ❏ may indicate the occurrence of the organisational fragmentation, segmentation and dissociation (described in the Author's *Principles of Management*) that results from (i) excessive scale and size, (ii) internal politicisation, (iii) ineffective protocols of performance management and control (Chapter 24), or (iv) failures of processes of external scrutiny; *and perhaps*
- ❏ indicate a potential impact of major change or destabilising events associated with political governance (such as Brexit); with excessive expectations; with the effects of globalisation; with emerging Kondriatev Waves or technology change; or with the potential for changes in the Knowledge Base, S Curve movements and S Curve Discontinuities which are described in detail by this Author in his *Principles of Strategic Management*.

SOME VERY SERIOUS DILEMMA MANAGEMENT CONSEQUENCES OF THE WEBBIST AND MORRISON MODELS

Most seriously from the viewpoint of this Author, the complacent legacy of the Webbist and Morrisonian models remains characterised by **several serious issues**, as follow:

❖ politicians and adherents in the UK civil, public and administrative services appear to remain blissfully aware of the *Management and Strategic Management processes* (as described by the Author) and their direct implications;

❖ these adherents have at best a poor grasp of the critical issue of *leadership* (Chapter 21);

❖ these adherents have at best a poor grasp of issues of *capability* (defined in this Book as capacity plus willpower) (Chapter 28);

❖ these adherents have at best a poor grasp of *competition strategy* (Chapter 23) in post-Imperial age, and of its implications for such as trade negotiations, Brexit, etc; *coupled with*

❖ an apparent unwillingness to encompass the effects on the UK of *aggressive state-sponsored mercantilism,* for instance as practiced by the French, the Japanese, the Chinese, the Russians and increasingly the USA.

Matters of executive commitment to major or defining decisions were also dealt with in Chapter 26.

Chapter Twenty Eight
Capability Management

If you are managing a professional football club, which comes first – the game-plan or the players?

WHAT IS CAPABILITY MANAGEMENT?

Capability is defined in this Book as *comprising two inter-related variables*, as follow.

Capacity – which includes necessary *resources* such as tangible and intangible assets (including reputation or brand), *time, finance, Human Capital* (to include expertise, competence and skill sets), *requisite bureaucracy* (defined in terms of operational systems and process, relationship architecture, responsibility allocation, accountability, performance measurement and management), *management process*, and *leadership*.

Willpower – by which choices and decisions are actively implemented by the enterprise on the basis (i) of *a clarity of governance and leadership purpose* and (ii) *an appropriate stakeholder and management drive*. In the context of this Book such willpower and motivation will be proactively applied (i) to the identification and definition of dilemmas, and (ii) to the making of decisions about how to deal with them.

The effectiveness of the Dilemma Management process, whether in the process of identification, mapping, decision, or resolution must then depend to a significant degree on the management of the relationship or *fit* between:

❏   the available capability; *and*
❏   the particular requirements associated with the dilemma or circumstances under consideration as (i) contingent variables with (ii) their potential impact on outcome or organisation.

SOME SELECTED EXAMPLES OF CAPABILITY MANAGEMENT ISSUES GIVEN IN THIS BOOK

Selected examples of capability management issues include:

❑ Dilemma Management;

❑ Bill's promotion dilemma;

❑ the management of finance, process and risk;

❑ managing value, commitments to decisions, and large projects;

❑ football club management;

❑ the ability of the media, the Attention Economy, social media, single interest / pressure groups (etc) to insinuate, to influence, to persuade, to distort, to corrupt Minors, and to create anxiety or crises; *and*

❑ crisis management itself.

SOME DILEMMAS OF CAPABILITY MANAGEMENT

A variety of dilemmas of Capability Management are described below, with their chapter references given as appropriate.

Equifinality – which is a concept derived from Systems Thinking. Equifinality is described in Chapter 4 and in the Author's *Principles of Management* as being predicated on the assumption that open systems can achieve in a variety of different ways the objectives required by the people who run them. There may be no one "best way" to achieve strategic, organisational or operational goals. Similar ends can be achieved by different paths and from different starting points, for instance depending on the character of the resources and contingencies prevailing in the relevant internal or external environments. A practical consequence of equifinality is that leaders, politicians, managers, administrators (etc) have greater scope and discretion in deciding how to achieve their objectives than would otherwise be suggested by other, more prescriptive schools of leadership and management thought, concept formulation or culture.

The application of the concept of equifinality to the establishment or development of capability therefore implies that decisions are made that are contingent on prevailing conditions and available resources as determinant variables. The ongoing creation and use of capability may become a matter of change, flexibility and innovation (etc). The concept of equifinality is related to that of "Best Fit", described in the next section below.

Best Fit – which describes the condition of a degree of *close congruence* between (i) decisions on the choice and specification of the capability to be established, maintained, or developed; and (ii) the purposes and contingencies for which that capability is specified. These two variables are seen of necessity to be coterminous. They are the two sides of the same coin. For instance, Chapter 21 described C.B.Handy's description of leadership operations in which success depends on the coterminosity between all of:

❑   the needs of the dilemma, the situation, the circumstances or the concept / event characteristics (Chapter 4) as prevailing contingencies; *and*

❑   the needs or objectives of governance, leadership, management and task relative to these circumstances; *and*

❑   the capability available or required to meet these needs or objectives.

Handy notes that a failure to achieve the requisite degree of harmony between these variables may lead to conditions (or new dilemmas) in which decision choices are rendered ineffective. Or instead, the mismatch between these variables may be sufficiently serious as to render decision outcomes negative or counterproductive.

Some criteria indicating congruence – Chapter 24 describes such decision criteria to include the degree of any or all of:

❑   the appropriateness of relative fit or congruence to the circumstances;

❑   the desirability of this fit;

❑   the feasibility of achieving this degree of fit;

❑   the likelihood of achieving specific outcomes such as comparative advantage, levels of reasonableness or proportionality, Six Sigma infection control, compliance (etc) described at various points in this Book.

Fitness for purpose – by which the relative degree of fit (i) between the available capability and (ii) the purpose for which its use is intended is such that outcomes (such as manufacturing, service provision, political process (etc)) are fit for purpose.

The avoidance of unnecessary Hidden Factory or Costs of Poor Quality (COPQ) – as described in Chapter 24.

The Voice of the Customer – such that in Six Sigma terms (Chapter 24) the available capability is closely congruent with, or fits the needs of the customer, client, or other Voices as described in Chapter 4.

Performance measurement and management – by which (i) the application of the available capability, and (ii) the performance measurement and management processes associated with the use of that capability are congruent and coterminous.

Time scale – decisions may have to be made as to whether the capability in question is relevant to current requirements, or to those of the time scales upon which future planning is predicated. Or does a management dilemma instead emerge in which it becomes apparent that this capability is obsolete or even redundant, unfit for current purpose. Does the inadequacy of the capability become a limiting factor? This might be the case of UK rail infrastructure which makes it impossible routinely to deploy double-deck container wagons as used for example in North America. Or are the skill sets upon which the capability depends subject to the negative effects of plateauing professionals or the working of the Peter Principle?

CASE EXAMPLE
The uniformed services – it must be self-evident that as far as the uniformed services are concerned:

❖ the existence of explicit laws or policies governing some issue or other will be no guarantee that any particular desired regulatory compliance therewith will be achieved if:-

❖ the capability required to achieve this compliance is neither present, congruent or fit for purpose.

By way of illustration:

❏ the implementation by the police of laws to prevent drivers using hand-held mobile phones, as described at various points in this Book;

❏ the non-pursuit of difficult cases where the lack of available police capability (and in consequence a lack of viable evidence) leads the Crown Prosecution Service to conclude that there is little likelihood of attaining any successful prosecution;

❏ the projection of military power, for instance by the Royal Navy, in situations where it has neither adequate numbers of ships nor the sailors to operate them.

Again, *the issue arises as to which must come first*. To what extent are decisions on the establishment, maintenance or development of capability to take priority in the scheme of things? And how congruent are these decisions likely to be with the conditions which will apply to the use of available or planned capability? Or do strategic or policy decisions take priority, regardless of whether or not the capability exists to achieve their implementation? This issue is also dealt with in the final section of this Chapter.

CASE EXAMPLE

The provision of Public Good – the concept of Public Good was described in Chapter 24 in terms of:

❏ a necessary value, utility or service from access to which no-one can or should be excluded; *and*

❏ the provision of which should not be subject to reduction or atrophy (wearing out) as a result of consumption over time by the people who are entitled to access it.

Public Good provision might be defined in the UK to include such services as Health and Social Care, Education and the development of Human Capital, Policing and safeguarding, Border Security, and Defence of the Realm (etc). These are essential to the welfare and safety of the nation. It may also be argued that many of these services should be provided by the State, or that, like defence, it is only the State that can make them available. However, by definition:

❏ the effective provision of Public Good must be dependent on the making available of the necessary capability. Those who plan for and authorise the requirements for Public Good cannot separate this provision from the establishment of the necessary capability. Again, these are the two sides of the same coin; *and*

❏ the capability needed to provide this Public Good is likely to be subject to atrophy or entropy over the time during which it is in use. Healthcare assets wear out, as do roads and railways. Specialist staff become plateau'd or retire – their replacements have to be recruited or trained. Those who plan the provision of Public Good will have to prepare for the necessary financing and refurbishment of the capability upon which its provision depends – now and into the future. This planning may throw up unexpected (and expensive) surprises over time like the emergence of a tidal wave of knife crime, the extensive internet programming and corruption of Minors, the discovery of sub-standard built assets such as weak bridges and dams, or flammable tower block cladding on public housing described in an earlier chapter (etc).

CAPABILITY MANAGEMENT OR CORPORATE PLANNING?

Chapter 27 described an approach to strategic management based on a centralised top-down or planning down style. This approach was described as being any of rationalistic, deliberate or universalistic. These concepts were defined and illustrated in that chapter.

The outputs from these processes were / are often handed down ("thrown over the wall") to subordinates or administrators to implement (or to try to implement). Such outputs were for many years post Morrison described as "corporate plans". Sometimes such plans might make reference to the capability required to implement them. Sometimes they might not. Practical or real-world issues of capability and implementation may or may not have been of significance to those in positions of governance, decision making, and authorisation. Nor necessarily were associated issues of performance measurement and management even when it came to the disbursement of public (ie taxpayers'money). Such a process of so-called "corporate planning" might work. Or it might not.

Strategic Management processes – Chapter 20 instead noted that Strategic choices made by decision makers in an institution in response to dilemmas (such as those created by the need to make policy choices) will have to be consistent with, or to fit the available or planned capability. Otherwise implementation and performance management processes may be unviable from the start. The enterprise will be unable to do what it has set out to do. This capability will in addition have to constitute a realistic entity, based on objectively identifiable resources, people, skill sets and finance. Decisions on what form this entity must take should not be based on emotion or ideology when public money is involved, or on wishful thinking about "what should be the case" or "what the Government ought to do", or on pure theory or fantasy. Worst of all, incongruent decisions on a governance / strategy / leadership fit with the capability needed to implement mission, business plan, policy or purpose may result, in terms of Chapter 20 in any of:

❏ the institution being unable to react on any of an incremental, proactive, emergent or opportunistic basis; *or*
❏ a reliance on serendipity (luck); *or at worst*
❏ alternative (and maybe undesirable) decisions or actions being forced upon the institution by uncontrollable outside forces.

Chapter Twenty Nine
Another Big Picture

A reference to the "Big Picture" was first made in Chapter 4. Chapter 29 now deals with the issue of a personal, leadership or organisational failure (or worse *a refusal*) (i) to encompass a prevailing Big Picture; and therefore (ii) any corresponding failure to acknowledge the presence of dilemmas that this Big Picture is likely to contain.

Clearly, if decision-makers or the organisation are unable or unwilling to accept the existence or veracity of this Big Picture, then any necessary dilemma diagnosis and resolution are unlikely to happen.

BIG PICTURE DILEMMAS (I)

The *first part* of this chapter focuses on how a failure to acknowledge the character of a Big Picture might come about. For instance:

The existence of the "canny administrator"– a failure to deal with a dilemma, however resolvable or unresolvable it appears to be, may in part be explained by *(a) an personal, organisational, or cultural reluctance – or instead (b) a leadership failure to look at the Bigger Picture* (i) in which the dilemma is contained, (ii) in which there are awkward questions that may have eventually to (or must) be answered, and (iii) in which clues exist about possible resolution for those people (if any) prepared to tackle the risks or leadership difficulties that this resolution might involve. This Author contends that such a failure to encompass the Bigger Picture is one consequence of the "canny administrator" syndrome that for example characterises much of the UK's political, public, security, healthcare and charitable sectors. This syndrome may be characterised (i) by a conditioned or semiospheric *obsession with analysis and detail only* (as described in a later section below); (ii) by a deliberate failure to allocate and to enforce meaningful overall personal responsibility and accountability for performance management (with its accompanying "blame culture" syndrome); (iii) by entrenched amateurism (reference has for example already been made in this Book to work being perceived to be a prolonged extension of middle class university life); associated with (iv) a prevailing intellectual displacement, denial or laziness; (v) an effectively non-existent requirement for any mandatory and validated Continuing Professional Development (CPD) process; and finally (vi) by the ineffective level of professionalisation (Chapter 1) and understanding of the management and performance management processes described throughout this Book and in the other Books listed in the Introduction.

Pragmatism (1): scepticism about planning – there exists in the UK a not unreasonable (or indeed a healthy) scepticism about the value and effectiveness of the *planning process*. Reference has already been made in this Book to the adage "no plan survives contact with reality". This scepticism has at least two components, as follow:

❏ however sophisticated might *forecasting processes* be, there may be a significant reluctance to place a great degree of reliance on them. This is particularly the case for *longer term* forecasting. It would have been difficult in recent years to predict (i) the Brexit process and its consequences (such as for the UK Regions); or (ii) the fall in demand for diesel cars; or (iii) the relative collapse of High Street retail as described in an earlier chapter. No one knows how accurate forecasts of climate change might be if they are predicated on time scales of decades into the future; *and*

❏ secondly a justifiable concern about the processes of *corporate planning*, for instance as developed in response to the work of the Webbs and Herbert Morrison described in an earlier chapter. Just because a corporate plan, for instance written by a Civil Service Department purports to address the Bigger Picture as conceptualised by it (i) at a particular point of time, or (ii) from the viewpoint voiced by its political masters, there is no guarantee that it is representative or viable, nor that it can or will in reality be implemented. Nor that it is anything more than an expensive form of political distraction, work creation, displacement activity, or attempt to make excuses for official shortcomings.

These are key criticisms laid at the door of traditional approaches to forecasting and planning by the proponents (such as this Author) of the **strategic management** process. This adopts a more flexible, more contingent and more capability-led approach to emergent conditions faced by the enterprise, the institution or the public service.

Pragmatism (2): the devil is in the detail – however much the need to look for a Bigger Picture might be accepted, UK culture is to a significant degree dominated by the powerful professional (or "fine print") conditioning demonstrated by the influence of the legal, also the accountancy and auditing professions (in particular Chartered Accountancy). The acute medical profession is similarly characterised by highly subject-specific practice, with only a low priority being given to wider issues of whole body, mental or social health. For these professions the devil is in the detail, necessarily so as society becomes more litigious and a so- called "compensation (or blame) culture" takes root.

The influence of Cross-Cultural Variables – these variables were summarised in Chapter 6. They are also dealt with in the Author's *Principles of Management*. Of particular relevance to this chapter are the following.

High Power Distance / Hierarchy / Uncertainty Avoidance – decision-making and strategic management processes (whether in the private, public or charitable sectors) remain generically characterised in the UK by high Power Distance in conditions characterised (i) by well-established Hierarchies of role, profession or class; and (ii) a high degree of uncertainty avoidance. This is particularly the case where there is centralisation and the existence of powerful semiospheres operating a closed control. People lower down in the organisation are seen as implementers of the detail described in the Section above, or as technicians and administrators. Not for them the access to the (relatively) open strategic management process conferred on their German colleagues under the system of *Mitbestimmung* and its two tier boards.

Analysis or Holism? – the traditional emphasis on Analysis (*deconstruction*) as a dominant mode in UK academic education and cognitive conditioning has to a degree relegated the conceptualisation of "wholes", integration or Big Pictures to an afterthought. Nowhere is this syndrome better illustrated by acute medical practice in the UK, where, again, the issues of whole body, mental and social care described above are at best given a secondary priority. Similarly, the Brexit saga was conceptualised (sometimes in a "story-telling", anxiety-creating and crisis-ready format) by a highly opinionated and aggressive media in terms of a competing, incompatible and fragmented variety of political and institutional pressures. The interests of those who voted to "Leave" were sometimes dismissed by strongly opinionated accusations of provincialism, irrelevance, feeble intellect, small- mindedness, racism and disinterest in the future.

Inner-Directness and Particularism – by which, again, the focus is placed on the detail already described above. Any concern with the Big Picture is subordinated to an over-riding focus on the detailed requirements of authority, role and task. Concepts of Big Pictures are instead secondary matters for *Outer-Directness*. The wider picture is a matter (if at all) for others elsewhere in the Hierarchy or the decision-making body; or indeed to be ignored as an unnecessary, and unwanted intrusion to the status quo. External or environmental concepts of Requisite Variety and Genetic Diversity (even if recognised) may be dismissed (i) as unwelcome, (ii) as a source of disturbance to the groupthink or semiospheres of entrenched, complacent or plateau'd professionals, and (iii) as something therefore to be resisted.

Time Span of Discretion – this Book would contend that the Time Span of Discretion concept described in Chapter 21 is a means of implementing a viable process of Dilemma, Strategic and Performance Management based on a realistic view of the Big Picture. However, this contention assumes that people, leaders and hierarchies possess the necessary willpower, knowledge base, cognitions, attitudes, training and skills to implement the concept. Where these necessary paradigms and capabilities are not in place, however, it may be difficult (if not impossible) for the enterprise or institution to recognise the Big Picture that it may have to deal with.

Critical Big Picture issues dealt with in this Book include personal responsibility, narcissism, the influence of social media on Minors, competition strategy, the need for nation-wide entrepreneurialism, performance management, security, environmental concern, and Public Value.

Reference to issues of amateurism, ineffective professionalisation; outdated or irrelevant bases of Knowledge and competence; failures of education, training and CPD; the effect of outdated Webbist conditioning and Morrison's corporatism; the Peter Principle (etc) have also been made throughout this Book.

BIG PICTURE DILEMMAS (II)

The *second part* of this chapter moves on to identify some risks that may emerge as a result of any failure to identify the Bigger Picture, or worse, to deny its existence.

Serendipity risk – a failure even to consider what is the nature of the Big Picture facing the enterprise or institution may be likely to place it at the risk of having to depend on *serendipity*. To a degree, such a reliance on serendipity has characterised the UK Brexit process. Things might work out for the best? Or they might work out for the worst? That is their dilemma.

The negative consequences of relying on serendipity may however best be illustrated at this time of writing by *the catastrophic increase in the incidence of UK knife crime*. This was preceded:

❏ by a politically deliberate, but massive, socially foolish, and unsustainable reduction in Police Officer numbers; *and*

❏ by a disastrous "politically correct" decision to limit essential "stop and search" activities associated with members of the public suspected of drug-dealing, carrying offensive weapons, or operating across so-called "county lines" (etc).

An unavoidable Big Picture – certain circumstances will *require* the identification of some kind of Big Picture, or at least of some scenarios that might make it up. This is undoubtedly the case in terms of *essential and unavoidable long-term thinking* about such issues as electricity and fuel supply, the calamitous impact of social media on Minors, vocational and professional education and training, mental health, climate change, infrastructure and transport investments, the healthcare of an ageing population, the role of High Street retail, etc.

Competition strategy – competition strategy was described in Chapter 23. A focus on the Big Picture of competitive positioning and competitive strategy, as described in that chapter, is as critical for politicians, the public and the healthcare sectors as it is for business enterprises, charities and the Third Sector. For instance (and whether they now like it or not) local and regional authorities have to bid for available funds on a competitive basis. Waving the "begging bowl" was for example a traditional historical means for local authorities to try to access state handouts. This begging bowl is now fast disappearing. It is being replaced in the UK by a central government or funding agency demand for the demonstration by potential recipients to show more enterprise in achieving public value for money than their neighbours. *Whether this is for good or for ill – that is the dilemma.*

Chapter Thirty
Causes of Dilemma
Decision-Making Delay

SOME FACTORS CAUSING DILEMMA DECISION-MAKING DELAY

This chapter identifies a number of factors which may (for good or ill) account for dilemma decision-making delay and an apparent or temporary failure of the Dilemma Management process. These factors are described as follow.

Overcentralisation – in which decision-making delay or inaction may be associated with a refusal or an inability at governance or senior management level to delegate authority and responsibility to others below them in the hierarchy. Overcentralised structures might be characterised by high Power Distance, autocracy, family control, or a semiospheric association with powerful membership or political groups. They might be associated with other National Culture variables such as a very high degree of uncertainty avoidance, or an entrenched masculinity and patriarchy. These were described in Chapter 6. The people who run overcentralised structures may only be prepared to appoint trusted family or party members, friends or cronies (etc) to subordinate roles. Or instead they may simply appoint "yes-men" from whom they will receive no question or challenge.

A potential result may be *decision-making overload*. Too many issues requiring decision flow up to the top of the organisation, only to have to wait their turn for attention or action – if at all. This syndrome may be exacerbated where:

❏ the occupants of the organisation reside in a powerful (or at the time unassailable) semiosphere, as described in Chapter 9; *or*
❏ there are obvious "blind spots" in patterns of perception or thinking, particularly in the case of unwanted dilemmas; *or*

❏   there is strong resistance (or an inability) to deal with change, ideological CD, or to accept decision solutions "not invented here"; *or*

❏   wealthy or powerful proprietors, decision-makers, or third generation sons are lazy or absent, perhaps spending their time at the races, on their yachts, or in the local casino instead of doing their job.

Overcentralised structures may be at their most vulnerable in the dilemma conditions described in Chapters 15, 18 and 26, where the chosen mode of operation (and an emerging fear of its consequences) could lead to *unsustainable commitments, crisis, or a direct threat of corporate collapse.* Overcentralisation may also be associated with:-

Ineffective information flows – in which information flows to a highly centralised decision-making process suffer from the classic symptoms of filtering, downgrading or distortion (to include the use of "creative accounting") for instance described in detail in the Author's *Principles of Management* to which reference is made in the Introduction to this Book. Ultimately, decision-makers will only receive information that (i) those below them believe that they will accept, which is (ii) consistent with their opinions and prejudices, and (iii) for whose upwards transmission neither the risks of personal sanction nor dismissal may be foreseen. This is akin to the "don't shoot the messenger" syndrome. Also see immediately below.

CASE EXAMPLE
A Dilemma Management illustration: "controlling the president's information flow" – Michael Wolff suggests in his book *Fire and Fury* (pps188-189) that a 'unique [US White House] problem … was partly how to get information to someone who did not (or could not or would not) read, and who at best only listened selectively … the other part of the problem was how best to qualify the information that he liked to get. **Wwww** had honed her instincts for the kind of information – the clips – that would please him. **Xxxx**, with his intense and confiding voice, could insinuate himself into the president's mind. **Yyyy** brought him the latest outrages against him.

[Then] there were his after-dinner calls – the billionaires' chorus. And the cable [TV] … programmed to reach him – to court him or to enrage him.

The information he did not get was formal information. The data. The details. The options. The analysis. He didn't do PowerPoint. For anything that smacked of a classroom or being lectured to – "professor" was one of his bad words … he got up and left the room.

This was a problem in multiple respects … but perhaps most of all, it was a problem in the evaluation of strategic military options. The president liked generals … [but] what [he] did not like was *listening* to generals who [had skilled themselves] in the new army jargon of PowerPoint, data dumps, and McKinsey-like presentations'. At one interview, '**Zzzz**, wearing a uniform with his silver star, came in and immediately launched into a wide- ranging lecture on global strategy. [The president] was soon, and obviously distracted, and as the lecture continued he began sulking.

"That guy bores the shit out of me"' he announced after **Zzzz** left the room.

Calculated indecision – whereby and on the basis of past experience the decision-maker consciously refuses to make some dilemma decisions on the grounds that the time does not appear to be right, and / or their "gut feeling" tells them not to act. Such refusal to act may in this case be based on a personal precedent that the decision-maker has in the past only got (say) 50% of such decisions right (and also therefore 50% wrong). This syndrome may affect airplane manufacturers such as Airbus or Boeing. Such organisations must "bet the company" on making huge investments in creating aircraft to meet their own future estimates of operating and market conditions *in a decade or so's time*. There is no guarantee that a market eg for more supersize jumbo jets will actually emerge (or in the case of the A380 be financially worthwhile), or that fuel-efficiency issues will not in the meantime change their parameters.

Politicisation and stalemate – dilemma decision making may become subject to delay or *stalemate* where the matter of concern has become *significantly politicised*. Earlier chapters of this Book noted that events or decisions may for example have become characterised by any of:

❑ the existence of multiple and conflicting objectives; *or*
❑ dilemma features which for whatever reason are (or instead may (i) be perceived or (ii) be promoted to be) currently irreconcilable; *or*
❑ an entrenched lack of agreement between (perhaps) equally powerful or influential stakeholders or ideologies; *or*
❑ the direct use of the political, negotiation or lobbying process by participants to delay or to block progress; *or*
❑ weak (or worse, an absence of) leadership capability, willpower or motivation to achieve a reconciliation or resolution; *or*
❑ the absence (again for whatever reason) of any opportunity or capability to resolve the impasse by means of direction, command or prescription. Unlike the Emperor Alexander, a Gordion Knot type dilemma cannot simply be sliced in two by a single sword-stroke; *and perhaps where*
❑ any proposal of an individual "back me or sack me" decision may be a deliberate creation (eg) of a political risk dilemma where (i) there is doubt as to whether the leader will actually do what he or she is threatening; and (ii) particularly if it could mean calling a General Election from which all may lose!

Such conditions of politicisation or stalemate might, at this time of writing, be illustrated by any of such UK contexts as:

❑ the future nature of the country's international political and trading relationships, as in the case of Brexit;
❑ aspects of the state's provision of healthcare, social welfare, or educational provision;
❑ public sector performance measurement and performance management;
❑ the interplay of, or lobbying by very powerful individuals, vested interests, and membership groups in business, finance, commerce, advertising, the media (etc); *as well as*
❑ the regulation of the media, social media, and the Attention Economy;

❑ the management and financing of professional football as a national sport;

❑ attitudes to certain forms of religious practice and behaviour;

❑ regional policy; the so-called "North – South Divide"; and equally the relationships with Scotland, Wales and Northern Ireland.

The current state of *Gun Control legislation in the USA* (Chapter 3) offers a catastrophic (and murderous) example of the direct consequences of dilemma management politicisation and stalemate – to which any resolution (i) does not appear in any way to be in sight, or (ii) to be likely in the foreseeable future.

"Slow burn" – in which the decision-maker is, for whatever reason, reluctant to act even though the need to do something is becoming more apparent and more urgent. Ultimately, some kind of critical "trigger" event or action, such as described in Chapters 15, 18 and 26, forces people to act. They themselves come to a realisation, however unwelcome and unwanted it may be, that they will have no alternative but in some way to act.

Passing the buck – whereby an apparently responsible decision-maker is, for whatever reason, unable or unwilling to visualise any suitable course of action by which to identify or to resolve a dilemma, or to deal with it. *He / she / they then pass the buck.* Their responsibility for the matter is somehow or other passed on to someone else. This person might be a member of the decision- maker's personal network who agrees to use his or her own contacts in order to "take care of the matter" on their behalf. They might instead be ordered to "sweep the matter under the nearest carpet", particularly if they are lower in the hierarchy and perceive that they might be at threat of sanction or dismissal if they are seen to fail. They might be poorly informed about the matter. They might be trying to curry favour, for instance in the hope of advancement. Or they might just be naïve.

This strategy might work if (for whatever reason) it is not clear "where the buck stops" in the organisation.

But *if it is very clear where the buck actually does stop*, then avoiding responsibility by passing the buck may be a risky strategy.

If discovered, the buck-passer may face sanctions for irresponsibility, incompetence, and a failure properly to do their job. Whatever may be the consequences, whether in terms of loss of face or credibility, reputational or career damage, etc.

Serendipity – in which decision making action or inaction are driven by (ie based on) a person's *perception of luck* or their "gut feel". Choice of action or inaction might similarly be based on the use of some kind of non-systematic risk-management technique such as tossing a coin, rolling a dice, visiting a bookmaker, or consulting an astrologer. Some cultures instead use the analysis of a person's hand-writing as a predictor. Reliance on serendipity may be likened to the saying of Dickens' Mr Micawber, who believed that "something or other is bound to turn up".

People who rely on serendipity may be tempted to deal with any display of scepticism by others by attempting to bully them; or to use aggressive interpersonal behaviour to deflect criticism; or to exploit other people's fear of conflict. In this respect there are parallels with the behaviour of the *chancer*, described immediately below.

Decision-making and the chancer – a chancer may variously be defined as:

❏ an opportunist or schemer who is habituated to "chancing his or her arm";
❏ an imposter who pretends (i) to be something that they are not, or (ii) to be able to do something that when put to the test they cannot accomplish;
❏ someone who takes advantage of poorly managed situations which they may then try to manipulate to their own advantage or profit;
❏ someone who may be skilled at talking their way out of difficult situations which they have created for themselves;
❏ a person who is by definition a source of an unpredictable risk or likely value loss to other people and institutions with which they come into contact.

Decisions made by chancers may be appropriate, or they may not. This will depend on how lucky they are (perceived luckiness was a quality sometimes sought by Napoleon when selecting his army officers). The chancer must try to hide any mismatch between his or her competence and the requirements of the task. So decisions likely to reveal the chancer's personal shortcomings may be avoided, whilst the decisions that are made might be defended by the aggressive behaviour described in the previous section above. Once, however, the chancer's lack of competence or their scheming has been revealed (that is, the person has been "rumbled"), their credibility may evaporate. This is when the chancer uses his or her in-built ability to spot trouble ahead. They may then seek urgently to move on to pastures new, prior to the eventual consequences of their decisions becoming clear to others (that is when "the pigeons come home to roost").

The presence of a skilled or ruthless chancer in the circumstances comprising large-scale commitments described in Chapter 26 may very significantly increase the risk associated with these circumstances. Ultimately the chancer may choose his or her opportunity and bail out with a fistful of profit well before the End Game described in that chapter.

Lucrative corporate positions as high level Information and Communication Technology (IT / ICT) consultants have in the past been particularly attractive targets for such skilled chancers. Subsequent havoc and huge financial losses have often been the result of their tenure.

Prevarication, obfuscation or "fudge" – in which inaction is the preferred decision (or rather non-decision) option. The individual or decision-making group will habitually or culturally seek excuses and opportunities to delay matters, (i) preferably for as long as possible, and (ii) perhaps hoping that in the end the problem will go away. This appears to be a syndrome associated with political, religious or religio-cultural organisations whose doctrine is coming under challenge, or is now being seen as outdated and irrelevant.

Lack of proactivity – some people appear to be unable or unwilling to identify and to make decisions, even when there is an obvious professional need (and responsibility) for them to act. This may simply be because they (and / or the people around them) are (and may also be pathologically) *lacking in the relevant motivation or proactivity*. They might be personally, professionally and administratively disorganised or incompetent. They may be unwilling or unable to accept personal responsibility. They might have become over-reliant on other people to do things for them. Worse, they may be unable to conceptualise any need to "get off their backside" in order to do something, nor more importantly to be motivated to recognise and to react to urgent professional cues requiring their action. Or they may have become habituated to personal prevarication, obfuscation and an addiction to the "conversations" and debate to which reference is made at various points in this Book. All of this might be a function of their:

❏ personal incapacity, lack of proper focus, outdatedness, laziness, CPD failure, or an outdated level of cognitive competence; *or*
❏ ignorance or denial of contemporary operational customer/ client service or performance management expectations; *or instead*
❏ lack of concern for, or an actually positive denial of the need for *organisational efficiency and assurance* (for instance in the use of taxpayer, charitable, or public funds); *or*
❏ entrenched personal complacency, social class or political arrogance; attachment to the status quo; *or ultimately*
❏ existence in a political, or wealthy, or luxurious "comfort zone" as semiosphere in which they do not perceive that they are really responsible for anything at all, in which talk is all that matters, or in which others will serve them as the need requires.

This might be associated with:

"Pathological" indecision – the responsible person or group is (for whatever reason) unwilling, or is instead unable to identify, to diagnose, describe or resolve a dilemma. *Nor is he / she / they prepared in any way to deal with it, nor to make decisions – however critical such decisions might be at the time.* For instance, see Chapters 3 and 26. The non (eg incompetent or refusing) decision- maker might suffer from *a mindset frozen* into the lack of proactivity described above, or worse remain inactive because for instance:

❏ they are simply out of their depth; *and / or*

❏ they are professionally unaware of, or unable (or unwilling in vocational terms) to come to terms with the demands of the management process which underpins this Book, and the four other Books to which reference is made in the Introduction;

❏ they realise (or are told) that in terms of the Peter Principle or Time Span of Discretion that they are well past their level of personal capacity (or indeed their "sell-by date"); *or instead*

❏ they suffer from significant personal doubt, associated with a lack of self-confidence in themselves or their professional competence; *or*

❏ they suffer from a psychological fear (i) of making decisions, (ii) of the commitments inherent in these decisions, and (iii) of the potential consequences; *or*

❏ their behaviour may have been conditioned (or exacerbated) by what may now be interpreted (i) as an *outdated and self- serving* twentieth century Higher Education culture of Webbist philosophy (Chapter 27), the vestiges of British Imperialism and social class arrogance, the supposed superiority of so- called "elite" academia in the UK and its continuing reinforcement of the non-vocational middle class prestige dealt with in earlier chapters; (ii) excessive analysis-paralysis and debate as a substitute (for example) for leadership, entrepreneurship, and action; (iii) for some an obsessive "even-handed" fear of favouring one side over another (even if for whatever reason and whether politically, financially and economically this is necessary or unavoidable); and (iv) the so-called "political correctness" described in Chapter 8; *perhaps associated with*

❏ the entrenched and non-responsible amateurism described above in which work continues to be perceived as a prolonged extension of middle class university life;

❏ a fear and avoidance of conflict and aggression on the part of peers, clients or others, with its perceived potential for political incorrectness or bullying; *or*

❏ a fear of the evaluation and the necessary staff appraisal and judgement by others that may be inseparable from the management process. This may be associated with the evaluation and comment on the level of personal professionalism, with its consequent potential for the questioning of personal competence, motivation and fitness to carry out a role; *or*

❑   they may have become culturally conditioned, for instance by a dominant home, school or national culture (Chapter 6) environment (i) to accept orders and instructions and (ii) to "know their place". They may have no experience of making decisions or giving orders, which behaviour is culturally alien (or has even been forbidden) to them; *or*

❑   again, they may as substitute take refuge in the (futile?) talk, "conversations", exhortations, dialectics and "debates", media blogs, and demand for actions that other people (but not themselves) "should" or "ought to" undertake (etc) described at various points of this Book. *These substitutes are mistaken for action.* These substitutes also act as a distraction from their own personal, professional or leadership shortcomings in the decision environments (i) that they face but fear, and (ii) from the personal responsibility from which they recoil.

This might also be related to:

Putting off the inevitable – ultimately (and as described in Chapter 26) the decision-maker (or the organisation he / she / they represent) may run out of time, credibility, options (and even friends or supporters). For instance, the consequences of past governance failures or institutional mismanagement begin to emerge and to catch out current government ministers or CEOs; auditors start to demur or to distance themselves in order to protect and to assure their own reputation and survival; exposés by the media or single interest groups as described in earlier chapters point to emergent crises in spite of the (possibly increasingly desperate?) efforts at the level of governance, political party, Trustee Board or CEO:

❑   to "hush them up"; *or*
❑   to deny them; *or*
❑   to "sweep them under the carpet"; *or*

❏ to "make them go away"; *or*
❏ to attempt to distract or to divert attention away from them to-wards what are internally perceived to be more positive events or stories; *or worst of all*
❏ to attempt – by whatever means – to hide them from outside scrutiny – whatever the legal, ethical, reputational, financial or career implications (etc). This might be characterised by such processes as "closing ranks" or implementing a "cover- up"?

Any or all of these actions may in the end lead to a *cascade* of (in-creasingly damaging) negative or destructive revelations and crises or public criticism; reputational, value and financial losses; litiga-tion; and perhaps official or regulatory investigation.

And finally – other factors which may give rise to decision making delay might include:

❏ the existence of *over-complexity*. The number of variables which must be taken into account, and the inter-relationships between them may make dilemma resolution hard to achieve. This issue has been dealt with at various points in this Book, for instance in the case (i) of dilemmas of negative value described in Chapter 15; of (ii) the wicked mess risk described in Chapter 17; and (iii) the unwitting creation of non- reconcilable complications in the performance management process described in Chapter 24;
❏ the use of *dispute and dialectics* to delay decision-making. This was a feature of the Brexit process where perceptions of necessary action and implementation were delayed by MPs and political parties for lengthy periods. Reference has been made to the issue of debate and dialectics as a dilemma source through-out this Book;
❏ the use of *creative ambiguity* by which a political party, an or-ganisation or a pressure group (etc) tries to "have its cake and eat it" by refusing (or appearing to refuse) to commit to any stated preferred course of action. There may, or may not be a finite limit to how long this strategy will work. It was a key feature of the UK Brexit process;

❏ the attempt to *buy time* by avoiding or delaying a decision. The UK has for instance a long tradition of using Commissions of Inquiry to investigate complex, dilemma-laden and often controversial matters. The timescale of these Inquiries means that decisions may be put off for the time being, or even quietly abandoned at a later date. The use of the strategy of buying time through the use of an investigative process may also be used as mechanisms for the diversion of public, media or stakeholder attention, or to enact displacement activity and obfuscation;

❏ the need for subordinates or government officials (etc) to interpret the reality of, or possibilities for implementation of otherwise generalised statements of purpose or intent made by governments or political parties. This may lead to decision making delay;

❏ personal, political or corporate *perceptions of indispensability*. Presidents and politicians, leaders, CE's / CEOs (etc) develop a sense that they are irreplaceable. At this time of writing such an Ultra High Power syndrome characterised the Presidential political dynamics in some African countries, Venezuela, Iran and Syria. The leader's indispensability and lack of accountability is likely to be defended by entrenched party members, cronies, family members, powerful interests, the military, kleptocrats, etc. It may be marked by isolation, megalomania, corruption and extreme violence towards critics. Whether therefore decisions are made (or not made) may simply be a function of leadership dynamics and a totally limited perception of internal greed or priority.

TREADING ON EGGSHELLS DEFINED

The process of "treading on eggshells" may be defined as a *caution-ary* action or stance. There may be any number of reasons for taking this stance. It may be chosen (i) when dealing with individual people, political parties or groups; (ii) when dealing with communities; (iii) when dealing with institutions or organisations; or (iv) when dealing with situations (etc).

The phrase "treading on eggshells" is a *metaphor* for being care-ful (or extra-careful) in handling sensitive situations. This might be because other people are perceived to be sensitive or may instead easily (or deliberately) become argumentative, angry or offended. That is, if you perceive that you are treading on eggshells, or walking on them you may choose to be cautious about what you say or do because, for whatever reason, you do not want to upset somebody or something.

The phrase "treading on eggshells" may then be applied as a met-aphor for some kind of *"relationship anxiety"* in which a person (or someone who represents an institution) feels that the "ground" they are walking on, or the relationship architecture in which they are in-volved, is unstable or unpredictable. Or other people (and events) are seen in some way to be semi-detached, dissociated or disconnected from whatever is going on around them. This might be because these people exist in a robustly self- contained semiosphere (such as that based on membership of a single interest group, or adherence to social media); are so-called "politically correct"; are Snowflakes; or are openly resistant or hostile to the issue involved (etc). The latter became a key feature of the UK Brexit process.

WHAT ARE "EGGSHELLS"?

Eggshells are defined for the purposes of this Book to be *metaphor-ical* sources (i) of dilemmas, and (ii) of drivers of division between

TREADING ON EGGSHELLS? 31-391

people, beliefs, groups, organisations (etc). Eggshells may be used for instance to form effective barriers (i) to communication, interaction or to the creation of understanding, or (ii) to the audibility and credibility of the various Voices described in this Book; or ultimately (iii) to delay or to impede action. Criticisms about care provision may for instance raise hackles on the part of NHS staff and social care administrators who are sensitive (or actually hostile) (i) to public complaints about society's elders (and long-term taxpayers) being described as "crumble" or "bed-blockers"; and (ii) criticisms about the traditional low priority of mental healthcare.

Eggshells may be any of fixed, established, variable or transient in character. They might include:

- ❏ attitudes eg in semiospheres;
- ❏ beliefs eg is the practice of religion a right or a privilege?
- ❏ Cognitions and Cognitive Dissonance;
- ❏ created anxieties and manufactured crises;
- ❏ received wisdoms eg leaving / staying in the European Union is best;
- ❏ conditioning eg the "lower orders" should know and keep to their place in the social pecking order;
- ❏ conditioning eg "niceness" should be maintained at all times even when it is clearly unproductive in the scheme of things;
- ❏ establishing understanding about what are requisite competencies and capacities eg professional, academic, vocational or entrepreneurial?
- ❏ the understanding of and adherence to specific paradigms, and the rejection of others eg the Snowflake syndrome; or the role of veganism (i) as a questionably nutritious and viable diet for young people, and (ii) in the wider ("Big Picture") context of the capability of the UK farming industry to feed the nation, to substitute for imported foodstuffs (with potentially high environmental, transport and distribution costs), to maintain high standards of animal husbandry and welfare, and to protect the UK countryside;
- ❏ perceptions eg of what is (so-called) "politically correct"?

- ❏ ideologies eg belief in Webbist and Morrisonian concepts (i) of "big state" intervention, and (ii) the continuing belief in the Oxbridge-type educated "disinterested expert" as an *amateur non-professional* described in Chapter 27;
- ❏ actual prejudices eg against the relevance, acceptance and application of the public value type methodologies described in Chapter 24.

Case Example: the mega Report – the Author was sitting next to a City Councillor at a meeting. She was bemoaning the receipt of an official 70,000 word Report with 50 Recommendations that she had received and had to read. With a weary expression she said to me "why can't they just do something instead of giving us these huge documents? It's all just displacement activity. And all these Reports do is to gather dust and end up in the recycler." Responding to my suggestion that the City Authorities request one-only page documents with a maximum of three objectives or recommendations, complete with required implementation timescales, she turned to me and said that the bureaucrats responsible would be most offended by such a suggestion. And besides, they were not trained or able to write short focussed reports the like of which she and the Author were familiar when working in industry.

SOME EXAMPLES OF MANAGEMENT DILEMMAS ASSOCIATED WITH TREADING ON EGGSHELLS

There could be any number of examples of Management Dilemma associated with the need *to navigate an eggshell-laden territory*. Some have already been described in the various other contexts identified in this Book. The following is simply a short list chosen for illustrative purposes in this chapter:

- ❏ managing a professional football club which has powerful owners and also employs very highly paid "star" players;
- ❏ agreeing Government spending priorities for defence, policing, pandemics, healthcare, education, housing, or infrastructure (etc);
- ❏ dealing with powerful stakeholders; "Big Data", "Big Pharma", etc;

❑ dealing with febrile conditions in political institutions (such as Parliament) or charities, etc;

❑ dealing with so-called "political correctness" (especially where the "politically correct" people or groups involved come into the categories of deliberate *eggshell creators or maintainers* described in a later section of this chapter);

❑ dealing with an opinionated, hostile, politically correct or "edgy" media. The objective of such a media (whether newspaper, broadcast or social, etc) may be to create artificial stress, anxieties or crises for others as forms of (potentially "fake"?) news stories;

❑ managing hospital clinicians or consultants;

❑ getting rid of (what may now have become unsustainable ?) free pensioner bus passes (!).

DILEMMA MANAGEMENT CONSEQUENCES

The (metaphorical) presence of eggshells, or an *eggshell divide* between the parties to the dilemma may give rise to any of the Management Dilemmas described in Chapter 1, and fit the reasoning given in that chapter. The assessment of the nature or impact of the eggshells might then be based on the event or concept characteristics described in another chapter. Dilemma management consequences might include any or all of:

❑ how and by whom is the nature of the eggshells to be perceived?

❑ deciding the reason for the existence of the eggshells; *and*

❑ deciding on their relative strength or brittleness?

❑ estimating what risk the eggshells are perceived to contain (i) if they are left alone, or (ii) if crushed?

❑ ascertaining how the eggshells might be used to create anxieties or crises (etc), and by whom?

❑ deciding whether the eggshells, or the eggshell divide should (i) be left alone, (ii) cracked, or (iii) removed completely; and by whom?

❑ estimating whether the cracking or removal of the eggshell or eggshell divide will be categorised by critics as "politically

incorrect", or as acts of anxiety creation, bullying, forced change, "Luddism" or even Fascism?
❑ deciding whether the dilemmas created by the eggshells have been consolidated ("concreted") or institutionalised into a further dimension (as in politics, the media, or in the budgetary disbursement of state funding, etc), adding additional complexity to the Dilemma Management process? The derivation of this extra complexity may be serendipitous, or equally it may result from a deliberate strategy;
❑ estimating the relative strength, determination or capability (capacity plus willpower) of the parties on either side of the eggshell divide.

SOME CHARACTERISTICS OF EGGSHELL PLAYERS
Decision and strategy makers, sources of influence, and people involved on either side in the eggshell divide are categorised in this chapter as being either of:

❑ *eggshell defenders – creators and maintainers; or accommodators;* **or**
❑ *eggshell breakers or removers.*

EGGSHELL DEFENDERS CATEGORISED [I] – CREATORS AND MAINTAINERS
The creation and maintenance of eggshells as a strategy, or the maintenance of an eggshell divide might be a function of any of the following *groups of drivers*:

❑ the influence of vested interests / powerful groups or semiospheres;
❑ strongly established cognitions, resistance to tolerating Cognitive Dissonance (CD);
❑ the existence of entrenched ideologies, negotiating positions;
❑ a belief in, and a motivation to further a particular cause;
❑ a belief in, and a motivation to protect the status quo; *or*
❑ attempts to protect status, terms and conditions; *or*
❑ a fear of loss; *or*

- ❏ "turf defending";
- ❏ a motivation to resist change, or to alter the nature of that change, or to remove the people who wish to bring about that change;
- ❏ an awareness of critical "Hidden Factory" performance variables that could be used by others to change the status quo;
- ❏ an awareness and application of the nature of the relevant concept or event characteristics;
- ❏ perceptions of potential for risk, anxiety creation, or crisis;
- ❏ an aggressive denial of the potential / actual / inevitable influence of requisite variety and genetic diversity.

The relative *strength* of these drivers may be reinforced by any or all of:

- ❏ a prevailing belief, ideology or opinionation;
- ❏ so-called "political correctness";
- ❏ the existence of strong Voices;
- ❏ conditioning;
- ❏ fear of conflict;
- ❏ strong Snowflake character;
- ❏ strong semiosphere values / ideologies;
- ❏ the likely existence of a critical endgame (Chapter 26); *and*
- ❏ otherwise the use of strong and proactive leadership in defence of eggshells and the eggshell divide.

The relative strength of these drivers may in particular *be reinforced* in conditions characterised by:

- ❏ a reaction to parties who hold different, opposing or threatening views;
- ❏ the power of ideology, belief or politicisation – of whatever sort and whatever the cause;
- ❏ a reaction to poor / non-existent Emotional Intelligence on the part of other people (eg Type "A") or stakeholders;
- ❏ an awareness and fear on the part of any of the participants of the workings of the Peter Principle;
- ❏ aggressive adherence to entrenched but obsolete paradigms; and / or

❏   a lack of awareness of, or rejection of critical / determinant financial and performance management methodologies (eg as summarised in this Book);

❏   otherwise by perceptions that an active defence is needed against the effects of incompetent or ineffective leaders, decision makers, administrators, chancers, cronies (etc) who for instance are perceived to be attempting to hide their professional shortcomings from others eg by using diversionary tactics, aggression, bullying, threatening behaviour, conflict (etc).

EGGSHELL DEFENDERS CATEGORISED [II] – ACCOMMODATORS

A strategy of accommodating to the existence and effects of eggshells, or an eggshell divide may be a function of any of the drivers already described above. In addition the following groups of drivers might also apply to *eggshell accommodators*:

❏   a fear of the big or wider picture – a syndrome described in terms of "the canny administrator" described in Chapter 29;

❏   fear of change expressed in the form of naivete or lack of motivation;

❏   a conditioning to fear or avoid conflict;

❏   actual awareness of the capability limitations of staff or incumbents, perhaps coupled with a history of CPD failures; *or*

❏   the cognitions, CD, and behaviour patterns of the plateau'd professional; *or*

❏   outdated adherence to a potentially obsolete installed base (i) of thinking, (ii) Knowledge, or (iii) paradigm base;

❏   an established or entrenched habituation to custom and practice or patterns of indulgence, such as Blake & Mouton's "Holiday Camp" style of management 1.9 (see *Principles of Management*);

❏   a lack of awareness (or denial) of alternatives, etc.

Caught in the middle – the eggshell management process may come up against people, groups or semiospheres who have become *caught in the middle* of an eggshell divide. These may have little choice but to accommodate to the prevailing eggshells because for instance:

❏ they perceive that they are uncomfortably close to powerful stakeholders, no matter on which side of the eggshell divide these may reside;
❏ they are aware of the personal, occupational or professional risks to them of both sides of the eggshell divide. This might include people such as school teachers, police officers, politicians, civil and local government servants, full-time charitable officers, etc;
❏ they have weak Voices, or represent those with weak Voices;
❏ their own leadership is weak or ineffective (or has been deliberately established to be so).

So, like Mr Micawber they might just hope that events will in the end take a turn for the better – that is that serendipity will intervene for the good.

EGGSHELL BREAKERS AND REMOVERS CATEGORISED

Eggshell breakers or removers may be people or organisations who (i) for whatever reason and (ii) however it might be accomplished, wish to break or crush the eggshells or the eggshell divide with which they perceive that they are confronted. Or instead their aim is to remove the people or the organisations associated with these eggshells. They might use the event or concept characteristics (Chapter 4) to categorise their perceptions of the eggshell divide. And they may have a high tolerance of conflict. This may especially be the case if they think that they are dealing with people whose "niceness" they perceive to be associated with a fear of, or a low threshold of conflict tolerance.

EGGSHELL STRATEGIES

There would appear to be at least three categories of *eggshell strategy*. The first strategy is *the specific*, as follows:

❏ strengthen and / or complicate the eggshells and the divide / barrier, then to defend it; *OR*

- ❑ weaken the eggshells by cracking them; *and / or*
- ❑ remove the eggshells by changing conditions or parameters, or removing their creators.

The second strategy is *the generic proactive*:

- ❑ strengthen own forces;
- ❑ attempt to weaken opposing forces;
- ❑ play to own capabilities (capacity plus willpower);
- ❑ attempt to play to opponents' weaknesses;
- ❑ reinforce own position (in terms of power or bargaining / negotiating position);
- ❑ attempt to weaken opponents' position;
- ❑ attempt to increase the cost to the opponent;
- ❑ attempt to increase level of CD, anxiety, conflict and / or risk to the opponent;
- ❑ attempt to exploit emergent opportunities.

The third strategy is *the generic reactive*:

- ❑ attempt to maintain the status quo;
- ❑ use obfuscation or denial;
- ❑ attempt to refuse to interact or negotiate;
- ❑ attempt to increase the cost to the opponent;
- ❑ attempt to avoid conflict;
- ❑ attempt to avoid antagonising opponents, ("let sleeping dogs lie");
- ❑ attempt to co-operate across the divide, or to seek compromise.

Issues of *competition strategy* were dealt with in Chapter 23. The application of a *Lewin Force Field* was described in Chapter 26.

SOME SKILLED EGGSHELL PLAYERS?
The Author might suggest that (*in his opinion only*) any or all of the following are highly skilled *exploiters* of eggshells and eggshell divides in the UK:

- ❑ the UK National Health Service as a highly powerful semiosphere, with its open strategy of public self-promotion and

politicisation (also see Chapter 27 on the Webbs and Herbert Morrison);
- ❏ the UK education system in general, but academia and publicly funded research institutions in particular;
- ❏ Big Data; *and*
- ❏ Social Media (now a highly destructive and self-sustaining force as far as UK Minors and their parents are concerned);
- ❏ powerful vested interests, of whatever sort;
- ❏ single interest and pressure groups; *but whose reputation may be affected (damaged) by the actions of*
- ❏ self-publicist and pressure group proponents eg of environmental, educational or dietary causes (etc) based on questionable, speculative, potentially damaging or unproven Knowledge and science who (i) are not in any serious position to suggest viable means of actually implementing their proposals (or any valid reasons why this should be the case) apart from demanding that "the government should / ought to do something", or (ii) who are reliant on the application of techniques of anxiety or crisis creation (Chapter 18), "political correctness", the Snowflake syndrome (etc) in order to attempt to create a layer of eggshell protection to bolster or defend their position in the scheme of things;
- ❏ certain Voices;
- ❏ the so-called "politically correct" and their agencies; *and*
- ❏ political parties;
- ❏ etc.

Chapter Thirty Two

Muddling Through, Dilemma Management, and the Public Service Organisation

What taxes or licence fees are you paying? What level of performance should you expect for your hard-earned money from those (i) who are spending it on your behalf, or (ii) receiving their salaries and retirement pensions from it? In particular, what are your expectations of someone in the public or media service who is paid more than £250 thousand per year?

CHAPTER PURPOSE

The Final chapter of this Book deals with Dilemma Management issues in some of the UK Public Service Organisations. These are referred to here by the use of the acronym "PSO". Such PSOs include the publically funded healthcare system, education (whether at school or college level), the civil and judiciary services, local government organisations, state corporations such as the BBC, government quangos, or the civil uniformed services.

By definition, the operations of these organisations *(and much more importantly the people who run them)* are critical to the functioning of civil society, for instance because:

❏ they provide the Public Good described in Chapter 24 and in later chapters in a context of expanding expectations, growing individualism and reluctance to accept personal responsibility, and "pass the parcel" behaviour at the level of government and its advisers or agencies aimed at trying to reallocate responsibility and to shuffle funding requirements to someone else. This pattern is being made more serious where:-

❏ the institution on the receiving end has become, or is in the process of becoming a provider or refuge of last resort as described in the Introduction to this Book, for instance in the cases of schools, the NHS, and the Police Service;

❏ their strategic management and operational process are inevitably politicised;

❏ they consume large sums of taxpayer and other public money; not unreasonably associated with:-

❏ public demands for demonstrable efficiency, transparent performance management, taxpayer value for money, and operational excellence for instance described in terms of Six Sigma.

The chapter applies (but does not repeat) appropriate Dilemma Management material from previous chapters as appropriate. It contains illustrative Case Examples. Its contents are ordered into three sections, as follow:

➤ Context
➤ Dilemmas facing the PSO
➤ Implications for PSO Dilemma Management capability

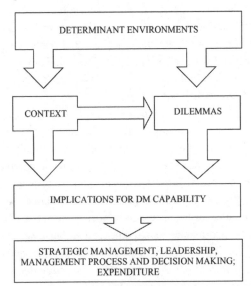

Figure 24
Dilemma Management and the Public Service Organisation

32-402   DILEMMA MANAGEMENT

A DEFINITION OF "MUDDLING THROUGH"

The concept of "Muddling Through" may be defined in terms of an action or process being carried out by someone, or by people in an organisation, which may or may not be successful. The person or people involved are unlikely to have much idea about what to do, nor how to do it. They may not have the proper capacity, the skills, the right tools or equipment, or the necessary experience. There may be little or no organisation or direction. Muddling through may be evidenced by behaviours made up on an personalised, aimless, inconsistent or improvised basis varying from day to day. Mr Micawber muddled through, depending on both willpower and serendipity for his survival. People who rely on muddling through may also try to "wing it" – see below.

ONE RECAP – "WINGING IT"

Chapter 8 referred to the habit of lazy journalists "winging it", hurrying to finish or to short-change their work in order to get away from their office "to have fun at the pub". In another case, the *Sunday Times* newspaper describes the record of a former UK politician as being that of a person who 'thought [he / she] could wing it [when what was needed was] serious and sustained application'.

The name of the politician is matterless here (and cannot in any case be reproduced). *What is important in the context of this Book is that "winging it" is an amateurish (and contemptible) pattern of behaviour.* After all, and especially in the case of government and state activities involving great responsibility, potentially calamitous consequences, and the expenditure of large sums of taxpayer money, a maximum degree of professionalism (and 'serious and sustained application') is the only default performance available. Such professionalism should, for instance also be seen to be at Six Sigma levels in terms of Performance Management. *Nothing else will do, and there is no excuse for not achieving it (i) in long-established state institutions with a massive reservoir of knowledge and experience, and equally (ii) when the taxpayer is footing the bill.*

CONTEXT

The dilemma context in which PSOs operate may be characterised by any of the following variables.

Multiple and conflicting objectives or agendas that result from:

❏ the nature of the determinant or authorising environment, whether characterised by pressures from the electorate, politicians, funding agencies, stakeholders, partners (etc);

❏ disagreement about priorities, complexity;

❏ an over-reliance on so-called "advisers", external consultants, and skilled chancers;

❏ an individual and institutional reluctance to encompass new ideas (such as Dilemma Management) that do not conform to established ways of thinking. This issue is also given extensive treatment in some of the other Books written by this Author and listed in the Introduction.

Disparate or conflicting external pressures associated with changing public attitudes and political expectations, and the demands from single interest groups (etc):

❏ the prevailing Voices, for instance as described in Chapter 4, their relative degree of strength, and the extent to which they are consistent or dissonant with each other;

❏ the opinionation and so-called "political correctness" described in earlier chapters, perhaps associated with:-

❏ the impact of patterns of (i) cognitive consonance and cognitive dissonance and (ii) Snowflakery;

❏ journalistic amateurism, media bias or pressure, or patterns of hostility.

Performance Management pressures associated with:

❏ again, the nature of the authorising environment, whether characterised by pressures from politicians, scrutineers such as the National Audit Office, the electorate, funding agencies, partners, stakeholder commitments as described in Chapter 26 (etc);

❏ the implications of any prioritisation of Public Good provision;

❏ public and media attitudes to the matters of the scale and nature of public expenditure, taxpayer value for money; and specifically:-

❏ criticisms of the waste of public money and asset value loss as described in Chapter 15.

Performance Management Case Example – Performance Management, asset management and public procurement

UK Government procurement performance has for many years faced a strong undercurrent of criticism and disapproval. Various examples have been given in this Book. Criticism has variously been levelled (in no particular order) at:

❏ the East African Groundnut Scheme; the Brabazon aircraft; Blue Streak and other missile systems; the Nimrod Air Surveillance system; Crossrail; HS2; SmartMeters; traditional warship construction (the US Navy has wooden and also fast shallow draft ships); weapon system failures experienced by the British Army during the Gulf wars;

❏ the use of Public-Private Partnerships (PPPs) for instance in major infrastructure projects; *and*

❏ what has proven the damaging environmental consequences of the Marple era focus on road building and the corresponding reduction in rail mileage through the Beeching Report. The closure of the former Great Central Line has meant for instance the unknowing elimination of what could have been a perfect and cost-effective part-route for HS2.

Comment on the handling by the Civil Service of Carillion plc was described in Chapter 15.

Issues of Amateurism

A consistent theme of this Book has been that of the lack of proper professionalism that characterises the leadership, management and operations of many UK institutions. These institutions are to be found throughout the business / commercial sector, the public sector, and the charity / Third sector. This Book has given many examples, and described the dilemmas that are associated with them. This chapter suggests that the consequences of amateurism and a lack of proper professionalism for PSOs include:

❏ a prevailing lack of real world, international, or "business" work experience that results in staff naivete and ineffective judgement, for instance in authorising environments, decision making, financial management, etc; apparently made worse by the growing phenomena of:-

❏ the lazy "winging it" described above; and the snowflakery and windbaggery described in earlier chapters;

❏ the issue of the use of formalised and externally accredited professional and vocational qualifications in order to complement internal programmes of work experience monitoring, development and CPD. Such qualifications might already exist (as in the case of accounting practice or procurement), or might instead be validated under NVQ (etc); *and*

❏ the excessive and expensive reliance on external advisers and consultants to which reference has already been made. There is no guarantee that the amateur will be able to judge whether the advice to be given is valid, nor that the price being quoted is right.

DILEMMAS FACING THE PSO

Dilemma Management issues dealt with in this Book are likely to affect all aspects of the leadership, management, and decision making within the PSOs under consideration in this chapter. These include any or all of:

❏ the direction, priority, and balance of the authorising process; operations, risk, financial and performance management; and the securing of asset values;

❏ niceness; the middle class cultural fear of conflict; and exploitation by those who make a deliberate targeted use of aggression against others. These were all evident during the Brexit process;

❏ inner directness, closed semiospheric attitudes, cronyism, etc;

❏ a reluctance to apply concepts of collective or corporate responsibility, for instance during critical negotiations such as Brexit;

❏ a reluctance to accept the consequences of, or to manage the rules and exceptions dilemma described in Chapter 6;

❏ the continuing reliance on badly outdated paradigms; an obsolete knowledge base; analysis-paralysis, vestiges of imperialistic attitudes; or an installed base of thinking; *and*

❏ outdated Webbist attitudes;

❏ shortcomings that derive from the planning down processes described in Chapters 27 and 28;

❏ shortcomings that result from the reluctance to accept or understand the Big Picture, and the failure of "joined up" thinking that is endemic to these sectors; exacerbated by

❏ the "canny administrator" syndrome described in Chapter 29;

❏ an inability to deal with or to manage the patterns of delay or eggshells described in Chapters 30 and 31; and

❏ the serious consequences of a continuing UK reliance, for instance in politics, the Civil and Foreign Services, and the Judiciary, on (i) elites (in some cases very wealthy) with an apparently limited understanding of the wider issues and difficulties affecting ordinary families and working people, and limited (or no) exposure to the personal, financial or collective risks to which their actions may give rise; as well as (ii) a reliance on entrenched ideologues and career politicians (etc) with outdated or limited mindsets, limited perceptions, and poor judgement. *This is a classic genetic diversity and requisite variety argument,* exacerbated (iii) by a growing London and Southern-centricity and hostility to the other Regions that make up the UK.

SOME DILEMMA IMPLICATIONS FOR PSO CAPABILITY

Dilemma implications for capability were analysed in Part Four, also in Chapter 28 and more widely in Part Five. In the case of the PSO these are likely to impact on any or all of the necessary processes of:

❏ *strategic management* – for instance, is it possible to reconcile Webbism (Chapter 27) or the "canny administrator" syndrome (Chapter 29) with the need to take into account the various Big

Picture issues, Time Span of Discretion, Competition Strategy (etc) as described in Parts Four and Five?

❏ *leadership process* – whether in terms of competence, capacity, motivation or willpower;

❏ *management process* – to include Mintzberg's four roles described in Chapter 22. The critical need for negotiation competence has for instance characterised government procurement or the Brexit process. The latter has also revealed the consequences of the limiting factor imposed by the vestiges of imperialist culture still to be found in the mindsets of some PSO staff;

❏ *financial and performance management* – which in some cases (i) do not form an effective part of the paradigms by which the organisation is run by its staff; or (ii) which are deliberately ignored because of the implications of their proper implementation. This may have been the case of the use of Public-Private Partnerships (PPPs), or may apply to the need for the application of Six Sigma to infection control;

❏ *risk and crisis management* – failings under which category have constituted an ongoing and long-term source of difficulty and value loss in PSOs.

CASE EXAMPLE: UK STATE SCHOOLS
Multiple agendas and conflicting objectives – singing from which Hymn sheet?

This chapter has already noted the syndrome in which institutions such as schools have become, or are in the process of becoming, national providers or refuges of last resort. This was described in the Introduction to this Book.

State schools in the UK are subject to a variety of externally imposed objectives and pressures. They face agendas set by the education authorities, by parents and governors, by the media, and by the Children's Commissioner (etc). They are also forced to deal with wide variations in the attitudes of children (and their parents) towards behaviour, motivation, discipline and achievement.

These objectives and agendas may, or may not be congruent or consistent. In some cases they are directly in conflict, and affect the capability of the education system to do its job – *if agreement can be reached as to how that job should be defined?*

School children have, in the main, the status of Minors (under 18) and remain the responsibility of their parents or guardians. Chapter 5 describes some of the distracting or corrupting influences of the Attention Economy and Social Media. These influences also have a direct impact on schoolchildren.

Some Dilemma Management consequences of the multiple agendas and conflicting objectives are listed below, and their implications for school capability identified.

Problem parents – The Week quotes an Ofsted Report which describes an apparently increasingly abusive attitude towards school teachers. It notes that the schools' watchdog says that 'teachers are coming under growing pressure from parents who expect instant responses to emails, complain when their children do not get top grades (regardless of effort), and defend their offspring's poor behaviour instead of siding with the school ... the report says the behaviour of children and parents is a key factor of low morale among teachers, who are leaving the profession in record numbers'.

Discipline and compliance – poor or disruptive pupil behaviour may limit what a state school can achieve in terms of the outputs for which it is supposed to be established. The discipline needed to achieve compliance, tough study, excellence, and the requisite level of development of the country's Human Capital has progressively been eroded by any or all of:

❏ middle class cultural niceness and fear of conflict; excessive pupil and parental individualism; so-called "politically correct" social (and Snowflake) hostility to the exercise of "authority" and discipline in society; and the lack of the resources or willpower to employ security staff who (on the US model) are licenced to make decisions on the exercise of classroom control, restraint or the removal of disruptive children.

Issues of classroom discipline, tough study (etc) are dealt with in the Author's *Equality, Diversity and Opportunity Management* to which reference is made in the Introduction to this Book.

External pressures, the last resort syndrome, and capability – the Commissioner for Children in England has at this time of writing called for:

❏ the appointment of a "Child and Adolescent Mental Health Service Counsellor" to every school;
❏ increased funding for the teaching of children with Special Educational Needs and Disabilities;
❏ School facilities to be open and available at evenings, weekends and holidays. This to include facilities for feeding children who for whatever reason are at risk of malnutrition during the holidays;
❏ the allocation of police officers and youth workers in schools in order to reinforce the security and safeguarding described in Chapter 16.

These are of course all worthy objectives and merit serious study by all concerned. But in Dilemma Management terms they must be categorised as having been "thrown over the wall" as described in Chapter 27. Issues of capability and implementation are to be someone else's responsibility. The location of this responsibility is not (and may not be) clearly defined. The Government or UK political parties "ought to do" or "should do". But Government departments will instead continue to pass the buck. Individualistic parents will continue to refuse to accept their responsibility for the children that they have brought into the world. And the media will continue its armchair and non-responsible criticism of hard- pressed schools and the teaching staff who are clearly trying to do their best under the most challenging of circumstances. All in all, the proper corporate responsibility of school governors and managements may remain unclear, or be difficult to define, and in any case be impossible to fulfil.

And in the meantime the issue of whether schools have, or instead may not have the capability to implement all of these highly desirable objectives will remain a matter of serendipity.

Mapping the fit of state school or school system capability – Figure 25 shows a dilemma map based on five cells numbered 1 to 5 where Number 1 is to the right and Number 5 is to the left. *Each cell is mapped against the fit (or appropriateness) of a given (fixed) level of available capability "C" at Time "t1"*. The cells are described as follows:

❖ Cell 1 – in which a school or school system wishes to meet all expectations and demands, even if these are multiple or conflicting. The achievement of good student results is seen either as (i) a priority, or (ii) *the* priority.

❖ Cell 2 – in which the school or school system espouses satisficing behaviour by attempting to meet at least some (but not all) equally valid expectations and demands. Adequate student results are the objective, however this is to be defined.

❖ Cell 3 – which is at best characterised by *muddling through*. Operations may have to be carried out with the use of some creative ambiguity. Student results obtained may be marginally acceptable, or they may not.

❖ Cell 4 – which is characterised by a declining ability to manage staff and resources. There is a loss of control, declining morale, and increasing teaching staff turnover. Student results are likely to be poor or unacceptable.

❖ Cell 5 – which is characterised by a significant loss of control. The failing institution can only produce unacceptable results. The school or system is likely to have to be placed in special measures. This will have major financial and resource implications for future capability – wherever this may have to come from given the fixed availability at Time "t1".

Worse, in Dilemma Management terms, the proportion of the fixed capability available at Time "t1" that needs (i) to be allocated to the maintenance of order and discipline, and (ii) to create a functioning learning environment is likely to increase from Cell 1 to Cell 5. The greater that proportion, the less capability will be available for other essential pedagogic or socially desirable processes. At the same time, it has now becoming abundantly clear that at this time of writing UK teaching conditions in Cells 3 to 5 are corrosive of teaching staff willpower where Capability is defined in this Book as Capacity plus Willpower.

Issues of school teaching were also described in Part Two.

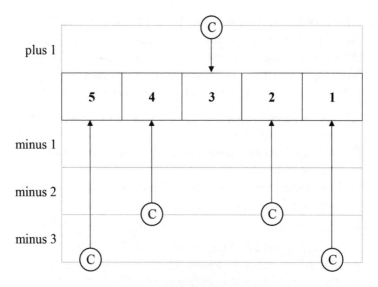

Figure 25
School system capability fit

And Finally

HERE IS SOMETHING FOR YOU TO TRY:
Using the framework described in this Book, construct your own Dilemma Management analysis, ultimately focussing on issues of capability, leadership, management process, decision making, performance management, professionalisation and implementation.

[1] You could do this for a work context, or an example in which you have a particular interest.
[2] You could do this as a part of your ongoing professional CPD or qualification.
[3] You could do this for something which you consider to be important, such as:

❖ energy provision;
❖ environmental and climate change issues;
❖ the prospects for UK agriculture;
❖ the prospects for UK woodland and forestry;
❖ the prospects for UK countryside;
❖ the provision of rail and other public transport services (perhaps to include the mass re-introduction of electrically powered trolleybuses associated with Park And Ride facilities);
❖ the provision of housing in the UK;
❖ the packaging of products for retail;
❖ the provision and priority of vocational education at 18 plus in the UK;
❖ issues of leadership and management training, development and professional certification in the UK;
❖ issues of public health.

[4] You could do this in respect of UK school classroom order and discipline. For instance, you might start from the viewpoint that the responsibility for the creation and maintenance of an

appropriate and positive learning environment that would foster tough study and student excellence should be passed in its entirety to school authorities and the state as funding agency. This might result in the empowerment of teachers who would be free to do their proper job. That is to teach and assess students as a means of improving the Human Capital upon which an economy like the UK depends absolutely.

ENJOY!

Index